spotlight

second edition

on Critical Skills in Essay Writing

CAROLE ANNE MAY
CAMOSUN COLLEGE

spotlight

second edition

on Critical Skills in Essay Writing

Pearson Canada
Toronto

Library and Archives Canada Cataloguing in Publication

May, Carole Anne, 1948–
Spotlight on critical skills in essay writing/Carole Anne May.—2nd ed.

Includes index.
ISBN 978-0-13-502925-1

1. English language—Rhetoric—Textbooks. 2. Essay—Authorship—Textbooks. 3. Report writing—Textbooks. I. Title.

PE1471.M39 2010 808'.042 C2008-908123-4

ISBN-13: 978-0-13-502925-1
ISBN-10: 0-13-502925-2

Vice-President, Editorial Director: Gary Bennett
Editor-in-Chief: Ky Pruesse
Acquisitions Editor: David Le Gallais
Marketing Manager: Loula March
Supervising Developmental Editor: Suzanne Schaan
Production Editor: Richard di Santo
Copy Editor: Colleen Ste. Marie
Proofreaders: Ann McInnis, Nancy Carroll
Production Coordinator: Avinash Chandra
Composition: Integra
Permissions Research: Lynn McIntyre
Art Director: Julia Hall
Cover and Interior Design: Anthony Leung
Cover Image: Adam Taylor/GettyImages

1 2 3 4 5 13 12 11 10 09

Printed and bound in the United States of America.

PEARSON

dedication

This book is dedicated to my brother, Ron, and to my sister-in-law, Cindy.
Thank you for your love, friendship, and support over the years.

brief contents

detailed contents

preface

Welcome to the second edition of *Spotlight on Critical Skills in Essay Writing*. The second edition contains many exciting improvements based on reviewer suggestions and student feedback. The text is primarily designed for first-year or college preparation students, but will be useful to all students who must develop their writing skills in order to succeed in future post-secondary courses. The text helps students progress by building the development of critical thinking, reading, and writing skills through a clear sequence that develops application with varied exercises—both individual and collaborative—from the prewriting phases, to college essay writing, and finally, to research paper writing.

The second edition of *Spotlight on Critical Skills in Essay Writing* offers excellent changes in sequence, format, and exercises. It features new separate chapters on critical reading, academic writing, APA style, MLA style, and grammar fundamentals. Also new is the addition of Review Tests for all chapters of the text. New academic readings are now found in Chapters 1 to 15.

Spotlight on Critical Skills in Essay Writing, Second Edition, retains the elements most instructors want to see in a textbook. The critical thinking skills of summarizing, paraphrasing, comparing and contrasting, evaluating, analyzing, developing argument, researching, and synthesizing information are taught directly through chapter work. Collaborative work for students is developed through a variety of exercises throughout the text. Chapters contain extensive explanations, examples, and exercises. Editing skills and the development of writing style find focus in Chapters 16 and 17, while developing a vocabulary for college is emphasized in Chapter 18. Two types of reading comprehension are expanded through general and critical questions accompanying the readings in Chapters 1 through 15. Review tests offer students practice in developing key skills for planning, composing, writing, researching, proofing, and editing.

Spotlight on Critical Skills in Essay Writing, Second Edition, offers clear and extensive explanations on many aspects of English study. For example, students learn format and structure from rhetorical modes, but they also learn to observe how writers express themselves and how to shape their own writing efforts. This means that while students become better at expressing themselves more concisely, they are also becoming familiar with academic discourse. In addition, planning strategies are crucial for developmental writers. Students require the opportunity to develop their written language capabilities through the interplay of thinking and writing. Moreover, academically-bound students require critical skill proficiencies in order to succeed in academic contexts. In recognition of this, this new edition is intended to amplify the tenets of sound principles of adult education which was also the foundation of the first edition: to develop students' belief in their own potential and academic success because positive educational experiences will transform their lives, and to provide them with the opportunities to learn what they need to know.

Summary of Changes

The second edition has been revised to capitalize on the strengths of the first edition while incorporating the following improvements:

- improved format
- new exercises
- changes in chapter sequencing; the chapter on expository writing (now Chapter 9) has been moved later in the book to follow some of the introductory skills, and the coverage of documentation styles (now Chapters 14 and 15) has been moved to follow the discussion of writing a research paper
- addition of a critical reading chapter (Chapter 1)
- addition of an academic writing chapter (Chapter 8)
- a separate APA chapter with an example paper (Chapter 14)
- a separate MLA chapter with an example paper (Chapter 15). This material, and the text as a whole, has been thoroughly updated to reflect the new seventh edition of the *MLA Handbook for Writers of Research Papers*, published in 2009.
- addition of a comprehensive English grammar fundamentals chapter (Chapter 17)
- inclusion of *Employability Skills 2000+* that dovetail with academic skills being developed in each chapter
- reorganization to place the readings, many of them new, in Chapters 1 through 15, rather than in a separate chapter
- comprehension questions, critical comprehension questions, and writing assignments to accompany readings

Key Features

- The text begins with a chapter on critical reading and thinking because this work is foundational to learning in post-secondary education.
- Chapter work also connects to *Employability Skills 2000+* prepared by the Conference Board of Canada in order that students develop and apply skills that are essential in today's workplace.
- Students gain the experience they need to cope with research reading. Most of the new readings come directly from professional journals in education, environmental science, biology, fashion, academic study, and other disciplines.
- Rather than providing a separate readings chapter, the new edition has readings, comprehension questions, critical comprehension questions, and writing assignments in Chapters 1 through 15. This bundling helps to provide continuity of concept development.
- Each chapter contains a review test. The answers to the review tests are found in the Instructor's Manual and not in the Answer Key, so instructors may choose to use these review tests for marks.

- Pre-writing and planning strategies for writing are discussed in two separate chapters (Chapters 2 and 3).
- A special chapter (Chapter 6) deals with summarizing and paraphrasing strategies and exercises. This academic skill is essential for post-secondary studies.
- In Chapter 7, the rudiments of evaluation for critical thinking and writing purposes are presented as a separate chapter to highlight their importance.
- Chapter 8, Academic Writing, introduces students to the components and purposes of academic writing, with an extensive discussion of plagiarism. This chapter will help students to recognize the features of academic writing.
- Chapter 9 introduces students to the rudiments of expository writing, including basic essay structure and common rhetorical modes.
- Chapter 10 examines some of the principles of written argumentation since effective argumentation is a cornerstone of academic writing.
- Chapter 11 discusses the structuring of argument for academic writing.
- Four chapters have research writing as their focus (Chapters 12 through 15).
- Chapter 14, Research Papers: APA Style, introduces writers to APA documentation and provides exercises, an example paper, two types of comprehension questions, and writing activities.
- Chapter 15, Research Papers: MLA Style, introduces writers to MLA documentation and provides exercises, an example paper, two types of comprehension questions, and writing activities.
- An extensive chapter on editing and style notes (Chapter 16) includes tips on editing and eliminating common errors in punctuation and grammar. It also contains style notes on special items like active and passive voice, logical constructions, sentence variety, and cohesive devices.
- Chapter 17, Grammar Fundamentals, comprehensively covers the basics of English grammar and mechanics with many exercises and two review tests.
- A special and comprehensive chapter develops college vocabulary (Chapter 18).
- Intense and varied opportunities offer students practice. Ideas are not merely introduced. Students work through practices designed to develop critical thinking via a series of steps and strategies that encourage engagement and reflection. The structure of the exercises encourages collaborative work among students.
- Bonus Exercises at the ends of most chapters give students the opportunity to learn about common errors college level students make in their writing and offer practices to hone editing skills and eliminate these common errors.

The approach of *Spotlight on Critical Skills in Essay Writing*, Second Edition, and its instructional content have been field tested over a number of years with college students. Overall, students reported their enjoyment of the approach, the nature of the exercises and assignments, and satisfaction about the improvement in their abilities to think critically, analyze, organize, and construct written material.

Through its philosophy and structure, the book encourages students to become capable and confident, ready to handle higher-level challenges in their writing. It emphasizes the conception of writing as a complex process, as a recursive undertaking, and as an individual project having phases. Most importantly, *Spotlight on Critical Skills in Essay Writing*, Second Edition, develops thinking, reading, and writing skills essential for post-secondary studies, the workplace, and the life world.

Supplements

Instructor's Manual

Spotlight on Critical Skills in Essay Writing, Second Edition, is accompanied by an Instructor's Manual that is an invaluable resource for anyone using this textbook. Included in the Instructor's Manual are self-tests for Chapters 1 through 15 that can be printed for student use (self-tests for Chapters 16 through 18 appear in the text), suggested activities, review test answers, and additional answers for exercises found in the text. This supplement can be downloaded by instructors from a password-protected location on Pearson Education Canada's online catalogue (www.pearsoned.ca/highered). Simply search for the text, then click on "Instructor" under "Resources" in the left-hand menu. Contact your local sales representative for further information.

CourseSmart

CourseSmart is a new way for instructors and students to access textbooks online anytime from anywhere. With thousands of titles across hundreds of courses, CourseSmart helps instructors choose the best textbook for their class and give their students a new option for buying the assigned textbook as a lower cost eTextbook. For more information, visit www.coursesmart.com.

Acknowledgments

I am especially grateful to Pearson Education Canada for their continued support and encouragement. My thanks go to Patti Riediger, Matthew Christian, Richard di Santo, Linda Cahill, Nancy Carroll, the reviewers, and my students and colleagues for their wonderful assistance in the first edition. For the second edition, I wish to acknowledge the clear direction and warm support of Christopher Helsby, Suzanne Schaan, and Richard di Santo once again from Pearson Education. They have been invaluable at all times. Thanks also to Colleen Ste. Marie, Ann McInnis, and Nancy Carroll for their editing and proofreading talents. Thanks are also due to the reviewers whose feedback on the original proposal or manuscript chapters has helped to shape this new edition, including the following people: Brent Cotton, Georgian College; Paula Crooks, Conestoga College; Tom Gwin, Red Deer College; Moira Langley, Kwantlen Polytechnic University; Aurelea Mahood, Capilano University; Norma-Jean Nielsen, Canadore College; Jill Singleton-Jackson, University of Windsor; Michelle Semeniuk, Northern Alberta Institute of Technology; and Tamara Stern, Sheridan Institute of Technology and Advanced Learning.

chapter 1

Developing Critical Reading

Chapter Objectives

After completing this chapter you will be able to

1. recognize what comprises critical reading as a skill set;
2. analyze organizational features of a text, such as main ideas and important details;
3. recognize writers' claims;
4. specify writers' evidence;
5. use some reading techniques, such as skimming and scanning;
6. employ annotations and marginal notes to deepen comprehension.

INTRODUCTION

It is no accident that *Spotlight on Critical Skills in Essay Writing*, Second Edition, begins with a chapter on critical reading and thinking. In your work as a student in college or university, you will be plunged into intellectual activities for which you must be prepared. You will be entering an intellectual life that presupposes inhabitants who are sophisticated readers, thinkers, writers, and speakers, accomplished in many skills and able to perform them with relative ease. These underlying basic skills are the foundation of your learning. Without them, academic life can be a struggle.

Employability Skills 2000+

At the ends of chapters throughout this text, you will find references to *Employability Skills 2000+*. The Conference Board of Canada created these sets of skills in order to develop Canadian workers who are ready to meet the demands of the Canadian contemporary workplace. According to its website, the Conference Board of Canada's mandate is to "build leadership capacity for a better Canada by creating and sharing insights on economic trends, public policy and organizational performance." The Conference Board of Canada's mission is to provide research in economic development, and governments develop policies based on that research. Consequently, many employers today will be looking for candidates who possess the "soft skills" that the research indicates as being essential for the job.

Students are the future workers and leaders of Canada, so these *Employability Skills 2000+*, which include a wide range of tasks and sets of competencies, are appropriate to post-secondary learning. You will be reminded that the skills you are learning in your

English classes and through this textbook are also transferable to your professional and personal life. Fundamental skills, such as the ability to communicate, manage information, use numbers, think, and solve problems, are essential. Personal management skills, such as the ability to demonstrate positive attitudes and behaviours, be responsible, be adaptable, learn continuously, work safely, work with others, and participate in projects and tasks, are all specified in the Employability Skills because they are completely necessary for success in the workplace. Therefore, chapter 1 of *Spotlight on Critical Skills in Essay Writing*, Second Edition, introduces you to one of the most important of the Employability Skills—critical thinking and reading. By increasing your proficiency in critical reading, you will be better equipped for the complex literacy demands facing workers today in Canada.

Most people need a helping hand to better develop their critical thinking, reading, and writing skills. Students need more opportunities to practise and develop as critical thinkers. That is the essence of this first chapter: to help you build a conceptual framework for thinking about thinking and to help you apply this meta-thinking as you read and write.

WHAT IS CRITICAL THINKING?

Thinking about critical thinking has been a focus in Western thought since the time of the ancient Greeks. Early Greek philosophers used a system of questioning techniques to help thinkers think clearly, reasonably, and logically about ideas in the society around them. Critical thinking does not imply throwing out all conventions and established beliefs; instead, thinkers engage in a careful examination of governing assumptions in the societies around them in order to sort out what is reasonable and should remain as foundational principles or ideas and what should be more closely scrutinized and questioned.

According to Dr. Robert H. Ennis, a prominent expert in the field of critical thinking, critical thinking is "reasonable reflective thinking focused on deciding what to believe or what to do" ("A Streamlined Conception of Critical Thinking," *Teaching Philosophy* 14 no. 1 (1991): 6. Also online in "Critical Thinking, What Is It?" 1992: www.ed.uiuc.edu/EPS/PES-Yearbook/92_docs/ENNIS.HTM). In their article, "Conceptualizing Critical Thinking," Bailin, Case, Coombs, and Daniels (1999) suggest that critical thinking skills involve "habits of mind" that "require the sensitive use of a variety of intellectual resources in the exercise of good judgement" (p. 298).

To progress as critical thinkers, then, people have to adopt a "critical thinking disposition." What experts suggest is to develop ways of thinking that become part of your thinking no matter where you are or what you are doing. In other words, you become disposed to thinking critically. Students may find they have to work at this just like any other skill. Sometimes they may find it difficult to apply this way of thinking when courses seem fragmented and learning seems passive to them.

Developing your critical thinking skills will open up possibilities; you will discover that ideas can be viewed from different perspectives or points of view and that each perspective is based on a set of values and beliefs that may not always correspond or be in harmony with others. The struggle for power and control is often the struggle over who controls the dominant values, so a large part of your critical investigation must also include an examination of who is making a claim and why. Applying critical thinking skills means analyzing and evaluating. You will consider what your investigation means to you by looking at how the results fit with what you think you know, have read, or have experienced.

Interpretation is a large part of thinking and research. Each major discipline has its own group of critical thinkers who have shaped their fields in various ways. However, depending on the examiner, data can be interpreted differently at different times and in different circumstances. For example, a perennial criminal justice debate centres around what constitutes evidence. Prior to the discovery of the molecular structure of human DNA by James Watson and Francis Crick, criminal investigations relied on fingerprints, eye-witness accounts, and physical clues found at the scene as the strongest pieces of evidence. Then, in the early 1980s an English scientist named Sir Alec Jeffreys invented DNA testing, and soon criminologists and forensic scientists began DNA profiling in violent crime and paternity cases. They proclaimed DNA matching as the most powerful tool available for gathering criminal evidence because of its reliability and scientific infallibility. In fact, this new form of evidence has overturned prior judgments and revealed that many innocent people had been wrongly convicted.

Critical thinking is linked to critical reading, an essential skill. When you assume a critical thinking stance when you read, you are developing useful habits and a clear disposition to become organized, analytical, questioning, and more able to extend what experts call "the intellectual resources" at your disposal.

The critical thinking and reading tools you will learn to use are not confined to your English studies only. You carry your thinking tools with you from course to course, field to field, and situation to situation. Learning to solve problems using different techniques and strategies is part of the larger picture of being a professional person in a complicated, changing world. Critical thinking and reading skills are indispensable.

WHAT IS CRITICAL READING?

Critical reading means using specific strategies in order to gain clarity and deepen comprehension. A reader goes beyond the basic skimming of a text—he is looking, rather, for the "deep structure."

Critical reading involves reading

- for understanding;
- to understand organization;
- to understand the claims a writer is making;
- to find out if a writer has provided facts rather than just opinion;
- to discover what evidence the writer provides;
- to discover if a writer has developed ideas in a clear, logical way;
- to discover if a writer has included reasonable ideas;
- to uncover bias.

Steps to Becoming a Critical Reader

If you want to become a more sophisticated reader, you will need a plan. Generally speaking, a plan offers you some steps to follow, and this section provides a variety of suggestions.

STEP 1: PREPARE TO ENGAGE

Your college or university reading will be more difficult than everyday reading because the writing is at a higher level; it often contains new vocabulary, concepts, and ideas; and it constitutes the material for which you will be examined in your courses. Everyday reading does not make the same demands, so expect to spend extra time on your course reading.

- Anticipate that higher-level reading cannot be done superficially.
- When you begin a reading task, set up a mental state of anticipation. Centre yourself by saying, "I am about to engage with this material."
- Work in a quiet, nondistracting area.
- Be prepared for the reading task by having what you need with you, such as writing materials, laptop, course outline, and course assignment. Preparation is key to becoming engaged in a reading task.

STEP 2: USE EXTERNAL CLUES

By using as many external clues as possible, you are giving yourself a "heads-up" about what is coming next. You are also helping your mind to engage with what is in front of you.

- Read all introductions carefully.
- Read all titles and headings carefully.
- Preview the article or chapter, page by page.
- Look for visual aids, such as graphs, pictures, charts, and so forth.
- Look at the length of the article.

Keep in mind that anticipation and prediction are important components of effective, deep reading.

STEP 3: KEEP AN OPEN MIND

To be a critical thinker and reader includes being open- and fair-minded. Read fully to give the writer an opportunity to develop his or her ideas. As you read, try to understand what the writer is saying. Many students think that critical reading means trying to criticize a writer's ideas, so they will start to argue with the ideas on the page before they have completely apprehended them. Train yourself to read for understanding first.

- Try to comprehend what the writer is communicating.
- Think about what claims the writer is making.
- Try to read with an open heart and mind.
- Read thoughtfully.

Remember that having an open mind is vital in developing critical thinking and reading.

STEP 4: PREPARE TO CHANGE YOUR SPEED AND PACE

Speed in reading means the number of words you take in; pace in reading means the manner by which you read or the rate of moving through the text. Some students think that speed reading is the answer; however, as the Learning Center at the University of Texas at Austin suggests, students who have "difficulty understanding what they read will not be helped by learning to misunderstand faster."

For complex pieces of writing, read at a different speed, and pace yourself differently than you would do when you are reading easy material. Reading a chapter in a philosophy text requires much more effort than reading an article in a newspaper. Newspapers keep their readability deliberately low, around a grade 8 level, while university or college texts or articles are written at anywhere from first-year to graduate level.

Furthermore, your reading assignment may involve language, sentence style, syntax, and vocabulary completely unfamiliar to you. As such, it will simply take you more time to process and understand. The more familiar you are with the concepts discussed in a text, the faster your speed and pace of reading will be. Therefore, if you are encountering concepts in your reading for the first time, you will find your speed and rate of comprehension decrease.

You must know your purpose in reading. It helps you keep in mind how you are to read the material; in other words, know the depth of knowledge of the material you must have, so that you can adjust your reading strategies, your speed, and your pace. Here are some typical purposes:

- If you will be examined on the materials in detail, then you must read deeply with a thorough knowledge of the concepts and ideas. You should expect your speed and pace to be slower, so allow for more reading time. Adjust your schedule accordingly.
- If you will be examined on the ideas in general, then you need not concern yourself with every detail. You should increase your speed and pace, but you should allow for gaining total comprehension of main ideas and key concepts. Adjust your schedule accordingly.
- If the material is part of the overall reading required in your course, then you will be expected to read and understand it. In this sense, you are reading generally, so you should increase your speed and pace to a fairly rapid rate.
- If you are reading material to decide whether or not you can use it for your research writing, you should skim. Skimming is a rapid reading method for gaining the overall meaning of a text. When you are skimming, you are getting the gist of the text.
- If you are studying for an exam and reading material in order to locate a particular name, date, number, term, or other item, you should scan. Scanning is a rapid reading technique enabling a reader to look over a text quickly in order to find a specific piece of information.

Remember to adjust your speed and pace according to your purpose in reading. And keep in mind that skimming is rapid reading to gain a general sense of a material and that scanning is a technique used to gain a specific piece of information rapidly from text.

STEP 5: UNDERSTAND THE TERMS

You must understand the terms being used in a text. Look up words that are unclear in meaning to you. Because each discipline has specialized vocabulary, taking a course in biology, sociology, law, nursing, computing science, and so forth can seem like a burden because having so many new terms to learn may be overwhelming. However, learning to familiarize yourself with new terms is part of the first steps in comprehension and in the development of your critical thinking and reading skills.

Sometimes readers do not understand a term because it is a cultural reference that they may not recognize. The reference could be to a product, movie, magazine, or television program; it could even be to something that is part of pop culture history, which makes it very difficult for someone new to North America to understand. A term or concept may also be related to a cultural narrative linked to the social and spiritual nature of a community and part of the belief system of the community. It is important to ask someone for an explanation and for examples when you come across complicated cultural terms because just looking them up in a dictionary is inadequate.

Develop a system for remembering. Here are some suggestions:

- If you are reading a term over and over again, it means that the word is an important concept in the writer's argument or in the field: take note of that term and its meaning.
- Write down new important terms, along with their definitions, because writing helps to reinforce short-term memory.
- Make a list of new important terms as they crop up in reading, and test yourself regularly: e.g., on a daily or weekly basis.
- Try to use some of the new important terms in your writing and speaking. This will help to reinforce meaning.
- Ask a friend or colleague for help in understanding terms that have cultural references. Dictionaries are useful, but discussing important cultural terms with someone can give you more in-depth knowledge.

Remember that understanding the meaning of key concept terms is critical for comprehension.

STEP 6: ANNOTATE AND MAKE MARGINAL NOTES

Annotating means marking text in various ways in order to understand its meaning, reveal its structure, and analyze its ideas. You can develop your own system of annotating in the white spaces of your textbooks, articles, or handouts.

Use some of these suggested annotation techniques:

- Highlight key terms in the same colour (yellow, for example); then underline those you do not understand.
- Underline thesis statements or main ideas, using pencil.
- Highlight major points in the same colour (blue, for example).
- Write *EX* in the margins beside examples in order to map the writer's evidence.

- Write *R* in the margins to note reasons in order to map the writer's reasons or explanations.
- Insert question marks in margins to note passages confusing to you.
- Insert exclamation points (!) in the margins to denote surprising claims or passages.
- Write *NB* (Latin for *nota bene*—i.e., "note well") in the margins beside important passages.

Marginal notes are jotting techniques to deepen comprehension and to develop the analysis of the writer's arguments. Use pencil in case you change your mind about a note or want to erase it.

Some suggestions for marginal notes are as follows:

- Write a single-sentence summary of a paragraph in the margin beside it in your own words. Trying to summarize in your own words helps you to know whether you understand the passage or not.
- Write questions in the margin that arise from the reading. Your questions may be ones that challenge the assumptions or claims the writer makes.
- Make notes when connections occur to you. Use arrows to indicate connections. (←→) For example, "Compare with what writer says on page 255. (←→)"
- Write *Claim* in the margins wherever you think the writer has made a claim or given a position. You may want to write the claim briefly in your own words.
- Annotate and make marginal notes for all material related to tests and exams. These materials need your full attention, so using annotation and marginal notes will be a boon to you come study time. Studying becomes much easier when you come back to your annotated pages and see at a glance how the text has been organized, what is important to remember, and what terms, ideas, or questions you noted.

It's important to keep in mind that annotating deepens analysis of text and improves comprehension.

STEP 7: READ MORE THAN ONCE FOR DIFFERENT PURPOSES

Generally speaking, you will need to read complex materials more than once, particularly those materials to be examined or tested.

- The first time you read, read to get a general impression or overall sense of the material.
- The second time you read, read more deeply. Use steps 1–7 to assist you to read more carefully and critically. Step 8 is the point at which you will put together what you have learned and apply more complex critical thinking principles.

Not all material must be read in the same way, however. If, for example, your instructor or professor assigns six readings, along with one chapter of a text for the next class, you must understand which materials you can skim and which must be read and understood more fully. If you are reading something in order to get a general sense of the material, you can skim it relatively quickly: look over titles, headings, major paragraphs, and conclusions. As mentioned in step 4, good readers adjust their rates according to their purpose in reading. Reading for different purposes is a feature of being an effective reader.

Generally speaking, your main goal is to be able to answer two questions: what is this about, and what major points is the writer making?

STEP 8: APPLY CRITICAL THINKING TECHNIQUES

As a critical thinker and reader, you want to be able to use the above steps as tools so that you are able to reflect and analyze more deeply. After you have completed steps 1–7, you will have a good notion as to how the writer has organized the text because you will have looked up key terms, identified the main points, marked evidence and reasons, and noted claims. In addition, you will have written summary statements and recorded questions to help you analyze the writer's claims. Before moving on, you will need to use the following critical thinking questions to help you synthesize the information and data you have collected in the previous steps:

- What assumptions does the writer make?
- What claims is the writer making?
- Does the writer adequately support his claims?
- Does the reader present ideas clearly and logically, fully developing the points by using good evidence, proof, or explanation?
- Does the writing indicate writer bias? Bias is a clear preference for a particular point of view, demonstrating the writer's partiality towards it.

Now it is time to practise these techniques. The following exercises are taken from a variety of sources. Some of the materials are easy to read while others are more complex and demanding. Scholarly writing will take all your critical reading powers to accomplish successfully. Prepare to engage.

Exercise 1 *Practising Critical Reading Steps*

The following two readings are related to one of the world's favourite flavours: chocolate. These articles come from popular sources: a current news website from the CBC and a trade magazine, *Canadian Grocer.* You can expect a certain ease of reading; therefore, you should adjust your speed and pace. Your purpose in reading these two articles is to gain a general sense of them in order to discuss the assumptions.

Use external clues, e.g., titles and subheadings, to help you prepare for reading. Skim each article first. Then annotate each of the articles as directed in step 6, and make marginal notes if you need to. Underline and then look up unfamiliar words. Use the chart following the two readings to write down main ideas, a summary statement, and assumptions made by the writers. Also note the writers' sources of evidence. Expect to share your ideas.

After completing the first part of the exercise, form a group of no more than five students. Discuss your findings, and be prepared to present them to the rest of the class.

Use chart paper, overhead transparencies, or a computer to record your ideas for presentation.

Chocolate: The Bittersweet Treat

by Michelle Gelok

Wondering whether you can indulge in that chocolate treat staring at you from the store counter without compromising your healthy diet? Well, if you're a lover of chocolate, you may be in luck. There is increasing evidence that chocolate can be part of a healthy diet—and that it may even offer some specific health benefits. However, not all chocolate is created equal. Read on to find out how to incorporate this treat into your diet and get the most of what it has to offer.

CHOCOLATE—A HEALTH FOOD?

While recent headlines might have you thinking chocolate is the next big health food, don't be fooled. You have to do a bit of homework to separate the types of chocolate that can contribute to better health from the ones that simply contribute to an expanded waistline.

The most important thing to realize is that the health benefits provided by chocolate are a result of the flavonoid content found in the cocoa bean. Flavonoids are natural compounds with antioxidant properties—the same compounds that give berries, red wine, and green tea their health benefits.

However, the more chocolate is processed, the fewer flavonoids it retains—therefore reducing its antioxidant abilities and its potential health benefits. Dark chocolate has the most flavonoids, almost four times as many as milk chocolate, while white chocolate has none.

To maximize the protective effect chocolate has to offer, your best bet is to reach for dark chocolate when the craving hits. To make sure you are getting the highest concentration of flavonoids, read the list of ingredients and choose bars that list cocoa solids or cocoa mass first, not sugar. Alternatively, choose a bar with a high percentage of cocoa—70 per cent or more.

Beware of highly processed, sugar-coated chocolate bars—these are nothing more than empty calories and contain little in the way of cocoa or flavonoids.

THE SCIENCE BEHIND THE SWEETNESS

Here's a rundown on some of the latest research in support of chocolate's health benefits:

Heart Disease—A study published in the March 2007 issue of the *American Journal of Clinical Nutrition* found that of more than 34,000 post-menopausal women who consumed the most flavonoid-rich food, 22 per cent had a lower risk of developing coronary heart disease. Chocolate was ranked as one of the top flavonoid-rich foods associated with a protective effect, along with bran, red wine, grapefruit and strawberries.

These findings support previous research published in 2006 in the *Archive of Internal Medicine*, which found men who consumed high amounts of cocoa products (2.3 grams or more per day) had a 50 per cent lower risk of developing cardiovascular disease, compared with men with the lowest consumption.

Blood pressure and cholesterol—In a study published in the July 4, 2007, edition of the *Journal of the American Medical Association*, researchers found that a little bit of dark chocolate may help lower your blood pressure. German researchers followed two groups of people with untreated high blood pressure for 18 weeks. Half got a bit of dark chocolate every day while the other half received white chocolate. In the end, those eating the dark chocolate saw a drop in their blood pressure and there was no change for the group that ate white chocolate. The bad news is, it only took about six grams of chocolate to do the trick.

A study two years earlier, published in the journal *Hypertension*, uncovered similar findings using more chocolate. Researchers randomly assigned 20 subjects with high blood pressure to receive either 100 grams a day of flavonoid-rich dark chocolate or 90 grams per day of flavonoid-free white chocolate. The group receiving dark chocolate experienced a drop in blood pressure. Researchers also found that levels of low density lipoprotein (or "bad") cholesterol dropped by 10 per cent in the dark chocolate group.

Psychological well-being—Heart health isn't the only thing with a link to chocolate. A 2007 study published in the *European Journal of Clinical Nutrition* found that men who preferred chocolate to other types of candy had a lower body mass index and waist circumference than men who did not eat chocolate. Chocolate lovers also experienced more feelings of happiness and better psychological well-being.

HOW MUCH IS TOO MUCH?

The optimal amount of chocolate to consume for health benefits remains unclear. Despite encouraging findings in some studies, one thing is certain: Dark chocolate is still a source of calories, fat and sugar, and therefore, like all foods high in fat and calories, should be enjoyed in moderation.

Limiting yourself to a few small pieces of dark chocolate a week is a reasonable way to enjoy the pleasures of chocolate without overdoing it. Excessive consumption could lead to weight gain, which in turn could cancel any potential health benefits it has to offer.

DARK CHOCOLATE VERSUS MILK CHOCOLATE EASTER CANDY

Here's a look at the nutrient content of 40 grams of 70-per-cent-cocoa dark chocolate:

Calories 213
Fat (grams) 16

Saturated fat (grams) 11
Sugar (grams) 12

Unfortunately, many commercial Easter products are not made with pure dark chocolate—instead they are usually milk chocolate with lots of added sugar. Here's a look at the nutrient content of 2 Kinder Surprise milk chocolate eggs (40 grams):

Calories 230
Fat (grams) 15
Saturated fat (grams) 9
Sugar (grams) 20

While dark chocolate tends to be lower in calories and sugar than milk or white chocolate, there are still plenty of other foods rich in antioxidants that are nutrient-dense and high in fibre, such as blueberries, oranges, broccoli and spinach. These foods are rich sources of vitamins and minerals, and are smart foods to add to a healthy diet high in antioxidants.

OTHER CONSIDERATIONS

Not only are specialty chocolates available from around the world in a variety of flavours, fortunately you can now use your chocolate purchases to benefit the well-being of others and the environment.

There are also an increasing number of high-quality chocolate bars available that are organic and "fair-trade" (fair trade products such as coffee or chocolate offer farmers in developing countries higher prices for their goods than they would typically receive on the world commodity markets, and money is directed to social and environmental development as well as fair labour wages). Consider choosing these to make your next indulgence guilt-free.

THE BOTTOM LINE

While there is increasing evidence that chocolate may have health benefits, the latest research doesn't warrant excessive consumption of all things chocolate. There is no reason why chocolate can't fit into a healthy eating plan, but if you are going to indulge, opt for dark chocolate for optimum health benefits.

Source: CBC.CA. Michelle Gelok, "Chocolate: The bittersweet treat," CBC News online, www.cbc.ca/news/background/health/chocolate.html (updated July 4, 2007).

Chocolate Lovers Delight

by Carolyn Green

Chocolate with chilli pepper? The untutored in the fine art of chocolate making might be forgiven for assuming that chocolate manufacturers are getting desperate in their efforts to come up with new extensions. In fact, for Aztec nobility, chocolate and chilli went together like chocolate and cream or almonds go for us now. Bitter chocolate, chocolate with peppermint filling, chocolate with matcha and goji berries, chocolate with ginseng and maca, chocolate with acai (the latter three made by Zazubean of Vancouver) are just some of the new "revolutionary" flavours in chocolates. Chocolate is a treat that conjures up images of indulgence and sated taste buds. But when the word "healthy" is thrown into the mix, chocolate takes on a whole new persona. In recent years this one word has given the delicious brown substance additional respectability.

"It's not a taboo product anymore," says Valerie Hyska, promotions manager for Moncion Grocers Petawawa Market in Petawawa, Ont. "People who are health conscious feel that they can treat themselves again to chocolate."

And that's just what they're doing. According to Nielsen's MarketTrack National Grocery Banner, the sale of chocolate in Canada for the 52-week period ending July 7 was $451.6 million, up 7% from the previous year. This comes on the heels of a 6% gain to $423.2 million a year earlier.

Unit volumes are experiencing a less robust increase, perhaps due to the proliferation of new 100 gram bars. Still, in the year ending July 2007, unit volumes in the total chocolate category rose by 1%, while bars increased by 10% and boxed chocolates soared by 15%. A year earlier, unit volume gains of bars were up a whopping 25%, while boxed chocolates rose a respectable 4%.

HEALTH BENEFITS

Industry watchers agree that recent scientific findings suggesting dark chocolate may help reduce the risk of heart disease and is a high source of antioxidants, believed to help prevent some forms of cancer, have energized to transform chocolate into a "good food." But most agree that the potential health benefits are only one piece of the puzzle.

John Rowsome, president of the Confectionery Manufacturers Association of Canada (CMAC), says the broadened selection of flavours and textures that are now available is also helping to boost increased consumption.

"People are looking at chocolate and the [different] beans that come from Madagascar or South America," says Rowsome. "They're looking at different beans and different flavours . . . so it goes from the everyday to the exotic."

Amy Snider, a home economist and vice-president of Dana McCauley & Associates, a Maple, Ont.-based food consulting firm, says what was once unheard of is now becoming mainstream. For instance, she points to chocolate that is "tarted up" with flavours such as cayenne or salt, which she says intensify the sweetness of the chocolate. There are also truffles that have been infused with green tea—a double whammy for folks looking for more antioxidants. Although chocolate has for some time been a baking ingredient, it's now being used to add pep to such foods as cereals.

SEARCH FOR FLAVOUR ADVENTURES

In addition to health benefits and an increased selection of chocolate flavours, Snider says chocolate consumption is growing because of a trend she calls "aficionadoism" where people are tasting new flavours with a spirit of adventure.

"A cookbook came out recently that talked about tasting parties and chocolate is one of those items you can do because there are differences between the different cocoa blends and strength of cocoa and the intensities and milk chocolate. So there really is a push toward chocolate right now where it's about quality and taste," says Snider. This trend is particularly appealing to young working urbanites, she adds. "They don't have a lot of time to put together a dinner party . . . but want something that's trendy and elegant, yet not troublesome," she says. "You just throw out a few bars and serve some drinks."

As well, with new portion-control products—often about 100 calories—now available, chocoholics can indulge without guilt. And for the purist consumer, a growing number of organic chocolate SKUs—including the Green & Black's brand imported from the U.K.—are finding their way to the confectionery aisles.

Despite the higher price tag, "the organic and natural food movement in Canada is really beginning to flourish as more and more consumers are drawn into the category," says Laurence Bass, international development manager for Green & Black's. Although Rowsome has no statistics to prove his case, he and others say that dark chocolate is clearly the category driver. As well, because of Canadians' adventurous leanings, high-end products are dropping into shopping baskets as fast as shelves can be restocked.

Responding to health and wellness trends, in August Mars Canada introduced Mars Dark. It's a new formulation that blends the familiar taste and texture of the original Mars bar in dark chocolate, and it's peanut-free.

While sales figures are proprietary, Toronto-based Kraft Canada Inc., which began distributing the Côte d'Or line of upscale chocolate in late 2004, says sales are continuing to grow.

"I think people are beginning to understand chocolate as a premium product, and are developing a greater interest and respect for it," says Barbara Cooper, Côte d'Or product manager.

To ensure potential customers truly understand the stature of the Côte d'Or line, the company recently launched a pairing campaign through the media and at food and wine shows attended by consumers. It is also considering sampling in the grocery-store sector.

UPSCALE OFFERS

Few chocolate makers in Canada have been asleep at the switch in developing new upscale lines. For instance, Toronto-based Laura Secord has recently launched a new line of 100 gram bars, available in three flavours.

Phil Guay, vice-president of sales for Laura Secord, says the new bars were introduced in June to fill in a gap of the "everyday" segment in confectionery that he defines as a product that a customer buys any time of the year, either for immediate or future consumption.

"We were not part of that," says Guay, who adds that Laura Secord has quadrupled its sales to the grocery, drug and mass banners to almost $13 million in two years. "The fastest growing segment right now in chocolate is everyday future consumption, which includes 100 gram bars."

Laura Secord also addressed the growing trend of portion control about a year ago when it launched its Sweet Therapy line targeted at the weight-conscious 25- to 45-year-old female.

"The problem we have with [regular] boxed chocolates . . . is that people buy them as a gift, not for themselves," says Guay. "Every time we talked to women, they would feel guilty if they bought a box of chocolates. If they didn't eat them all and threw some in the garbage, they'd feel guilty and if they ate the whole box, they'd feel guilty."

WOMEN LEAD THE WAY

Women represent a huge chunk of the chocolate market. "Most women lead very hectic lives with shared commitments between spouses, work, children and home, and that makes the time they take for themselves even more precious," says Monica Tenorio, director, chocolate, Cadbury Adams Canada. "Today's women have a new focus on a balanced lifestyle that includes decadent indulgences. They're looking for a personal gratification in their day that helps them maximize the little time they have for themselves."

To address the above perceived need, Cadbury Adams Canada recently launched Caramilk Deluxe. To market the new product, the company created the Caramilk Deluxe Lounge where women received a five- to 10-minute massage with the accompaniment of soothing music, followed by a sampling of the new chocolate.

With chocolate sales—particularly the up-market variety—on the rise, there's little doubt that strong growth will continue. A key reason for the positive outlook is Canada's low consumption rate. According to CMAC, in 2005 per capita figures showed that Canadians gobbled up only 2.92 kg compared with 5.57 kg in the U.S. and 6.55 kg in the European Union.

Perhaps Rowsome of CMAC sums it up best: "My crystal ball would say that in seven years we've seen a constant growth of confectionery sales in this country through good times and bad . . . This is going to continue and when you look at the consumption in Canada versus other countries, the opportunities are boundless."

Source: Carolyn Green, "Chocolate Lovers Delight," Canadian Grocer, 121 *(8): 70–73. Copyright Rogers Publishing Limited, October 2007.*

Reading Chart

	Main Ideas	*Assumptions*	*Sources of Evidence*	*Summary Statement*
"Chocolate: The Bittersweet Treat"				
"Chocolate Lovers Delight"				

Exercise 2 Putting Critical Reading to Work

The following two articles come from scholarly journals. Your purpose in reading is to comprehend the writers' ideas so that you can understand the structure of their arguments. Conceptual terms and specialized vocabulary are underlined. Look up unfamiliar terms.

Note that one article is from a sports journal, and although you may think sports reading is easy work, you will see that reading about sports theory can be just as complex as reading about philosophy. Also notice that the third reading contains APA style citations, which means the writer has used the American Psychological Association style of referring to authors and their works. These citations appear in parentheses and indicate the date of publication. You will learn much more about research and research writing in chapters 12–15 of *Spotlight on Critical Skills in Essay Writing*, Second Edition.

Using the chart that follows the next two readings, write definitions for terms you do not understand. Write down main ideas. Then summarize the writer's argument, if possible.

After completing the first part of the exercise, form a group of no more than five students. Discuss your findings, and be prepared to present them to the rest of the class.

Use chart paper, overhead transparencies, or a computer to record your ideas for presentation.

Archetypes

by Julie Stevens

The notion of archetypes originally emerged from discussions in organization theory that supported a holistic as opposed to a particular approach. Mintzberg (1979) built upon early work that emphasized structural components of organizations to present different typologies. Miller and Friesen (1980a, 1980b, 1984) developed a holistic perspective that included both organizational and environmental properties, termed gestalts. Ranson, Hinings, and Greenwood (1980) expanded the notion of an archetype beyond simply an organization comprised of structural elements to an entity that embraced a distinctive interpretive scheme of values and ideas. Hinings and Greenwood (1988) defined archetype as "clusters of prescribed and emergent structures given order or coherence by an underpinning set of ideas, values, and beliefs, i.e. an interpretive scheme" (p. 22). For example, the Kitchen Table archetype presented by Kikulis et al. (1992) outlined how volunteer-based values were manifest in an unstandardized yet centralized structure led by executive volunteers. For the purpose of this discussion, archetypes are viewed as tightly coupled value-structure designs. Here, core values and practices come to be tightly coupled with organizational structures to create a stable and coherent configuration.

Source: Julie Stevens (2006). "The Canadian Hockey Association Merger and the Emergence of Amateur Sport Enterprise." Journal of Sport Management, *20: 74–100. Excerpt, p. 76. © 2006 Human Kinetics, Inc.*

Adolescent Passengers of Drunk Drivers

by Christiane Poulin, Brock Boudreau, and Mark Asbridge

Motor vehicle collisions are the leading cause of death for youth in Canada and the United States [1–4]. Among licensed drivers, adolescents 16–19 years of age have the highest collision involvement rate relative to any other age group [5]. The highest risk of a vehicle collision occurs among drivers 16 and 17 years of age who have just graduated from a learner's permit to an unsupervised driving licence [6–8]. Alcohol figures prominently in adolescent fatalities arising from motor vehicle collisions. In 2000 in Canada, 39% of the 329 adolescents 16–19 years of age who died in motor vehicle collisions were deemed to be alcohol-related fatalities [9], and in 2004 in the United States, 23% of the more than 2400 driver fatalities among youth 16–19 years of age had a blood alcohol concentration equal to or greater than 0.08 [1].

Adolescents are at high risk of motor vehicle collisions, and of fatality in such collisions, not only as young drivers but also as the passengers of young drivers. Of the nearly 5000 motor vehicle fatalities that occurred in 2004 among adolescents 13–19 years of age in the United States, 46% were passengers and, of those, 62% were passengers in vehicles operated by drivers who themselves were 13–19 years of age [1]. Adolescent drivers with adolescent passengers are more likely to operate the vehicle while impaired, or to become distracted, or to engage in other behaviour that increases the risk of a collision [10]. Several studies have demonstrated that all occupants in the vehicles of newly licensed young drivers are at increased risk when adolescent passengers are in the car [5, 6, 11].

Riding with a drunk driver (RDD) has become recognized as a high-risk behaviour [12, 13]. In the United States in 1997, 37% of students in grades 9–12 reported having been a passenger under these circumstances [14]. In Canada, 29% of students in grades 7–12 in Ontario in 2003, and 39% of their counterparts in Manitoba in 2004, reported RDD [15, 16]. RDD has been found to be associated with heavy episodic drinking, cannabis use, cigarette smoking [17–20], increasing age [16, 20, 21], rural residence [18], early age onset of alcohol use [22], staying out at night without permission, negative social behaviours and participation in social activities [23]. Grube & Voas [24] found that expectancies of arrest and loss of licence were related negatively to both RDD and driving under the influence of alcohol. The evidence is mixed as to the association between RDD and gender. One study found females to be at higher risk [25], one study reported that males were at higher risk [14] and several studies failed to demonstrate that gender was an independent risk factor [21, 26, 27]. RDD has also been found to be associated with the behaviour of driving under the influence of alcohol. Yu & Shacket [22] explored the apparent reciprocity between these two behaviours among youth 16–24 years of age in the state of New York. They found that driving under the influence of alcohol was predictive of RDD but not the reverse and concluded that driving under the influence of alcohol was a valid and powerful predictor of RDD.

In the present study, we sought to determine the prevalence and risk factors associated with being a passenger of an alcohol-impaired driver among adolescents in the Atlantic provinces of Canada. The risk factors we have drawn upon allow us to consider both the individual-level predictors of RDD along with the broader structural and ecological forces that may shape the choice to take part in this behaviour. We were interested in alcohol and other drug use, as these behaviours may be viewed as resulting from powerfully conditioned social environments. We were also interested in two key social determinants of health—socio-economic status and rural residence. Socio-economic class has been found to be a persistent determinant of health [28, 29]. More recently, rural and remote residence has been examined as a source of inequities in health status and behaviours (e.g. [30]). In the case of RDD, adolescents who come from families with a lower socio-economic status may have preferentially fewer options for safe rides home. For example, less economically advantaged families may not have a vehicle, they may not be able to give the adolescent access to the family vehicle, or they may be unable to provide alternative transportation such as a taxi. Rural residence may be a structural determinant of adolescents' choosing to be a passenger with an alcohol-impaired driver, due to the mechanism of having little if any access to public transportation, particularly at weekends and at night. In Canada, rural residence has also been found to be associated with a higher prevalence of drinking among adolescent males [30]. We therefore hypothesized that at the individual level, a lower family socio-economic status, rural residence and substance use would be independent risk factors of RDD. We also hypothesized that students living in less advantaged neighbourhoods and neighbourhoods with a high prevalence of substance use would be at greater risk of RDD. Understanding RDD from a multi-level environmental perspective can ultimately provide insights as to policy and programme options operating at the provincial level.

Source: Christiane Poulin, Brock Boudreau & Mark Asbridge. "Adolescent passengers of drunk drivers: a multi-level exploration into the inequities of risk and safety." Addiction, *102: 51–52. © 2006. Reproduced with permission of Blackwell Publishing Ltd.*

Reading Chart

"Archetypes"		
Terms	Main Ideas	Summarize the Writer's Argument
"Adolescent Passengers of Drunk Drivers"		
Terms	Main Ideas	Summarize the Writer's Argument

Exercise 3 Presenting the Author's Ideas

The following longer reading will be particularly interesting to readers who are concerned about the environment and, specifically, the health of the world's oceans. The piece is striking in its details.

Read the article and prepare to engage with the material. Your purpose in reading is to present your understanding of the writer's main ideas, assumptions, and recommendations. You are also reading to detect bias. Prepare to share your writing with the rest of the class.

Part 1

1. Annotate the material.
2. Make marginal notes where you need them.
3. Write questions in the margins.
4. Underline terms you do not understand, and look them up.
5. Indicate key pieces of evidence.
6. Highlight statements that indicate the writer's bias.
7. Write assumptions in the margins.

Part 2

Write a paragraph of 200 words, outlining the writer's ideas and setting out the writer's assumptions and arguments. If you notice bias, include a statement or two about that. Also provide the writer's recommendations. Do not comment on the material. Instead, use critical thinking and reading skills to understand what this writer is suggesting. Prepare four extra copies of your paragraph to distribute to your group.

Part 3

In a group of no more than five people, exchange compositions. On chart paper, record the differences you see in the compositions as related to assumptions, arguments, bias, and recommendations.

Plastic Ocean

by Susan Casey

Susan Casey is an accomplished writer and editor who was born in Toronto. She has written the *New York Times* bestseller *The Devil's Teeth: A True Story of Obsession and Survival Among America's Great White Sharks* (2005). From 2003 to 2006, Casey was the development editor of Time Inc. and the editor of *Sports Illustrated Women.* She has also worked as the creative director of *Outside* magazine. Her pieces have been published in *Sports Illustrated, Esquire, Time, Fortune, The New York Times, Best Life,* and *Outside.*

Fate can take strange forms, and so perhaps it does not seem unusual that Captain Charles Moore found his life's purpose in a nightmare. Unfortunately, he was awake at the time, and 800 miles north of Hawaii in the Pacific Ocean.

It happened on August 3, 1997, a lovely day, at least in the beginning: Sunny. Little wind. Water the color of sapphires. Moore and the crew of *Alguita,* his 50-foot aluminum-hulled catamaran, sliced through the sea.

Returning to Southern California from Hawaii after a sailing race, Moore had altered *Alguita*'s course, veering slightly north. He had the time and the curiosity to try a new route, one that would lead the vessel through the eastern corner of a 10-million-square-mile oval known as the North Pacific subtropical gyre. This was an odd stretch of ocean, a place most boats purposely avoided. For one thing, it was becalmed. "The doldrums," sailors called it, and they steered clear. So did the ocean's top predators: the tuna, sharks, and other large fish that required livelier waters, flush with prey. The gyre was more like a desert—a slow, deep, clockwise-swirling vortex of air and water caused by a mountain of high-pressure air that lingered above it.

The area's reputation didn't deter Moore. He had grown up in Long Beach, 40 miles south of L.A., with the Pacific literally in his front yard, and he possessed an impressive aquatic resume: deck-hand, able seaman, sailor, scuba diver, surfer, and finally captain. Moore had spent countless hours in the ocean, fascinated by its vast trove of secrets and terrors. He'd seen a lot of things out there, things that were glorious and grand; things that were ferocious and humbling. But he had never seen anything nearly as chilling as what lay ahead of him in the gyre.

It began with a line of plastic bags ghosting the surface, followed by an ugly tangle of junk: nets and ropes and bottles, motor-oil jugs and cracked bath toys, a mangled tarp. Tires. A traffic cone. Moore could not believe his eyes. Out here in this desolate place the water was a stew of plastic crap. It was as though someone had taken the pristine seascape of his youth and swapped it for landfill.

How did all the plastic end up here? How did this trash tsunami begin? What did it mean? If the questions seemed overwhelming, Moore would soon learn that the answers were even more so and that his discovery had dire implications for human—and planetary—health. As *Alguita* glided through the area that scientists now refer to as the "Eastern Garbage Patch," Moore realized that the trail of plastic went on for hundreds of miles. Depressed and stunned, he sailed for a week through bobbing, toxic debris trapped in a purgatory of circling currents. To his horror, he had stumbled across the twenty-first-century leviathan. It had no head, no tail. Just an endless body.

"Everybody's plastic, but I love plastic. I want to be plastic." This Andy Warhol quote is emblazoned on a 6-foot-long magenta and yellow banner that hangs—with extreme irony—in the solar-powered workshop in Moore's Long Beach home. The workshop is surrounded by a crazy Eden of trees, bushes, flowers, fruits, and vegetables, ranging from the prosaic (tomatoes) to the exotic (cherimoyas, guavas, chocolate persimmons, white figs the size of baseballs). This is the house in which Moore, fifty-nine, was raised, and it has a kind of open-air earthiness that reflects his '60s-activist roots, which included a stint in a Berkeley commune. Composting and organic gardening are serious business here—you can practically smell the humus—but there is also a kidney-shaped hot tub surrounded by palm trees. Two wet suits hang drying on a clothesline above it.

This afternoon Moore strides the grounds. "How about a nice fresh boysenberry?" he asks, and plucks one off a bush. He's a striking man wearing no-nonsense black trousers and a shirt with official-looking epaulettes. A thick brush of salt-and-pepper hair frames his intense blue eyes and serious face. But the first thing you notice about Moore is his voice, a deep, bemused drawl that becomes animated and sardonic when the subject turns to plastic pollution. This problem is Moore's calling, a passion he inherited from his father, an industrial chemist who studied waste management as a hobby. On family vacations, Moore recalls, part of the agenda would be to see what the locals threw out. "We could be in paradise but we would go to the dump," he says with a shrug. "That's what we wanted to see."

Since his first encounter with the Garbage Patch nine years ago Moore has been on a mission to learn exactly what's going on out there. Leaving behind a twenty-five-year career running a furniture-restoration business, he has created the Algalita Marine Research Foundation to spread the word of his findings. He has resumed his science studies, which he'd set aside when his attention swerved from pursuing a university degree to protesting the Vietnam War. His tireless effort has placed him on the front lines of a new, more abstract battle. After enlisting scientists such as Steven B. Weisberg, Ph.D. (executive director of the Southern California Coastal Water Research Project and an expert in marine environmental monitoring), to develop methods for analyzing the gyre's contents, Moore has sailed *Alguita* back to the Garbage Patch several times. On each trip the volume of plastic has grown alarmingly. The area in which it accumulates is now twice the size of Texas.

At the same time, all over the globe there are signs that plastic pollution is doing more than blighting the scenery; it is also making its way into the food chain. Some of the most obvious victims are the dead seabirds that have been washing ashore in startling numbers, their bodies packed with plastic: things like bottle caps, cigarette lighters, tampon applicators, and colored scraps that, to a foraging bird, resemble baitfish. (One animal dissected by Dutch researchers contained 1,603 pieces of plastic.) And the birds aren't alone. All sea creatures are threatened by floating plastic, from whales down to zooplankton. There's a basic moral horror in seeing the pictures: a sea turtle with a plastic band strangling its shell into an hourglass shape; a humpback towing plastic nets that cut into its flesh and make it impossible for the animal to hunt. More than a million seabirds, 100,000 marine mammals, and countless fish die in the North Pacific each year, either from mistakenly eating this junk or from being ensnared in it and drowning.

Bad enough. But Moore soon learned that the big, tentacled balls of trash were only the most visible signs of the problem; others were far less obvious, and far more evil. Dragging a fine-meshed net known as a manta trawl, he discovered minuscule pieces of plastic, some barely visible to the eye, swirling like fish food throughout the water. He and his researchers parsed, measured, and sorted their samples and arrived at the following conclusion: by weight, this swath of sea contains six times as much plastic as it does plankton.

This statistic is grim—for marine animals, of course, but even more so for humans. The more invisible and ubiquitous the pollution, the more likely it will end up inside us. And there's growing—and disturbing—proof that we're ingesting plastic toxins constantly, and that even slight doses of these substances can severely disrupt gene activity. "Every one of us has this huge body burden," Moore says. "You could take your serum to a lab now, and they'd find at least one hundred industrial chemicals that weren't around in 1950." The fact that these toxins don't cause violent and immediate reactions does not mean they're benign: scientists are just beginning to research the long-term ways in which the chemicals used to make plastic interact with our own biochemistry.

In simple terms, plastic is a mix of monomers linked together to become polymers, to which additional chemicals can be added for suppleness, inflammability, and other qualities. When it comes to these substances, even the syllables are scary. For instance, if you're thinking that perfluorooctanoic acid (PFOA) isn't something you want to sprinkle on your microwave popcorn, you're right. Recently the Science Advisory Board of the Environmental Protection Agency (EPA) upped its classification of PFOA to a likely carcinogen. Yet it's a common ingredient in packaging that needs to be oil- and heat-resistant. So while there may be no PFOA in the popcorn itself, if PFOA is used to treat the bag, enough of it can leach into the popcorn oil when your butter deluxe meets your superheated microwave oven that a single serving spikes the amount of the chemical in your blood.

Other nasty chemical additives are the flame retardants known as polybrominated diphenyl ethers (PBDEs). These chemicals have been shown to cause liver and thyroid toxicity, reproductive problems, and memory loss in preliminary animal studies. In vehicle interiors, PBDEs—used in moldings and floor coverings, among other things—combine with another group called phthalates to create that much-vaunted "new-car smell." Leave your new wheels in the hot sun for a few hours, and these substances can "off-gas" at an accelerated rate, releasing noxious byproducts.

It's not fair, however, to single out fast food and new cars. PBDEs, to take just one example, are used in many products, including computers, carpeting, and paint. As for phthalates, we deploy about a billion pounds of them a year worldwide despite the fact that California recently listed them as a chemical known to be toxic to our reproductive systems. Used to make plastic soft and pliable, phthalates leach easily from millions of products—packaged food, cosmetics, varnishes, the coatings of timed-release pharmaceuticals—into our blood, urine, saliva, seminal fluid, breast milk, and amniotic fluid. In food containers and some plastic bottles, phthalates are now found with another compound called bisphenol A (BPA), which scientists are discovering can wreak stunning havoc in the body. We produce 6 billion pounds of that each year, and it shows: BPA has been found in nearly every human who has been tested in the United States. We're eating these plasticizing additives, drinking them, breathing them, and absorbing them through our skin every single day.

Most alarming, these chemicals may disrupt the endocrine system—the delicately balanced set of hormones and glands that affects virtually every organ and cell—by mimicking the female hormone estrogen. In marine environments, excess estrogen has led to *Twilight Zone*-esque discoveries of male fish and seagulls that have sprouted female sex organs.

On land, things are equally gruesome. "Fertility rates have been declining for quite some time now, and exposure to synthetic estrogen—especially from the chemicals found in plastic products—can have an adverse effect," says Marc Goldstein, M.D., director of the Cornell Institute for Reproductive Medicine. Dr. Goldstein also notes that pregnant women are particularly vulnerable: "Prenatal exposure, even in very low doses, can cause irreversible damage in an unborn baby's reproductive organs." And after the baby is born, he or she is hardly out of the woods. Frederick vom Saal, Ph.D., a professor at the University of Missouri at Columbia who specifically studies estrogenic chemicals in plastics, warns parents to "steer clear of polycarbonate baby bottles. They're particularly dangerous for newborns, whose brains, immune systems, and gonads are still developing." Dr. vom Saal's research spurred him to throw out every polycarbonate plastic item in his house, and to stop buying plastic-wrapped food and canned goods (cans are plastic-lined) at the grocery store. "We now know that BPA causes prostate cancer in mice and rats, and abnormalities in the prostate's stem cell, which is the cell implicated in human prostate cancer," he says. 'That's enough to scare the hell out of me." At Tufts University, Ana M. Soto, M.D., a professor of anatomy and cellular biology, has also found connections between these chemicals and breast cancer.

As if the potential for cancer and mutation weren't enough, Dr. vom Saal states in one of his studies that "prenatal exposure to very low doses of BPA increases the rate of postnatal growth in mice and rats." In other words, BPA made rodents fat. Their insulin output surged wildly and then crashed into a state of resistance—the virtual definition of diabetes. They produced bigger fat cells, and more of them. A recent scientific paper Dr. vom Saal coauthored contains this chilling sentence: "These findings suggest that developmental exposure to BPA is contributing to the obesity epidemic that has occurred during the last two decades in the developed world, associated with the dramatic increase in the amount of plastic being produced each year." Given this, it is perhaps not entirely coincidental that America's staggering rise in diabetes—a 735 percent increase since 1935—follows the same arc.

This news is depressing enough to make a person reach for the bottle. Glass, at least, is easily recyclable. You can take one tequila bottle, melt it down, and make another tequila bottle. With plastic, recycling is more complicated. Unfortunately, that promising looking triangle of arrows that appears on products doesn't always signify endless reuse; it merely identifies which type of plastic the item is made from. And of the seven different plastics in common use, only two of them—PET (labeled with #1 inside the triangle and used in soda bottles) and HDPE (labeled with #2 inside the triangle and used in milk jugs)—have much of an aftermarket. So no matter how virtuously you toss your chip bags and shampoo bottles into your blue bin, few of them will escape the landfill—only 3 to 5 percent of plastics are recycled in any way.

"There's no legal way to recycle a milk container into another milk container without adding a new virgin layer of plastic," Moore says, pointing out that because plastic melts at low temperatures, it retains pollutants and the tainted residue of its former contents. Turn up the heat to sear these off, and some plastics release deadly vapors. So the reclaimed stuff is mostly used to make entirely different products, things that don't go anywhere near our mouths, such as fleece jackets and carpeting. Therefore, unlike recycling glass, metal, or paper, recycling plastic doesn't always result in less use of virgin material. It also doesn't help that fresh-made plastic is far cheaper.

Moore routinely finds half-melted blobs of plastic in the ocean, as though the person doing the burning realized partway through the process that this was a bad idea and stopped (or passed out from the fumes). "That's a concern as plastic proliferates worldwide, and people run out of room for trash and start burning plastic—you're producing some of the most toxic gases known," he says. The color-coded bin system may work in Marin County, but it is somewhat less effective in subequatorial Africa or rural Peru.

"Except for the small amount that's been incinerated—and it's a very small amount—every bit of plastic ever made still exists," Moore says, describing how the material's molecular structure resists biodegradation. Instead, plastic crumbles into ever-tinier fragments as it's exposed to sunlight and the elements. And none of these untold gazillions of fragments is disappearing anytime soon: even when plastic is broken down to a single molecule, it remains too tough for biodegradation.

Truth is, no one knows how long it will take for plastic to biodegrade, or return to its carbon and hydrogen elements. We only invented the stuff 144 years ago, and science's best guess is that its natural disappearance will take several more centuries. Meanwhile, every year we churn out about 60 billion tons of it, much of which becomes disposable products meant only for a single use. Set aside the question of why we're creating ketchup bottles and six-pack rings that last for half a millennium and consider the implications of it: plastic never really goes away.

Ask a group of people to name an overwhelming global problem, and you'll hear about climate change, the Middle East, or AIDS. No one, it is guaranteed, will cite the sloppy transport of nurdles as a concern. And yet nurdles, lentil-sized pellets of plastic in its rawest form, are especially effective couriers of waste chemicals called persistent organic pollutants, or POPs, which include known carcinogens such as DDT and PCBs. The United States banned these poisons in the 1970s, but they remain stubbornly at large in the environment, where they latch on to plastic because of its molecular tendency to attract oils.

The word itself—nurdles—sounds cuddly and harmless, like a cartoon character or a pasta for kids, but what it refers to is most certainly not. Absorbing up to a million times the level of POP pollution in their surrounding waters, nurdles become supersaturated poison pills. They're light enough to blow around like dust, to spill out of shipping containers, and to wash into harbors, storm drains, and creeks. In the ocean, nurdles are easily mistaken for fish eggs by creatures that would very much like to have such a snack.

And once inside the body of a bigeye tuna or a king salmon, these tenacious chemicals are headed directly to your dinner table.

One study estimated that nurdles now account for 10 percent of plastic ocean debris. And once they're scattered in the environment, they're diabolically hard to clean up (think wayward confetti). At places as remote as Rarotonga, in the Cook Islands, 2,100 miles northeast of New Zealand and a twelve-hour flight from L.A, they're commonly found mixed with beach sand. In 2004, Moore received a $500,000 grant from the state of California to investigate the myriad ways in which nurdles go astray during the plastic manufacturing process. On a visit to a polyvinyl chloride (PVC) pipe factory, as he walked through an area where railcars unloaded ground-up nurdles, he noticed that his pant cuffs were filled with a fine plastic dust. Turning a corner, he saw windblown drifts of nurdles piled against a fence. Talking about the experience, Moore's voice becomes strained and his words pour out in an urgent tumble: "It's not the big trash on the beach. It's the fact that the whole biosphere is becoming mixed with these plastic particles. What are they doing to us? We're breathing them, the fish are eating them, they're in our hair, they're in our skin."

Though marine dumping is part of the problem, escaped nurdles and other plastic litter migrate to the gyre largely from land. That polystyrene cup you saw floating in the creek, if it doesn't get picked up and specifically taken to a landfill, will eventually be washed out to sea. Once there, it will have plenty of places to go: the North Pacific gyre is only one of five such high-pressure zones in the oceans. There are similar areas in the South Pacific, the North and South Atlantic, and the Indian Ocean. Each of these gyres has its own version of the Garbage Patch, as plastic gathers in the currents. Together these areas cover 40 percent of the sea. "That corresponds to a quarter of the Earth's surface," Moore says. "So twenty-five percent of our planet is a toilet that never flushes."

It wasn't supposed to be this way. In 1865, a few years after Alexander Parkes unveiled a precursor to manmade plastic called Parkesine, a scientist named John W. Hyatt set out to make a synthetic replacement for ivory billiard balls. He had the best of intentions: save the elephants! After some tinkering, he created celluloid. From then on, each year brought a miraculous recipe: rayon in 1891, Teflon in 1938, polypropylene in 1954. Durable, cheap, versatile—plastic seemed like a revelation. And in many ways it was. Plastic has given us bulletproof vests, credit cards, slinky spandex pants. It has led to breakthroughs in medicine, aerospace engineering, and computer science. And who among us doesn't own a Frisbee?

Plastic has its benefits; no one would deny that. Few of us, however, are as enthusiastic as the American Plastics Council. One of its recent press releases, titled "Plastic Bags—A Family's Trusted Companion," reads: "Very few people remember what life was like before plastic bags became an icon of convenience and practicality—and now art. Remember the 'beautiful' [sic] swirling, floating bag in American Beauty?"

Alas, the same ethereal quality that allows bags to dance gracefully across the big screen also lands them in many less desirable places. Twenty-three countries, including Germany, South Africa, and Australia, have banned, taxed, or restricted the use of plastic bags because they clog sewers and lodge in the throats of livestock. Like pernicious Kleenex, these flimsy sacks end up snagged in trees and snarled in fences, becoming eyesores and worse: they also trap rainwater, creating perfect little breeding grounds for disease-carrying mosquitoes.

In the face of public outrage over pictures of dolphins choking on "a family's trusted companion," the American Plastics Council takes a defensive stance, sounding not unlike the NRA: plastics don't pollute, people do.

It has a point. Each of us tosses about 185 pounds of plastic per year. We could certainly reduce that. And yet—do our products have to be quite so lethal? Must a discarded flip-flop remain with us until the end of time? Aren't disposable razors and foam packing peanuts a poor consolation prize for the destruction of the world's oceans, not to mention our own bodies and the health of future generations? "If 'more is better' and that's the only mantra we have, we're doomed," Moore says, summing it up.

Oceanographer Curtis Ebbesmeyer, Ph.D., an expert on marine debris, agrees. "If you could fast-forward ten thousand years and do an archaeological dig . . . you'd find a little line of plastic," he told the *Seattle Times* last April. "What happened to those people? Well, they ate their own plastic and disrupted their genetic structure and weren't able to reproduce. They didn't last very long because they killed themselves."

Wrist-slittingly depressing, yes, but there are glimmers of hope on the horizon. Green architect and designer William McDonough has become an influential voice, not only in environmental circles but among Fortune 500 CEOs. McDonough proposes a standard known as "cradle to cradle" in which all manufactured things must be reusable, poison-free, and beneficial over the long haul. His outrage is obvious when he holds up a rubber ducky, a common child's bath toy. The duck is made of phthalate-laden PVC, which has been linked to cancer and reproductive harm. "What kind of people are we that we would design like this?" McDonough asks. In the United States, it's commonly accepted that children's teething rings, cosmetics, food wrappers, cars, and textiles will be made from toxic materials. Other countries—and many individual companies—seem to be reconsidering. Currently McDonough is working with the Chinese government to build seven cities using "the building materials of the future," including a fabric that is safe enough to eat and a new, nontoxic polystyrene.

Thanks to people like Moore and McDonough, and media hits such as Al Gore's *An Inconvenient Truth*, awareness of just how hard we've bitch-slapped the planet is skyrocketing. After all, unless we're planning to colonize Mars soon, this is where we live, and none of us would choose to live in a toxic wasteland or to spend our days getting pumped full of drugs to deal with our haywire endocrine systems and runaway cancer.

None of plastic's problems can be fixed overnight, but the more we learn, the more likely it is that eventually wisdom will trump convenience and cheap disposability. In the meantime, let the cleanup begin. The National Oceanographic & Atmospheric Administration (NOM) is aggressively using satellites to identify and remove "ghost nets," abandoned plastic fishing gear that never stops killing. (A single net recently hauled up off the Florida coast contained more than 1,000 dead fish, sharks, and one loggerhead turtle.) New biodegradable starch-and corn-based plastics have arrived, and Wal-Mart has signed on as a customer. A consumer rebellion against dumb and excessive packaging is afoot. And in August 2006, Moore was invited to speak about "marine debris and hormone disruption" at a meeting in Sicily convened by the science adviser to the Vatican. This annual gathering, called the International Seminars on Planetary Emergencies, brings scientists together to discuss mankind's worst threats. Past topics have included nuclear holocaust and terrorism.

The gray plastic kayak floats next to Moore's catamaran, *Alguita*, which lives in a slip across from his house. It is not a lovely kayak; in fact, it looks pretty rough. But it's floating, a sturdy, 8-foot-long two-seater. Moore stands on *Alguita*'s deck, hands on hips, staring down at it. On the sailboat next to him, his neighbor, Cass Bastain, does the same. He has just informed Moore that he came across the abandoned craft yesterday, floating just offshore. The two men shake their heads in bewilderment.

"That's probably a six-hundred-dollar kayak," Moore says, adding, "I don't even shop anymore. Anything I need will just float by." (In his opinion, the movie *Cast Away* was a joke—Tom Hanks could've built a village with the crap that would've washed ashore during a storm.)

Watching the kayak bobbing disconsolately, it is hard not to wonder what will become of it. The world is full of cooler, sexier kayaks. It is also full of cheap plastic kayaks that come in more attractive colors than battleship gray. The ownerless kayak is a lummox of a boat, 50 pounds of nurdles extruded into an object that nobody wants but that'll be around for centuries longer than we will.

And as Moore stands on deck looking into the water, it is easy to imagine him doing the same thing 800 miles west, in the gyre. You can see his silhouette in the silvering light, caught between ocean and sky. You can see the mercurial surface of the most majestic body of water on Earth. And then below, you can see the half-submerged madhouse of forgotten and discarded things. As Moore looks over the side of the boat, you can see the seabirds sweeping overhead, dipping and skimming the water. One of the journeying birds, sleek as a fighter plane, carries a scrap of something yellow in its beak. The bird dives low and then boomerangs over the horizon. Gone.

Source: From The Best American Science and Nature Writing, *edited and with an introduction by Richard Preston, Tim Folger, Series Editor. (New York: Houghton Mifflin Company, 2007) 9–20. Reprinted by permission of International Creative Management, Inc. Copyright © 2006 by Susan Casey. First appeared in* Best Life.

REVIEW TEST

Try the following review test. It will help you assess what you have learned from the chapter. Be prepared to share your responses with others in the class.

1. What distinguishes critical thinking? How can you tell that you are thinking critically?
2. Name four things that critical reading involves.

3. Name the eight steps of critical reading as outlined in the chapter.
4. What does it mean to use "deep structure" when you read critically?
5. What will you do to help develop your critical thinking and reading skills? Name at least three strategies you will use.

CHECKOUT

Here are some of the ideas you will take away with you after you have completed the chapter:

- Critical thinking is deliberate.
- Critical thinking requires you to be open to the process.
- Critical thinking involves including different points of view in your analysis.
- Both critical thinking and reading require a change of habit on the part of the thinker and reader.
- Developing critical thinking and reading skills takes time, patience, and practice.

Mastering the concepts in this chapter will also help you develop and apply the following employability skills highlighted by the Conference Board of Canada in *Employability Skills 2000+*:

Communicate

- read and understand information presented in a variety of forms (e.g., words, graphs, charts, diagrams)

Manage Information

- access, analyze and apply knowledge and skills from various disciplines (e.g., the arts, languages, science, technology, mathematics, social sciences, and the humanities)

Think & Solve Problems

- seek different points of view and evaluate them based on facts

Source: Adapted from *Employability Skills 2000+* Brochure E/F (Ottawa: The Conference Board of Canada, 2000).

chapter 2

Writing as Process: Prewriting

Chapter Objectives

After completing this chapter you will be able to

1. recognize phases of writing;
2. develop ways to deal with procrastination;
3. encourage yourself about your own writing;
4. generate writing ideas;
5. determine your purpose in writing;
6. choose a suitable writing tone.

INTRODUCTION

Writing is the development of ideas, the expression of thoughts using words, and a set of practices. As such, writing is a process because it involves a series of interrelated steps, producing changes that result in some sort of written outcome—a review, an essay, a journal, a research paper, or something else, such as a poem, a short story, a play, a film script, or a novel. Almost all students engage in some kind of writing activity in the course of their studies, and almost all learn and improve.

As a writer, you must recognize that writing is a process: you write, revise, edit, rework, and often rethink a piece of writing. The process is not like taking a bus from point A and arriving in a more or less straight line to point B. Although writing, like bus travel, has many stops along the way, it can move in different directions: backward, sideways, in circles, randomly, and so on. Unlike the bus, you cannot predict exactly which direction the writing will take you. If bus travel were like writing, some passengers might find themselves ending up in strange and surprising destinations.

It is quite fine and normal to find the writing process a little bit messy. You may have to rework the introduction of a paper after you have adjusted other parts. With some trepidation, you may discover an outline needs reworking or may find out a great idea that came to you at three in the morning looks pretty weak in the hard, cold light of noon. Recognize that unexpected turns are part of the bumpy journey in writing. *Spotlight on Critical Skills in Essay Writing*, Second Edition, offers the writing process as six phases: chapter 2 presents phase 1, prewriting, while chapter 3 discusses phases 2–6: planning, drafting, revising, editing, and presenting.

OVERVIEW: PHASES OF WRITING

Writing does not always "happen" in the same way, but writing does usually occur as a process that includes several phases. As a writer, you think about what you are going to write: you might make idea notes, you might discuss your ideas with friends, and you might do some research on your topic. You might be doing more than one thing at a time when it comes to your preparation for writing; it all depends on what the situation is, how much time you have, how much time you are willing to commit, and what your purpose in writing is.

The phases of writing are not clear-cut, but experts do agree that most writers experience most or all of them at different times. Each writing experience you have will be unique—an interesting combination of what you have learned and what you choose to apply to the task at hand. Clearly, more complex writing tasks, such as research papers, will require more preparation, while simpler or shorter tasks will require less.

The following section introduces you to the prewriting phase of writing; the subsequent phases are described in chapter 3. Remember that you may not use all of the phases every time you write; however, you should be utilizing the important phases in most academic writing situations.

PHASE 1: PREWRITING

Prewriting refers to the preparatory work you put in before you begin to write a draft: a draft is an attempt at writing, and most longer academic assignments require several drafts. Prewriting is a stage wherein you think and prepare to write. It may include reading and taking notes, sketching ideas, outlining, and discussion, but it may include other activities that help generate ideas and keep you inspired.

To Procrastinate or Not

One of the most important parts of the writing process comes at the start. Have you noticed how difficult it seems at times to get something started? You can think of examples from your own life. Perhaps, for instance, you have work to do around your home, yet you find yourself putting it off in order to do something else, usually of lesser importance. Do you find yourself doing the laundry when what you really need to do is get started on a research paper? Do you find yourself watching a silly television program instead of doing the reading for your English literature class? You might say yes to a group of friends who want you to go out with them when you really ought to say no. Almost all students will report similar experiences, and they will also talk about the guilt they feel at not making the best choices for time management. That's the starting point: to recognize that procrastination, the putting off of a task or assignment, is a normal response, maybe even a useful one. Like everyone else, you need to learn strategies to deal with it.

Procrastination is the result of a number of issues but rarely laziness. Procrastination might indicate you feel uncertain. Maybe the challenge seems too great. Maybe you feel shy about asking your instructor to help clarify an assignment. Perhaps previously you have had negative experiences with a subject such as English and feel anxious about it. Examine your feelings: do you put off doing an assignment for any of these reasons?

It is true that frequently students put off course-related things, not necessarily because they are bad planners or incompetent people but, rather, because they are really not sure what they are supposed to do in an assignment. If this is the case for you, then try the following strategies:

Strategy 1. Find someone else in the class who looks organized. Ask this student if she would mind talking with you briefly after class because you want to make sure you have understood each assignment correctly. Tell your new colleague that you often misunderstand assignments and need help with clarification.

Strategy 2. Contact your instructor. Email is an excellent tool. In your email, tell your instructor that you need help with clarification. Don't write a long-winded message, full of excuses and apologies. Be polite, direct, and concise. Most instructors will respond quickly to your request. If an assignment is complex, use email to book an appointment with your instructor, or visit her during posted office hours.

If you procrastinate because you feel anxious due to some previous history with the subject, you can develop coping strategies.

Strategy 3. Look for another student in your course or program who you think is a good listener, well-organized, trustworthy, and friendly. Ask to meet for coffee and tell the student why you want to talk to her. When you meet, be fairly straightforward about your experiences and try to be specific. You might say something like this: "When I was in high school, I didn't do well in English. Now that I think about it, I'm not really sure why. I do know I had a habit of putting things off until the last minute. Then I would hand in whatever trash I had written. Soon I formed a habit of doing this, and my teachers started getting the impression that I was lazy or lacking ability. I didn't like that feeling much. Now I have a chance to start again, but I'm not sure how. Have you ever experienced the same situation? What did you do about it?"

Strategy 4. Every college and university campus has a Learning Help Centre and special resource counsellors who can help you. If you are not comfortable talking with another student, then consider getting some advice from an on-campus expert. Learning counsellors often offer free courses that help with time management, test stress, coping with course loads, and other related issues. Find out what your campus has to offer to support you in your learning.

Whatever you do, don't feel that you're stuck. Putting something off for a short time may actually allow you to develop some "thinking space." Cognitive psychology now suggests that thinking takes many forms—what you believe to be procrastination may be something else: i.e., working something through or a kind of mental mulling over. Here are some other tips that might help you:

Tip 1. Recognize when you are procrastinating. Think about your reasons: Are you feeling anxious? Are you unclear about the assignment? Have you made some poor choices about what to do with your time?

Tip 2. Set a deadline, and immediately start taking action. Procrastination ends when you take action. Do something right away. You can read for 10 minutes. You can work on an internet search. You can write in your journal. You can read your text and take notes. You can pack up and head off to the library. You can read on the bus on the way to work. You can always take action of some sort, no matter how small it might seem. The old saying, "A journey of a thousand miles begins with a single step" is certainly true.

Tip 3. Set small goals. Write them in your Day-Timer or journal. Make the goals achievable. Don't promise yourself something you cannot deliver. In other words, make your first step a reasonable one. For example, you might say, "This evening I plan to reread what my assignment is and to brainstorm for ideas for 30 minutes."

Tip 4. When you begin to feel bogged down, talk with someone. The person does not have to be in the same course as you. She can be a friend or family member who is a willing and sympathetic listener. Conversation can help in so many ways: It can generate ideas or clarify them. It can lift your spirits. It can help you take action.

Tip 5. Use a journal to express and discuss your delay. Take a fresh sheet in your journal and write—without stopping—for 10 minutes. Write about anything connected to your procrastination and your assignment. Write without pausing. Write without stopping to think out what you have to say. Start with this sentence: "I think I know why I am procrastinating over my term paper. . . . " After 10 minutes (set a timer), read over what you have written.

Now you are ready to work. Start with phase 1, prewriting. Prewriting is a preparatory step to writing. It is an activity or set of activities to help focus your attention, ideas, and writing. In chapter 3, you will read about the rest of the phases. After you have worked through some activities to get you started, you can assess what you have, sort through it, and then set up a plan for writing.

THE IMPORTANCE OF INTEREST IN YOUR WRITING

Interest is a motivator. When you write, think of interest in two ways. Think of you—what interests you and what gets you interested in writing—and your reader and how your writing might interest her. Obvious as it may seem, the more interested you are in a topic or assignment, the more engaged you become with your writing and, ultimately, the better the paper you will write. Sometimes you have to work at being interested. Boredom will seldom produce an outstanding assignment. Not everything you do in your post-secondary studies will excite you, so recognize that fact and be prepared to deal with it.

How do writers pique their own interest? How do they get started? What sorts of tricks do they have?

Developing Your Interest

First of all, consider what interests you. Interesting topics can lead to interesting papers. Not all courses will offer you choices in assignments, but many do. Begin by asking yourself some questions:

- What sorts of topics do I find myself reading about?
- Do I really want to know about something?
- Are there topics I want to explore that are related to a future career path?

- What do I usually do to pursue a topic I am interested in?
- Where do I go to look for new, interesting ideas?

For a writer, a good tool to use is an ideas book. An ideas book is exactly what it sounds like: it is a book you carry with you in which you write down ideas you have throughout the day. Perhaps they are story ideas if you are considering taking a creative writing course. Maybe they are ideas for research. Possibly you have ideas about books, stories, or articles you want to read, or authors you wish to research. You might list literary criticism and comment, and topic ideas for papers.

The effectiveness of the ideas book comes from using one on a regular basis. For the ideas book to be effective, you must have it with you, and you must make entries by habit. Journals, for instance, have become very popular with students. Many write in their journals on a daily basis. Journal writing can be extremely beneficial to you if you happen to be one of those people who consistently develop this habit.

An ideas book is somewhat different from a journal. It is really a kind of repository, a place for you to collect and record specific ideas for specific study and research work as the ideas occur to you. While a journal is a place to discuss feelings and events, your ideas book is a gathering place for inspired thoughts, ideas, and study directions.

The ideas book need not be difficult to use or expensive to purchase. You can find three-hole notebooks for less than $2.00 at the dollar store. However, different writers have different preferences. You might favour a smaller, palm-sized memo book since it is an item you can easily tuck into your backpack, purse, or pocket.

If you prefer to take a laptop to campus, you can set up a special folder called "Ideas." Inside the folder, set up files, either by assignment, by subject, or both. For instance, set up a file for each upcoming assignment. List the deadline dates, instructions, professors' names, and the number of marks each assignment is worth. Then sketch in a rough outline and a timeline. Now you are ready to add ideas whenever they occur to you or whenever you find something interesting to add from your reading or discussions.

Tips for an Ideas Book

- Date each entry.
- Make brief notes.
- Develop your own shorthand for these brief notes. For example, you could make up your own code: NG for "not good," EX for "excellent" or "example," and so on. Even add your own commentary, such as "I'm excited about this idea because I think it will really help me shape the second part of my paper."
- Keep the book with you wherever you go. Warn your family and friends that you might have to stop to make a quick note from time to time, or make a note on your laptop.
- Do not tear out any pages or delete any of your files in your ideas folder. Sometimes a mediocre idea can lead to more engaging ones.
- Review your ideas book or files from time to time. Create some plans based on an idea from your book. In other words, if you are about to make a trip to the library, you might check out your ideas book to consolidate some of your research.

Asking Questions for the Ideas Book or Ideas Folder

Do you recall these questions from an earlier part of this chapter?

1. What sorts of topics do I find myself reading about?
2. Do I really want to know about something?
3. Are there topics I want to explore that are related to a future career path?
4. What do I usually do to pursue a topic I am interested in?
5. Where do I go to look for new, interesting ideas?

Use these questions after you have purchased your ideas book or set up your ideas folder on your laptop. Look at the first question. Take a few minutes to answer it. Make a list of topics of interest to you. Write down all ideas—do not censor yourself. Write down the current date, and list as many topics of real interest to you as possible. In about one week's time, do the same thing again. Compare the two lists: Are they different? Have you expanded your areas of interest a little since the first entry?

Question 2 asks you what you really want to know about. Write down as many items as you can think of. Your list can contain a wide diversity of queries. For example, you might want to read about a famous sports personality you admire. You might want to know something about her life. On the other hand, you might want to know how to organize a conference, train a dog, service a piece of machinery, or practise making a speech. All of these items are arranged according to knowledge of "how to" do something. Similarly, you might want to consider questions relating to abstract ideas, conceptions, or theories. For example, you might want to know what a famous philosopher thought about social conventions, such as marriage; what an artist's views on the viewer are; what constitutes a human freedom; or what a feminist might say about *Hamlet*. Write down such questions as they occur to you, but keep them brief and clear.

Review what you really want to know every two weeks. As you revisit your lists, you might suddenly decide to expand one of these questions into a term paper or research essay. You might find some excellent ideas buried in among the questions.

Question 3 links to question 2. As you explore what you really want to know about, questions relating to your future career goal may emerge. For example, you may find that the most interesting and relevant questions connect to art, art theory, or art criticism if you are a visual arts student.

When you explore your answer to question 4 you will actually be examining what procedures you use when you investigate something. The question will help you focus on what process you follow, what techniques you use, or what method you develop. Think about what you usually do. Think about what steps you take. Write them down. Then consider whether this process has been effective for you. If you want to improve it, write down some questions you need to answer to improve your research techniques.

Consider this example: Someone assigns a task for you to do; perhaps it is your supervisor, an instructor, or a friend needing help. How do you go about solving the intellectual problem? Do you look for answers on the internet? Do you talk to someone you trust? Do you look up possible references at the library? Do you take notes? Do you ask an expert? All of these possibilities are valid, but some are more useful than others.

Prior knowledge is important. To select an effective method, you must have some knowledge to begin with. For instance, some tasks require a particular line of inquiry that is more thorough and scholarly. To do a general search on the internet requires that you know about the process of making an inquiry using a browser and search engine. However, as an academic student, you must also know about the scholarly research available online and about how to access it through huge academic databases accessible only through your college or university library site.

To answer question 5 requires an active search. You can find many new and exciting ideas in the professional journals of your academic library on campus. You can note new topics or areas of interest emerging from newscasts, newspaper articles, internet news, reputable magazines, television, podcasts, and radio programming. The seminar and discussion groups in your courses will also become important sources for the exchange of ideas and opinions. Even having coffee with a group of your friends from class can be exciting and entertaining if the discussion revolves around ideas. You might want to form a group of interested people from your class who want to meet to discuss two or three important social issues, to debate points in articles or materials given out in class, or to organize and plan collaborative projects. Another idea is to go to bookstores, too. You'll see new book releases on current issues or find sections in the store you may not have investigated before. Your campus bookstore may be the place to start. Large universities have excellent campus bookstores with particularly interesting reference sections. In all cases, take advantage of the opportunity to participate, investigate, and learn.

Considering Your Reader's Interest

After you have given some thought to your own interest in a topic and writing about it, you are ready to consider your reader's interest. Obviously, it is not always easy to tell exactly what interests your reader or whether what you have to say will interest her. However, it is important to consider what factors may be important. This section discusses your audience—the reader—and in that discussion, you will think about which aspects of your reader are most critical to you as the writer.

Your audience is your reader or group of readers. Of course, in most post-secondary courses, your instructor or professor will be your most important audience because that is who will be evaluating your work. In addition, in many cases, she may be the sole reader of your work. However, this scenario is changing. Many courses now include other audiences for students' writing. Here are three other audiences for academic work:

1. Collaborative projects demand that you work together with three to five other members of your class to produce one written assignment. In such a situation, you will find sharing your own writing an important feature of the group project. Some students find it rather odd to share their writing with anyone other than their instructors. In short order, however, they find they must write publicly as part of many post-secondary courses, particularly business, nursing, education, English, community studies, First Nations studies, and social sciences.

2. Peer-reviewed projects are assignments based on evaluations completed by fellow students of written work done in the class. Some students have not experienced peer reviews before. You, too, might find it somewhat difficult to have another class member review, comment on, and grade your work, yet peer-reviewed assignments are a common practice in post-secondary studies today.

3. Public assignments may include letters to editors, articles written for a class magazine, articles for electronic journals and magazines, or assignments posted for online course

work. Some instructors ask students to write letters to the editor as part of their course work. Students must then read and respond to comments others may make about their letters. In other circumstances, you may be asked to contribute by writing a short article for a magazine your class assembles. In another situation, if you are taking an online course, you may discover that you must post one of your assignments to your classmates and visitors. *Posting* means you must put your work in a special section of the course site online where others may read it and make comments about it.

An audience may also be someone you imagine. For example, in a sociology course, you might be asked to write an essay about the life your grandparents experienced and then compare it to yours in terms of changes in social structure. As you write, you might imagine your grandparents reading the piece. You might think of how they would react, what they would say about your work, or what they would want you to explain. In so doing, you begin to revise your work according to what your imagined (and intended) audience might have to say. Your writing begins to be shaped, then, not only by the topic but also by the intended audience, either real or imagined.

As you write, visualize your reader, imagined or otherwise. If your audience is a "real" one, such as colleagues, class members, instructors, or professors, you write with a more informed perspective of your reader. You know, more or less, what to expect. You really do know your audience because you have met them. If, on the other hand, you are writing with an imagined audience in mind, you will have to construct some sort of profile of your reader as you write. The profile should take into consideration the following:

- What does your intended reader know about the topic? Are you writing for an expert or an amateur?
- What level of interest do you expect your reader to have? Do you expect your reader to be deeply engaged by the topic or to have merely a passing interest in it?
- What do you think is most important in regard to this particular audience's interest?

Exercise 1 *Thinking about Audience*

Form a group of three to five members. Answer the following questions. Be prepared to share your answers with the class.

1. You are writing a short paper for an online class. What considerations would you make for an audience?
2. You are writing a letter to the editor for an assignment. What considerations should you need to make for your audience? What other considerations might this assignment entail in terms of audience?
3. You are writing an essay for a course in criminology. As part of the course, your instructor asks you to share your paper with a group of social service sector workers. What considerations should you give to your paper in regard to audience and audience interest?
4. You are being asked to write an essay about relationships in families. No specific audience is being named. What would you do in regard to imagining your audience and your audience's interest?

THE IMPORTANCE OF PURPOSE WHEN WRITING

Your purpose in writing provides focus. Purposes vary from writer to writer, or from discipline to discipline. However, every writer should understand why she is writing something, beyond getting marks for a course.

Before you read more about the writing process, try the following exercises.

Exercise 2 Thinking about Purpose

Write down a purpose for each of the following writing scenarios. Think of purpose as the reason or reasons you are writing. Be prepared to share your answers.

1. You have been asked to write a letter to the editor about the crowding on the city buses that take you to college or university each day.

   ____

   ____

2. You have been asked to write a piece about coaching hockey.

   ____

   ____

3. You have been asked to write a piece about poverty and the elderly.

   ____

   ____

4. You have been asked to contribute three pages to a collaborative writing assignment on women in the workplace. Your section of the report is to cover pay equity.

   ____

   ____

5. Your assignment is to describe the typical adult learner. The assignment is for the Continuing Education Department of your college or university. The piece will be posted on its website.

   ____

   ____

Writing can serve different purposes, audiences, and interests. You can think of writing as having four basic purposes:

- to describe;
- to narrate (tell a story);
- to convince;
- to explain, evaluate, or investigate.

Exercise 3 Purposes in Writing

Write down which purpose or purposes each of the following assignments might have. Check your answers with the Answer Key. Be prepared to explain your answers.

1. The assignment is about environment and clear-cutting practices. The purpose or purposes: ____

   ____

2. The assignment is about grading practices in schools. The purpose or purposes:

   ____

   ____

3. The writing assignment is to interview a person living on the streets and then write, using the interview as material for the piece. The purpose or purposes:

   ____

   ____

4. The writing assignment is to compare two writers' use of metaphor in their fiction. The purpose or purposes:

   ____

   ____

5. The writing assignment is about amateur soccer in Canada. The purpose or purposes:

   ____

   ____

THE IMPORTANCE OF TONE IN YOUR WRITING

Tone in writing has to do with your attitude toward your subject or your readers. A writer's tone may be formal or informal, optimistic or pessimistic, serious or comical, angry or joyful, bitter or hopeful; in fact, any emotion or mode of expression may indicate the writer's tone.

An ironic tone and a satirical tone need to be mentioned separately because these two expressions describe special circumstances, not emotions. Irony is the opposite of what you expect from a situation or an action: it often expresses something sarcastically or humorously. For example, the statement, "Kim and Bo lost the set of plans they had worked on for eight months" is ironic. What is the irony in the situation?

Satire is a form of ridicule; the writer wants to expose the foolishness or immoral conduct of an individual, group, corporation, or government. Often satire targets some aspect of society, or some "class" in society. Sometimes satires are referred to as spoofs.

Some examples are the Austin Powers movies, which spoof the spy films of the 1960s, and political cartoons, which satirize political life, heads of state, and government policies and mistakes.

You will find plenty of examples of irony and satire in writing, but life itself has many examples, too. Read the newspaper and look for examples of irony and satire. You might be surprised at what you find.

The tone is also created by the way you say something, including word choice and connotation. **Connotation** means the ideas that are implied or suggested by words. These ideas can have positive, negative, or neutral emotional effects. Connotations are largely culturally based. In other words, certain words will affect people in different ways depending on how those words are viewed by their culture. However, the media and popular language usage of words can change the connotation of words: from negative to positive, by making them more socially acceptable, or from positive to negative by using them in socially unacceptable contexts. Here are some examples of the connotative power behind words:

Positive	***Negative***	***Neutral***
fan	follower	supporter
friend	crony	colleague or associate
bond	tie	relationship
home	hovel	dwelling

Therefore, if you want your tone in writing to be positive, use words with a positive connotation. Your choice of words and their connotations should support your attitude.

Examples:

> Some <u>naive</u> governments tend to <u>meddle</u> in the domestic affairs of other <u>foreign</u> countries. (What is the writer's tone? What is the writer's attitude? What is the connotation of the underlined words?)

> Some <u>well-intentioned</u> nations want to provide <u>assistance and aid</u> to <u>less fortunate</u> countries. (What is the writer's tone? What is the writer's attitude? What is the connotation of the underlined words?)

THE IMPORTANCE OF CHOOSING AN APPROPRIATE POINT OF VIEW IN YOUR WRITING

When you consider the tone of a piece or the tone you wish to use in an assignment, also think about the point of view—that is, the perspective from which the piece is written. If a writer uses the **first-person, singular** point of view ("I"), then she is talking from a personal perspective.

Example:

> I remember my prairie childhood with affection.

If, instead, the writer chooses a **first-person, plural** point of view, then she wants to include you, the reader, in the discussion. Of course, such a point of view is more intimate and makes the assumption that you are really part of the discussion.

Example:

We all want to try our best to raise money for the Society of Wayward Poodles.

Sometimes *we* as a point of view can be condescending, as in, "We all want to take our medicine, don't we?" The first person, plural can also be patronizing, as in, "We all want to own the best car on the road."

A **third-person, plural** point of view is the one recommended for academic writing. By choosing third person, plural (e.g., *they*, *people*, *students*, and so on) rather than third person, singular (e.g., "each student should bring his lunch"), you will avoid sexism in your language. Sexism uses a particular point of view, usually male (as in "his lunch"), as if both genders share that point of view.

Examples:

All people have the right to personal privacy.

All students should bring their lunches to school.

Use the third-person point of view in your academic writing unless your instructor or professor tells you otherwise.

Passive voice is a construction often used to report an event or occurrence. This point of view is selected if the person doing the action (the subject or agent) is not important, or if the writer wants to blur responsibility for action.

Examples:

The children were moved into another classroom in the school.

Two people were arrested for drunken driving at the same intersection on the same night.

In the example sentences, the reader does not know who did the action; that is, the reader does not know who did the actual moving or arresting. However, it is not actually important to know those facts: it is the moving and the arresting that take precedence in the sentences.

Sometimes authorities use a passive construction to convey a "blameless" point of view.

Examples:

Gas prices were increased again today.

The public was notified of the changes to the policy.

In this example, the reader cannot locate responsibility. Those answerable for raising and controlling gas prices or making changes to public policy are missing from the sentence.

Points of View

first person, singular	I
first person, plural	we
second person, plural or singular	you
third person, singular	he, she, it
third person, plural	they
point of view indistinct	often found in passive voice constructions

Example: The criminal was stopped at the border. (Who stopped the criminal?)

Exercise 4 Recognizing Point of View

Work in pairs. Read each of the following examples. Tell what point of view you see in each. Explain how the point of view works in the example. Be prepared to share and discuss your answers.

1. I love the way summer brings out casual clothing, relaxed meals, and a sense of fun.
2. Economic indicators are pointing to a drop in prices in the housing market.
3. "The Prime Minister, a specialist in calling in the locksmith after the horses had fled—the whole herd in fact—and the barn in ruins, ended the week with a great raft of ethics proposals for cabinet, leadership candidates, backbenchers and lobbyists. I think it is more than fair to ask: Why wait for the middle of his third term to institute what the public would have welcomed at the beginning of his first?" (Rex Murphy, Canadian Broadcaster)
4. Marshall McLuhan said, "Canadians are the people who learned to live without the bold accents of the natural ego-trippers of other lands."
5. "I read and learned and fretted more about Canada after I left than I ever did while I was home. I absorbed anything I could on topics that ranged from Folklore to history to political manifestos . . . I ranted and raved and seethed about things beyond my control. In short I acted like a Canadian." (Will Ferguson, *How to Be a Canadian*)
6. Three people were arrested on Thursday at the main gates of the Montreal airport's main loading dock.
7. The Canadian beef industry estimates it has lost $7 billion since the Canadian–U.S. border was closed due to mad cow disease.
8. It is time for all of us to roll up our sleeves and get our annual flu shots.
9. A person needs to decide whom he should elect for the position of president of student council.
10. You must understand our return policy does not permit us to accept an item after 14 days of purchase.

Exercise 5 *Identifying Tone*

In each of the following passages, identify the writer's tone. Check your answers with the Answer Key. Be prepared to explain your answers.

1. Use these two general categories: formal and informal.
2. Then try to be more precise by adding another descriptor like *angry*, *upset*, *playful*, *hopeful*, and so on.
3. Underline words that helped you to recognize the author's tone.
4. What is the predominant point of view in each passage?

PASSAGE 1: Each Saturday morning at this time of year, my neighbourhood observes the ritual known as Getting Rid of Stuff. Front lawns teem with relics from attics and basements: orphaned plates, dented toys, jackets with killer shoulder pads, and a turntable with the hopeful sign "Still works!"

Strolling past with my grocery bags, I marvel at the useless junk some pack rats have hoarded for years. Then I remember my own hoard: the mouldy vaporizer, the half-dozen maps of San Francisco (one per trip because we never arrive prepared) and a cocktail dress in a screaming shade of fuchsia, last worn when Madonna and Sean Penn were still an item. There's more, but you get the idea. While my neighbours purge their flotsam and jetsam, mine explodes from every drawer, which means I'm hopelessly behind the times. This is, after all, the golden age of organizing, when the ultimate status symbol is a pristine closet full of storage bins in fashion colours, and the virtues of "conquering clutter" fill websites, magazine layouts and entire TV shows.

Source: Rona Maynard, "My Cluttered Life," Chatelaine *Jul. 2005: 40. Reprinted by permission of Rona Maynard.*

PASSAGE 2: Architecture is a knowledge-intensive business. When clients retain the services of an architect, they seek knowledge ranging from aesthetics to technical know-how to effective relationship-building skills. Firms compete on the basis of how clearly they understand stakeholder priorities as well as their insight in ways that far exceed standard "we listen to you" marketing promises.

Source: Sharon VanderKaay, "The Business of Selling Knowledge, Part 1," The Canadian Architect *Feb. 2005: 27.*

PASSAGE 3: Robert Louis Stevenson said: "Life is not a matter of having good cards, but of playing a poor hand well." To stress proof our children, we need to teach them how to play poor hands well. One of the best ways is to show them how to take something stressful or negative and look at it in terms of advantages and opportunities, or in some way to see it in more positive or very neutral terms. This is called "reframing."

The person who learns how to quickly reframe stress will feel more empowered, regardless what obstacles life places before them [sic]. Even the most severe stress, perhaps caused by an accumulation of losses, can be the source of incredible personal and spiritual growth for them. They will feel those losses, and will certainly grieve them. More importantly, eventually they will find a way to use those experiences to enhance and enrich their lives.

Here's an example of reframing I found a few years ago (source unknown): A man and his two young children were riding a city bus late in the afternoon. The children were constantly running up and down the aisle, yelling at each other. The man seemed oblivious to their activity. One woman was bothered by their behavior, and tapped the man on the shoulder. She said, "Don't you see that your children are bothering the other passengers?" He replied, "Oh, yes, I guess they are." He paused, and with tears in his eyes said: "We just came from the hospital. Their mother died an hour ago, and I don't know how to comfort them." The woman instantly perceived the situation much differently, and was no longer bothered by the children's behavior.

Source: Judy Neal, "Making Diamonds: Helping Children Benefit from Stress," Natural Life *Mar.–Apr. 2002: 21. Reprinted by permission of Judith M. Neal, M.A.*

Exercise 6 Using Tone in Your Writing

Using each of the following topics, write a sentence or two, expressing the tone shown in parentheses after each topic. Think about the connotation of the words you choose. Bring your answers to class, and be prepared to share and discuss them with others.

Example:

shift work (informal, negative):

Working the late shift at the hospital creates constant disruption in my home life and keeps me "out of synch" with the rest of the world.

1. Your wages (informal, positive)

____

____

2. Your wages (formal, negative)

____

____

3. Health (informal, ironic)

____

____

4. City government (informal, satiric)

____

____

5. Home entertainment systems (formal, angry)

____

____

6. Choosing a career (formal, hopeful)

____

____

7. Fashion (informal, playful)

____

____

8. Cooking (formal, authoritative)

____

____

9. Parents (informal, respectful)

____

____

10. Skiing (informal, ironic)

____

____

THE IMPORTANCE OF FINDING IDEAS FOR YOUR WRITING

How do writers get ideas? Once you have selected something of interest that will please both you and, with any luck, your audience, you must create some ideas. Prewriting involves preparing to write. Usually, writers start by thinking about what they have to say, but they find it is not always easy to come up with ideas. Writers use strategies: some they have learned along the way, but many they have borrowed from other writers.

Generating ideas means using techniques and tricks to find or invent ideas so that you have some raw material to work with. Use a variety of methods to assist you in creating thoughts for your writing since the same strategy does not necessarily work in all situations.

Writers will tell student writers to develop some techniques and personal habits. Writers use a variety of techniques. Some fiction writers keep notebooks for ideas. Barnaby Conrad, author of over 24 books, says, "If you, as an embryonic writer, are not keeping notes regularly, you deserve the guilty feeling that is oozing into your body right now" (*Writer*, June 1992, 9).

Other writers like to haunt bookshops and hang out near magazine stands. They claim that looking over the pages and spending time browsing reading materials gives them lots of ideas.

Writers who like to work with the internet can also peruse a wide range of websites, searching for items of interest. They find that online newspapers are excellent sources of timely topics. You might be one of these writers, but you must use caution not to borrow too freely from pages on the internet. All writers must respect copyright: they must not plagiarize others' written materials. However, all writers can certainly learn by reading other writers' works.

Tools for Generating Ideas

As in other situations in life, good tools are important. Still, you can have excellent tools but not know how to use them. It is the techniques and applications that make you better at using tools. The more you write, the better the tools you have to get the job done because you have developed more techniques to use those tools. Overall, the writing job becomes easier. It is critical that you do not "get stuck" in writing assignments because you do not have the right tools at hand. Tools for writing are really strategies to use when you realize you are not moving forward with the job.

TOOL 1: BECOMING A READER AND LEARNING TO RESEARCH

Writers get lots and lots of ideas from reading. Writers learn about writing by reading other people's work; they also gain ideas from reading widely.

In "How I Write," Anne Rice says this about where she finds ideas: "The best come from my research. I read nonfiction, history, archeology, and some New Age material about people who claim to see ghosts or have had near-death experiences" (*Writer*, Feb. 2001).

Canadian filmmaker Atom Egoyan, director of such award-winning films as *The Sweet Hereafter* (1997), *Where the Truth Lies* (2005), *Citadel* (2006), and *Adoration* (2008), attributes his career start to some early reading and research he did when he was a high school student. He claims his first film instruction book came from his high school library in Victoria, British Columbia.

TOOL 2: FREE-WRITING

Free-writing is a term used to describe a technique for creating ideas. To free-write means to allow yourself to write freely, without constraints of any sort, on a topic of interest to you. As you free-write, you begin to understand what you know about something. You start to recognize if you do have something to say. To free-write, try using the following steps:

Steps to Free-Writing

- Choose a topic of interest among those assigned.
- Choose a place to free-write where you will not be interrupted for 20 minutes.
- Choose five or six fresh sheets of paper or open a new computer file.
- Have a watch or clock available to view as you write.

- Look at the time and write it down on a piece of paper beside you.
- Since you will write for 20 uninterrupted minutes, add 20 minutes to the start time, and write the stop time in large numbers underneath your starting time. Write "STOP" beside the second number.
- Write in a continuous fashion for 20 minutes. Do not stop keyboarding or writing.
- Write anything that comes into your mind on the topic—anything at all. Do not censor yourself. Do not stop to think about your writing. Do not correct anything. Keep writing for 20 continuous minutes.
- When you reach the "STOP" time, cease writing.
- Rest for a few minutes.
- Reread what you wrote.
- Select ideas of interest by underlining the words, using a brightly coloured highlighter pen, or highlight the words on your computer pages. Put the ideas that seem to go together into a group; this is called "clustering" and is a useful method to help you see how ideas may connect.
- On a fresh sheet of paper or in a new computer file, write down the ideas you have highlighted.
- Look over your new list.
- Save the list as an ideas file. Give the computer file a distinct and easily recognizable name.

Example:

Suppose someone wants to write about buying a computer. The writer has chosen to free-write for about 20 minutes. Below are the notes from the imaginary writer's free-writing session.

Topic: Tips for Buying a Computer

I've got a fixed budget of $2000. What about the power of the processor? What brand name? Should I worry about the brand or not? I should think about the size of the RAM and the system speed, especially if I'm going to run games—a huge memory-eater! Speaking of a graphics card . . . Maybe I should use my own experience. I can talk to others; Blake is my favourite techno-geek; he has tons of information. I can read what's on the internet and pay attention to some blogs. Sometimes there are pretty good reviews, too. I can check the flyers and talk to salespeople, maybe even do some tryouts in the store. I guess I should figure out my main purpose for computer use and users—they always ask you that in the store—who's going to use it? I should take my time and not make a rush purchase. I know good bargains come up in back-to-school September sales and Christmas sales.

Notice the writer does not use complete sentences and does not pay much attention to grammar and punctuation. Free-writing is not an assignment you will be marked on—it's for your own personal use to help you get started with your writing. If you do decide to share it with another person, she should understand these are "thinking notes"; they are not your best academic prose!

TOOL 3: DRAWING

Many writers find that drawing helps them to develop ideas. You need not worry about your beliefs about your artistic talents. Remember, you are not trying to develop drawing skills: you are attempting to develop thinking skills. You are drawing in order to help you think.

You can use diagrams, geometric figures, lines, squiggles, boxes, faces, or whatever else seems interesting to use. For example, think of a map. Isn't a map really a way of thinking about a concept? After all, the world does not really look the way a map does, but its hills, distances, terrain, sub-structures, and so forth may be represented by a map. As you know, there are many kinds of maps that are designed for different purposes. A navigational "map" is not the same as a road map. A treasure map is not the same as the "map" of the shopping mall.

The map or drawing you make may also serve different purposes. You may draw one map to help you "see" the overview of something, like the plot of a story, for instance.

Another map may help you understand the relationship between characters. For instance, a novel may have a complex set of characters that develop a variety of ways of relating to one another. Planning a piece of writing by drawing out the relational lines and then examining those lines in detail may help you to visualize your project in a new way. Some people have used a tree drawing with the trunk as the main idea or thesis, larger branches as main points, and smaller branches as examples, proof, evidence, or other support. One writing student drew a geometric figure: the base was a flat plane, representing the central idea; a number of equilateral triangles represented each paragraph, with the base of each triangle as the topic sentence, and the corners of the triangle as the "structure" of each paragraph: i.e., the major points. If you like to draw, try using your skill to draw your plan, rather than using words. You might be very satisfied with the results.

Exercise 7 Drawing Ideas

Take each of the following topics or assignments and "draw your way through" to some ideas. Be prepared to show your "drawings" to others, to talk about them, and to explain how they helped you.

1. You have been assigned this topic: "Men and Women in Professional Sports."
2. You have been assigned this topic: "Pluralism in Canadian Society."
3. You have been assigned this topic: "Canadian Television."

TOOL 4: KEEPING A RESPONSE OR DOUBLE-ENTRY JOURNAL

A response journal is somewhat different from an ideas book. A response journal is a means of keeping notes as you read. Sometimes these journals are called "double-entry" journals because you divide the page in half: one side of the page is a place for you to record your ideas, thoughts, feelings, drawings, diagrams, and incidental notes as you read. The other half of the page is for you to record what the writer says. Here is where you would record direct quotations, paraphrases, and short summaries, with appropriate page numbers. The response journal is useful in three ways:

1. It gives you a place to jot down responses to an idea or to the author's words.
2. It gives you a place to collect an author's words, thoughts, and ideas.
3. It provides you with a permanent set of notes that will become more and more valuable to you over time. You can keep all of the response journals you make, and file them away by date. Having an archive of your own response journals will be helpful to you in a number of courses.

You needn't spend a lot of time and money on response journals. Buy a packet of the cheapest notebooks you can find. Always have one on hand as you read. Date each entry and make the two types of notes as you read. What a worthwhile source these journals will become!

Example of a Response Journal

Response Journal: Entry: May 12, 2008
The Life of Pi by Yann Martel, Vintage Canada, 2002.

My Responses and Ideas	*Writer's Words*
• I like how the writer starts his story about how difficult writing is and how he had to struggle to get over the fact that his novel wasn't selling. It must be hard to face that fact. Maybe he thinks, "My writing isn't very good—nobody likes it!" Maybe he is experiencing a "crisis of confidence"; I think all writers must go through that, me included!	• He says "readers ignored it" (v).
• He also talks about how that lack of confidence spills into his next writing project.	
• Well, he may have lost confidence, but at least he keeps his sense of humour!	• Martel says, "I mailed the notes of my failed novel, I mailed them to a fictitious address in Siberia, with a return address, equally fictitious, in Bolivia" (vii).
• I am starting to really like the humour in the book. I'll have to pay attention to how Martel uses it. What role will humour play?	

TOOL 5: USING DISCUSSION

An excellent way of checking your understanding and perspective on an issue is to debate it with a friend or a group of friends. Many people feel comfortable if they can verbally express their ideas. In fact, you may be the sort of person who likes to "talk out" ideas with someone else.

Discussion can be a great way to help express and clarify underdeveloped notions. Engaging in a lively verbal exchange with someone else, particularly someone who is interested in the topic, can be stimulating and motivating. A good example of discussion groups at work today is book clubs: thousands of these clubs meet every week online and in person across Canada and the United States.

Healthy and respectful debate should also be part of your life as a student and as a citizen. Suppose, for instance, you have a strong interest in public housing and are planning on becoming an urban geographer, a city planner, an architect, a social worker, or a civil engineer. Perhaps you choose this topic as a research project. You might find other students with similar interests who might want to meet and discuss issues relating to public housing. Interested individuals usually speak passionately about their topics, and they, along with information, are often good sources of inspiration.

You might even decide to form a discussion group, particularly if you are working collaboratively on a group project for a course. Small group projects can be very rewarding, or they can be a disaster. Frequently, having some ground rules to foster discussion can be helpful. When everyone agrees to follow the "rules," then discussion can flow in a civil manner without egos getting in the way.

Ground Rules for Discussion Ground rules are guidelines that everyone agrees to follow in a discussion. Your group may decide to add others to the list below:

- Do not interrupt someone when she is speaking.
- Do not insult the speaker because you do not agree with the speaker's point of view.
- Be sure you understand the speaker's points. Ask for clarification of a point if you do not understand it.
- Be respectful to speakers in the group.
- Stick to the topic.
- Ask questions to help clarify understanding.

When your group first meets, the members may decide to appoint one member as the "watchdog," the individual who calls someone when she is breaking one of the agreed-to rules. As members of the group become more familiar with one another, the watchdog may no longer be.

Exercise 8 Using Discussion as a Tool

Follow these directions for a small-group discussion. Your instructor will assign five or six topics.

1. Select one of the topics.
2. Gather together with others who have also chosen the same topic. Remember, you should have three to five members in your group. If there are not enough members, choose another discussion group.

3. Use the ground rules for discussion.
4. Go to another part of the campus for your discussion. The classroom gets very noisy when too many people are talking at the same time. Your instructor will tell you how much time you have for your discussion.
5. When your discussion is ending, talk with others in the group about the discussion itself. Was it worthwhile? Did you follow the ground rules? Did the discussion help you gain ideas?
6. When you return and the class reconvenes, be prepared to share your reactions to the discussion with the whole class.

REVIEW TEST

Try the following review test. It will help you assess what you have learned from the chapter. Be prepared to share your responses with others in the class.

Part 1: Without looking back in the text, write definitions for each of the following terms.

1. Prewriting ______________________________
2. Procrastination ______________________________
3. Tone ______________________________
4. Point of view ______________________________
5. Free-writing ______________________________
6. Ideas book ______________________________
7. Response journal ______________________________
8. Audience ______________________________
9. Passive construction ______________________________
10. Connotation ______________________________
11. Satire ______________________________
12. Irony ______________________________

Part 2: Name three points of view.

1. ______________________________
2. ______________________________
3. ______________________________

Part 3: Give three tips for generating ideas.

1. ______________________________

2. ______________________________

3. ______________________________

Part 4: Write a sentence for each tone and point of view asked for in the following.

1. You are a new student at the University of Bravo. You write a letter to the dean of Student Affairs because you want to volunteer for her new committee: Making Campus Life Better. Write a sentence that expresses your reasons for wanting to join the committee. Write from a first-person perspective.

   ____

   ____

   ____

2. You want to write for the student newspaper, called *Campus Spoof.* You are asked to write a satirical article about the food in the cafeteria. Write a sentence from your article, using a third-person point of view.

   ____

   ____

   ____

3. You are writing a paper for your English class. Your paper is about the high cost of getting a university or college education. In one of the paragraphs, you want to have an ironical point of view. Write from a third-person, plural point of view.

   ____

   ____

   ____

Assignment

Do an internet search on how writers write. Choose one writer who interests you. Read online what the writer says she does to prepare to write. Answer the following questions and bring your answers to class:

1. How does the writer select a topic or theme?
2. How does the writer generate ideas?
3. What does the writer say about preparing to write?
4. Are there special circumstances the writer needs to have in order to write?

5. What likes and dislikes does the writer mention about her writing preparation?
6. What does the writer say about writer's block?
7. What tips or techniques did you pick up from the writer?

Bonus Exercise Tone

Find a short article of interest about fashion using the internet or a current magazine. Read the article. Underline words that convey the author's tone. Consider the point of view. Then write a paragraph of 150–200 words on how the tone works in the article. Bring the article and your work to class. The instructor will ask you to post your article and writing in the classroom. You and the rest of the class will circulate to read the articles and student writing. The class will then discuss what students learned about writing from the assignment.

READING

How Scientists Party

by Alastair Bland

Alastair Bland was born in San Francisco and has written for a variety of publications, including the *San Francisco Bay Guardian*, the British quarterly *Petits Propos Culinaires*, the food website Egullet.com, and the Canadian literary publication *Brick, A Literary Journal*. He has a degree in anthropology and geology from U.C. Santa Barbara. Bland writes about his travels and his experiences. In the following selection from *Brick*, Bland describes what it is like to be at a party full of scientific types; it is not the dull event you might imagine. Everyone has a process, even partying scientists.

Every year around finals time, scientists from San Francisco State University gather at the house I was raised in for the Holiday Physics and Astronomy Party. My father, Dr. Roger Bland, a veteran physicist at the university, has hosted this event for the past fifteen years, and I've attended nearly every time. The party, which has achieved near-legend status among the faculty, is a rare opportunity for brilliant scientists and their burnt-out students to mingle, to revel in the underlying silliness of their field, to loosen their neckties after the long semester, to have a few drinks, and to light up the night with electricity and fire.

The first group of guests this year arrived at 7 P.M., tromping in the front door with a spark-generating Tesla coil, a pot of liquid nitrogen, some blowtorches, and a case of Heineken. By 8:30 the alcohol was flowing, the music was thumping, and the whole place was swarming with nerds. There was hardly room to move, yet the throngs parted gracefully for my dad as he made his way from the kitchen to the living room to announce the first event.

He clinked his wineglass with a fork and hollered, "Now begins the Equation-Editing Shootout!"

There were a few cheers, but many of the students looked puzzled. They'd heard about this annual gathering from the old-timers, about how their professors historically got drunk, set things on fire, and acted like delinquents, and they wondered if the party, like an aging rock band, had finally lost its edge.

It was certainly a slow beginning to the famous fete. A Microsoft Word window was projected onto the living room wall as the first contestant, a professor, took a seat at the computer desk. A man with a stopwatch said, "Go!" and the professor began to type. Her goal was to transcribe from a textbook a long and tedious quantum mechanical wave function—and to do it in the least time possible. As a configuration of numbers and Greek lettering began to unfold on the wall, the grad students paid close attention. They sipped their beers and nodded in approval as the equation filled out. It took a full six minutes for the professor to finish, and when she did, there was a round of applause, and a voice shouted, "Yeah! That's what I'm talkin' about!"

I looked up at the screen, but all I saw was this:

$$\Psi_{\text{nhm}}(r,\theta,\phi) = \left[\frac{2\mu Z}{m_r a_0}\right]^{3/2} \quad \begin{matrix} \text{r.u}-l-1 \\ e^{uo}\,\boldsymbol{\in} \\ n1-0 \end{matrix} \quad \frac{2n+1\ (n-m)!}{4\pi\ (n+m)!}\ (1-x^2)m^{l2}\ e^{imp}$$

In past years at the Physics and Astronomy Party, I've seen Ph.D.s get high on helium, vacuum-sealed oil drums collapse under the weight of our atmosphere, a giant weather balloon expand across the living room, and balloons full of propane go up in flames in the backyard, so this new event did seem a bit tame. I spotted my father hovering near a huge bowl of tamales, waved him over, and suggested that we get a new act in motion for the laymen in the crowd: "I think they're hoping to see something explode."

"Yeah," he said through a mouthful of pork and cornmeal, "I'd say it's about time for the liquid nitrogen."

From behind the Christmas tree, my father produced a vat of super-subfreezing liquid, a common light bulb, and a half-dozen safety goggles. While the next contestant in the Shootout stationed himself at the keyboard, Dr. Bland plugged in some wires, handed out the glasses, and prepared to lower the glowing bulb into the steaming pot. "This," he said, "is what happens when three thousand Fahrenheit meets seventy-seven kelvin! Fire in the hole!"

The bulb dropped, and the crowd collectively held its breath—but nothing happened. The light bulb remained lit for three seconds in the vat, then fizzled. Dr. Bland furrowed his brow like a man immersed in thought; synapses in his brain fired and sent off electrical currents this way and that to retrieve notes and textbooks from the cerebral shelves, to check the facts and figures related to the matter, to try to understand what had—or had not—happened.

But the semester was over, and it didn't really matter. He shrugged and grabbed a carrot from a nearby vegetable platter. I saw what was coming—the Liquid Nitrogen Smash-Out, a foolproof, tested-and-true crowd-pleaser. He dunked the carrot for ten seconds and then shattered it like glass over the coffee table. "Anyone else want to try?" he asked as he set the bubbling vat on the floor.

Everyone did, of course, and frozen shrapnel began to fly. When the vegetables ran out, the participants went for napkins, tamale husks, flowers from the vase, and branches from the Christmas tree. Almost everything except fingers became fodder for the smashing, and the carpet was soon littered with debris.

It has long been a tradition at the Physics and Astronomy Party to plug wires into a dill pickle and set it aglow. It's a simple trick that takes place on the back-deck table, and at this year's gathering, a student was given the job of sinking the wires into either end of the vegetable. "The tough part," my father joked, "is not to get electrocuted." The young lady set down her beer, securely lodged the wires, then plugged in the cord. The pickle turned an alien yellow, began to hum like a spaceship, and started cooking from the inside out. For thirty minutes, the students played this game, laughing and rearranging the wires, adding more pickles, pouring beer over them, and somehow managing not to fry one another.

In the living room, an astronomy professor took his place in the Equation-Editing Shootout, but it was nearing Saturday morning by now, and few were watching. Wine and beer had numbed senses, and even the most respectable Ph.D.s had taken to sipping liquid nitrogen and then gargling it like mouthwash. They giggled and cheered as clouds of vapour blasted from their mouths. Bystanders covered their eyes, fearing that someone's tongue would crack and fall off, but there were no such accidents.

Actually, surprisingly, no one has ever filed an official complaint over the Physics and Astronomy Party. Like an experienced rock band, my father and his colleagues know how to put on a show *and* keep things in order.

But one incident from four years ago deserves mention. After a long and happy night, Dad and company goaded me into dumping a gallon of liquid nitrogen onto a hot barbecue. A violent mushroom cloud of burning ash enveloped me while twenty drunken guests went diving over chairs and tumbling into the doorway for shelter. The insulated vat dropped from my hands and shattered while I fell backward. I bumped my head on the wall, landed on shards of glass, and was temporarily blinded by dust. I might have had grounds for a lawsuit, but even in America, a fellow can't sue his parents and still expect a room to stay in.

This year, it had been my level-headed father's plan to ignite rocket fuel on the back porch as the grand finale, but only one of the required ingredients—pressurized nitrous oxide purchased from a novelty shop in the Castro—had been located. "We won't be going to the moon tonight," my father apologized to the half-dozen remaining students, "but this stuff will still burn." He lit up a blowtorch while a student opened an N_2O cartridge and filled a large red balloon with the gas. One student forced the nitrous oxide through a length of PVC piping while another ignited the gas on its way out the opposite end. It was true, nobody went to the moon; but the gas flared brilliantly like a miniature space shuttle for several seconds.

"This guy's so rad," a student said quietly to me. "He's such a cool professor."

"I know," I told him. "He's my dad."

Source: Alastair Bland, "How Scientists Party," Brick, A Literary Journal, *Issue 75, Summer 2005: 49–51. Reprinted by permission of Alastair Bland.*

Comprehension Questions

1. Without using a dictionary and using context clues, what does the underlined term *goaded* mean in the selection?
2. What does the writer mean when he says the party is a chance to "light up the night with electricity and fire"?

3. What is the author's tone? What clues help you to decide?
4. What is the purpose of this article, do you think?
5. According to the writer, what assumptions are made about science?

Critical Comprehension

Discuss the irony in the article. Use examples and the third person.

Assignment

In a paragraph of 200 words, discuss the concept of *science* and *scientist* as depicted in the article, comparing it or contrasting it with conventional ideas. Use a third-person point of view.

CHECKOUT

Here are some of the ideas you will take away with you after you have completed the chapter:

1. Complex writing tasks, such as research papers, will require more preparation, while simpler or shorter tasks will require less.
2. Free-writing is meant to help generate new ideas.
3. Prewriting is a stage wherein you think and prepare to write.
4. Interest is a motivator; as you write, visualize your reader, imagined or otherwise.
5. Discuss your writing ideas with friends.
6. Be on the lookout for writing ideas; try using a pocket notebook.
7. Journal writing can be extremely beneficial.
8. Break free of procrastination by taking control of your learning.
9. Use tools, such as an ideas book or a double-entry journal, to help you generate ideas.

Mastering the concepts in this chapter will also help you develop and apply the following employability skills highlighted by the Conference Board of Canada in *Employability Skills 2000+*:

Think & Solve Problems

- be creative and innovative in exploring possible solutions

Participate in Projects & Tasks

- select and use appropriate tools and technology for a task or project

Source: Adapted from *Employability Skills 2000+* Brochure E/F (Ottawa: The Conference Board of Canada, 2000).

chapter 3

Writing Phases: Planning to Presentation

Chapter Objectives

After completing this chapter you will be able to

1. put together a plan for your next writing project;
2. decide which organizing tools are best for your writing tasks;
3. work with drafting to develop your ideas into a written, organized form;
4. recognize that revision is necessary in your writing;
5. consider editing and proofreading skills as part of the writing process;
6. benefit by presenting your writing assignments correctly.

INTRODUCTION

Despite the fact that some writers make writing sound and look "easy," writing takes a lot of planning if you want your writing to be good. Good writers plan what they are going to say. Their writing may seem flawless to you—it flows, is well organized, captures your interest, and has many exciting ideas. You can see only what the writers have produced; you cannot see what the writers have gone through to get there.

Planning can take many different forms and is connected to purpose. If you want to build a house, you will need blueprints to express your plans. If you are presenting ideas to your colleagues at work, you will need to condense your points and highlight the important ones. You might choose Microsoft PowerPoint or another software program like it as the means to put your presentation together, but you will have to plan each slide carefully, using point form. Whatever your project may be, the planning you choose should suit the project.

As a writer, you also have choices of planning tools, depending on your project. A major term paper requires a much more extensive planning tool than a short-answer writing assignment does. Of course, to start planning, you will need to gather some ideas through prewriting, the first phase, as you learned in chapter 2. Once you get some ideas, what do you do with them?

PHASE 2: PLANNING

In chapter 2, you read about ways to generate interest and ideas in phase 1, the prewriting phase. In phase 2, you will learn about planning. Academic writing requires organization. When you are assigned a project or paper, you will notice it usually includes using a variety of elements. These components include your ideas, your research notes, and a particular format. You must combine these elements effectively, and that requires planning.

Writers have preferences about which organizing tools they like to use. Some writers say they do not like formal outlines but prefer less formal or "sketch outlines" to help guide their writing. Other writers suggest that formal outlines are the best organizers for them because ideas are clearly mapped out in detail. Although writers differ on their choice of organizing tools, they all agree that ideas must be organized well in advance of the actual writing. Organizing tools, then, are essential to writers.

Writers also recognize that outlines can be changed because writing is a recursive activity, not a linear one. **Recursive** means repeating the process as needed in order to achieve a satisfactory outcome. It means revisiting earlier steps to see how they fit with current ones. Therefore, although outlines provide structure to the organization of a piece of writing, they should never be rigid or inflexible. As you work through your research and your writing, you may find new, exciting ideas cropping up. You should feel comfortable adding these new ideas to your outline while, perhaps, even deleting others.

As an organizing tool, outlines are somewhat plastic: they can be shaped and moulded, depending on your purpose. The following section provides information about two types of outlines.

Planning Tool 1: The Formal Outline

A formal outline is a popular, traditional organizing tool. It uses a series of numbers and letters to indicate the level of ideas.

- Roman numerals I, II, III, IV, V, and so forth stand for major ideas.
- Capital letters A, B, C, D, and so forth represent main points.
- Numbers 1, 2, 3 appear as minor points under the main points.
- Small letters, a, b, c, d, and so on can represent subpoints under the numbers if you want a finely detailed formal outline.
- Small Roman numerals i, ii, iii, iv, v can represent the smallest details of all underneath the subpoints (a, b, c, d).

When you construct a formal outline, write a single statement at the top of the page to indicate what the paper will be about. This statement is called the **thesis statement**. This sentence is the most important one because it frames your discussion—what will be included in the frame and what will be left out.

In the essay chapters of this book (chapters 5 and 9), you will learn more about thesis statements and how to frame them. For the purposes of outlining, your thesis statement can be quite fluid because you are just in the planning phase of your paper. You may find as you gather ideas and make an outline that you want to adjust or rewrite your thesis according to what changes emerge.

A formal outline is most useful when you are planning a longer paper, such as a research paper. A formal outline includes major categories of discussion with lots of supporting details. You will need to do research in order to support major ideas, so formal outlines will take some time to prepare.

Review the formal outline below. Then answer the questions that follow it.

Thesis: The Harry Potter series by J.K. Rowling has been the biggest publishing success of the past 100 years.

I. Astonishing sales (MAJOR IDEA)
  A. Global (MAIN POINT)
    1. Over 250 million copies sold (MINOR POINT)
    2. Translated into 47 different languages
  B. U.S. market
    1. More than 350 million copies sold worldwide (*CNN Money*, August 2, 2007).
    2. Thousands of Harry Potter groups and websites
  C. Canada and the U.K.
    1. Bloomsbury, British publisher of the Harry Potter series, says 750 000 copies of *Harry Potter and The Half-Blood Prince* were pre-ordered before the release date.
    2. Raincoast Books has the exclusive publishing rights in Canada and has sold more Harry Potter books than any of the other bestsellers in Canada combined.

II. Success of the author, J.K. Rowling
  A. Financial
    1. Received $105 000 for first in the series, *Harry Potter and the Philosopher's Stone*
    2. Told not to expect too much more
    3. Personal fortune of at least 545 million pounds reported in several British newspapers (*The Telegraph*, *The Independent*) and BBC News, March 23, 2008
    4. Now on the Forbes list of the world's richest people
  B. Personal
    1. Came from being a poor, single mother
    2. Manages her personal fame well
    3. Believes that reading enriches children's lives

III. Creation of new marketing strategies
  A. Use of the internet to sell books online
    1. Millions of copies sold through Amazon
    2. Cross-referenced on hundreds of thousands of websites
  B. Fan pages on the internet
    1. Thousands of fan clubs
    2. "Fanzines"
    3. Wizard clubs online
  C. J.K. Rowling's strategy of dealing with the press
    1. No personal promotions necessary
    2. Has meetings with fans, and media are invited
    3. Includes children in all promotional materials

Exercise 1 Questions on the Formal Outline

Answer each of the following questions. Be prepared to share and discuss your answers.

1. How many paragraphs do you expect the writer to write, using this formal outline?

 ____

2. How many main points are there in the first paragraph?

 ____

3. What are the minor points of the first paragraph?

 ____

4. How many major ideas are there in the second paragraph?

 ____

5. What are the main points of the second paragraph?

 ____

6. How many major ideas are there in the third paragraph?

 ____

7. What are the minor points of the third paragraph?

 ____

8. What tone do you think the writer has chosen?

 ____

9. What do you think of the writer's plan?

 ____

10. Do you think the formal outline will produce a good piece of writing? Why or why not?

 ____

Exercise 2 Making a Formal Outline

Suppose you are writing an article on party planning. Construct a formal outline to show your overall content and organization. Your instructor may ask you to hand in your outline.

Planning Tool 2: The Informal Outline

An informal outline is much sketchier than a formal outline. The informal outline is useful for shorter assignments or for answering questions on exams or in-class writing sessions. This type of outline does not commit you to a detailed plan and does not take much time to prepare. There are different ways to organize ideas in an informal outline. It may just be a list of broad headings, such as the following:

- Harry Potter series
- Sales success
- Success of the writer J.K. Rowling
- New marketing strategies introduced

These headings give you a general direction for writing, but details are missing. If you already have a good working knowledge of a topic, then you may be able to use an informal outline effectively.

You may also use boxes, circles, or other geometric figures of different sizes. Large boxes could represent the major points; smaller boxes the minor ones. You can arrange an informal outline so that only a few items show, perhaps just the major ideas.

THE SKETCH

A sketch outline is a type of informal outline that is used only as a starting point for writing, unlike the formal outline, which has already been well planned out. A sketch outline can consist of questions, phrases, short notes, or headings. A sketch outline might look something like this:

- What about the Harry Potter series?
- How many copies in the series have sold?
- Why?
- What about the writer, J.K. Rowling?

The sketch outline above gives you something to use as a starting point. In other words, you have simply "sketched in" some broad ideas, categories, or questions. As you research and write, you may find your ideas take shape and become slightly different than you originally anticipated. As you work, your sketch outline fills out. After working with it for a short time, you might decide to construct a more fully developed, formal outline.

Other Planning Tools: Checklists, Questions, Notes

Some writers like to work with even less formal tools. Checklists are simple but can be quite effective, too. Checklists can be a series in a form like this:

Harry Potter Series

British origin
the author
the sales
marketing strategies
the reason for popularity
the reader

You might start with a list of ideas you have researched on a topic of interest. You can then check the ones you want to use in your writing and start from there.

Other writers recommend brainstorming for a few minutes, thinking of all the possible questions about a topic. The questions can also be used to guide your research. You may then select the questions that produced the richest information and ideas, and use those questions as a writing guide. Your set of questions may look something like this:

- Who is J.K. Rowling?
- Why are her books so popular?
- Who reads them?
- How many books have sold?
- Who markets them?
- How are the books marketed?
- Who owns the publishing rights in Canada?
- What about the movies based on the books?

These organizing tools, both formal and informal, are not demanding to use. The informal ones are wonderful for you to use after you have done some thinking, prewriting, and research. Very quickly they will help you get started writing. You can construct more formal outlines after the prewriting phase, as long as you feel you are ready to do that. Or, you might use a sketch, checklist, or set of questions as your first organizer, and a formal outline after you've had a chance to see how the "flesh" of the ideas fits on the "bones." After you've done some preparation work with prewriting strategies and you've used some organizing tools, you are ready to write your first draft.

Study Tool: Outlining

Organizing tools, such as outlines, are indeed useful for your writing, but did you know they can also help you study and learn? You can use formal outlines and even informal ones to chart how written material has been organized. Understanding the organization of something develops your comprehension of the material. The speed and depth of your reading comprehension will depend on how familiar you are with the texts of a particular academic community.

You have to read a great deal of material for your courses that is densely packed with information; to do this, you will benefit from being able to use learning and thinking tools in a variety of ways. Outlines can really help you with your study reading.

Example:

Read the following text:

> Life stages affect how individuals and their families cope with illnesses and injuries. Lifespan development theory states that each individual will go through a sequence of orderly, distinct stages in life. At each stage, a person has to master some developmental task. Each task is a growth responsibility that appears at a certain stage of an

individual or family's life, and has emerged from biological needs, cultural imperatives, and family goals. These tasks must be successfully completed in order to secure present satisfaction, social approval, and future success. Failure to do so will result in dissatisfaction, social disapproval and difficulties with later tasks and life. Because individuals and families interact, individual and family life cycles often juxtapose and intertwine with each other. Understanding life-cycle theory can help the physician to assess and intervene appropriately.

Source: Vincent Poon and Ed Badner, "Life-Cycle Theory: Make Use of It in Your Practice," Patient Care *Mar. 2005: 62.*

FORMAL OUTLINE AS STUDY GUIDE

The following example shows one way study notes, using an outline and the paragraph from *Patient Care*, could be organized. This outline is not the only way the ideas from the passage could be organized; however, the outline helps the reader to know if he has understood the passage. Besides, the clear set of outlined notes will make an excellent study aid.

Notice that the writer has included a list of unfamiliar terms used in the passage. When it comes time to study, the student can glance over the list of terms to check understanding of them. Also notice that there is only one major idea (I. Lifespan development theory), with three main points (A, B, C) and several minor points (1, 2, 3, or 4) beneath each main point. Because this passage has only one paragraph, it will not have a thesis statement, but it will have an overarching major idea.

I. Lifespan development theory
  A. Everyone goes through a sequence of separate life stages.
    1. These stages affect how we cope with crises.
  B. What is involved in the stages?
    1. Each stage includes a "developmental task" of some sort.
    2. Each task furthers growth.
    3. Each task comes from biological, cultural, or family needs.
  C. What results?
    1. Successful task completion ensures satisfaction.
    2. Noncompletion of developmental tasks leads to social difficulties and later life problems.
    3. Contrasting life cycles in individuals can complicate family life.
    4. Physicians who understand lifespan development theory and the cycles can assist individuals and families.

Key Terms: lifespan development theory, cultural imperatives, juxtapose, intervene

Exercise 3 Making an Outline from a Reading

Use the above example as a model. Construct a formal outline, based on the passage provided below. Also include a list of unfamiliar terms at the end of your outline. Your instructor may ask you to hand in your outline or may ask you to share it with others.

First Nations are the largest of the three constitutionally recognized Aboriginal peoples in Canada. Within Manitoba, the Cree (mid north and north), Dakota and Assiniboine (southwest), Dene (far northwest), Ojibway (south) and Oji-Cree (mid northeast) are the indigenous peoples of Manitoba who have contributed greatly to the economy and vitality of Manitoba and Canada through community and individual achievements, traditional and westernized knowledge, philosophy, arts, science, and culture. First Nations do share a belief in a holistic balanced approach to life as necessary to maintain good health. Yet the diversity of language, culture, geography and history of the 63 First Nations communities necessitates their full involvement in changing policies and approaches in health.

According to the Statistics Canada Aboriginal Peoples Survey 2001, the Manitoba First Nations population is 107,146, which is approximately 10% of Manitoba's total population with 47% of First Nations people living on reserves. The remaining 53% live in rural communities, often close to their reserve communities, or in urban centres. The median age of Manitoba First Nations people is 22.8 years, while that of the non-Aboriginal population is 38.5 years. Thus, First Nations planning for future employment and services must consider that this youthful population "bulge" is a decade behind the mainstream population. While mainstream society is concerned with preparing for the retiring baby boomers' needs, including housing for "empty nesters" and senior homes, First Nations are planning for more schools and family housing.

Source: M. MacKinnon, RN, Grand Rapids Cree Nation, "A First Nations Voice in the Present Creates Healing in the Future," Canadian Journal of Public Health *Jan.–Feb. 2005: 96 (Suppl.1): S13–S16. Reprinted by permission of the Canadian Public Health Association.*

PHASE 3: DRAFTING

After you have used some prewriting strategies to help you think of ideas, and you have organized those ideas using an organizing tool, such as a formal or informal outline, you are ready to write your first draft. You will often hear the term *drafts* associated with phases of writing. **Drafting** is the development of ideas into a written, organized form: it entails writing several versions, called *drafts*.

You will work through the process from draft 1, the initial draft, to the final draft. Different assignments may require a different number of drafts, depending on how complex the assignment is and how familiar you are with the texts and resource materials relating to the discipline. If, for example, you have never written a literature paper before, you can expect to write more drafts than usual. Even if you have written a literature paper but have not completed one on poetry, you will be learning as you go. Anticipate doing extra drafts.

All writers use drafts when they write. Some writers work with fairly detailed outlines, even at the first draft phase. Others like to move freely with their ideas through the first draft in order to see where the writing ends up. If you are a person who is comfortable with a more freewheeling style, then you may get your best results from a kind of free-writing approach to the first draft. However, if this idea makes you tense or fearful, use a sketch outline or a more formal outline to write your first draft.

Bear in mind that *drafting* means a series of attempts. Your first draft will not be your final because ideas need to be developed over time and through effort, revising, and editing. Your drafting process might look like this:

- Your ideas follow an arc—you start with ideas, and then you move forward with them, writing as you go along until you reach a peak in the process, at which point thoughts and ideas begin to slow down.
- At this point you stop, and you begin to review your first completed draft.
- You might revisit earlier points and make changes or revisions to them or to the organization of ideas.
- Then you begin to write again, based on the changes, and moving along the arc again.

You cannot actually predict how long or wide the writing arc will be, but sometimes you can make a good guess based on how difficult the assignment is and how familiar and comfortable you are with the material.

When you are drafting, you are composing or getting ideas down on paper. You are not editing or revising. **Composing** means you should feel relaxed and allow the ideas to come out onto the page.

Writing the First Draft

Writing your first draft should be a fairly enjoyable experience if you have planned for it. After you've done some prewriting work, chosen an organizing tool, and have a plan for writing, you can begin with some confidence. Remember, your first draft is your first attempt, not your last.

Begin writing the first draft as soon as you can. Having ideas down on paper in a developmental form is important. Following are some tips for writing your first draft:

Tip 1. Be organized: gather all the materials you will need (your notes, your plan for writing, laptop, notepaper, pens, and so forth).

Tip 2. Be organized: try to set aside one uninterrupted hour to start.

Tip 3. Be organized: find a quiet and relatively private space. If your home is a busy, noisy place, stay on campus for an extra hour and work in the library or learning centre. Some writers can work in a noisy, busy place, but most people find a library, a private study space, or a quiet room at home works best to enhance, not distract from, concentration.

Tip 4. Be organized: work either on computer or on paper, whichever is more convenient and comfortable. Double-space your work, so you can add ideas.

Tip 5. Be organized: use your plan. Begin to write, according to your plan. Keep writing, and don't stop until your hour is up.

Tip 6. Be aware: don't let the proofreading bog you down on the first draft. As you write, do not concern yourself with errors. Don't stop to correct spelling, grammar, or punctuation. Don't worry a sentence to death; if you stop often, you will interrupt the "flow," and flow is what composing is all about!

Tip 7. Be aware: take breaks. After the hour is over, stop for a break.

Tip 8. Be aware: review what you have written when you return to your draft.

Tip 9. Be aware: when you feel that you have finished the entire first draft, stop.

Tip 10. Be organized: save the file and then print a copy of what you have written if you have worked on a computer. Always be sure to make a backup copy.

Tip 11. Be your own critic: review what you have written. Use a pen or pencil in a bright colour, and add notes here and there in the draft as you read. The notation may be as simple as an asterisk (*) to indicate that a section needs revision; it may be an underlining that shows that a sentence needs work; or it may be a comment in the margin. Use the first draft checklist below to help guide your review.

Tip 12. Be organized: back up all your notes, the printed draft, and your other materials, and leave the task overnight or for a few hours. It is important to begin the second draft with fresh eyes.

Using a Checklist

Having a variety of tools at your disposal is really beneficial. A checklist is a marvellous device because it is so flexible and simple, yet so effective. You can have lots of different checklists for lots of different purposes. The checklist below is for you to use as you are reviewing the first draft of an assignment. You can also develop your own checklist, which you custom fit to your own needs.

First Draft Checklist

I have met the assignment objectives.
I have a clear beginning.
I have provided clear points.
I have included some convincing examples.
I have good variety in my sentence structure.

Using a Computer

If you prefer to write, i.e., compose and edit, using a computer, then you probably have already learned a number of writing strategies. However, some of the following tips may be new to you and may prove to be useful.

Tip 1. Be organized in your process: each time you write a draft, open a new file. This practice will prevent you from overwriting. Call the file, "Draft 1," and add an abbreviated title and the date to the file name. Save it the same way, but make sure your title is not too long. The next time you return to the computer to write, open Draft 1, copy it, and then paste it to a new file. Save the new file as "Draft 2," using the same abbreviated title but with the new date. You will have a number of drafts in various files at the end of your writing, but this way, you will never lose any of your work.

Tip 2. Be organized: make a backup of your work. Use a flash device or some other portable means for the backup. If your hard drive dies unexpectedly or if your computer becomes infected, you have backed up your work and can use another computer to continue with your projects. Often students save only to the hard drive. Although this is usually fine, it is heartbreaking and frustrating to lose all your work, so take a little time and back up your projects!

Tip 3. Be aware: always keep a hard copy of every assignment you turn in. Hand one copy in to your professor or instructor, and keep the other one on file. Sometimes, papers are mislaid. If you have a hard copy at the ready, you will be able to turn in a misplaced assignment. Of course, if your assignment has been backed up in your computer files, you can always print another hard copy as needed.

Tip 4. Be organized: open another file for notes. Save the file as "Notes for ________________________ (abbreviated title of your paper)." As you read, research, and take notes, you can place any useful ideas in this file. It is doubtful you will use all of the notes and ideas, but, should you decide to use one, you will know where to look for it. You can continue to add comments as you work through your assignment. Do not delete these files because some of them may be useful for more than one course.

Tip 5. Be aware: keep files up-to-date. Manage your files well, and the work will seem easier. Keep your files focused: don't try to do too many things with one file. Instead, create a folder for each assignment. In the folder, put all of your draft files and your note files, along with anything else relating to the assignment. Be aware of your process when you are writing on computer. You can train yourself to become more efficient when working with electronic files. You can also learn a lot from your own technological mistakes.

PHASE 4: REVISING

Samuel Johnson said, "What is written without effort is in general read without pleasure." What do you think Johnson meant when he said that? What is Johnson saying about the reader–writer connection?

His comments may capture why writers revise. However, sometimes student writers have a mistaken impression of what revising a written composition means.

Some students think revising equals repairing a few sentences, running their work through a spell checker, and adding fancy title pages with catchy titles in appealing fonts. Nothing can be further from the truth. Surprising as it may seem, revising is one of the most important phases of writing, yet many students resist the need to do it. They do not realize how much they can learn and earn by devoting time to this phase.

Why don't most students spend more time on revisions? Perhaps they have run out of time—the deadline always seems to be just around the corner, especially with a heavy course load to juggle. Or, perhaps they are so tired of the paper that they cannot bring themselves to rework it and make any major changes to it at all. Finally, perhaps they cannot evaluate their own work very efficiently.

Students can change all of these circumstances by better planning and by opening their hearts and minds to other ways of doing things.

Why Revise?

Revising is the critical process of evaluating your work in order to improve it.

The process looks something like this:

Reread
↓
Rethink
↓
Revise

The prefix *re* looms large in the above words: it means "again"—read again, think again, work again. Revising is so important that if you do a good job of it, your assignments will likely receive better grades; if you do a poor job or make no effort at all in this phase, your marks will reflect your lack of effort. Moreover, learning to revise will help you become a better writer.

It is at the revising phase that you can go "back" over your work to read it as a whole, judging how a piece "sounds." You can mark parts that sound unconvincing, are badly worded, seem illogical, look out of place, appear unsupported, or lack effectiveness. Then, you can rework these parts and then, if needed, adjust the whole.

At this stage, you can also consider if the piece matches your initial purpose and intended audience. Does the work answer the assignment? Does it have the tone, structure, argument, evidence, and overall organization that will make it effective and convincing?

Finally, planning for revisions will help your overall time management. You will learn to be sure to allow time in your schedule for the revision of papers. You will actually plan to revise. Even if you have only a few hours to spend revising, you will learn how important it is: you will catch errors, rework parts of your paper that might have proved embarrassing, and, generally, pull the piece together for a better presentation and mark.

What Are the Levels of Revision?

Although experts may not agree exactly on how many levels of revision are possible, they will agree on three types. In *Spotlight on Critical Skills in Essay Writing*, Second Edition, we will refer to these levels as macro-level revisions (large-scale), micro-level revisions (smaller-scale), and editing. You will read more about editing in the next section. For the time being, consider what comprises macro-level and micro-level revisions.

MACRO-LEVEL REVISIONS

This level includes rereading the whole paper to discover its overall strengths and weaknesses. You note areas where more evidence is required, where an additional step must be added, where a conclusion does not follow, where an idea needs clarification, and so forth. Then you rewrite sections, tailoring them to the rest of the paper. Finally, you reread the paper again to see if the improvements you've made are satisfactory.

MICRO-LEVEL REVISIONS

This type of revision has to do with a particular section of your paper. Perhaps you notice that the body of your paper is strong but that your conclusion is weak. You reread the paper, paying particular attention to the conclusion. Then you spend extra time reworking the conclusion to give it what you want: a sense of summary and a sense of closure with some punch. You then reread the paper, seeing what the new conclusion "sounds like."

Checklists for Revising

Macro-level
My paper answers the assignment.
My paper has a consistent tone that I like.
My paper addresses a certain audience.
My paper has an effective overall arrangement.
My paper is well-developed with good support overall.
My paper is convincing.

Micro-level
My paper has an effective and interesting introduction.
My paper has a clear thesis or organizing statement in the introduction.
My paper has clearly developed and well-supported body paragraphs.
My paper has few faults in logical thinking.
My paper presents lots of good evidence: examples, explanations, statistics, or reasons.
My paper has an effective and forceful conclusion.

How Do I Get Feedback When Revising?

Feedback means having others read your work and gathering their comments and suggestions in order to improve the piece of writing. As you do this, you will also be improving your general skills as a reader. You may see two types of feedback used in courses: peer reviews or peer feedback, and self-assessment.

PEER REVIEWS

Peer reviews or peer feedback means having other members of the class read your work and comment on it. You, in turn, will do the same for them. Most of the time, instructors provide criteria for peer reviews to give focus to the reviewers' comments and to make them as constructive as possible to the writer receiving the review.

Often, peer reviews include written comments on a peer review form. After the peer review, you will be able to discuss the written comments with the reviewer. You can find many examples of peer review sheets on the internet. Try downloading one and using it for one of your own papers.

Examples Taken from Various Peer Review Sheets

Is the writer's purpose clear?	yes	no
Does the writer have a clear thesis statement?	yes	no
Is the writer's tone appropriate?	yes	no
Has the writer provided sufficient support?	yes	no
Are points well developed?	yes	no
Do conclusions follow from the arguments presented?	yes	no

Sometimes you may ask a friend or relative to read your paper. Some outside reviewers can do a good job, providing you give them a list of criteria for the review. However, not all feedback is going to be useful. Value-laden criteria (the "goodness" or "badness" of something) does not offer you much help, unless the person using this type of criteria can provide you with clear reasons for his likes and dislikes.

In most cases, getting an outside reviewer is a good idea. The reaction you get to your paper can be beneficial, in general. Common instances of useful feedback may include helping you to pinpoint confusing areas of your paper. For example, a reviewer may not understand what you are saying in a passage, although to you it may be perfectly clear. He may question you on the paper's organization, but you may have thought the paper was sensibly structured.

SELF-ASSESSMENT

You can learn to be a good reviewer of your own work, but it takes some time, patience, and self-training to do so. You may find assessing your own written work is a bit more difficult than assessing someone else's. Why that is so may have to do with learning to be self-critical in a positive and constructive way.

Some Tips for Self-Assessment

- Keep track of your writing strengths and weaknesses. Most writers know what gives them trouble in the writing process. Each time you write a paper, try to recognize what is giving you trouble. Write it down in your ideas notebook. Work through the problem, and write down the action you took.
- Keep track of the instructor's feedback. For example, if the instructor tells you to give more specific examples in a paper, make a note of that in your ideas book. Date the entry. Use the feedback constructively.

When you are revising, go back over the instructor feedback notes you have taken. Then check this feedback against your new work. For example, you might ask yourself, "Have I provided enough specific examples in this paper?"

- Develop your own checklist. For instance, if you know that you often forget to check your papers for effective conclusions, put "check conclusion" on your checklist.
- If you are serious about improving your writing, read what other writers have to say about what they did. Every year publishers produce collections of essays on writing by writers.

Exercise 4 *Optional: Other Writers' Tips*

Try an internet search for what other writers have to say about assessing their own writing. Can you find new words of wisdom to guide you in your reflections of your own work? If you find useful tips or strategies, bring them to class. Be prepared to share them with others.

PHASE 5: EDITING AND PROOFREADING

After you have completed a number of drafts, done some macro- and micro-level revising, and satisfied your checklists about organization and content, you are ready to edit and proofread. Editing and proofreading are not the same.

- **Editing** means you are trying to clarify the meaning or style of sentences and their "fit" in paragraphs.
- **Proofreading** means looking for errors in the paper at the sentence level. You consider the mistakes in sentences—grammar, usage, spelling, and punctuation.

For an excellent discussion about editing, proofreading, and the distinction between them, along with some solid tips, visit the University of Toronto's Applied Science and Engineering website. You can find it at the following address: **www.engineering.utoronto.ca/about/programs/communication/Online_Handbook/The_Writing_Process/Revising_Editing_and_Proofreading.htm**.

Your instructors and professors will expect you to have proofread your papers well before handing in the final drafts. Without a doubt, you will lose marks if you have not done so. More important, concise and clear written communication means a great deal in the professional world. Poor editing results in bad impressions.

Proofreading for Grammar and Usage Errors

Do you know which errors plague you? Do you have trouble with subject–verb agreement, parallelism, verb tenses, or pronoun references? Do you forget certain forms of verbs? Writers know what kinds of difficulties they have with grammar and usage. However, in order to improve, you have to do something about the errors—namely, eliminate them! Try following these steps:

1. Keep track of which mistakes you tend to make in your papers.
2. When you edit and proofread, print a hard copy of the paper.

3. As you read, pay attention to the errors particular to your writing.
4. Read each sentence out loud.
5. Highlight any sentence that contains an error.
6. Try to read for one type of error at a time. In other words, if you have some problems with subject–verb agreement, for example, then read through your paper, looking only for subject–verb agreement mistakes. What this tells you is that you will have to read your paper several times for editing and proofreading purposes.

Chapter 16 offers a close look at some of the common sentence-level errors. Pay particular attention to this chapter as it can help you overcome some of your mistakes.

Proofreading for Spelling Errors

Some spelling errors can be repaired by running your paper through the spell checker in your word-processing program, but this practice does not always guarantee that all mistakes will be caught. Although you should use the spell-check, do not rely on it completely. The spell-check program cannot read context: in other words, it cannot tell which spelling is appropriate because it does not comprehend subtle differences in the use of a word. If you have trouble with synonyms in spelling (words like *there*, *their*, and *they're*), then you cannot rely on spell-check to help you make corrections.

Remember that some instructors penalize heavily for spelling errors in papers. They believe students should know how to clean up spelling by using spell-check, a dictionary, or a proofreader.

Proofreading for Punctuation Errors

All academic writers need to learn how to use punctuation correctly, particularly commas, semicolons, apostrophes, and quotation marks. Here are some steps to help you catch those pesky punctuation problems.

1. Read your paper line by line, looking for errors in punctuation.
2. If you are not sure if there is an error in a sentence, ask someone.
3. Look up punctuation usage on the internet; there are thousands of sites, particularly those hosted by colleges and universities.
4. Invest in an excellent English handbook. Many new versions appear every publishing year. Get used to using the handbook. When you don't know how to use a mark in punctuation, look up its use in the handbook. The more often you look it up, the more likely you are to remember the correct usage.
5. Pay attention to the details of punctuation. Your message can be misleading or inaccurate if your punctuation is off. Instructors and professors will deduct marks for punctuation errors.

Chapter 16: Editing and Style Notes contains some information on common punctuation errors. Review that information from time to time.

PHASE 6: PRESENTATION

After you have completed all of your drafts, you are ready to prepare your final, the one you will hand in for the assignment. This is the last phase of the writing process. The presentation of your paper includes the following elements:

- Font
- Format
- Title page (if one is required)
- Line spacing
- Pagination
- Overall appearance

You want to make a good impression, so be sure your presentation does that. The presentation also sets a tone: it shows your attitude to the assignment. If you have spent quite a bit of time on it and given lots of effort to the first five phases of writing, you will want to complete your project on a high note—i.e., with a polished and pleasing presentation.

Preparing the Final Draft

The final draft is the version ready to be handed in for reading and evaluation. It is the culmination of all the efforts of the previous drafts. Before you submit your paper, proofread one final time. Surprisingly, you will catch some errors you missed previously.

THE FIRST PAGE OF THE FINAL DRAFT

Some instructors or professors want to see a title page as the first page of your final draft. However, if you are preparing a paper according to MLA (Modern Language Association) style, you will not produce a title page.

THE TITLE PAGE

Following is a sample title page. Your instructor may ask you to produce a title page slightly different from the sample. If your instructor has handed out special instructions regarding the title page, you should follow them to the exact detail. Most instructors are very particular about students' following correct format.

Use an 11- or 12-point clear font. Do not use any font larger than that, and do not use a script type of font. Most instructors do not want the assignment to be submitted in a presentation folder. Instead, staple the paper together in the upper left-hand corner.

Example: Title Page

Parasites, Nematodes, and Sushi:
The Allergy Connection

I.C. Topgradz
90765432
Biology 161 Sec 5
Prof. R.U. Sharpe
April 10, 2008

- About three inches (7.5 cm) from the top of the page, centre the title of your paper. Be sure the title shows the focus of the paper. If the title in the above example had been "Parasites and Nemotodes," it would have been too broad. It would not reveal the specific focus of the paper. The title as given above shows the paper's clear direction. All words in the title must be spelled correctly.
- About one inch (2.5 cm) from the bottom of the page, type your name, your student number, the name of the course and your section number, the name of your professor or instructor, and the date the paper is due. (Do not date the paper the day you complete it; date it the day you hand it in.)

MLA-STYLE FORMAT

MLA-style format has specific requirements. English courses and most humanities courses use the MLA (Modern Language Association) style of formatting and presentation. You will read more about MLA-style papers in Chapters 13 and 15.

Below is a sample of the presentation format of an MLA-style paper. Generally speaking, MLA papers do not have title pages.

Polly Pepperpot
ID 507999325
Prof. U.B. Tokswell
English 161 Sec 5
November 4, 2008

Pepperpot 1

Natural Optimism: Folk Wisdom and Characterization in W.O. Mitchell's
Who Has Seen the Wind?

- The title should show the focus of the paper. If the title in the example above had been "Characterization in W.O. Mitchell's *Who Has Seen the Wind?*" it would have been too broad. It does not reveal a specific focus. The title as given above shows the paper's clear direction by relating specific concepts.
- Use a running header on the upper right-hand side of the page, showing your last name and the page number.
- On the first page about one inch (2.5 cm) down in the upper left-hand side, key in your name, your student number, the instructor's or professor's name, the course and section number, and the date of submission.
- On the first page, centre your title about a half inch (1.25 cm) below the date of submission. Do not put the title on every page.
- Double-space the paper.

REVIEW TEST

Try the following review test. It will help you assess what you have learned from the chapter. Be prepared to share your responses with others in the class.

Define each of the following terms in one or two sentences. Use separate paper.

1. Informal outline

____

2. Revision

____

3. Feedback

____

4. Title page

____

5. Micro-level revision

____

6. Draft

____

7. Peer editing

____

8. Formal outline

____

9. Final draft

____

10. Proofreading

____

Assignment

1. Prepare a formal outline for an essay using one of the following topics:
   - Hiking
   - Child care
   - Smoking salmon
   - Blogs
   - Kids and being street smart
2. Develop an informal outline about a popular television series.

Bonus Exercise That *or* Which?

Use *that* to introduce a restrictive clause—a clause necessary to a sentence because it helps to define the subject of the sentence. It clarifies the subject. Use *which* to introduce a nonrestrictive clause—a clause not necessary to defining the subject. A *which* clause adds information not really needed in the sentence. It does not clarify the subject.

Use commas with nonrestrictive clauses. Do not use commas with restrictive clauses.

The house that burned was built in 1912.

(Restrictive: It defines which house specifically.)

My salmon sandwich, which was wrapped in plastic, tasted delicious.

(Nonrestrictive: The clause adds information but is not needed.)

Add *that* or *which* to each sentence below. Check your answers with the Answer Key.

1. The alarm ___________ sounds like a whistle wakes the baby every night at eight.
2. *Oryx and Crake*, ___________ is speculative fiction, is Margaret Atwood's 11th novel.
3. Mimi prefers to eat low-fat snacks ___________ she prepares herself.
4. The steel table ___________ has only two legs should be sent to the junk pile.
5. Mr. Taki bought blue and white wallpaper, ___________ was on sale, to use in the small dining room.
6. The accident ___________ claimed the victim's life occurred at this intersection last Thursday morning.
7. The conference on eco-globalism, ___________ was held in Helsinki in 2006, had over 5500 delegates.

READING

The following article offers some interesting viewpoints on how language arts has been and could be improved in public school so that students would be better prepared for post-secondary education. Read the article carefully. Then answer the questions. Be prepared to share and discuss your answers.

Reading, Writing, and Thinking for All

Critical thinking, cultural awareness, impassioned writing. These skills aren't just for the college bound.

by Mike Schmoker

Dr. Mike Schmoker is an author, speaker, and consultant. His interests include educational reform of assessment and curricula in schools that are student-centred and that look toward student success. His most recent book is *Results Now: How We Can Achieve Unprecedented Improvements in Teaching and Learning (ASCD,* 2006).

Harvard president Derek Bok recently appeared on National Public Radio emphatically endorsing the value of a basic liberal arts education. Bok extolled such an education not only for its contribution to intellectual and personal growth, but also because a liberal arts education is "what employers are really asking for":

> They feel that graduates don't write well enough, they don't think clearly enough, they don't have a good enough ethical sense, they don't understand the relationship of business to the larger social and public policy problems of the United States—they aren't globally aware. (Rehm, 2006)

Listening to Bok, I thought, aren't these the skills and dispositions we want all students to possess, whether or not they attend college? One recent study confirms that such skills are needed in 120 of the most common high-paying jobs and professions that *don't* require a college education (Olson, 2005). Moreover, a liberal arts education helps students develop judgment and confidence and equips them to more fully contribute to the world they live in.

But can we really hope to provide all students with an intellectually challenging education that fosters critical thinking, understanding of domestic and global realities, and exposure to important cultural touchstones? I believe we can. To see one curricular strategy for doing so, let's look at a high school in Arizona where a strong emphasis on reading and analyzing powerful texts provides students with world-class preparation.

A CHARTER WHOSE CHOICES PAY OFF

Six years ago, Arizona administered the first version of its Arizona Instrument to Measure Standards (AIMS) test. Initial scores were shockingly low—even at traditionally high-scoring schools. Curiously, at two schools, 100 percent of students passed all three portions of the test. One, predictably, was a magnet school that only enrolled high-achieving students. But the other school, Tempe Preparatory Academy, in suburban Phoenix, is an open-enrollment charter high school. Its student population is almost exclusively from middle- and lower-middle-class families; 15 percent of the students are nonwhite, and 5 percent are identified as having special needs. When Tempe Prep's success hit the newspapers, the number of students on its waiting list soared overnight.

Tempe Prep's students continue to score virtually 100 percent on all portions of the AIMS test. Their average SAT score is 1250. Why do students at Tempe Prep succeed academically? There is no question that the school attracts intelligent, industrious students from supportive families. But the explanation goes beyond this to a curricular choice Tempe Prep made. If other high schools followed suit, they too could provide a rigorous liberal arts education to all.

A SIMPLE, DEMANDING CURRICULUM

From 9th through 12th grade, every student at Tempe Prep attends a daily two-hour Humane Letters block, which combines content from the areas of language and history. The curriculum of this course is stunningly simple: Students spend almost all of in-class time reading, writing, or discussing the issues they encounter in their readings. This emphasis on in-class reading, discussion, and writing is exactly what literacy experts like Richard Allington (2001) recommend for all schools, including—if not especially—high-poverty schools. But it's rare to see it in action.

The school makes its expectation for abundant amounts of reading, writing, and discussing—as well as assigned texts—clear to students, teachers, and parents. The assigned readings are almost exclusively classics that will broaden students' horizons and generate deep questions. For example, among the assigned texts in 9th grade are *Walden, Othello,* and *Our Town.* In 10th grade, students read *1984* and *Pride and Prejudice;* in 11th grade, dialogues of Plato and Aristotle's *Poetics*; and in 12th grade, *Don Quixote* and writings by Karl Marx, among others. Some modern authors, such as Ernest Hemingway and F. Scott Fitzgerald, are also on the list.

By graduation, students have spent about 1,400 hours in these college-style seminars and have read and discussed thousands of pages of high-quality text. Students analyze and argue, agree or disagree with the ideas they encounter, and evaluate the ethics of various characters' actions. And—significantly—student work incorporates mastery of Arizona's standards for language arts: displaying logic and clarity, making inferences, doing character analysis, supporting one's arguments, synthesizing, evaluating, and discerning an author's bias or perspective.

But Tempe Prep's success is also a result of what they *don't* do. There is none of what Allington (2001) calls a "recitation script" that emphasizes "known-answer questions" (p. 88). Time isn't wasted on what he calls "stuff"—worksheets and assignments that can consume precious class time.

Rigor and focus are also part of the writing curriculum. Students write nine argumentative or thesis-driven essays every year, and they must revise each essay using the Six-Trait writing rubric (Culbam, 2003). That's 36 multiple-draft essays by the end of high school. In addition, every student writes a 15- to 20-page thesis in his or her senior year, which the writer must defend to a panel of teachers and community members.

As William Eitzhugh (2006) observes, the opportunity to deeply explore an issue and write an extended essay about it is one of the quintessential intellectual experiences, important not only for preparation for college but also for success in innumerable lines of work.

THE CENTRALITY OF ARGUMENTATIVE LITERACY

Gerald Graff (2003) has called the kind of ability Tempe Prep nurtures in its students "argumentative literacy." A recent study sponsored by the Association of American Colleges and Universities found that argumentative literacy may be the most essential skill students need to succeed in college. The study's recurring theme is that students abandon college chiefly because K–12 education does not prepare them to think, read, and write argumentatively (Conley, 2003).

Being skilled in argument equips all students—college bound or not—to become intelligent, contributing employees and citizens. There is a strong convergence of opinion here. For Christopher Lasch (1995), learning to argue is "the essence of education," which not only prepares us for every aspect of life and employment, but also "strengthens civil society" (p. 101). Gerald Graff (2003) estimates that only 20 percent of students are prepared for the argumentative culture of the university; he asserts that "argument literacy . . . is central to being educated" (p. 3).

FOSTERING ARGUMENT AT VIEW PARK PREPARATORY

To see how these strategies work with students for whom pursuing a college education is far from a given, consider View Park Preparatory High School in Los Angeles. Ninety-eight percent of View Park's 375 students are black; half receive free or reduced-price lunch. View Park uses a curricular approach similar to Tempe Prep's, with a focus on developing students' analytical and argumentative skills. From 9th through 12th grade, English instruction focuses almost exclusively on reading, argument, and persuasive writing.

The curriculum is built around debating questions like this one connected to Ken Kesey's novel *One Flew Over the Cuckoo's Nest:* "Does McMurphy liberate or imprison his fellow patients in the ward?" Through such reflective questioning, teachers train students to back up any inference they make in their own writing or in discussions of literature. Students learn to use Stephen Toulmin's (1958) Model of Argumentation—which recognizes the four key elements of argument as claim, clarification, evidence, and warrant—to produce college-level written arguments.

View Park students not only outperformed their white peers in the district on the 2005 California English Language Arts Exam, but they also have the highest test scores among black high school students in California (Hernandez, Kaplan, & Schwartz, 2006).

OVERCOMING OBSTACLES

To implement curriculums that foster argumentative literacy, schools must overcome two crucial obstacles: "curricular chaos" and misconceptions about students' intellectual capabilities.

Curricular Chaos Evidence suggests that a high-quality, common curriculum—including purposeful reading, writing, and discussion—is the most powerful factor that affects learning (Marzano, 2003). Unfortunately, in too many schools, curricular chaos prevails (Schmoker & Marzano, 1999).

For a time, my daughters attended secondary school at a highly touted preparatory academy. Ironically, this school did very little to prepare them as effective thinkers, readers, and writers because there was no set curriculum. Many classes relied on lectures, movies, and worksheets. Even in honors courses, assessment was rare, haphazard, and patently lower order. There were no school or department guidelines for what texts students should read or how many written assignments they should complete, and teachers did not use scoring guides to assess writing. One administrator admitted that after a full decade of existence, the one issue the school had not addressed was curriculum.

Schools don't have to mimic Tempe Prep's curriculum to ensure that students receive key intellectual preparation. But we must make sure that teachers explicitly define—and monitor—what students will learn, which texts they must read, which scoring guides they should follow, and how many written assignments they must complete.

Administrators must also audit the curriculum by meeting with teacher teams each quarter to review which standards teachers covered and to examine the results of common assessments. We must conduct occasional, unannounced classroom walkthroughs, followed by reports to the faculty on whether instruction is adhering to the established curriculum—or whether "stuff" is supplanting the necessary reading, writing, and debating.

"Students Aren't Up to It" The second obstacle to implementing a powerful curriculum is the misconception that some students—particularly the non-college-bound—aren't capable of a more intellectually viable curriculum or would find it boring. Not so. John Goodlad's studies in the early 1980s, based on visits to more than 1,000 classrooms in seven regions of the United States, revealed that language arts as traditionally taught has usually been students' least favorite class. But when the curriculum centers around reading, writing, and discussion as catalysts for inquiry, language arts becomes students' favorite class (Goodlad, 1984; Marino, 1998).

CREATING CATALYSTS FOR INQUIRY

Virtually all courses can become catalysts for inquiry—and a means to teach the skills that the future demands of all students—when we build the curriculum around good questions. Success relies on these elements: a good text (a section in a textbook, an article, or a book chapter); a provocative question; and a structured way for students to respond in written and oral form. In choosing texts, look for high-quality fiction and nonfiction that are likely to provoke strong opinions and varied interpretations, such as two texts in which the authors present opposing views, and ask students to write a synthesis defending or criticizing one of these views, referencing evidence from both texts.

Teachers need to spend planning time with their colleagues to develop questions and prereading prompts that will spur inquiry, meaty discussion, and high-quality writing. Certain types of questioning work best in this regard: asking students to compare and contrast; defend a position; or rank a list of historical people or events from most to least influential, providing justification from key readings. Teachers can refine generative questions such as these to work at many grade levels: In the folk tale "Hungry Spider and the Turtle," who would make a better friend—Spider or Turtle? (for 1st graders). Is Zeus just? Was it wise for the United States to enter World War 1?

The best prompts and questions will be generated through collaboration. The most stimulating questions can be used in various forms throughout a class or a whole school. Teachers at Tempe Prep are continually refining the questions they use in Humane Letters.

THE PROOF: HIGH-QUALITY WORK

Like all students, reluctant readers in high-poverty schools are eager to discuss and argue from the moment they learn to decode even very simple texts. In the white heat of argument, students learn to organize their interpretations into a persuasive essay. This consistently leads to polished, passionate written work. The proof that this approach is worth the effort is found not only in the fact that Tempe Prep students name Humane Letters as their favorite class, but also in the thinking and writing they produce.

There is nothing complicated about the way that students at schools like Tempe Prep and Park View acquire an education that sharpens their critical thinking and writing skills for life. It's time we realized that teachers can adapt this approach to prepare all kinds of students in any kind of school for full engagement with their world, while demonstrating that, in Ted Sizer's words, "We don't know the half of what these kids can do."

Source: "Reading, Writing, and Thinking for All," by Mike Schmoker. In the April, 2007 issue of Educational Leadership, *64(7), pp. 63–66.* *Learn more about ASCD at www.ascd.org.*

References

Allington, R. (2001). *What really matters for struggling readers.* New York: Addison Wesley Longman.

Conley, D. T. (2003). *Understanding university success.* Eugene, OR: Center for Educational Policy Research, University of Oregon.

Culham, R. (2003). *6 + 1 traits of writing: The complete guide for grades 3 and up.* New York: Scholastic.

Fitzhugh, W. (2006, October). Where's the content? *Educational Leadership, 64* (2), 42–47.

Goodlad, J. (1984). *A place called school.* New York: McGraw Hill.

Graff, G. (2003). *Clueless in academe.* New Haven and London: Yale University Press.

Hernandez, A., Kaplan, M. A., & Schwartz, R. (2006, October). For the sake of argument. *Educational Leadership, 64*(2), 48–52.

Lasch, C. (1995). *The revolt of the elites.* New York: Norton.

Marino, J. (1998, February). Between the lines of Goodlad, Boyer, and Sizer. *English Journal,* 77(2), 19–21.

Marzano, R. (2003). *What works in schools.* Alexandria, VA: ASCD.

Olson, L. (2006, May 10). Skills for work, college readiness are found comparable. *Education Week, 25*(3), 1.

Rehm, D. (2006, April 14). U.S. college education. *The Diane Rehm Show* [Radio broadcast] Washington, D.C.: WAMU.

Schmoker, M., & Marzano, R. (1999, March). Realizing the promise of standards-based education. *Educational Leadership, 56*(6), 17–21.

Toulmin, S. (1958). *The uses of argument.* Cambridge, UK: Cambridge University Press.

Comprehension Questions

1. Who do you think is the intended audience for this article?
2. What are the two obstacles to developing a quality curriculum, according to Schmoker?
3. How does the author view "the classics"?
4. What does the writer mean when he says, "Virtually all courses can become catalysts for inquiry"?
5. What viewpoints does the author have about the preparation high school students are receiving in the United States?

Critical Comprehension Questions

1. What is your assessment of Derek Bok's statement that appears at the beginning of the article?
2. What are "soft skills" and how do they relate to the modern workplace?

Assignment

Choose one of the following topics. In two paragraphs, each about 150 words, provide your answer. In the first paragraph, discuss what your opponent may have to say about the topic. In the second paragraph, provide your position, but use a third-person point of view. You may use research to support your views, but be sure you reference your sources.

1. Agree or disagree with this statement: A liberal arts education is essential for today's workplace.
2. Agree or disagree with this statement: Canadian high school students are effectively prepared for post-secondary education.
3. Agree or disagree with this statement: Poverty has a direct effect on a student's educational experience.

CHECKOUT

Here are some of the ideas you will take away with you after you have completed the chapter:

1. Organizing tools help you plan your writing.
2. Writing is a recursive activity.
3. Feedback is useful for developing revision checklists.
4. An effective internet search can display helpful writing tips.
5. Be aware of your writing process to help you improve.
6. Think of the writing process as having six phases in order to take a step-by-step approach.

Mastering the concepts in this chapter will also help you develop and apply the following employability skills highlighted by the Conference Board of Canada in *Employability Skills 2000+*:

Think & Solve Problems

- be creative and innovative in exploring possible solutions

Be Responsible

- plan and manage time, money and other resources to achieve goals

Learn Continuously

- set your own personal learning goals

Source: Adapted from *Employability Skills 2000+* Brochure E/F (Ottawa: The Conference Board of Canada, 2000).

chapter 4

The Paragraph

Chapter Objectives

After completing this chapter you will be able to

1. describe the important elements of an academic paragraph;
2. recognize the purpose of a topic sentence;
3. construct a clear topic sentence;
4. provide effective supporting ideas for your paragraph;
5. write an effective wrap-up sentence for your paragraph;
6. recognize the use of transitions;
7. use transitions in your paragraphs.

INTRODUCTION

Your purpose in academic writing is usually to explain, inform, or convince. A paragraph, the most important element in your academic writing, is a collection of sentences centring on one major idea. The more well thought out each of your paragraphs is, the more likely you will achieve your purpose in writing.

The paragraph is unified when every sentence in it develops the *topic sentence*—the sentence that contains the main idea of the paragraph. Usually the topic sentence is the first sentence in academic paragraphs because it lets the reader know immediately what the paragraph will be about.

Components of an Academic Paragraph

- *The topic sentence* that tells what the paragraph will be about.
- *Major points* that support the topic sentence.
- *Three major points* (occasionally two major points may be enough) that support the main idea in your topic sentence.
- *Supporting details*: examples, reasons, statistics, anecdotes, research, or experiences that fully explain and develop each of your major points.
- *The wrap-up sentence* if you are writing a one-paragraph composition. The wrap-up sentence ends the paragraph in a logical and satisfying way. If your paragraph is a body paragraph within an essay or research paper, paragraphs should not end in

concluding or wrap-up sentences. Instead, longer pieces of writing use *transitional sentences* between body paragraphs. In this case, transitional sentences at the ends of body paragraphs help to ease the reader out of one paragraph discussion and into the next.

To add coherence to your paragraph, use transitions between major points. **Transitions** are words, phrases, or sentences that act as bridges between ideas. They make the writing style more fluid.

In the case of essays or longer multi-paragraph pieces, each body paragraph should end in a satisfactory manner and lead to the next major idea in the discussion. As mentioned, these transitional sentences help ideas flow nicely for the reader because the development of ideas is moved along logically and smoothly.

HOW TO USE OUTLINES FOR YOUR PARAGRAPHS

You will recall from chapter 3 that an outline is a blueprint for your writing ideas and is one of the most useful writing tools you can use. Basically, for paragraphs, you can use one of two types: the full-sentence outline or the point-form outline. Use complete sentences for all of the points in your paragraph in the full sentence outline, while in the second type, use short notes rather than full sentences. In either case, write out your topic sentence in full.

Example: Sentence Outline

Topic sentence:

Deadbolts are the most effective locks for home security.

Major point 1:

These locks have a square-faced bolt.

Support major point 1 (explanation and a statistic):

The shape of the bolt prohibits the forcing open of a door with a knife blade, screwdriver, or similar instrument. (explanation)

According to a June 2006 Canada Council for Safety report, deadbolts proved to be a deterrent in 95 percent of home entry attempts by thieves. (statistic)

Major point 2:

These locks have a longer bolt, usually 2.5 cm.

Support major point 2:

The longer bolts make the door virtually impossible to pry open because of the tight closure; there are no gaps between the door and the frame. (explanation)

Conventional night latch locks often leave a gap, allowing for "credit card" entry robberies. (example)

Major point 3:

Some deadbolts provide extra security for French doors by locking from the inside with a key.

Support major point 3:

The homeowner locks the deadbolt from the inside by the turn of a key. The homeowner can then remove the key, and even if the burglar breaks the glass, he cannot open the lock. (explanation)

Wrap-up and transitional sentence (if inside an essay):

The many advantages of a deadbolt make it a good investment for a homeowner; however, the type of door frame is another consideration in home security. (wraps up the ideas and leads to the next paragraph in the essay)

Example: Note-Form Outline

Topic sentence:

Deadbolts are the most effective locks for home security.

Major point 1:

- square-faced bolt.

Support major point 1 (explanation and a statistic):

- shape prohibits the forcing open of a door with a sharp instrument. (explanation)
- June 2006 Canada Council for Safety report deadbolts deterrent in 95 percent of burglary attempts. (statistic)

Major point 2:

- a longer bolt, usually 2.5 cm.

Support major point 2:

- door impossible to pry open because tight closure; no gaps between the door and frame. (explanation)
- night latch locks leave gap, allowing for "credit card" entry robberies. (example)

Major point 3:

- extra security by locking from inside with key.

Support major point 3:

- locks the deadbolt from the inside by a key, can then remove key, and burglar cannot open the lock. (explanation)

Wrap-up and transitional sentence (if inside an essay):

- advantages of a good investment; however, door frame is consideration in home security. (wraps up the ideas and leads to the next paragraph in the essay)

Example: Completed Paragraph

Here is the completed paragraph. Please note the writer has added transitions between the points to add emphasis, new ideas, and flow. The transitions are shown in italics.

Deadbolts are the most effective locks for home security. To begin with, these locks have a square-faced bolt. The shape of the bolt prohibits the forcing open of a door with a knife blade, screwdriver, or similar instrument, for example. According to a June 2006 Canada Council for Safety report, deadbolts proved to be a deterrent in 95 percent of home entry attempts by thieves. Furthermore, these locks have a longer bolt, usually 2.5 cm. The longer bolts make the door virtually impossible to pry open because of the tight closure; there are no gaps between the door and the frame. Conventional night latch locks often leave a gap, allowing for "credit card" entry robberies. In addition, some deadbolts provide extra security for French doors by locking from the inside with a key. The homeowner locks the deadbolt from the inside by the turn of a key. The homeowner can then remove the key, and even if the burglar breaks the glass, he cannot open the lock. The many advantages of a deadbolt make it a good investment for a homeowner; however, the type of door frame is also a consideration in home security.

Exercise 1 Developing an Outline

Choose one of the following topics. Develop an outline—either in sentence form or note form. Write out your topic sentence in full. Be prepared to hand in this assignment or have a peer from class evaluate your work. Your outline should be easily transformed into a paragraph. Be sure to include three major points to support your topic sentence.

1. Raising horses
2. Employment programs for youth
3. Building your own gazebo
4. Problems with bills
5. Easy credit
6. Rock climbing
7. Online magazines
8. Recreational snorkelling
9. Family vacations
10. Extreme sports
11. Urban camping
12. Wine tasting
13. Computer animation
14. Herbal teas
15. Financial investments

HOW TO STRUCTURE A BASIC ACADEMIC PARAGRAPH

Your academic paragraphs should look like this:

Topic sentence (contains the main idea of the paragraph)

↓

First major point (in a separate sentence)

↓

Support for first major point (proof or explanation in separate sentence or sentences: use examples, reasons, statistics, research, anecdotes, or facts)

↓

Second major point (in a separate sentence)

↓

Support for second major point (proof or explanation in separate sentence or sentences: use examples, reasons, statistics, research, anecdotes, or facts)

↓

Third major point (in a separate sentence)

↓

Support for third major point (proof or explanation in separate sentence or sentences: use examples, reasons, statistics, research, anecdotes, or facts)

↓

Wrap-up sentence (logical closing to the paragraph or leads to the next paragraph as a transitional sentence or device)

HOW TO DEVELOP TOPIC SENTENCES

The topic sentence expresses what the paragraph will be about—in other words, its main idea. Usually you find topic sentences placed at the beginning of paragraphs. It is most important to write clear topic sentences that direct both you and your reader through the writing. Topic sentences control the scope of a paragraph, so do not make them too broad or too general in nature. By the same token, do not make them so narrow that they are really a supporting detail rather than a major idea. If your topic sentence is too narrow, you will not have anything much to discuss in the paragraph.

Examples:

Topic sentence too broad: Government should be investing in alternative sources of energy.

Topic sentence too narrow: Switchgrass on the Canadian prairies is a useful source of ethanol.

Topic sentence is workable: The Canadian government should investigate the potential of using ethanol as a new energy source.

Exercise 2 Identifying Topic Sentences

Work in pairs. Tell whether the topic sentence is workable, too narrow, or too broad. Be prepared to provide reasons for your answers.

1. Caribou have a terrible smell.
2. Most of the students at Rona College like to participate in rollerblading sports.
3. Although the Smart Fortwo is proving to be popular, it does not provide an alternative for most consumers.
4. Baseball, unlike soccer, relies on the mental agility of its players.
5. Wayne Gretzky is a really important figure in hockey.
6. Nine out of ten participants chose Flako pastry made from non-transfat margarine.
7. Cordless tools have their drawbacks.
8. Orange and pink are a horrible colour combination.
9. The police in Toronto have learned a good deal from the London police based on their experience of the terrorist attacks in London in 2005.
10. No child should have to go to bed hungry.
11. This sleeping bag uses the marvellous new material, microheat, as an insulator.
12. The children from the grade 4 class of Roseberry Elementary learned three important lessons about helping others.
13. Marijuana laws need to be updated.
14. Aboriginal leaders have four claims in the North Battleford, Saskatchewan, area.
15. Cruelty to animals is outrageous.

Exercise 3 Developing Topic Sentences

Write a clear, effective topic sentence for each of the following. Your instructor may ask to see your work or may ask you to share your work with others.

1. Making a difficult decision

   ____

   ____

2. Studying sharks of the North Atlantic

____

____

3. Escorting a friend to court

____

____

4. Owning your own business

____

____

5. Making perfect muffins

____

____

6. Selecting a birthday gift for your partner

____

____

7. Selling real estate

____

____

8. Choosing a college or university

____

____

9. Preparing an effective resumé

____

____

10. Talking to your children about stealing

____

____

Exercise 4 *Peer Editing Topic Sentences*

Form a group of three to five people. Make three to five copies of the topic sentences you developed in the previous exercise. Exchange them with members of your new group. Edit these sentences together by examining each topic sentence according to the following ideas:

1. Is the topic sentence workable, or is it too broad or too narrow? Why?
2. What ideas would you expect the writer to include in her paragraph?
3. What advice could you give to help the writer improve her topic sentence?

HOW TO DEVELOP SUPPORT FOR YOUR MAJOR POINTS

Support means providing evidence or proof for your major points. The more specific and convincing your evidence, the more likely it is you will persuade your reader. You can build support in a number of ways.

- Provide more explanation:

  State your point; then, in the sentences that follow, elaborate or explain the point.

  Example:
  Historically, pandemics begin in very isolated regions and take quite a number of years to spread. (major point) In other words, diseases that are communicated by human or animal contact do not suddenly infect huge areas or populations. (supporting explanation)

- Provide examples, statistics, or facts.

  Example:
  Historically, pandemics begin in very isolated regions and take quite a number of years to spread. (major point) In other words, diseases that are communicated by human or animal contact do not suddenly infect huge areas or populations. (supporting explanation) For example, the World Health Organization names six stages in the development of a pandemic, with each stage taking some time to progress. (example)

- Provide a reason or a chain of reasoning.

  Example:
  Historically, pandemics begin in very isolated regions and take quite a number of years to spread. (major point) In other words, diseases that are communicated by human or animal contact do not suddenly infect huge areas or populations. (supporting explanation) Viruses are found in ducks, chickens, whales, seals, pigs, and horses, but according to the World Health Organization, only birds host all subtypes of influenza virus. The virus can be transmitted directly from the animal or the animal's environment to humans, but often, there is an intermediate animal host. Pigs, for instance, can act as the intermediate host, so the virus travels from the bird, to the pig, to humans. By this time, however, health protection intervention will have stopped the mass transmission among humans. (chain of reasoning)

Exercise 5 Providing Support

Work in pairs or small groups. You will see major points given in the exercise below. Provide the type of support asked for in each item. Write down your answers, and be prepared to share them with others in the class.

1. Major point: Skateboards on city streets are annoying.

   Support: Provide a chain of reasoning. ______________________________

   ____
   ____
   ____
   ____
   ____

2. Major point: Teen marriages are not generally sanctioned in the Western world.

   Support: Provide a fact or statistic. ______________________________

   ____
   ____
   ____
   ____
   ____

3. Major point: Positive body image is stronger among young males than females in North America.

   Support: Provide a fact or statistic. ______________________________

   ____
   ____
   ____
   ____
   ____

4. Major point: Recreational activities bring families closer together.

   Support: Provide more explanation. ______________________________

   ____

   ____

   ____

   ____

   ____

5. Major point: Mutual sympathy and open communication engenders community.

   Support: Provide a chain of reasoning. ______________________________

   ____

   ____

   ____

   ____

   ____

Exercise 6 *Providing Reasons*

Provide three reasons that support each of the following. Your instructor may ask to see your work. Be prepared to share your answers.

- Three reasons why procrastination can harm a student.

  1. ______________________________

  2. ______________________________

  3. ______________________________

- Three reasons why having a brother (or sister) is important.

  1. ______________________________

  2. ______________________________

  3. ______________________________

- Three reasons why video games are so popular.

  1. ____________________
  2. ____________________
  3. ____________________

- Three reasons why I love going to parties.

  1. ____________________
  2. ____________________
  3. ____________________

- Three reasons why I should get an A in my English course.

  1. ____________________
  2. ____________________
  3. ____________________

HOW TO DEVELOP UNITY IN PARAGRAPHS

Unity in your paragraph means that every idea you provide in the paragraph relates to its central theme or main idea. All of the ideas in the paragraph contribute to the topic sentence (which states the central or main idea of your paragraph).

As you think of new points and support in your paragraphs, think of how they relate to the topic sentences. Do they relate? Are they on topic or not? If they are not, then your writing will be disjointed to the reader.

HOW TO DEVELOP COHERENCE IN PARAGRAPHS

Coherence in your paragraphs involves the linking of your ideas. Each part of the writing connects to the others, so the overall writing has a logical sense to it. Coherent writing has a flow of ideas and an effective style. You may consider unity as part of coherence since unifying all ideas will make pieces of writing flow logically.

To add to the coherence in a paragraph, use transitions. Transitions like *furthermore*, *also*, *on the other hand*, *consequently*, and so forth provide direction to your idea flow. They tell the reader, "Now I want to add to that," or "Now I want to contrast that," or "Now I want to leave that point and start another." The next section discusses transitions and their uses.

Use Transitions

Transitions are words, phrases, or sentences used to express a change of ideas. One idea might be ending and another idea beginning. They can show relationships between ideas in terms of time, logic, or explanation. The next section reviews the kinds of transitions at your disposal as you write.

Transitions to Show Emphasis or Addition of Ideas

1. and
2. also
3. finally
4. as well as
5. too
6. in addition
7. moreover
8. furthermore
9. in the same fashion
10. another
11. again
12. further
13. to begin
14. first, second, etc.
15. next

Example Paragraph 1:

My neighbours just purchased a really unusual new dog, a Hungarian Puli. Its appearance is a little startling at first. Poldi, the Puli, has an amazing coat, which seems to have the ability to form dreadlocks unless it is combed. Moreover, the dreadlocks hang in long rope-like strands, giving the dog a distinctive, almost Rasta look. In addition, the thick dread coat makes it difficult to tell which end of the dog is which. My neighbours' children love to walk Poldi so that they can trick passersby into patting the wrong end of the dog. Also, the Puli's floppy style of walking and running emphasizes its long corded coat.

Transitions to Show Time Order or Chronological Order

1. first
2. in the first place
3. second
4. later
5. then
6. last
7. until
8. as soon as
9. while
10. soon
11. now
12. eventually
13. at last
14. after that
15. early
16. whenever
17. in due time
18. before
19. to begin with
20. afterward
21. third
22. next
23. during
24. when
25. finally
26. after
27. prior to
28. meanwhile

Example Paragraph 2:

Canada's relationship with hockey began with a geographic and meteorological fact—we have a white and snowy winter, and <u>when</u> it gets cold, we get ice. That's how the very game of hockey began, and we took to it with pre-lapsarian pleasure. As the game grew and developed, every aspect of it became a part of our lives. The mounds of Zambonied snow that sit behind arenas in the middle of the summer speak to this. The Eaton's catalogue with table lamps, bed sheets, and bath towels adorned with the logos of NHL teams are likewise manifestations of how hockey is represented in even our most non-hockey accoutrements. Ads in the paper that mention a "hat trick" of sales at the local furniture emporium also speak to this. Popular players promote cars and clothes and beer and every other kind of merchandise from milk (Doug Gilmour) to Viagra (Guy Lafleur). And <u>then</u>, of course, there is Tim Hortons®. The Hall of Fame Maple Leafs defenceman, <u>now</u> long dead, lives on in the taste buds of millions of Canadians every day who gulp down his coffee and savour his doughnuts. Hockey is not just a sport and it's more than a passion; it is an ingrained part of who we are, how we live our lives and go about our business. Grown men play the game <u>until</u> they're too old and their bones too brittle to endure the rigours of skating. More girls and women play in Canada than anywhere else in the world. Hockey books, hockey cards, hockey videos, hockey posters, and hockey pucks are part of kids' bedrooms from coast to coast and are stashed away in nearly every family basement or garage. "Hockey helmet" is a way to describe a particular coiffed look. No one would know what vulcanized rubber is were it not for the puck. Indeed, the game has a language all its own, from "slot" to "cherry-picker", and "lid" to "hat trick", words that have become part of our everyday vocabulary in and out of the arena. According to a recent poll conducted by CBC, Don Cherry, Wayne Gretzky, and Paul Henderson are among the greatest Canadians in the country's history, every bit as famous as great prime ministers, scientists, artists, and activists.

Source: Andrew Podnieks, A Canadian Saturday Night: Hockey and the Culture of a Country, *(Vancouver: Douglas & McIntyre, Greystone Books, 2006), 3–4. Reprinted by permission of the publisher.*

Transitions to Show Contrast or Difference

1. but
2. in contrast
3. however
4. yet
5. despite the fact
6. although
7. opposite
8. on the contrary
9. on the other hand
10. nevertheless
11. otherwise
12. still
13. even though
14. different
15. than
16. whereas
17. conversely

Example Paragraph 3:

Unlike the honeybee, a beneficial insect, the yellow jacket is considered a pest by most people. It is considerably more aggressive than the honeybee and can sting repeatedly. The yellow jacket is interested in garbage and protein materials early in the season and fresh fruit in the fall. In contrast, the honeybee is interested only in flowers. It will not pester people for their food at picnics, opposite to the yellow jacket. Even though both the honeybee and the yellow jacket belong to the same genus of insects, their food, social habits, and nest-building activities are widely different.

Transitions to Show Similarity or Comparison

1. both
2. each
3. like
4. likewise
5. respectively
6. similarly
7. also
8. and
9. in the same fashion
10. just as
11. compared to

Example Paragraph 4:

Both porcelain and bone china are desirable types of pottery throughout the world. Known in various forms by most cultures of the world, each type is highly prized. Collectors comb the globe looking for rare and important pieces. Some are so valuable that only world-class museums or billionaires can afford them. For example, at Sotheby's Imperial Sale, held in October 2000, a fine Ming porcelain jar from the 16th century sold for $5 567 640. Likewise, both porcelain and bone china are held in high esteem because they are considered works of art. Artisans from different continents were employed specifically to hand-paint elegant designs on vases, plates, and bowls. Even Picasso tried his hand at plate paintings. In the same fashion, china and porcelain are collected by millions as a hobby. Some of the most sought-after pieces depict famous historical scenes or moments. Great Britain, for example, commemorates its royal and historical figures of importance in china specially manufactured for a notable occasion. Prince Charles's two weddings, for instance, to Diana and then to Camilla, have been celebrated, respectively, in commemorative plates, dinner sets, mugs, teacups, and saucers. After centuries, these two types of ceramics continue to be popular for their elegance, historic importance, and desirability to collectors.

Transitions to Show Cause and Effect

1. as a result
2. consequently
3. therefore
4. thus
5. accordingly
6. so
7. to conclude
8. then
9. hence
10. if
11. for this reason

Example Paragraph 5:

Watching the news before going to sleep can cause sleep disturbance or insomnia. The late-night news is often filled with depressing events. As a result, an individual is put into a kind of stage of alert. Images, sounds, or phrases may remain in a person's immediate consciousness, and therefore may plague the person as she tries to settle down and relax for sleep. Consequently, overstimulation and restlessness follow. Thus, a person becomes centred on worry and stress. Accordingly, the person becomes aroused rather than calmed into a state of sleep, so late-night news watching is not recommended.

You can find more information about transitions and transitional phrases in this edition by looking in the index at the back of the book.

Exercise 7 Using Transitions

Work in pairs. In the following sentences, add a transition that would make sense for each sentence relationship. Pay attention to how the ideas in each sentence relate to one another. Be prepared to share your answers. Note that you may require a semicolon in front of some transitions.

1. Dentists advise patients to floss their teeth; _______________, they might suffer from periodontal disease.
2. Anwar enjoyed the tour of the museum, _______________ he did not care for the meal in the cafeteria.
3. My sister claims that farmed salmon and wild ocean salmon taste the same, _______________ I maintain the texture and flavour are different.
4. The force of the tsunami of December 26, 2004, was formidable; _______________ it killed more than 150 000 people, which is _______________ the entire population of cities like Barrie, Ontario, or Kelowna, British Columbia.
5. Mieux-Mieux, the long-haired cat, has a velvet cushion for her bed, _______________; Boozer, the family dog, has to sleep in an old basket under the kitchen stairs.
6. Stilton Chesterson is the world's highest paid security chief, _______________ he will not allow himself to be photographed due to the nature of his job.
7. _______________ there is a heavy rain, we can hear foghorns as ships pass through the narrow passage between the islands.
8. _______________, to start the engine, turn the key to the left; _______________ hold down the green button for five seconds.
9. The muffins from that take-out restaurant are really high in calories; _______________, they contain about five tablespoons of sugar each.

10. _______________ Freemont had inherited a great fortune from his parents, he squandered his money on gambling and expensive cars, _______________ within five years, he was destitute.

Exercise 8 Developing Unity and Coherence

Below is a paragraph that lacks both unity and coherence. Read the paragraph and answer the questions that follow.

Paragraph: Poor Unity and Coherence

Sports and fitness trends are related to what John Kelly, a University of Illinois sociologist, calls "the Olympic effect." Since the Olympic Games get such an abundance of media coverage and promotion, adult viewers tend to participate more just before, during, and immediately after the Olympics. The Olympics occur every four years. I do not tend to watch the Olympic Games coverage too much, although many of my friends do. After the Olympic flurry is over, participation in sports and fitness activities tends to spiral downward again, according to Dr. Kelly. However, casino gambling and poker have increased interest and participation since 2004. I do not gamble, either.

1. Why does the paragraph lack unity?

   Give some examples.

   ____

   ____

2. Why does the paragraph lack coherence?

   Give some examples.

   ____

   ____

3. Does the writer use transitions or transitional phrases? Which transitions might the writer have chosen? Why? Give examples.

   ____

   ____

HOW TO USE POINT OF VIEW IN PARAGRAPHS

Point of view means from which perspective a piece of writing is told. If you want to write about a childhood experience, for example, you will write using a *personal* point of view or using the first-person pronoun *I*. Most of your academic writing assignments in post-secondary courses will not ask for this point of view, but some instructors may encourage you to use it. Psychology essays, for instance, may ask you to talk about yourself in a particular situation, as might cultural studies courses. Some instructors, however, ask you to avoid the personal or *I* point of view.

Keep in mind that different points of view serve different purposes. On occasion, you might find it is appropriate to use the first person, yet at others, the first person is unacceptable. Your journal, for example, is written from a personal point of view, but your physics lab report is not.

What points of view are recommended in academic writing? Most of the time, you will write using a *third-person point of view*, either *he*, *she*, or *they*. Use a third-person, plural point of view if you want a nonsexist position. Since *they* does not name a gender, it tends to remove sexism from discussion. Also, *you* as a point of view is often discouraged. Some instructors regard *you* as presenting problems in writing because the writing style may seem sermonizing in tone. However, some instructors will allow the second person point of view, particularly if the writer must give instructions.

Points of View and Purposes

- *I* (first person, singular) → the writer is involved in the events; the point of view is more subjective (personal involvement)
- *We* (first person, plural) → the writer and the reader are together involved in the events; the point of view is more subjective
- *You* (second person, singular or plural) → the reader is the focus
- *He or she* (third person, singular) → the point of view is more objective (at a distance), but a gender is named
- *They* (third person, plural) → the point of view is more objective (at a distance), but no gender is named
- *One* (third person) → the point of view is neutral. However, some instructors do not accept *one* as a point of view because it can make the writing style sound strained.

Check with your instructor about which points of view are acceptable in your assignments and which are not. Often your instructor will mention this information in your course outline.

HOW TO USE WRAP-UP AND TRANSITIONAL SENTENCES IN YOUR PARAGRAPHS

You should end each paragraph in order to satisfy one of two purposes. First, if your paragraph is a single paragraph composition that stands by itself, use your wrap-up or last sentence to draw discussion to a close. You may summarize the main points of your paragraph, or you may simply restate your topic sentence. On the other hand, if your paragraph is part of the body of an essay or longer multi-paragraph piece, you should link this paragraph to the next one. Make the last sentence of your paragraph tie off discussion and lead your reader logically to the next main idea. In other words, last sentences of body paragraphs should be transitional, bridging between the paragraphs. Reread the five example paragraphs in the section titled "How to Use Transitions," paying attention to the last sentence in each.

REVIEW TEST

Try the following review test. It will help you assess what you have learned from the chapter. Be prepared to share your responses with others in the class.

1. Define a paragraph.

____

____

____

2. What is the topic sentence of a paragraph?

____

____

____

3. What is a main point in a paragraph?

____

____

____

4. How can you provide support for your ideas in a paragraph?

____

____

____

5. What is point of view in writing?

____

____

____

6. Name the third-person, plural point of view.

____

____

____

7. Name the personal point of view.

____

____

____

8. What is the purpose of a second-person, plural point of view?

____

____

____

9. What is unity in a paragraph?

____

____

____

10. What is coherence in a paragraph?

____

____

____

11. What are transitional words or phrases (transitions)?

____

____

____

12. Name five transitions.

____

____

____

Assignment

Write a paragraph of 150–175 words about one of the following topics. Start with a clear topic sentence. Use transitions in your paragraph. Use a third-person point of view.

1. Babysitting
2. Exercise classes
3. Surfing
4. Reading to young children
5. Bingo
6. Sewing your own clothes
7. Getting tickets for a game

8. Worrying too much
9. Making a container garden
10. Raising fish
11. Going to the movies
12. Working in a restaurant
13. Saving money
14. Keeping up with trends
15. Grooming your dog

Bonus Exercise *A Case of* Who *or* Whom

Who and *whom* are pronouns. As you may recall, pronouns are words that function as nouns and stand in for nouns. Pronouns can have three functions: They can be the subjects of sentences or clauses. They can be objects of verbs or prepositions. They can also show possession.

Examples:

Who knocked at the window?

The subject of the sentence is *who.*

He gave whom some money?

The object of the verb is *whom.*

Whose wallet is this?

The possessive case of *who* is *whose.*

Hint:
Who is the subject case.
Whom is the object case.
Use the subject case after a linking verb.

Use the correct form of the pronoun to match its function in the sentence. Check your answers with the Answer Key.

1. To ______________ was he speaking at the dinner table?
2. We have decided ______________ we will invite to the conference.
3. Ally and Samantha wish to know ______________ you are.
4. The tourist sights are plentiful in Halifax and ______________ knows best where to find them but my friend, Bert, ______________ lives there.
5. It was Rico, I think, ______________ was the best dancer in the competition held last weekend in Hamilton.
6. Mr. Daliwal consulted a lawyer ______________ he met in Winnipeg during a business meeting.

7. Buster Keaton was the man ______________ everyone loved in the silent movies.

8. The women, two of ______________ are Finnish, told stories of their grandmothers.

9. To ______________ do you turn in times of trouble?

10. Martial law was applied to those ______________ were considered terrorists.

READING

So What if Stories Can't Promise a Happy Ending?

by Russell Smith

Russell Smith is an acclaimed columnist for *The Globe and Mail* and writer of six works of fiction. His latest novel, *Muriella Pent,* was released in 2004 and nominated for several prizes for fiction writing. The following selection comes from Smith's former weekly column, "Virtual Culture," written for *The Globe and Mail.* Although Smith writes on a wide range of topics, he is particularly interested in art and what constitutes art in the 21st century. As you read "So What if Stories Can't Promise a Happy Ending?" think about the changing face of the narrative today.

I gave a reading in a university class, of a short story that I had published recently. The story was conventional: past tense, third person, a significant moment at the end.

The class was in philosophy at the University of Toronto. They're studying the philosophy of art and aesthetics, so the professor, Mark Kingwell, asks an artist to come in and talk about what he or she does. So I gave my reading and I got the usual intelligent and interested questions afterwards—about the writing process, about truth and fiction, about all those serious things that show that students are engaged with the idea of art as a part of intellectual life.

But this is a rarefied world, and I know that the world outside is not like that. Outside, art, as opposed to, say, an Asian-fusion meal at a modernist restaurant, is not satisfying. It doesn't have a high enough fat content: It doesn't give you information, it doesn't make you rich, it doesn't get you a husband, it doesn't give you 10 simple redecorating ideas.

So when one student approached me afterwards and began asking the aggressive questions about contemporary fiction and how opaque it all is, I felt something like relief: It wasn't what one expected from a university, but at least it was familiar. These are the hard issues that publishers' sales reps have to deal with. She didn't want to ask the question in the class, possibly because it would have seemed dumb. But it was a good question, a question that is constantly asked of all the contemporary arts outside the universities. The question was simple: What is the point of short stories? The student admitted that she never got them. There didn't seem to be any message. They just ended. And then she wondered if there was a message that she was too stupid to get. Was she stupid, or was she looking for the wrong thing?

The question is interesting because it is commonly asked of visual art. What is the point of something—an object, an installation, a weird video—that does not appear to say anything, that just is? What is the point of a room full of metal boxes, or a building wrapped in plastic? What is it saying? Art objects are not, on the whole, narratives. And when they are neither representations nor narratives, it's hard to look at them as anything other than riddles.

But stories are stories. One would think that human society has been telling each other stories for long enough that the activity is understood as an entertaining one even when it doesn't have an immediately practical function. This student's question illuminates the fact that stories are not what they used to be: They are not like 19th-century novels, which told the story of a life or a society over time, nor are they like some 19th-century stories (say, those of Poe or Maupassant) that contained a surprise or twist, rather like the punchlines of jokes. Since Chekhov and his descendants, the modernists, stories have been about glimpses: They let you into a moment in someone's life. That moment is significant in ways that are not usually explained. These stories are growing, into the 21st century, even more cryptic. They may end with a poignant image but no other resolution.

Simultaneously, popular entertainment grows ever more didactic. Hollywood movies do, in fact, have messages, and they are often just as obvious as Aesop's (family is more important than career; stupid people can be good; there's no place like home for the holidays). So the short stories in the literary quarterlies, by contrast, are beginning to appear more and more like the art objects in white-walled galleries: riddles with no answers.

I asked the student if she felt as frustrated by paintings. Even representational paintings usually don't have messages either. What's the point of them? She answered that stories were different. They tickled a different part of the brain. Which is true, I concede, since language is a different process of representation, but why can't they be like paintings in their aims? She didn't know. But she did know she wanted stories to have messages, sure, even messages that were like morals, why not?

Kingwell and I asked her, What about simple escapism? Don't you want to just be with some fictitious characters in a foreign world for half an hour? She wasn't excited by that idea either. Literary stories still made her feel that she was missing something.

So we explained to her the tradition of the modernist epiphanic-story—the story that ends with a character whose realization about something comes as a surprise to the reader and casts the first part of the story in a different light—and asked her, did she not see that as a message of a sort? She agreed to that, mostly, I think, to humour us; I could tell that slice-of-someone-else's-life stories were never going to interest her much.

The exchange made me think, strangely, of gossip, and its popularity: There is no point to the stories released daily about celebrities' marriages and affairs, and we don't know the characters in those stories either, not personally. They may as well be fictional.

And we like to hear them because we understand the world through them, in ways that Plato and Hegel spend many hundreds of pages trying to explain, and that I cannot.

Source: Russell Smith, "So What if Stories Can't Promise a Happy Ending?" The Globe and Mail *23 October 2003: R1–R2. Reprinted by permission of Russell Smith.*

Comprehension Questions

1. What is an epiphanic story?
2. Find the underlined word *opaque* in the selection. Without using a dictionary and using context clues, write down what you think *opaque* means.
3. According to Smith, how have stories changed?
4. How do stories about celebrities' lives seem fictional?
5. Considering how modern stories have developed, what would you expect stories to be like in 100 years?
6. How does the writer use contrast in the piece?

Critical Comprehension

1. What do you think the writer means when he says, "Outside, art, as opposed to, say, an Asian-fusion meal at a modernist restaurant, is not satisfying."
2. What assumptions are made about "art"?

Assignment

Discuss in a paragraph of 200 words the contrast in these two statements the writer makes in the article: "Since Chekhov and his descendants, the modernists, stories have been about glimpses" and "Simultaneously, popular entertainment grows ever more didactic." Use a third-person point of view.

CHECKOUT

Here are some of the ideas you will take away with you after you have completed the chapter:

1. Full-sentence and point-form outlines are planning tools useful to writers.
2. Between supporting points, transitions promote emphasis and flow.
3. Transitions may be words, phrases, or sentences.
4. In multi-paragraph pieces, the last sentences of body paragraphs should be transitional.
5. The topic sentence of a paragraph shapes its main idea.

6. Major points provide arguments and evidence to support the topic sentence.
7. Most of the time, you will use a third-person point of view in academic writing.

Mastering the concepts in this chapter will also help you develop and apply the following employability skills highlighted by the Conference Board of Canada in *Employability Skills 2000+*:

Communicate

- use relevant scientific, technological and mathematical knowledge and skills to explain or clarify ideas

Manage Information

- locate, gather and organize information using appropriate technology and information systems

Source: Adapted from *Employability Skills 2000+* Brochure E/F (Ottawa: The Conference Board of Canada, 2000).

chapter 5

The Essay

Chapter Objectives

After completing this chapter you will be able to

1. write better essays by adopting a conventional academic essay form;
2. organize, clarify, and enhance your writing ideas by using rhetorical modes;
3. recognize that academic essays should be clearly, though not rigidly, organized;
4. adopt a thoughtful approach to the organization and presentation of all your writing;
5. write successful essays that attract and inform interested readers.

INTRODUCTION

Everyone agrees: writing takes work. Stephen Leacock, a famous Canadian humorist, once said, "Writing is no trouble: you jot down ideas as they occur to you. The jotting is simplicity itself—it is the occurring which is difficult." The essay is the conventional form of expression in academic writing. Most of the courses in the humanities, social sciences, nursing, and business require essay answers. Although essays are commonly assigned to be written outside of class, in-class essay writing has become more popular during the semester and in examinations. Therefore, essay writing will follow you wherever you go in your post-secondary studies.

This chapter introduces you to the basic form of the essay. You will learn throughout the course of this book to write more extended essays, too, in order to prepare you for the demands of your academic course work.

WHAT IS AN ESSAY?

Definitions of *essay* vary. One common definition is "a written composition on a specific subject." Another conventional definition adds another dimension: "an essay is a short, controlled composition giving the writer's views on a specific subject or expressing his or her opinions on a specific subject." Finally, you find another element in this definition: "an essay is a short composition that attempts to inform and convince the reader."

By amalgamating the definitions, you will have captured an essay's key components: "an essay is a short, controlled piece of writing expressing an author's views or opinions on a specific subject in an attempt to inform and convince the reader."

The essay, then,

- is short and controlled;
- expresses views or opinions;
- is on one specific subject;
- attempts to inform and convince.

On first reading this, you might think that an essay is just a fancy name for a written argument, and in a sense, you are right. The term *argument* suggests controversial issues and clear reasoning. Although essays can deal with controversial issues in a reasoned way, they can also discuss a wide range of topics—from light and amusing to heavy and sombre—meant to convince readers. In other words, "Why cousins should not be invited to weddings" is just as much an essay topic as "Capital punishment should be reinstated in Canada." The first essay topic is not as serious in tone as the second, but it, too, is controversial. Both topics will try to convince readers of each writer's position or views.

Now you might ask, "What good will essay writing do me in my future career or studies?" Many courses in English, the social sciences, nursing, business and commerce, biology, engineering, history, philosophy, and so forth require students to explain and convince. Today, companies are hiring new people based on their "soft skills," as well as on their academic or technical training. Communication is a major component of a soft skills set. According to many industry experts, the most important element in the modern professional workplace is the ability to communicate well in speaking and writing. *Employability Skills 2000+* places "Communicate" first on its list of skills needed for today's workforce.

Even in your daily life, you will do some writing that involves trying to explain, inform, or convince somebody of something. If you write a letter of application, you are attempting to convince a prospective employer to hire you. If you write a letter to Bell Canada, complaining about a billing for unauthorized phone calls, then you are attempting to convince or persuade. If you have a dispute with your landlord or a car salesperson and you find yourself in court, the organization of your argument, written or spoken, will assist your attempt to convince. If you write a proposal for a new project that your community group might be interested in taking on, you must explain why the project should go ahead; you must inform your readers of the facts as you understand them, and you must try to convince them that your project idea is a good one.

Essay writing can become a useful learning tool to you in a number of ways. It can become a tool

- to sort out what you think about some issue or topic;
- to convince others your points are valid;
- to organize written ideas;
- to coordinate and complete a thinking/writing project;
- to revise ideas;
- to incorporate others' advice about revision and improvement;
- to present a well-edited, thoughtful written piece;
- to gain the satisfaction that you are capable of all these things.

WHAT ARE THE MODES OF ORGANIZATION FOR ESSAYS?

Essays can have patterns of development called rhetorical modes or ways in which the information can be organized. *Spotlight on Critical Skills in Essay Writing*, Second Edition suggests five basic modes: process analysis, comparison and contrast, classification and division, cause and effect, and definition, all of which are discussed in more detail in chapter 9. These modes are essentially the same as those you might use for writing paragraphs.

Of course, few people write essays by deciding first on the rhetorical mode and then on the topic. The rhetorical modes are simply tools. You can choose to use one or not. You will find that most writers use a blended approach: they may choose to compare and contrast two ideas, but they may also include the history of the ideas (process analysis or time order) and their impact (cause and effect).

Essays are a lot like people; each one you write will have its own personality. Some of your essays will fall into place easily, while others are stubborn and won't want to work for you. But our flexibility as learners allows us to accept the fact that things are not always the same. It is better to survey the tools in front of you, consider the essay designs, and then choose one that fits your taste and your purpose. You will write essays on various topics of interest to you, but your instructor will not ask you to write *pure design* types of essays. Some essays you write may contain a mixed pattern—a little cause and effect with a little contrast because this is what seems to work best for a particular essay. This makes sense, so don't panic: mixing essay designs, unlike mixing drinks, has no ill effects.

You will see, though, that a clear directing sentence that contains the main idea of the essay is essential. This sentence is called the **thesis statement**, and it controls the ideas and the organization of the essay.

Basic Structure of an Essay

Introductory paragraph with a thesis statement

↓

Body paragraphs with topic sentences, main points, and supporting evidence (minimum of three)

↓

Concluding paragraph

You will write essays that have these same components. Academic essays must have an introductory paragraph with a thesis statement—a main idea sentence controlling the whole essay. The body of your academic essay should have a minimum of three separate paragraphs, but more often than not, the body of an essay at the post-secondary level has more than three. Every body paragraph discusses a major idea of the thesis and develops points and evidence to support claims made by the thesis. The conclusion sums up the major ideas in the essay and leaves the reader with a general thought on the topic. Check with your instructor or professor about her preferences regarding essay writing because you may find some variations. For example, some do not want a summary statement in the conclusion of a short essay; others may not require transitional sentences between paragraphs in a short piece.

An academic essay must have the following:

- introductory paragraph containing a thesis statement (controlling idea);
- body paragraphs (at least three that support the claims of the thesis);
- conclusion (summing up and providing a general thought);
- strong evidence;
- good editing;
- clear presentation (word-processed with title page, 11- or 12-point font, good spacing).

WHAT ARE THE PURPOSES OF WRITING AN ESSAY?

1. To meet the requirements of a course or exam
2. To provide a challenge in thinking an issue or topic through in an organized way
3. To develop a sense of language
4. To clarify thinking
5. To develop intellectual powers using language
6. To communicate an opinion or idea on a theme, special topic, or issue
7. To provide a point of view on a theme, special topic, or issue
8. To persuade readers to consider your point of view

An essay can test and develop your skills in a variety of ways. Good written expression is one of the most important capabilities you can have today. As mentioned, employers are looking for good communicators, not just those who are articulate and convincing in their speech, but those who are equally adept in their writing. As well, specialized writing, such as technical writing and argumentation, have become fundamental to many courses in colleges and universities.

As you write, you will make discoveries of different sorts. You will find out what you think about an issue. You will read what others have to say on the same topic. As a peer editor, you will read other students' work, and they may read yours. You will discover how you react to doing revisions and how you will incorporate suggestions and corrections into your writing routine. You will discuss ideas, and possibly debate them with a good deal of passion. You will find your own writing voice. You will surprise yourself at times, but in the final analysis, you will develop and improve as a writer.

WHAT ARE THE PARTS OF AN ESSAY?

Clearly, academic essays are part of your writing life as a post-secondary student. You will need to know how to construct essays that are logical and convincing. The following section will provide you with important information about writing short prose compositions called "essays."

The Introduction

Your essay begins in a paragraph called the **introduction**. Your introduction should start in an interesting way. It should provide some background on your topic. You may choose to give your reader some general information on the topic in order to build a bridge of common understanding between you and your reader. Finally, end the introductory paragraph with a thesis statement. It expresses the main idea of the essay. It focuses on a topic and then angles it to show the author's point of view and usually the rhetorical mode of development—how you will develop and organize your ideas.

The Body

The body of an essay extends over several paragraphs. The body of the essay develops the ideas. Each paragraph of the body contains a major idea of the thesis and supporting points. It provides specific and convincing evidence for the major ideas. Sometimes you might have to do some research in order to provide convincing proof for the points in your paragraphs. The body should contain a minimum of three paragraphs, but usually it contains more. Each paragraph begins with a topic sentence, which controls the ideas in each paragraph.

Develop your discussion in each paragraph in a thorough way. Set out a point in a separate sentence; then provide proof, explanation, or other support for each point. The proof can consist of examples, quotations, facts, statistics, illustrations, or specific reasons. Balance each paragraph so that you discuss each point equally well. The body of the essay should show balanced discussion throughout the paragraphs. At the ends of body paragraphs, except the last one, use **transitional sentences**—sentences that close one discussion and lead to another. These transitional sentences bridge ideas between the paragraphs.

The Conclusion

The conclusion wraps up the ideas of your whole essay. You may summarize the points to refresh them for the reader. End the essay by leaving the reader with a general thought on the topic. Try to have a forceful ending to ease the reader out of the topic. Remember that flat endings leave flat impressions. Do not introduce new ideas in the conclusion; instead, use the conclusion to tie off the ideas in the essay and to leave an impression on the reader.

Key Terms Connected to Essays

introduction	body paragraph	supporting evidence
conclusion	topic sentence	thesis statement
coherence	unity	narrative
expository writing	persuasive	rhetorical mode
editing	revisions	draft
outline	brainstorm	transitions
peer editing	documentation	

HOW DO I GET STARTED?

One of the most difficult activities for all writers is getting started. Even the most experienced writers can have trouble putting the first words down on the page. You, too, may find this happening when you write. Use the tips from chapters 2 and 3 to help generate ideas: try free-writing for a few minutes. Try drawing. Try opening a new file on your computer and writing without stopping for five minutes, with a first sentence that begins like this: "I'm having trouble getting started today. . . ."

Consider the topic you have chosen. Usually you will be assigned a selection of topics to choose from. Select the one that interests you the most. Spend a few minutes thinking about the topic. Ask these questions:

1. What do I think I know about the topic?
2. What interests me about the topic?
3. What opinions do I have on the topic?
4. What experience have I had with the topic?
5. What do I need to know about the topic?
6. Should I do some research on the topic?

Exercise 1 *Free-Writing to Generate Ideas*

Use the ideas from chapter 2. Free-write for a few minutes on the topic of your choice. Use the above questions to guide you. Spend time thinking about your answers to these questions. Use brief notes. Work quickly so that you are moving along. Flow is important to the writing process. After you have spent some time making notes, try to write out a rough thesis statement. Be prepared to share your answers.

Writing the Thesis Statement

The thesis statement is important—it is the engine in the machine, so to speak. Expository writing—writing that explains or informs—will comprise most of your writing assignments, but there will be occasions when you will write argument pieces. Most of these assignments will be in essay form. Your instructor will want to see a powerful, driving thesis statement in the introductory paragraphs of these assignments.

Do not make your thesis statement take in too much—this will make it too broad. On the other hand, do not make your thesis statement a single detail—then it will be too narrow. Think about an effective thesis in this way: if someone handed me this sentence, would I be able to use it to start writing because I would know the direction to take?

Characteristics of a Good Thesis Statement

1. Reveals the issue or topic to be discussed
2. Reveals a clear point of view
3. Reveals a particular focus or position on the issue or topic to be discussed
4. Usually shows the direction of the discussion (rhetorical point of view—contrast, compare, define, classify, and so forth)

Exercise 2 Group Activity: Writing Thesis Statements

Form a group of three to five people. Write thesis statements together for each of the following topics. After you have finished, you will then exchange your set of thesis statements with another group. You will decide if the other group's thesis statements are effective. Be prepared to explain your answers.

1. Professional women's hockey
2. Buying shoes
3. Exploiting animals
4. Preparing a special meal for a festival
5. Buying school supplies
6. Volunteering your time
7. Fixing a plugged sink

Exercise 3 Deciding the Effectiveness of Thesis Statements

Work in pairs to decide if each sentence below would be an effective thesis statement in an essay. In the spaces provided, write "too broad," "too narrow," "too vague," or "effective." Also write a comment on how you think the writer would handle the topic based on the thesis statement. Be prepared to defend and share your answers.

1. Children can be taught to share.

____

____

2. Young marriages never work.

____

____

3. Some games are just plain dumb.

____

____

4. Fresh herbs can make a meal.

____

____

5. Caring for elders has changed over the past 50 years in Canada.

____

____

6. Dogs have personalities.

____

____

7. Watching television is a waste of time.

____

____

8. Good discussion includes analysis, listening, commitment, and humour.

____

____

9. Groceries are too expensive, and rents are too high in this city.

____

____

10. Keeping exotic pets is a crime.

____

____

Writing the Introductory Paragraph

Various ways of starting an introductory paragraph of an essay are given here. You may choose the one that seems to best serve your purposes or style. Do not try to use all of them because each is meant to do the same thing—kick-start the essay.

The introduction has three plain purposes: to get the reader interested in the topic; to provide some background information for the reader; to provide the thesis statement for the whole essay. The introduction should be at least five sentences long. If it is too short, it will not fulfill the three purposes. However, the introduction should not be lengthy, either, because you might disengage your reader. Since most academic writing you will do will be for courses, do not make your instructor or professor wade through a cluttered introduction.

Approaches to Getting the Reader Interested and Providing Background

1. ***Head-On***

   Use an approach that tackles the issue in a direct and somewhat startling way. For example, suppose that you were writing about AIDS. If you were going to use a head-on approach, your introductory paragraph might look like this:

   > AIDS—today the word makes people stop and listen. Only about a decade ago, AIDS was a small concern to a handful of people. Most Canadians thought little about the topic and never dreamed it would someday touch their lives. But AIDS is multiplying at a terrifying rate; as much as a 67 percent increase has been noted by the medical community in Canada during the past two years. AIDS could become a modern-day epidemic, and everyone should know about the risks, the effects, and the prevention.

   Notice the first statement: it gets your attention. The last statement of the introductory paragraph is the thesis.

2. ***Quotation***

   Your opening statement can be an effective quotation from a newspaper, a magazine, or a TV or radio program. Suppose that your essay was going to be about the high cost of living in 2008. Your introductory paragraph might look like this:

   > "Forty-three percent of Canadians are living below the poverty line. Many children are going to bed hungry and families are breaking up over money stress," claims Doreen Saunders, a member of the Canadian Coalition Against Poverty in a speech given to public educators on November 8, 2008, in Red Deer, Alberta. Further she says, "If someone with some power doesn't try to intervene in the process, our social services systems will become so inadequate that street families will become as common as those in Third World countries." Few Canadians would admit that Canada has a problem in this regard. However, the high cost of living in most Canadian cities is beginning to have devastating effects.

   The first statements are direct quotations: the person is an expert, and her comments come from experience and knowledge. The last statement is the thesis statement.

3. ***Personal Experience or Anecdote***

   Please note that the first-person point of view is usually not recommended unless you are writing for observation or description purposes in a social science class, or you are writing for a creative writing course. If the first-person point of view is acceptable in your course, you could begin your essay by relating something that happened to you that bears on the topic. It could have been a critical event in your life, or it could have been something that seemed hardly noticeable at the time. Read the example below:

> We were going to a family fun fair put on by a local community group, and I was feeling rather confused about taking my little boy and going with this new person in our lives. The place was very stuffy, crowded, and noisy, and my son was behaving like a brat because all of the excitement was overwhelming him. Just when I thought the whole idea and day had been a disaster, I noticed our new friend in a quiet corner of a stairwell with my son. He was talking to my little boy calmly and at the same time was doing up the little guy's shoelaces. It was at that moment that I realized I loved those two people deeply. The love for someone is not the glamorous, wildly romantic notions shown in movies or magazines; instead it is peaceful and made up of small, almost invisible things.

The personal anecdote sets the tone of the essay—it shows a tender, compassionate side of the topic. The last statement is the thesis statement.

4. ***Question***

   Sometimes beginning an essay with a question or a series of questions can startle a reader into reading further. Note that the writer answers the question in the introduction; otherwise, the question or questions become a cheap rhetorical trick. Look over the introduction below:

> How can anyone survive on just fruits, vegetables, and grains? Isn't a person going to end up being malnourished on such a diet? People can and do exist well on such diets, and vegetarianism is perhaps one of the most misunderstood styles of eating. Prejudices exist against vegetarianism in North America, yet it has proven to be a far more healthful diet than any other.

The questions are answered. The last statement is the thesis statement.

5. ***Engaging Fact or Statistic***

   You can begin with any interesting statistic or fact that relates to your topic. Be sure to cite your source (show where you got your information).

   Here are some examples:

> According to one parenting group, 70 percent of birth control methods do not work! (PHT, 2007).
>
> One out of three marriages ends in separation or divorce (StatsCan, 2003).
>
> According to Wilfred J. Mudpie, pigs make the best pets! (Pet Noodle, 2008).
>
> Eighty-three percent of accidents happen in the home (Canada Safety Council, 2008).
>
> According to a study completed by the University of Western Canada, men make up to one-third times more money than women for the same job (2008).

Start the essay with a shocking fact or statistic; then move the reader on to some background information. Place the thesis statement at the end of the introduction.

6. ***Definition***

You may open your essay with a definition that runs one or more sentences long. Your thesis statement would then capture the main ideas of your definition. Be careful when you open using a definition. You do not want to reveal everything you will be saying in your essay in the introduction. It can become boring for the reader. In other words, do not tell everything through your definition. Here is an example:

> Being a writer is seen by some as exciting and rewarding. Others say it really amounts to being a famous person, one who is always in the limelight. Some even say that it is being the popular wit who is invited to every party and is the "talk of the town." However, being a writer is for the most part not any of these things. Instead, being a writer is a lonely, heartbreaking profession full of doubts and shadows.

The first statements are different definitions or conceptions of being a writer. The thesis is the last statement and provides a contrasting definition.

You may also divide the topic into parts, and define each. Following is an example:

> Vancouver is an important port on the west coast of Canada. It is a prominent place of industry and trade. Vancouver is a city of parks and gardens. In the day, Vancouver is a metropolis busy with commerce and the comings and goings of people. At night, it transforms itself into a centre for fun, food, and entertainment. Vancouver is a city of many faces.

The thesis is the last statement.

You can see then that the introduction can be handled in various ways. Try using one of these openers, then fill in some background for your reader, and finally give the reader the thesis statement. A thesis statement may be placed anywhere in the introductory paragraph, but most instructors prefer to see the thesis statement at the end of the introductory paragraph.

After you have formed a good working thesis and have some idea of what you want to include in the body paragraphs, go ahead and write a first draft of your essay. The next section provides some information about writing the body of support in an essay.

Exercise 4 Writing Clear Introductions

Work in pairs. Write an introductory paragraph for three of the following topics. Use a different way of opening each introduction each time. Place your thesis statement at the end of the introduction. Be prepared to share your introductions.

1. Mountain climbing
2. Part-time work
3. Fitness

4. Bargains
5. Good books
6. Losing
7. Winning
8. Cell phones
9. Travel
10. Dieting

Writing The Body of the Essay

When you write essays, you try to inform, explain, or convince. First, you want to show the reader that you have thought ideas through and given consideration to your topic. Then you must provide appropriate and convincing examples or pieces of evidence that support the topic.

CHOOSE GOOD EVIDENCE

Choose good evidence by selecting powerful examples. Most instructors claim that students do not think of enough specific, effective examples or reasons for their major points. Therefore, think of at least two reasons why the point you are establishing could be true. Three reasons are even better. You must think of or find several real examples or illustrations or facts to support each point.

Find examples or quotations to add weight to your argument. Keep the point you are trying to establish separate from the proof. Do not mix them in the same sentence.

Example:

In *Breaking Smith's Quarter Horse* by Paul St. Pierre, Smith is a man who may be too independent for his own good. He goes off to rescue some cattle in bad weather without letting anyone know where he is going.

The point: Smith may be too independent for his own good.

First piece of evidence to support the point: He goes off to rescue some cattle in bad weather without letting anyone know where he is going.

Choose evidence that is the most convincing you can find or think of. A weak example does not convince anyone.

Be confident in your statements. Say things like, "Mr. B. was a selfish character in the story who caused the ruin of several important people in his life." You may use a quotation: "Mr. B. knew no one else by name, paid little attention to what others told him and considered his own career as the most significant in the firm." The first sentence sets out the point—the character was selfish. The second sentence provides proof that the first statement has merit.

Characteristics of the Body of Support

- Clearly laid out
- Points clearly established
- Points supported by strong examples, reasons, or facts—good evidence
- Convincing through its well thought-out organization
- Concise and specific examples

USE TRANSITIONS

Transitions are words that help bridge ideas. In the previous chapter on paragraphs, you saw lists of transitions that work for different purposes and in different rhetorical modes or patterns of organization.

Use transitions between major points. Use transitional sentences between body paragraphs. Transitions keep the flow in writing. They help the writing "stick together" logically; in others words, they help to provide coherence in your writing.

Writing the Conclusion

The last paragraph of your essay is called a concluding paragraph or a conclusion. Your concluding paragraph may provide three things for the reader:

1. In a longer essay or research paper, it should restate the thesis. Write the thesis again, but use different words.
2. It should highlight the main points of the essay. Look at each body paragraph and summarize each in a few words. In a short essay, summarizing main points may not be as important as in a long paper. Ask your instructor or professor about preferences.
3. The conclusion should leave the reader with a general thought on the topic. Instead of simply summing up your ideas and leaving the reader there, add a worldly thought on the topic. This general thought provides closure in the reader's mind.

Note, however, that the conclusion is not the place to introduce new ideas or points that you have not mentioned previously in the essay. Instead, the last paragraph is the closing stage of a presentation—a place where you tie off the ideas and then impress the reader. You want to leave the reader thinking about what you have said.

As you write, it is important to learn to read other writers' works as a writer would read. Begin to learn to examine much more than the content of writing. Begin to look for the style and the structure of what you read. Writers learn to write from reading other writers. You will, too.

HOW DO I WRITE THE FIRST DRAFT?

After you have developed your ideas and evidence and composed your thesis statement, develop a sketch outline. Fill in the topic sentences, major ideas, points, and evidence. Think about your opening sentence. Then begin to write your first draft. You may recall that chapter 3 provides lots of information about outlining. Review the chapter to refresh those ideas.

Allow yourself to compose. Write ideas as they occur to you and do not worry about correcting all the mistakes. Editing out errors is part of the polishing of the piece. It has no place at the beginning of the writing process.

As Henriette Anne Klauser suggests in *Writing on Both Sides of the Brain: Breakthrough Techniques in Writing*:

> When you edit and write at the same time, the result is often a disaster: a disaster for you as a writer and eventually for your reader. Purple patches come from the unrestricted pen. Go back and edit later. Later is when you invite the logical sequential strength side of you to come forward and apply all the techniques of good grammar and construction that have been drilled into you since the beginning of your school days.

HOW DO I CHECK MY WORK?

Many instructors use a technique called *peer editing* in their classes. **Peer editing** means another student from your class is going to read your paper and comment on it. You will do the same. Peer editing can be very useful, particularly if everyone is committed to the task, and the criteria for evaluation are clear. Criteria are often embedded in checklists.

Review the following three peer editing checklists. The first checklist helps you to focus on organization and evidence—the content—in essays. The second concentrates on grammar and mechanics features of the writing. The last checklist centres on writing style.

Peer Editing Sheet 1 *Organization and Evidence*

Writer's name: __________ Editor's name: __________ Date: __________

Read the piece of writing, paying attention to organizational structures and development features. You will read for grammar, usage, spelling, and punctuation errors using a different editing sheet. Check the appropriate spaces. Be prepared to provide reasons for your answers.

Introductory Paragraph:

Begins with an effective "grabber"	yes _____	no _____
Provides one to two background sentences	yes _____	no _____
Thesis statement: end of introduction	yes _____	no _____
Thesis statement: clear, directing	yes _____	no _____

Rhetorical mode of the thesis statement: __________

Body Paragraph 1:

Begins with a clear topic sentence	yes _____	no _____
Provides three main points	yes _____	no _____
Provides specific support for points	yes _____	no _____
Provides transitional sentence to next paragraph	yes _____	no _____

Body Paragraph 2:

Begins with a clear topic sentence	yes _____	no _____
Provides three main points	yes _____	no _____
Provides specific support for points	yes _____	no _____
Provides transitional sentence to next paragraph	yes _____	no _____

Body Paragraph 3 (4, 5+):

Begins with a clear topic sentence	yes _____	no _____
Provides three main points	yes _____	no _____
Provides specific support for points	yes _____	no _____
Provides transitional sentence to next paragraph	yes _____	no _____

Concluding Paragraph:

Restates the thesis	yes _____	no _____
Sums up main ideas	yes _____	no _____
Last sentence effectively wraps up discussion	yes _____	no _____

Comments: (Name one thing you liked and one thing you didn't like about the piece.)

____

____

____

Peer Editing Sheet 2 *Grammar, Mechanics, and Spelling*

Writer's name: __________ Editor's name: __________ Date: ________

Read the piece of writing, paying attention to grammar, spelling, usage, and punctuation. Check the appropriate spaces.

Types of errors: A problem?

Grammar:

Subject–verb agreement errors	yes _____	no _____
Misplaced or dangling modifiers	yes _____	no _____
Comma splices	yes _____	no _____
Fragments	yes _____	no _____
Run-on sentences	yes _____	no _____
Punctuation:		
Comma use	yes _____	no _____
Semicolon use	yes _____	no _____
Colon use	yes _____	no _____
Apostrophe use	yes _____	no _____
Other Features:		
Point of view shifts	yes _____	no _____
Pronoun agreement errors	yes _____	no _____
Sentence logic problems	yes _____	no _____
Verb tense shift errors	yes _____	no _____
Spelling Problems:	yes _____	no _____

Comments: (Name one thing you liked and one thing you disliked about the editing of this paper.)

____

____

____

____

____

Peer Editing Sheet 3 *Reviewing Writer's Style*

Writer's name: ________________ Editor's name: ________________ Date: __________

Read the piece of writing with the intent of looking at the writer's style: how the writer says something. Check the appropriate spaces.

Style Feature	**Effective?**	
Sentences:		
Sentence variety (different patterns)	yes _____	no _____
Variety in sentence length	yes _____	no _____
Words:		
Appropriate selection	yes _____	no _____
Good use of adverbs	yes _____	no _____
Concise words chosen	yes _____	no _____
Effective diction	yes _____	no _____
Punctuation:		
Interesting variety	yes _____	no _____
Effective	yes _____	no _____
Tone:		
Writer's tone is appropriate	yes _____	no _____
Audience:		
The intended audience seems clear	yes _____	no _____
Tone and audience seem to fit together	yes _____	no _____

Comments: (Name one thing you liked about this writer's style. Name one thing you did not like. Add a recommendation to help the writer improve his or her style.)

____

____

____

____

____

____

REVIEW TEST

Try the following review test. It will help you assess what you have learned from the chapter. Be prepared to share your responses with others in the class.

1. What are the parts of an essay?
2. What is the most important part of the essay? Why do you think so?
3. Write a clear thesis statement for the following topic: camping as recreation.
4. What should an introduction contain?
5. Where should you place the thesis statement in the introductory paragraph?
6. How can peer editing help you?
7. Name five purposes for writing essays.

Assignment

In-class writing: Write a short essay (500 words) on one of three topics the instructor provides. You will have one hour to write. Use five minutes to generate ideas. Use five minutes to make a sketch outline. Write for 35 minutes. Leave 15 minutes for editing. Double-space your work.

Bonus Exercise *Avoiding Sexist Language*

Sexism in language use has to do with favouring one gender's point of view over another. If one point of view is the only one presented, then readers and writers may think that it represents all points of view. Use the third person, plural point of view to eliminate sexism. The internet provides some interesting information about sexism in language. Visit sites connected to college and university libraries and writing centres for quality information and examples. Check your answers with the Answer Key.

Rewrite each sentence, eliminating sexism:

1. Every man wants the freedom to find happiness for himself.
2. Most of the time, corporations try to find the best man for the job.
3. Everyone decided to vote with his own conscience.
4. Everybody should do what she can to help.
5. The reporters were trying to find out who was responsible and if he was available for comment.

READING

The following reading comes from an academic journal. The writer argues for the teaching of the "formula essay" or five-paragraph essay. Read the article carefully; then answer the questions that follow it.

In Defense of the Formula Essay

by Jan Charles Haluska

Jan Charles Haluska has been professor of English at Southern Adventist University, Collegedale, Tennessee since 1982, teaching literature and writing courses. He has also taught courses in aviation.

My advisor looked at me, perplexed. "Hasn't anybody ever taught you to write an essay?" he asked. It was 1970, and we were considering my bungled attempt to answer a final exam question for another teacher's literature class. Unfortunately the course had been a test of my ability to succeed as an English major, a plan my advisor himself had recommended based on my high grade in his "Advanced College Writing" a few months before. It seemed wise not to bring up that particular irony, though, in light of his question.

"No sir," I answered, studying my shoes.

What followed next was a revelation in two ways. He went to the board and sketched a frontal view of the Parthenon. "The roof is the thesis—what you are trying to prove," he said. "The columns are paragraphs giving explanation and evidence for your idea, and the floor is the conclusion that reaffirms the thesis." Thus in a brief diagram he outlined what is commonly known as the "five-paragraph essay."

As if a flashbulb had gone off, the concept was instantly, joyfully, obvious. So *that* was how you did it! Make your claim, support it in steps with evidence, and declare victory. The structure was as straight-forwardly effective as a left jab and right cross. I'd been writing essays that tried to get by on creative razzle-dazzle rather than rhetorical power. Why had none of my former English teachers ever shown me that simple drawing, or the fundamental rhetorical pattern it represented? For that matter, why hadn't *he* shown me before?

One clue was his discomfort in making that sketch. He really didn't want to do it. In grabbing the chalk he had paused, saying, "Now, I hope you don't get the wrong idea, because this is pretty mechanical, but. . . ." Incredibly, that fine man actually felt guilty for explaining such a simple, lucid pattern for essay writing.

After 35 years of using that diagram with secondary and college students, I still have no satisfactory answer as to why it inspires such fear and loathing. Of course I've heard the counter-arguments plenty of times.

"It's artificial."

"It stifles creativity."

"It suppresses individual expression."

"It produces lifeless writing."

"It discourages thinking."

Those kinds of accusations and more appeared in the most influential writing theory book of the 1970s: *Uptaught,* by Ken MacRorie.[1] A single word from that book—"Engfish"—caught on among English teachers. MacRorie used it to denote phony prose from students forced to write mechanically instead of self-expressively. In the flowering Age of Aquarius, the word seemed to encapsulate everything that was wrong with writing instruction, not to mention traditional education generally, and one heard it incessantly during presentations at the NCTE, MLA, and CCC conferences of the period. No wonder my well-meaning advisor was so reluctant to recommend a stylized, formal approach to writing essays.

A quick survey of books outlining the history of writing in American schools turns up an equal unwillingness to address the subject. For instance, Arthur N. Applebee's *Tradition and Reform in the Teaching of English: A History* (1942); James A. Berlin's *Rhetoric and Reality: Writing Instruction in American Colleges, 1911–1985* (1987); James J. Murphy's *A Short History of Writing Instruction from Ancient Greece to Twentieth Century America* (1990); and editor Maureen Daly Goggin's *Inventing a Discipline: Rhetoric Scholarship in Honor of Richard E. Young* (2000) all exclude any mention whatsoever of the five-paragraph essay. This is all the more astounding since a Google search lists the expression four-and-a-half million times online. The majority of hits seem to be from teachers' essay instructions for their classes. Next most common are in bloggers' debates. The majority of those seem to favor the formalized essay pattern, though plenty of people dismiss it with contempt. But since the technique is a major feature of writing instruction in America, why do so many historians ignore it? I have no answer.

To their credit, a couple of critics since MacRorie actually have been willing to enter the debate. For instance, Bruce Pirie offers a succinct criticism as follows: "What does a five-paragraph essay teach about writing? It teaches that there are rules, and that those rules take the shape of a preordained form, like a cookie-cutter, into which we can pour ideas and expect them to come out well shaped."[2] The mixed metaphor aside, one can understand his position, especially when he discredits such essays as being akin to training wheels on bicycles and paint-by-the-numbers kits.

A couple of other analogies make better sense, though. Consider the minivan, a good choice for a person who can afford only a single vehicle for both business and home. No, it cannot haul flea-market treasures as ruggedly as a pickup truck or look as nice as a convertible on a date, but it is useful in those roles all the same. The right "one-model" approach to school essays can be equally useful if followed with some common-sense flexibility.

Or take the analogy of aviation training. Because student pilots have a hard time learning to land, flight instructors teach a formalized system for doing it. The new flier learns to follow a standard rectangular pattern featuring a series of events—power reduction, lap extension, precise decreases in airspeed, and so on. Because weather and traffic conditions make every landing different, that pattern can be adjusted here and there each time, lengthening this, shortening that, doing this action earlier or later, etc.

But what if flight instructors taught landings as many English teachers present essay assignments? Student pilots would have to improvise each approach with no customary structure whatever. The sure result would be clumps of crushed aluminum dotting the neighborhood of every airport in the country.

Actually, "cookie-cutter" designs are indispensable to many practical activities, including the very realistic task of persuasion. For over two thousand years people patterned their speaking and writing techniques better to influence hearers or readers through language. For example, in *The Rhetoric* Aristotle acts like a good flight instructor, walking us through the steps of a model argument one might expect to deliver before a court or legislative assembly.

Romans like Cicero and Quintilian crafted their own work with the same purpose of preparing people for persuasive skill in political, legal, religious, and philosophical arenas. The idea of rhetorical structure as an aid in convincing others—and its corollary that writing must take a position convincingly for a reader/audience—went unchallenged for centuries.

Then in the late 1500s, Michel de Montaigne changed everything with so-called "personal" essays that simply exposed his subjective outlook rather than trying to apply rigorous, inductive logic to the external world of facts. He himself coined the term "essay" from the French word for "attempt," and used the form to show his personal reactions to various aspects of life. Pixie sums this up very accurately with the words of Peter Womack: it was "the cultivated response of a man of taste."[3]

Less often noticed is how Montaigne's innovation was prompted by the fear that he knew too little for authorship. "And then," he wrote, "finding myself entirely unprovided and empty of other material, I proposed myself to myself for argument and subject."[4] In other words, this approach was a way to accommodate his own ignorance and still write. For the first time, then, an essayist's inner feelings were presented as stand-alone subject matter, whether or not they related to objective truth in any provable way. Of course Montaigne used historical references and personal anecdotes, but he was interested more in sharing perceptions on this or that topic than in presenting formally organized factual persuasion. That turned the emphasis to *subjective* reality, the world of a person's interior musings. Since it was subjective, it could be free-form, like a rambling stroll through the countryside. To some, such writing seems like a preference for raw dough instead of freshly baked cookies; we may remember Samuel Johnson's famous dictionary definition of an essay as "a loose sally of the mind, an irregular piece."

Nevertheless, Montaigne's sweetly informal style was instantly popular. James Shapiro even suggests that his style influenced Shakespeare's writing of the soliloquy from *Hamlet*.[5] I find the connection telling, especially since the prince's famously quotable reflection gets him no closer to the decision he wants to make.[6]

Certainly Montaigne's approach has had enthusiastic imitators ever since. Students are particularly thrilled to have their informal essays published, if only in school literary booklets. Until that day with my advisor, I hadn't found one English teacher who wanted anything different from me.

But Montaigne-esque essays do present a grading problem. How does a teacher assign anything less than an A to an honest account of a student's thought process, however disjointed it might be on paper? If that's how the student's imagination has worked, anything else would be an inaccurate report of the experience. Thus a teacher in that situation tends to fall back on fairly narrow grading criteria, evaluating grammar and creative wording while largely ignoring the question of substance apart from emotional appeal.

If the student has shared his/her love for pickles, the teacher can only suggest more supposedly winsome language. Thus one might find notes like this on the margin: "Instead of saying 'I like biting into one,' Tommy, you need to be more creative. Write something like 'As I nip off a pungent piece, the sharp juice wakes up my tongue,' so the reader can get a feeling of the experience." No wonder many students get the idea that good writing simply involves loading a text with the subjective appeal of adjectives, adverbs, and metaphors.

By contrast, if the assignment is inductive persuasion, then the grade rests on objectivity, that is, the paper's effectiveness in clarifying and supporting a point of view whether the teacher actually empathizes with the student's opinion or not.

Perhaps that is why the formal school essay became so popular in the first place. Jeanne Donovan Sanborn traces its first appearance to a 1909 writing textbook, *Composition: Oral and Written* by Charles Sears Baldwin.[7] Sanborn quotes Baldwin's definition of an essay as "an exposition by paragraphs of a single controlling idea."[8] Whether or not a teacher agrees with an essay's point of view, Baldwin's definition opens the way for a very objective evaluation of the student's success in arguing for it.

Baldwin's own model for powerful writing was the celebrated Thomas Babington Macaulay, one among several notables who wrote so effectively for the *Edinburgh Review* in the early 1800s. Sanborn quotes Baldwin as praising Macaulay for trying "to carry a reader through a definite course of thought to a definite conclusion," and referring to others whose essays followed an "orderly, logical, definite development by paragraphs."[9] We may note in passing that Baldwin does not say "by *five* paragraphs."

More to the point, Baldwin's little definition hints at a formal essay's usefulness in helping our students to attain their full educational potential. As a student myself, I had long recognized that something was missing from the essay assignments I had been given. Like Montaigne, I knew too little for authorship, and so what I really needed was for a teacher to say, "Well, go out and learn enough about something to have a worthwhile opinion concerning it, and then write a firmly grounded account of why that opinion is valid." That kind of obligation is a win-win for teacher and student. It spurs the desired process of self-education while allowing the teacher to judge the essay as an intelligently supported opinion on the subject. Moreover it frees teachers from having to assign fair grades to mere collections of facts strung together, or worse, wandering accounts of the writers' perplexities better left to student journals.

Without that kind of enabling challenge, as a student I had to rely on creative pizzazz rather than substance in my essay tests or term papers. I wrote chronicles that tried to wander endearingly among the required facts and quotes. When the assigned number of words had been reached, I would try to sum up the whole mess with a conclusion sounding noble or wise enough to get by. This would only work decently with teachers whose thinking was not terribly rigorous, but what other way was possible?

Actually there was one rare, lucky moment in which the narrative technique won for me: a paleontology term paper about the stratification of fossils. In that essay I combined scientific tidbits with my own recent mule-back ride to the bottom of the Grand Canyon, producing a kind of travelogue noting fossil changes offhand as we descended through the dust and heat. Short on scientific content but full of folksy anecdotes from the trail, the paper won giddy praise from the professor. Maybe the poor man was tired of reading compilations of random facts about trilobites anyway. But ordinary term papers and test-essays went badly until the day my advisor drew that Greek temple.

He was certainly wise to avoid calling it a "five-paragraph essay," thus saving me from fixating on too rigid a structure. After all, what is the sense of insisting on exactly three interior paragraphs? Why couldn't a student's opinion rest solidly on two points? Or twenty?

This is why we must help our students avoid the *Cliffs Notes* kind of reductionism shown in the following formula:

Introduction, which ends with your thesis statement
Topic A that supports your thesis
Topic B that supports your thesis
Topic C that supports your thesis
A re-cap of your thesis statement, which leads off the Conclusion paragraph[10]

The idea is not to wind up with a set number of "topics." Rather we want the student to practice genuine thinking, beginning with an inductive process of gathering and weighing facts that build into a solid opinion, and then organizing a presentation of that case for a neutral audience. For instance, what if the facts fall into a pair of incompatible piles? Here is where some critics find a basic weakness in formula essays. "The 'authoritative voice' requires a pretense of uniformity," says Pirie, "a pretense that conceals productive stress and honest ambivalance."[11] Actually, a little flexibility of form can remove that problem without much trouble.

We can just ask the student to decide which pile of evidence seems bigger, and to adjust his or her essay structure to accommodate it in four steps as follows:

1. Introductory paragraph/thesis statement leaning toward idea #2.
2. Early interior paragraph(s) "Admittedly, idea #1 is attractive."
3. Later interior paragraph(s) "Idea #2 is a slightly better choice, though."
4. Concluding paragraph which either restates the thesis that the second idea is more desirable, or perhaps suggests how to accommodate both somewhat.

Notice that this follows the standard "yes, but" pattern known to every skilled lawyer and salesperson. More importantly, these steps could represent ten paragraphs or more, as appropriate.

Thus the flexibility of an intelligently formulaic essay can accommodate virtually every persuasive need, and I submit that this kind of exercise produces more actual practice in thinking than all the ambivalent rambling in the world. After all, it would not be surprising if a student started out his first draft with one choice for the better option, only to find through research that the demands of proving his/her claim with evidence led to a tilt in the opposite direction. What better way is there for the student to develop mental muscle?

So, yes, this formulaic style of essay needs a name free of numbers. One teacher online terms it a "keyhole essay." I have generally referred to it as a "Baconian essay," since it somewhat resembles the writing of Sir Frances Bacon in its controlling thesis and prediction of points, and its reliance on the persuasiveness of induction. When I'm in a playfully bombastic mood in front of students, it becomes "The Haluska System." Perhaps the best title is simply "the formal essay." In any case, just getting away from dogmatic numbering is the important consideration. That alone should destroy fully half the objections of its critics.

Whatever we call it, I have seen abundant evidence of its value in helping college students win high grades in writing assignments across the curriculum, even from teachers who specify narrative essays in their instructions. One such non-English colleague distributes a sample story-essay for the term paper required in his course. My students who take his class come to me in a panic: "You haven't taught us this kind of writing!"

"If you have the courage to stick to the formula," I tell them, "you'll do better than most others in the class who try to follow his suggestion." It works. Semester after semester their term papers get high grades from him. He may not really know what he's looking for, but he obviously senses the superiority of rigorously persuasive writing when he sees it. Most teachers across the curriculum here seem to have a similar reaction, reporting that my students, along with those from other freshman writing teachers who emphasize formulaic essays, do superior writing in their classes. Like a good minivan, the formal model does a lot of jobs pretty well, with enough flexibility to accommodate reading reactions, term papers, doctoral dissertations, letters home pleading for money, and so forth. It carries another hidden benefit, too. Although the personal essay favors our most artistic students who can charm their teachers with creative metaphors and clever phrasing, it is murder for others. One of the nicest moments in each semester comes when I tell the new class of college freshmen, "You don't need to be creative to get a high grade in this course. If you are, that's good, but if not, you can still get an A." The relief on many faces is telling.

Best of all, students freed from the requirement to invent a new, creative pattern with every essay can concentrate on learning the real fundamentals of good persuasion, principles they can apply to any kind of writing they need for the rest of their lives, formula-controlled or not. By keeping the model simple, we can focus on teaching the basic principles of rhetoric, the actual qualities that make for good essays of all shapes and sizes. Unity, development, and coherence head the list. Let's look at those in some detail.

UNITY

Every essay needs a thesis, an *opinion* clarified in the thesis statement, and every part of each paragraph should validate that opinion in turn. Sometimes, of course, a paragraph does this by admitting exceptions to that opinion or answering the objection directly.

Help me test the value of requiring an opinion. Imagine that you have assigned students to write a short report on one journal article in your field from a list you have provided. Which essay(s) would you respect more, judging by the thesis statements below?

A. The article talks about __________ and __________.

B. This is an excellent article because of how clearly it explains __________ and __________.

C. This article seems pretty uneven; although the author explains ______ well enough, his main points, __________ and __________, are presented in such a confusing way that I could hardly keep track of them.

If you chose either B or C, we agree. In both cases, the student has read the article with enough mental vigor to have formed an intelligent opinion about it. If that student gives specific details demonstrating each claim about the article, you will probably grade him or her pretty respectably whether you share that opinion or not. Conversely, you are likely to regard a simple list of topics in the article as feeble writing on the student's part. After all, educated people have well-supported opinions about things within their scope of learning.

The essay will be unified if every part of it stays on the subject stated in the thesis. Interesting side trips are possible, especially in longer papers, but the writer must stick to the main job or, like Hamlet, "lose the name of action." If that main job is validating a thesis, keeping the essay unified is a much simpler task, especially with a formula to lean on.

DEVELOPMENT

Formal analytical structure makes it more natural for every point to be supported by clear explanation and firm evidence. Attempts at persuasion most often degenerate into a series of passionate assertions without solid evidence for the writer's belief. Nor can that evidence consist of generalities or made-up events. Actual evidence is essential to persuasion, and consists of specific, real-world experience or the testimony of experts, just as in a court of law.

Thus each point in the essay should include standard elements: topic sentence, explanation, evidence—TEE. In a small essay, these elements will appear in one paragraph, but larger pieces can use several paragraphs for each point, perhaps intermingling explanation and evidence for maximum impact. But always, always, the claims must be grounded in real evidence, beginning with students' own experience. As students mature in their writing, we can easily lead them to other forms of evidence which are gathered, not from their memories, but from books, magazines, or the Internet, for example. The requirement that our students back up their assertions with anecdotal confirmation at first, and in later papers with other kinds of evidence, teaches a crucial lesson that many of today's college graduates still do not understand the need for evidence. Odds are that throughout their careers they will lose to their competitors who do.

There remains the objection that formula essays produce wooden, mechanical writing—so-called "Engfish." But, if we invite students to write about things that excite them, their interest will produce livelier prose. I encourage my students to concentrate on things they love or hate, and to continue the practice right through college so far as possible in planning papers for other classes.

The formula's emphasis on evidence offers one more benefit as well. All too often the research paper is taught after a series of Montaigne-like informal essay assignments, leading students to wonder what good the "research" is supposed to do. Without having learned the need for thesis-supporting evidence from the beginning, such students tend to regard a research paper as a mere exercise in learning the picky details of documentation for no particular purpose. What an insulting position to be in!

"But this kind of development has no application in the real world outside academia," say objectors. That is far from true. Consider a book that spent decades as a nonfiction best-seller: Dale Carnegie's *How to Win Friends and Influence People.* Yes, the subject matter helped, but so did the easy-to-read persuasiveness of Carnegie's stylized structure. Each chapter begins with a thesis statement about some beneficial action, explains it briefly, then presents a wealth of anecdotal evidence from various people's experiences demonstrating the validity of that chapter's thesis statement. It's the perfect TEE pattern, repeated over and over in chapter-length chunks. Mr. Baldwin would have approved. Some might claim that such a reiterated blueprint makes boring reading, but Carnegie's book is remarkably compelling. Nobody minds a recurring pattern of really interesting development, especially through anecdotes.

COHERENCE

Students are often shocked at the requirement to present their points in some kind of sensible order. When asked why a certain paragraph needs to come just at that place in their paper, some reply, "Because that's how the idea occurred to me." Although that is a good answer in a Montaigne-style essay, where the emphasis is on the writer's meandering thought-processes, it makes no sense for persuasive rhetoric. After all, the best sequence of points for explaining something convincingly is rarely the order in which the thoughts originally occurred to the writer. Formal structure lends itself to the intelligent order of presentation, with transitions that indicate for the reader why the next thing comes next.

Thus the successful analytical writer will lead his or her reader efficiently, step-by-logical-step, to agreement. The easiest order is very formulaic: it is the order of emphasis. For instance, the first point might show a good reason or piece of evidence, the next a stronger one, and so on until the final point covers the best reason. This so-called "emphatic order" comes naturally to both writer and reader if the aim is persuasion. "Cause/effect" is another good pattern, while chronological order, the sequence of the writer's experience, is generally very weak. True, everybody's model narrative essay, George Orwell's "Shooting an Elephant," is a masterpiece, but few students will succeed with a narrative about, say, the economic causes of the War of 1812. Much more impressive would be an essay presenting evidence and explanation of those causes in order of importance.

GRADING

Objective questions such as "What is the writer's thesis and how well does the essay keep track of it?" or "Does the writer provide convincing explanation and evidence for each supporting point?" put evaluation on a firm footing. Those three great virtues of any persuasive essay along with two others—clear, succinct wording and good grammar—suggest a total of five grading criteria. Ten points for each area of concern add up to a 50-point assignment. One's scoring can be much more analytical, and thus fairer, with a formally framed essay.

THE WRITING PROCESS

One great advance during the time I've been teaching has been the emphasis on finding an efficient system for writing. We now help students recognize that one-draft-and-turn-it-in essays are generally not a good idea. Still, here again there is a divide between informal and formal essay assignments. Informal essay writers often start with a "discovery draft" that wanders aimlessly through a writer's thoughts. Once completed, that draft is to be "polished" until it becomes an engaging composition. In practice that technique is awkward and unnecessarily time-consuming. It is much better to get organized before writing the first draft.

The most efficient process involves four distinct steps: thinking, planning, writing, and revising. Like a golf swing, that stylized sequence keeps its character while adapting to various situations. Normally a student should take several *days* on a paper, going from decisions about subject matter (loves or hates), a reader (someone who really needs or wants to know about this subject), a thesis, an ordered outline of steps and evidence to back the thesis, a first draft, and then revisions of that draft until the essay reaches its final form. A teacher can monitor each stage, making suggestions about objective effectiveness.

This coupling of an efficient writing process with a standard essay format allows a writer to produce effective persuasion for a number of uses beyond the classroom, whether to ask the boss for a raise, to present a proposal to the city council, or to win any other battles in the real world. The combination can work very rapidly, too. Recently I received this letter from a former student. He had not been at the top of the class during that semester, yet he had become familiar enough with the standard essay pattern and writing process to make them work for him at a moment's notice. Here is the letter:

> This semester I applied for a nursing scholarship that required a 500-word essay on "What I Can Contribute to Nursing." The awards would range from $250 to $1,000 depending on the quality of the paper. I found out about the scholarship the day it was due, and only had about 30 minutes to write. But I sat down at the computer and said a prayer. Then the idea came: why not try the Haluska method? So I picked an answer based on experiences I'd had, listed the stories in order of importance, and began to write TEE paragraphs around them under a brief introduction/thesis paragraph. I finished the whole paper in about fifteen minutes, proofread quickly, printed it out, and turned it in. The next week they told us the results: mine was the only entry out of twenty-three to receive the $1,000, and the paper had taken just fifteen minutes to write. The Haluska system had worked for me!

No, that student did not get a story published in a literary booklet or teen magazine. But learning how to write a formal essay had given him something much better: a powerful and efficient ally in the battles of life.

We may call it an "analytically persuasive essay," "formal essay," "inductive essay," "keyhole essay," "Baconian essay," or the shamelessly self-promoting "[insert your name here] system." As long as we stand unapologetically for a general formula that produces clear, objective writing from our students, we will do them a great service.

Notes

1. Ken MacRorie, *Uptaught* (Portsmouth, NH: Heinemann, 1970).
2. Bruce Pirie, *Reshaping High School English* (Urbana, IL: National Council of Teachers of English, 1997), 76.
3. Ibid., 75.
4. Michel de Montaigne, *Essays*, tr. John M. Cohen (New York: Penguin, 1993), 113.
5. James Shapiro, *A Year in the Life of William Shakespeare: 1599* (New York: HarperCollins, 2005), 292–99.
6. William Shakespeare, *Hamlet*, III, i.
7. Ibid., 126.
8. Ibid., 125.
9. Jeanne Donovan Sanborn, "The Essay Dies in the Academy" in *Pedagogy in the Age of Politics: Writing and Reading (in) the Academy*, ed. Patricia A. Sullivan and Donna J. Qualley (Urbana, IL: NCTE, 1994), 124–25.
10. http://www.cliffsnotes.com/WileyCDA/Section/id-131126.html.
11. Pirie, 90.

Source: Jan Charles Haluska, "In Defense of the Formula Essay," Academic Questions, *Vol. 20: 1, January 2007, pp. 46–55. With kind permission from Springer Science and Business Media.*

Comprehension Questions

1. What is the opposition to the five-paragraph essay?
2. What does the underlined word *lucid* in paragraph 5 mean?
3. What does the writer mean in paragraph 12 when he says "in the flowering Age of Aquarius"?
4. To whom is Haluska speaking, and why do you think he wrote this article?
5. What are the analogies Haluska makes, and in your opinion, do they work? Why or why not?
6. What contrast does Haluska provide for models of essay writing and writing instruction?
7. What does Haluska mean by unity, development, and cohesion?

Critical Comprehension

1. What view of creativity is presented in the article?
2. Can the most important features of Haluska's defence be related to everyday activities? How?

Assignment

Write a 500-word, five-paragraph essay about the importance of five-paragraph essay writing, using Haluska's ideas as your source.

CHECKOUT

Here are some of the ideas you will take away with you after you have completed the chapter:

1. The writing preferences of individual instructors may vary.
2. Conventionally, an academic essay has three parts.
3. A thesis statement is a sentence that states the main idea of an essay.
4. Most student writing assignments require expository writing.
5. Peer editing checklists can improve your editing and writing skills.
6. Being organized and clear are part of good communication.
7. Clear, effective communication is a key "soft skill" most employers are looking for in their employees.

Mastering the concepts in this chapter will also help you develop and apply the following employability skills highlighted by the Conference Board of Canada in *Employability Skills 2000+*:

Communicate:

- share information using a range of information and communications technologies (e.g., voice, e-mail, computers)
- use relevant scientific, technological and mathematical knowledge and skills to explain or clarify ideas

Manage Information:

- locate, gather and organize information using appropriate technology and information systems

Source: Adapted from *Employability Skills 2000+* Brochure E/F (Ottawa: The Conference Board of Canada, 2000).

chapter 6

Critical Skills: Summarizing and Paraphrasing

Chapter Objectives

After completing this chapter you will be able to

1. recognize and understand what a summary is;
2. identify summary purposes;
3. write a paragraph summary;
4. determine what plagiarism is.

INTRODUCTION

The completion of your assignments in post-secondary education will be shaped by the reading, interpretation, and discussion you do based on the work of thinkers in your field. Most courses will require you to do research for your academic papers. You can involve original material in your papers in one of three ways: you can directly quote the material (direct quotation); you can paraphrase the material (indirect quotation); or you can summarize the central ideas of the material (indirect quotation). In all three instances, you must name the author of the ideas (cite your sources). This chapter will introduce you to some of the ideas and techniques of summarizing and paraphrasing.

DEVELOPING CRITICAL READING SKILLS

As you recall, to read critically means to be involved actively with what you read. As a reader, you are thinking about not only what a writer says but also how a writer says it. As a critical reader, you think beyond the facts by trying to interpret them.

In several sections of *Spotlight on Critical Skills in Essay Writing*, Second Edition, you will find discussion and practice related to critical reading. Chapter 10: Critical Skills: Argumentation and Chapter 11: Structuring Argument provide more information and opportunity to practise the elements of critical reading and thinking.

Goals of Critical Reading

As a critical reader, you want to engage in a lively way with what you read. Following are some of the main goals of critical reading. You may have others you wish to add to the list; however, the six given below will act as strong guidelines and will help you to develop your criticality as a reader.

1. Thinking actively about what you are reading
2. Reflecting on what you are reading
3. Recognizing the elements of the writer's argument
4. Making judgments about the writer's argument
5. Evaluating the strengths and weaknesses of the writer's argument or ideas
6. Detecting the writer's bias

Active vs. Passive Reading

Active reading means you are engaged and interested in the text you are reading; **passive reading** means you are simply going through the mechanical aspects of reading—moving your eyes across lines of text and turning pages. To read actively is important because sometimes you can fool yourself into thinking you comprehend something you are reading when you actually do not. Active reading takes practice.

Tips

- Read with a pencil. Take notes, make notations in the margins, draw diagrams, make single- or two-sentence summaries, write key phrases or terms in the margins.
- Highlight cautiously. Sometimes over-highlighting ends up being the colouring of pages rather than the reading of them. If you do like to highlight, restrict how much you highlight on a page. For example, decide to highlight only the important features of the writer's argument or thesis, not examples, data, or other facts. After you have completed the highlighting of a page, look away and write a summary of a few sentences.
- As you read, write questions in the margins or in your notebook.
- Pay attention to how ideas are organized in the text. Does the writer compare or contrast? Does the writer discuss the most important ideas first or last? Does the writer provide clear proof as support for his claims?
- Pay attention to the writer's style. What is the writer's tone? What is the writer's diction like? To whom is the writer speaking, do you think?

Strategies for Critical Reading

Following you will find some strategies to use and practise in your academic reading.

Tips

1. Read the material more than once. The first time you read something, you may be simply getting the gist of the material (gaining a general understanding), but each time you read the same material, you will

have a different purpose for doing so. Do not expect to pick up everything you will need from a single reading; that is somewhat like thinking you can pack everything you will ever need into a single suitcase. Different trips require different things, and similarly, reading for a variety of purposes requires diverse tactics.

2. Diagram or outline the writer's argument, particularly if the writing is difficult or dense with detail and explanation.
3. Use active questioning. Think of several questions about the text prior to reading it. As you read, use these questions to focus your attention. Some examples of questions you can use might centre on the writer's evidence, the kinds of reasoning the writer uses, or the writer's ideas compared to another's.
4. Evaluate as you read. In your second or third reading, analyze and evaluate the writer's ideas. You might consider the strengths and weaknesses of a writer's arguments, for example, or you might concentrate on the conclusions the writer draws. Your evaluation will depend on your purpose in reading, too.

LEARNING TO SUMMARIZE AND PARAPHRASE

According to experts like Dr. Mike Rose, a celebrated professor at the UCLA Graduate School of Education & Information Studies, one of the most needed skills you will require as a student at college or university is the capability to summarize and to paraphrase accurately. Despite the fact that your reading workload will be substantial, you must still have a working understanding of the material in order to complete your projects and various assignments.

To **summarize** means to sum up the central ideas in a concise way. Summaries are useful for a number of reasons. First, they enable you to determine whether you have a general understanding of something. You do not need to have detailed knowledge about everything you read. At times, your instructors will want you to have a general grasp of a theory, a textbook chapter, or a journal article. Understanding and remembering the smallest details will not be very important. For example, if you were studying educational philosophy at a first-year level, you would be expected to be acquainted with the theories of John Dewey or Paulo Freire, but you would not be expected to be aware of every detail of their thinking.

Paraphrasing, like summarizing, is putting something you have read or heard into your own words; however, when you paraphrase, you wish to stay as close as possible to the source's meaning. In other words, a paraphrase captures the essential meaning of something while a summary encapsulates the central idea or ideas. Paraphrases are longer than summaries. Both paraphrases and summaries should balance the ideas as they are represented in the original. In summarizing or paraphrasing, you should strive to represent all ideas fairly.

Therefore, many of your academic tasks will rely on being able to distinguish significant ideas or main ideas from less important, minor, or supporting details.

main ideas	**most important**
↓	↓
minor details	less important
↓	↓
sub-details	of least importance

Characteristics of Summaries and Paraphrases

Summaries

- sum up the central idea(s)
- brief (about 20 percent of original)
- given in your own words

Paraphrases

- sum up the meaning of a source
- longer (often roughly the same length as the source)
- given in your own words

Examples:

The Original

Pictures can help us organize our ideas, and a picture of a writer can help us organize our ideas about the writer. The tight-drawn line of T.S. Eliot's mouth, the broad bare chest of Ernest Hemingway, the Druid-in-tweeds look of Robertson Davies—all these are with you in your imagination as you read. Is this a face we can take into our reading of Shakespeare? In particular, how does it relate to what we know of the man and his work in 1603? I stress 1603 because while the Droeshout portrait in the Folio is Shakespeare in black and white, dead and collected, setting his stamp on a posthumous anthology of his work, the Sanders portrait is Shakespeare alive, in colour, in mid-career. The Droeshout face is for book buyers; the Sanders face is the one you might have encountered if you were hanging around the Globe Theatre. (148 words)

Source: Alexander Leggatt, "The Man Who Will Not Meet Your Eyes," Shakespeare's Face, *ed. Stephanie Nolen (Toronto: Alfred A. Knopf Canada, 2002) 281.*

A Summary

We imagine a writer from his or her picture. The new colour portrait of Shakespeare fits his vibrant image more than the former black and white one. (27 words)

A Paraphrase

Since pictures can be organizational tools, a writer's portrait can assist us in thinking about a writer by helping us construct notions about him or her. We imagine the look of T.S. Eliot, Ernest Hemingway, or Robertson Davies from their photos as we read their work. Is the new portrait of Shakespeare in 1603 more fitting with what we know about him? While the earlier Droeshout black and white portrait seems to have marked the image and work of Shakespeare for all time, the new colour Sanders portrait seems more in keeping with the lively figure we conjure up from Shakespeare's work. One image seems lifeless, while the other represents someone who was very much alive. (word count: 117—79 percent of the original word count)

Goals of Summaries and Paraphrases

Summaries and paraphrases have similar purposes:

1. To gain a general understanding of what you read or hear
2. To condense others' ideas accurately and effectively using your own words
3. To bolster reading comprehension throughout college or university
4. To prepare for research writing and other research projects
5. To demonstrate understanding of material to your professor or instructor

Exercise 1 *One-Sentence Summaries*

Work in a group of three. Together, write a single-sentence summary for each of the following short pieces. Use your own words. Your one-sentence summaries should be no longer than 20 percent of the length of the source. Be prepared to share your answers with the class.

PASSAGE 1: Treasured by Chinese carvers for 5,000 years, the stone was created between 50 and 185 million years ago, when two massive tectonic plates smashed together and buckled upward to create the Cordilleran mountain region that stretches from the Yukon to Mexico. In rare cases, this collision drove serpentine, rich in iron and magnesium, into igneous rock like granite. At the contact zone, the pressure and heat transformed the soft serpentine into hard nephrite jade. These surface deposits are found as boulders, some weighing many tonnes, and as outcrops. (word count: 88)

Source: Chris Tenove, "Romancing the Stone," Canadian Geographic *Jul./Aug. 2005: 44.*

PASSAGE 2: One of the most striking—and unsettling—experiences I've ever had is to travel by car to a place I've never visited before, then travel back along the same route. The trip out always seems to take longer than the trip back—not just a little longer, but much, much longer. I vividly remember travelling by car a few summers ago to a town in Eastern Ontario that I had never been to before, expecting that each twist and turn of the lakeside road I was following would be the one to finally reveal my destination, hoping that the crest of every hill should provide a glimpse of a church steeple, yet I drove and drove and drove with nothing but farmers' fields on one side and docks and beaches on the other. By contrast, the trip back the next day was a very different story, a brisk little drive completely free of tension, insecurity, and surprise. (word count: 157)

Source: Jay Ingram, "The Tourist Illusion," The Velocity of Honey and More Science of Everyday Life *(Toronto: Viking Canada, 2003) 79.*

PASSAGE 3: Virtually all fruits and vegetables, from apples to zucchini, have become substantially inferior nutritionally. Many vegetables and fruits have lost nearly all of their iron, necessary for healthy blood. The most depleted nutrients were found to be Vitamin A, down an average of 68 percent; iron, down 76 percent; and calcium, with an average loss of 80 percent. (word count: 58)

Source: "Incredible shrinking nutrition," Better Nutrition *Oct. 2002: 22.*

AVOIDING PLAGIARISM

When you are preparing your notes for research papers or other written projects, you must be careful to name or cite all your sources. If you directly quote someone's words, you must say whose words they are. If you do not do so, then you are plagiarizing or claiming someone else's words and ideas for your own. Plagiarism is cheating. Colleges and universities have policies, often called "academic dishonesty," addressing plagiarism.

With the rise in the use of the internet, illegal use of someone else's material and breach of copyright are commonplace. Many people believe it is quite acceptable to "borrow" someone else's work, to cut and paste it into their own papers from a web page, and claim it as their own because "everyone else is doing it." However, plagiarism is wrong, and the academic administration of your institute will treat plagiarism as a serious offence: some post-secondary schools fail students caught plagiarizing; others go as far as deregistering or expelling these students. Check your university's or college's website for its policy on plagiarism. Look for its definitions and penalties.

Generally speaking, plagiarism includes

1. copying someone's words or ideas without crediting the source;
2. paraphrasing someone else's words or ideas without crediting the source;
3. summarizing someone else's words or ideas without crediting the source;
4. having someone else write, heavily edit, or completely revise a paper you claim to be your own;
5. manipulating information so as to make it appear it is a result of your own research and thought—"fudging the results."

Sometimes students may plagiarize without realizing they have done so. They may forget to acknowledge the writer, or they may believe that the information is common knowledge and that, therefore, sources do not need to be cited. Some students who are new to academic research may also believe that copying someone's words or ideas is a form of flattery—they may be copying because they admire a writer or thinker. However, claiming ignorance or innocence when it comes to plagiarism will not work. Your school's administration is interested in upholding academic standards and applying codes of ethics in regard to the research done within its purview.

You do not need to cite or acknowledge common knowledge or information in the common domain in your research papers, but at times, you may have difficulty determining whether something is in the common domain or not. *Common knowledge* means knowledge that is widely accessible to the public; this information could be found in several places and is not cited. For example, the population of the Atlantic provinces of Canada is in the public domain—you could find this information in different places without its being documented. However, if you wanted to know whether the population of

Newfoundland and Labrador has been impacted by employment issues, then you might find that information only in one source. In that case, you would have to cite the source because the ideas seem original to the author.

If you are in doubt whether to cite a source or not, check with your instructor or on-campus writing centre staff. If you are unable to do so and you are uncertain if the information is common knowledge or not, acknowledge the source.

Is It Plagiarism or Not?

In the following section, you will see examples of what constitutes plagiarism and what is acceptable.

Example:

- *The original quotation from Lionel K. McPherson:*
  The language of guilt and innocence can be misleading since it brings to mind an unqualified contrast between being culpable or not.
- *Student writing—Sample A*
  It is my opinion that the language of guilt and innocence can be misleading since it brings to mind an unqualified contrast between being culpable or not.
- *Student writing—Sample B*
  I think that language connected to guilt and innocence is deceptive because it seems to make us think in terms of being culpable or not.

In sample A, the student merely copied Dr. McPherson's words but did not acknowledge or credit him. In sample B, the student has produced a partial paraphrase and partial direct quotation but does not credit the original writer. Both are examples of plagiarism, even though the writer of sample B may have thought what he had written was his own writing since it contains some paraphrasing.

Correction:

Sample A—Using MLA style citation:
According to Lionel K. McPherson, "The language of guilt and innocence can be misleading since it brings to mind an unqualified contrast between being culpable or not" (485).

Sample B—Paraphrase:
Lionel K. McPherson believes that how we talk about guilt and innocence can be confusing because it seems to make us judge in an unexamined way who is responsible and who is not.

Exercise 2 Eliminating Plagiarism

Work in pairs. Read each of the quotations and then the student writing that follows. Decide if the student writing is plagiarism or not. If you uncover plagiarism, then correct it either by directly quoting, paraphrasing, or summarizing.

1. *Original source:*

According to the Statistics Canada Aboriginal Peoples Survey 2001, the Manitoba First Nations population is 107,146, which is approximately 10% of Manitoba's total population with 47% of First Nations people living on reserve. The remaining 53% live in rural communities, often close to their reserve communities, or in urban centres. The median age of Manitoba First Nations people is 22.8 years, while that of the non-Aboriginal population is 38.5 years. Thus, First Nations planning for future employment and services must consider that this youthful population 'bulge' is a decade behind the mainstream population. While mainstream society is concerned with preparing for the retiring baby boomers' needs, including housing for 'empty nesters' and seniors homes, First Nations are planning for more schools and family housing.

Source: Melanie MacKinnon, RN (Grand Rapids Cree Nation), "A First Nations Voice in the Present Creates Healing in the Future," Canadian Journal of Public Health *Jan/Feb 2005: S14.*

Student writing:

Fifty-three percent of Aboriginal people living in Manitoba live off reserve with the median age of 22.8 years, in contrast to the non-Aboriginal population of 38.5 years, and therefore planning for First Nations, concerned with employment and housing for youth and families, is about 10 years behind the mainstream population which is now preparing for the baby boomers who will soon be retiring and leaving their family homes.

2. *Original quotation:*

"The nation is bound together by its creative artists," Berton wrote in the *Globe and Mail* in 1999, "and not by parallel lines of rusting steel."

Source: Pierre Berton, Canadian CBC News Online, *30 Nov. 2004,* www.cbc.ca.

Student writing:

I think that Canada is held together by its artistic creativity.

3. *Original source:*

Youth homelessness is an understudied area in the Canadian context. Estimates on the enumeration of homeless youth vary depending on the criteria used. It has been estimated that there are about 150,000 runaways in Canada, while within the nation's biggest city, Toronto, the estimates of street youth vary greatly, from 5,000 by a Coalition of Youth Work Professionals to 12,000 by the Evergreen Drop-in Centre.

Source: Kelly N. Cameron, Yvonne Racine, David R. Offord, and John Cairney, "Youth at Risk of Homelessness in an Affluent Toronto Suburb," Canadian Journal of Public Health *Sept.–Oct. 2004: CBCA Reference 352.*

Student writing:

In my opinion, homelessness and youth have not been studied enough. For example, in the Toronto area, between 5,000 and 12,000 kids are said to be homeless, and we're just not doing much about it.

Exercise 3 Deciding the Purposes of Writing a Summary

Different reasons a student might have for writing a summary include these:

- To use as a study tool
- To make research information more accessible
- To understand a writer's argument
- To show your professor or instructor that you understand the material
- To deepen your own comprehension
- To provide a tool for someone else to get the information quickly

Below are some possible summary assignments you might receive at university or college. Work in pairs: use the list of purposes above and decide the purpose or purposes of each assignment. Be prepared to share your answers.

Assignment 1: In an anthropology class, you visit a field site. You are to provide a summary of your visit. What is the purpose of this summary?

Assignment 2: Your business instructor asks you to summarize two leadership theories given in two different articles. What is the purpose of this summary?

Assignment 3: Professor Megaphone, who teaches music theory, asks you to read the first three chapters of a textbook for next week's class. The professor asks you to provide a summary of 500 words on the chapters. What is the purpose of this summary?

Assignment 4: Your philosophy instructor asks you to critique the arguments found in several articles about ethics in professional life. What is the purpose of this summary?

Assignment 5: You are given a group assignment called Roles of First Nations Women in Early Canadian Political Life to complete in your Canadian history course. You must work collaboratively with two other students. Each of you is responsible for reading and summarizing three different articles as a foundation for your project. What is the purpose of this summary?

Exercise 4 Paraphrasing Quotations

Work in a small group. Together, read the quotations and construct a paraphrase for each one. Write your paraphrase on the chart paper your instructor or professor provides or on the classroom whiteboard.

1. The die is cast in Canada: there are two ethnic and linguistic groups; each is too strong and too deeply rooted in the past, too firmly bound to a mother culture, to be able to swamp the other. But if the two will collaborate inside of a truly pluralist state, Canada could become a privileged place where the federalist form of government, which is the government of tomorrow's world, will be perfected.

   Source: Pierre Elliott Trudeau, Library and Archives Canada website, www.collectionscanada.ca.

2. Metrical and rhymed poetry also has the huge advantage of being mnemonic. Listen to any child delight in repeating nursery rhymes; there's an intrinsic pleasure in similar sounds, in regular rhythms. The rhythmical movement of metre connects us with the rhythmical patterns we live by: breathing, pulse, walking; sleeping and waking; day and night; the seasons, etc.

   Source: Christopher Wiseman, "Opposing the Dark Side: An Interview with Christopher Wiseman," Interviewer Carmine Starnino, Books in Canada *March 2005: 32.*

3. There's a financial incentive to publishing a book that I haven't overlooked. But also your lifespan is always in doubt, and a writer's lifespan in particular, so take advantage of the situation while you can because you never know when it will end.

   Source: Judith Isabella [citing Laurence Gough], "Vancouver author not yet famous in hard-boiled genre," The New Islander *16 Nov. 1997: 10.*

4. I first met her in Vancouver in 1965, when her incisive criticisms disillusioned me from the fond belief that my adolescent effusions constituted poetry; I last saw her on the steps of the B.C. Legislature, old and frail but still determined, protesting against the logging of the Carmanah.

   Source: Stephen Scobie [about poet Dorothy Livesay], "Livesay Lived: Local poet's career spanned Canadian literary history," Monday Magazine *23.3: 14.*

5. You were bringing up something that had been worrying me for a long time. I had realized that the real establishment of the literary world did not consist of the best writers, just as the establishment of the art world did not consist of the best painters. It consisted of publishers and editors and literary columnists and opinion makers like Bill French and Ken Adachi and the bureaucrats in cultural agencies like the Canada Council, the CBC and various arts councils. I recognized there was a difference between an elite, which might consist of the best writers, and an establishment. I did not particularly like either, but to belong to an elite at least implied quality, while to belong to an establishment implied only power. And I knew all about what Lord Acton and the anarchist thinkers had to say about power.

   Source: George Woodcock, Essays on Canadian Writing *(Toronto: Summer 1993) 134.*

6. As if this heresy isn't enough, I've begun to think that perhaps the murder of the short story by Hemingway's and Carver's emulators and by schools of creative writing is the factor that has resulted in the current great swell of interest in creative non-fiction and especially in memoir writing, or as the *New Yorker* termed its featured essays, 'Personal History.' Here we once more have recovered feeling; here feeling is considered appropriate; here it is once again cherished and nourished; here there are no restrictive conventions killing the expression of emotion, or truth-telling from inside the teller of the story. Here, also, human truths are once again more important than any artificial form, structure, or convention. Here we are reading about real life again, and every reader recognizes it, and is grateful for it. Because memoir writing hasn't been a form much used by our most serious, professional writers in the last century, such writers are free to write in whatever way seems best to them, whatever way lends itself best to full and profound expression of experience.

   Source: Sharon Butala, "What's the Point," University of Toronto Quarterly *Fall 1999: 875.*

WRITING PARAGRAPH SUMMARIES

You may be asked to write a paragraph summary of a longer passage or article. In this case, you should apply some of the following guidelines when you prepare your summary. It is crucial that you use your own words whenever possible. Otherwise, you may be plagiarizing rather than summarizing a writer's ideas.

Guidelines for Paragraph Summary Writing

When you write summaries as paragraphs, use the following six rules, adapted from Jeanne D. Day from the University of Notre Dame:

1. Leave out unnecessary information.
2. Delete information that repeats.
3. Cluster information under larger categories whenever possible.
4. Select a topic sentence. (A *topic sentence* is a sentence in a paragraph that sums up the main ideas of the paragraph.)
5. If there is no topic sentence, invent one that fits.
6. After following steps 1–5, rewrite using your own words. Sometimes special terms must be used. Avoid quoting the author's own words, unless it is completely necessary to do so.

Exercise 5 Writing a Summary Paragraph

Work in pairs. Choose one of the articles below, all relating to sleep. Use the guidelines for paragraph summary writing, and together, write a paragraph summary that is approximately 20 percent of the original length. Be sure to start your paragraph with a topic sentence. You may use the topic sentence in the original if a topic sentence is supplied; otherwise, you must invent your own. Write out your summary and be prepared to share and discuss it. Include the word count at the end of your paragraph summary.

Article 1: Majority Suffer Sleep Loss, Study Says

by Siobhan McDonough

Getting a good night's sleep is hard for many adults and that often means poorer health, lower productivity on the job, more danger on the roads, and a less vibrant sex life.

"By three to four in the afternoon, I'm starting to feel brain-drained and I need that caffeine to pick me back up again," said Becky Mcerien, 50, of Philadelphia.

She gets 6.5 hours of sleep a night—slightly less than the adult average of 6.9 hours reported by the National Sleep Foundation.

Many experts say adults need a minimum of seven to nine hours of sleep a night.

A poll for the foundation, released this week, indicates that three-quarters of adults say they frequently have a sleep problem, such as waking during the night or snoring.

Most people ignore the problem and few think they actually have one. Only half of those polled were able to say they slept well on most nights.

"I get what I need to function," said Guillermo Sardina, 55, of Hamilton, N.J., who averages six or seven hours a night. "I sleep through the night. I'm a sound sleeper. . . . I don't even remember my dreams."

One-quarter of adults say sleep problems have some impact on their daily lives.

Richard Gelula, the foundation's CEO, said there's a link between sleep and quality of life.

"People who sleep well, in general, are happier and healthier," he said. "But when sleep is poor or inadequate, people feel tired or fatigued, their social and intimate relationships suffer, work productivity is negatively affected, and they make our roads more dangerous by driving while sleepy and less alert."

Symptoms of a sleep problem include difficulty falling asleep, waking a lot during the night, waking up too early and not being able to get back to sleep, waking up feeling unrefreshed, snoring, unpleasant feelings in the legs or pauses in breathing.

It's not just how much sleep a person gets, but the quality of sleep that matters, the report said.

Some of the country's sleep habits can be attributed to an always-on-the-go society, said Chris Drake, senior scientist at the Henry Ford Hospital Sleep Center in Detroit and co-chairman of the 2005 poll task force.

"In an increasing 24-hour society, people are staying up much later," he said. "They can go to a 24-hour pharmacy or supermarket. They can do anything at any time of the night and day. That can impact on people's decisions to stay up later watching TV, doing work, being on the Internet."

Mary Cuffee, 64, of Washington, says she stays up watching TV and has a stressful job. For her, seven hours of sleep aren't enough. She says she needs at least 10.

The study found:

- Six in 10 adult motorists said they have driven while drowsy in the past year; four per cent reported that they have had an accident or near-accident because they were too tired or actually fell asleep while driving.
- Three-fourths said their partner has a sleep problem, and the most common is snoring.
- Roughly one-fourth of respondents who have partners report that their sexual relationship has been hurt because they have been too sleepy. (word count: 526)

Source: Siobhan McDonough, "Majority Suffer Sleep Loss, Study Says: Bad Night's Rest Linked to Poor Health, Dangerous Driving," Times Colonist *[Victoria] 1 April 2005: C6. The Associated Press, April 1, 2005. Used with permission of The Associated Press, Copyright © 2008. All rights reserved.*

Article 2: Sleep Helps Us Solve Problems, Study Shows

by Patricia Reaney

Advice to "sleep on it" could be well founded, scientists said yesterday.

After a good night's sleep, a problem that seemed insurmountable the night before can often appear more manageable, although the evidence until now has been anecdotal.

But researchers at the University of Luebeck in Germany have designed an experiment that shows a good night's sleep can improve insight and problem-solving.

"If you have some newly acquired memories in your brain, sleep acts on these memories, restructures them, so that after sleep, the insight into a problem which you could not solve before increases," said Dr. Jan Born, a neuroscientist at the university.

To test the theory, they taught volunteers two simple rules to help them convert a string of numbers into a new order. There was also a third hidden rule that could help them increase their speed in solving the problem.

The researchers, who reported their findings in the science journal *Nature*, divided the volunteers into two groups.

Half were allowed to sleep after the training while the remainder were forced to stay awake.

Born and his team noticed the group that had slept after the training were twice as likely to figure out the third rule as the other group.

"Sleep helped," Born said.

"The important thing is that you have to have a memory representation in your brain of the problem you want to solve and then sleep so it can act on the problem."

But Born admitted he and his team do not know how restructuring of memories occurs or what governs it.

Pierre Maquet and Perrine Ruby of the University of Liege in Belgium said the experimental evidence supports the anecdotal suggestions that sleep can stimulate creative thinking.

"The authors [of the study] have applied a clever test that allows them to determine exactly when insight occurs in the time-course of learning," they said in a commentary.

Although the role of sleep in human creativity will still be a mystery, the research gives people good reason to fully respect their periods of sleep, they added. (word count: 342)

Source: Patricia Reaney, "Sleep Helps Us Solve Problems, Study Shows," National Post *22 Jan. 2003: A13.*

Article 3: Don't Snooze? You Lose.

by Brad Evenson

"Type A" people who practise all night or rise too early in the morning could be hampering their brains' capacity to learn and remember.

Harvard University researchers say the brain takes advantage of sleep to refresh the mechanisms it uses to perform tasks. Even a 60-minute catnap is enough to ward off mental burnout.

However, "life's modern erosion of sleep time could shortchange your brain of some learning potential," says Matthew Walker, a professor of psychiatry at Harvard Medical School. The new findings, published in the journal *Neuron,* have implications for a broad range of tasks, from swinging a golf club to playing a Mozart sonata.

These endeavours all depend on what brain scientists call "procedural memory."

Many dancers, athletes and musicians know they perform best when they stop practising a day or two before the show or competition. But it has never been clear whether it was passage of time or sleep that caused the improvement.

The Harvard University researchers say sleep is definitely the answer. In the study, they asked 62 right-handed volunteers to type the numbers 4–1–3–2–4 with their left hand as quickly and accurately as possible for 30 seconds. After 12 practice sessions of 30 seconds, subjects had improved their speed and accuracy by 60%.

A group that stayed awake for 12 hours after the morning training session showed no improvement when re-tested.

But after a night's sleep, their performance rose by almost 19%.

A second group that trained in the evening scored a 20.5% improvement after a night's sleep.

Dr. Walker and his colleagues say sleep may enhance motor skills by synchronous nerve firings called spindles—not unlike a crowd of sports fans doing the "wave" in a football stadium. These spindles peak during stage 2, non-rapid-eye-movement sleep, which most people enjoy in the two hours before waking.

"It's specifically those two hours that we have found to be most important," he said.

So people who get only six hours of sleep may be shortchanging their brains, Dr. Walker said.

In a related study published this week, another group of Harvard sleep researchers found a nap might help performance.

Reporting in the journal *Nature Neuroscience*, Sara Mednick and Robert Stickgold showed that irritation, frustration and flagging performance on a mental task could be halted with a nap.

In the experiment, subjects were asked to report the horizontal or vertical orientation of three diagonal bars against a background of horizontal bars in the lower left corner of a computer screen. Their scores on the task worsened over the course of four daily practice sessions.

When subjects took a 30-minute nap, the burnout factor was halted and their performance stopped deteriorating. A 60-minute nap actually restored performance to fresh, morning levels.

Brain recordings of naps show they contain significant amounts of "slow save sleep" which appears to be an antidote to burnout, scientists say. (word count: 477)

Source: Brad Evenson, "Don't Snooze? You Lose," National Post *4 Jul. 2002: A1–A2. Material reprinted with the express permission of: "National Post Company," a CanWest Partnership.*

Exercise 6 Paraphrasing Exercise

Use the same article you used in Exercise 5 and work with the same partner. Paraphrase the article. Use your own words. Write your paraphrase on a clean sheet of paper or on an overhead your instructor has supplied. You will be sharing your answer with the rest of the class. Put the word count at the end of the paraphrase.

REVIEW TEST

Try the following review test. It will help you assess what you have learned from the chapter. Be prepared to share your responses with others in the class.

1. What is the difference between a summary and a paraphrase?

____

____

____

2. Name three purposes of a summary.

____

____

____

3. What is plagiarism?

____

____

____

4. Give an illustration of plagiarism.

____

____

____

5. Write a summary of no more than 27 words for the following passage:

   Life stages affect how individuals and their families cope with illnesses and injuries. Lifespan developmental theory states that each individual will go through a sequence of orderly, distinct stages in life. At each stage, a person has to master some developmental tasks. Each task is a growth responsibility that appears at a certain stage of an individual or family's life, and has emerged from biological needs, cultural imperatives, and family goals. These tasks must be successfully completed in order to secure present satisfaction, social approval, and future success. Failure to do so will result in dissatisfaction, social disapproval and difficulties with later tasks and life. Because individuals and families interact, individual and family life cycles often juxtapose and intertwine with each other. Understanding life-cycle theory can help the physician to assess and intervene appropriately. (word count: 134)

   Source: Vincent Poon and Ed Bader, "Life-Cycle Theory: Make Use of It in Your Practice," Patient Care *[Mississauga] Mar. 2005: 62.*

____

____

____

____

____

6. Use the same passage and write a paraphrase.

____

____

____

____

____

____

Assignment

The purpose of this assignment is to demonstrate to your instructor that you understand the similarities and differences in two writers' views on the same topic. Both discuss the uses of the cell phone.

Steps:

1. Read each of the two articles below.
2. Write a one-paragraph summary of each article. Include the word count after each summary. Your summaries should be no longer than 20 percent of the source material.
3. Then write a comparison and contrast paragraph between the two articles, using your summaries as the basis of your discussion.
4. Hand in your assignment, using double spacing between the lines and a font that is 11 or 12 point in Times New Roman or another serif font.

   Your assignment should look like this:

   Summary paragraph 1 of article 1 (word count)

   ↓

   Summary paragraph 2 of article 2 (word count)

   ↓

   Comparison and contrast paragraph of the two summaries

Article 1: Digital-cam Voyeurs Lurking at UVic

by Sarah Schmidt

Hunting season is indeed open at the University of Victoria.

An online database of revealing photos of female students secretly photographed on campus, posted under the heading "Hunting season is open," has been growing since September 2003. The administration learned about the Web site a few weeks ago when a member of the university community complained, but didn't inform students of its existence.

The most recent submission of a "victim" to the "Hunted T-bars" section of the site was posted Thursday. The pictures, taken from behind at various public areas on campus, including the campus bar, library and student centre, focus on female students' buttocks and thong underwear. The young women are usually sitting.

Visitors are asked to rate each picture and provide commentary. Comments include: "I wouldn't hesitate" and "Umm . . . brb (be right back)." The photos are being taken with either camera phones or digital cameras.

Cellphone cameras, a technological craze particularly among young people, have been banned in some campus athletic facilities and private gyms in Canada for fear people would surreptitiously snap revealing photos. Saudi Arabia's highest religious authority has barred the popular gadget outright, blaming the cellphone with a built-in camera for "spreading obscenity."

David Clode, head of student services at UVic, said the school can do nothing about the Web site because the shots of women's derrieres are being taken in public places on campus and the site can't be traced to a member of the university community.

Clode added, "This person is clearly working as though people are not aware of what he's doing, although as somebody pointed out to me, how can you not be aware that you're being revealing?"

Referring to the students being photographed, he said: "Their choice of attire is their choice. I can't imagine that you don't know what the effect is of how you dress."

Joanna Groves, chairwoman of the student union, said the administration should have informed students about a photographer or photographers trolling the campus for candid shots of female students.

"It's just a violation of someone's privacy," Groves said. "It's like taking a picture up someone's skirt in a public place. It's going to make women feel unsafe. I think it's reasonable for the administration to inform women so they can be at least on guard . . . that someone might be around them trying to take those kind of pictures."

Bill C-2, legislation to amend the Criminal Code currently before Parliament, includes the creation of "an offence of voyeurism and the distribution of voyeuristic material." The proposed law makes it an offence to "surreptitiously observe or make a visual recording of a person in circumstances that give rise to a reasonable expectation of privacy, where that is done for a sexual purpose."

Const. John Price, spokesman for the Saanich police, said because the campus pictures are snapped in public places, the proposed law would not apply.

"Although it would probably be an affront to a group of people within society, it is not a criminal act. If they were photos of women in a bathroom stall or through a bedroom window, where there is a strong expectation of privacy, then yes, it would be a criminal matter."

Legal issues aside, Ottawa-based author and media critic Shari Graydon, said the Web site is a disturbing cultural artifact. It denies women's humanity by creating images focused on particular body parts, she said.

"Although the fashion statement that combines low-riding pants and thong underwear would seem designed to attract viewer attention to the underwear that's often exposed, the images are being taken without the women's knowledge.

"The images are being captured and disseminated surreptitiously, and their use on the Web site alongside the words 'hunted victims' is particularly creepy and unfortunate," said Graydon, author of *In Your Face: The Culture of Beauty and You.*

The Web site, www.peepingthong.com, is registered to a Jeff Smith, who lists an address not far from the UVic campus as his residence. The phone number provided to the Internet provider is not in service. Smith, listed as both the administrative and technical contact for the Web site, did not respond to an e-mail request for an interview.

Source: Sarah Schmidt, "Digital-cam Voyeurs Lurking at UVic," Times Colonist *[Victoria] 4 Feb. 2005: A1, A2. Material reprinted with the express permission of: "CANWEST NEWS SERVICE," a CanWest Partnership.*

Article 2: Cellphone Poses as Diet Conscience

by Sarah Staples

Jack Lavoie might have looked like just another annoying restaurant patron flipping out his cellphone in the middle of dinner. But like thousands of Canadians, Lavoie has been trying to lose weight, and his phone has been his "virtual" diet coach.

The musician and landscaper is one of the first health conscious technophiles to try MyFoodPhone: a Canadian-designed camera phone embedded with software that forwards pictures of its owner's meals to a registered dietician.

During testing of MyFoodPhone this winter at the Universite Laval, in Quebec City, Lavoie volunteered to upload images of everything he ate to a personal web page at www.myfoodphone.com.

Once a week for two months, he received a 90-second video clip response from "Caroline," a dietician in private practice, offering feedback on his food choices and tips for improvement.

MyFoodPhone, the brainchild of Quebec City-based NATS Inc., has been offered in New York City, New Jersey and Connecticut since February, and is set to make its Canadian debut this summer.

"It's like you get a video commentary of your week in the food world. (Caroline) would tell you, 'You're not eating enough vegetables,' or 'Don't forget to drink your water.' She'd direct you along the six or seven main food types," said Lavoie.

"You really become sensitive to what you're putting in your body."

At $150 US a month, plus the cost of the phone, the service is still cheaper and more efficient than booking weekly appointments with a dietician or fitness coach, its creators say.

With no advertising other than word-of-mouth, some 150 residents of the tri-state area have signed up to take virtual consultations from 50 dieticians.

And MyFoodPhone is only the latest of a slew of software-laden cellphones, PDAs and other web-enabled diet aids aimed at helping people take control over their weight loss as never before.

"Tele-dieting" technology and services represent an expanding slice of a weight-loss market worth more than $240 billion US globally, according to the Institute of Food Technologists.

It's an opportunity projected by Marketdata to reach $61 billion US in the United States alone by 2008.

Among newly released diet novelties is "Powerseed": a pod-shaped gadget launched in January. Powerseed acts as a sort of Pavlovian egg timer, encouraging dieters to chew their food slowly by discreetly beeping or flashing a green light every thirty seconds when it's time to take a bite.

Hundreds of diet and exercise software programs are becoming available for hand-held PDAs. They include versions of the popular Atkins, Keyoe, South Beach, and WeightWatchers diets released this winter that have been adapted for palmOne Zire, Treo and Tungsten hand-helds.

For more detailed calorie monitoring there's "Bodybugg," from Pittsburgh-based BodyMedia: a web-enabled armband resembling a heart monitor that advertises "92 per cent accuracy" in calculating the energy consumed and burned daily.

The system wirelessly uploads calorie counts to a computer progam that keeps track of weight loss, and offers menu suggestions to help dieters reach their desired weight.

A different kind of calorie counter is the breathalyser-style device called "BodyGem," by HealtheTech, which calculates a person's daily Resting Metabolic Rate, or calories burned by the body while at rest.

RMR accounts for as much as 75 per cent of bodily metabolism, meaning BodyGem can theoretically be used to estimate a person's ideal caloric intake for the day. It's a nifty concept, though pricey at $1,799 US for the starter package.

Source: Sarah Staples, "Cellphone Poses as Diet Conscience," CanWest News Service Times Colonist *26 May 2005: B4. Material reprinted with the express permission of: "CANWEST NEWS SERVICE," a CanWest Partnership.*

Bonus Exercise Reported Speech

Reported speech is sometimes called **indirect speech**. It means you are usually talking about words someone said in the past, either the immediate past or a long time ago. You report the words spoken in the past.

Examples:

- Lina said, "I'm leaving right after the concert." (direct quotation)
- Lina said (that) she was leaving right after the concert. (reported speech or indirect quotation. Usually "that" is left out in the construction. However, it is not incorrect to include it.)

Notice that when Lina spoke she talked about her intentions at the time in the present tense; however, when you report what she said, you will use a past tense verb.

Reported speech can be called indirect speech because the person is not saying the words directly; you are indirectly reporting them.

Notice, in the direct quotation, that the quotation marks go around the words the speaker says. If a direct quotation is broken up or interrupted by a signal statement of some sort (who has said the words), then use commas around your signal statement. Begin the rest of the quotation with opening quotation marks and end with closing quotation marks. Place your end punctuation (a period, a question mark, or an exclamation mark) inside the closing quotation marks. (MLA style works differently with direct quotations. Please review the MLA section for more information.)

Example:

"My boss expected the outcome," Sunny declared, "but I was certainly surprised!"

Notice that what Sunny said is interrupted by the signal statement. The exclamation mark stays inside the quotation marks.

Work in pairs. Use reported speech for each of the direct quotations in the following exercise.

1. "Be sure to check as you prepare to make a lane change," advised the driving instructor.
2. The police officer said, "I've noticed a number of people still refuse to wear their seat belts."
3. One of the students observed, "The instructor has purple hair!"
4. The caller asked, "Would you mail me one of your brochures?"
5. My sister shouted, "I'm terrified of heights!"
6. The television reporter stated, "I will be meeting with the Prime Minister on Tuesday."
7. Tama replied, "I don't want any sugar in my tea."

READING

The following reading is about an issue that concerns many health-care workers who are on the front lines: health literacy and health literacy education. Read Dr. Quigley's article carefully, attempting to understand the problems he unfolds. Then answer the questions that follow.

Knowledge Is Not Enough: Advancing Health Literacy Through Lessons from History

by B. Allan Quigley

B. Allan Quigley is a professor of adult education at St. Francis Xavier University in Antigonish, Nova Scotia.

"Research that produces nothing but books will not suffice."

—Kurt Lewin

Health literacy is an area of practice and study that is expanding so quickly in the United States and Canada that it is difficult to keep up with the literature—not to mention the steady stream of conference notices. While this is an exciting new development for both adult education and the health professions, the history of adult literacy is crisscrossed with the tracks of "bandwagons" (Quigley, 1997). It seems that few in the current health literacy race are pausing to ask what adults with low literacy skills have actually experienced, or need, or will accept. Even fewer are seeking to hear their voices. Is this the best way forward?

The findings of a 2001 medical study are instructive. After reviewing 72 controlled experiments concerned with training for self-management of Type 2 Diabetes, the researchers concluded: "It is apparent that factors other than knowledge are needed to achieve long-term behavioral change" (Norris, Engelgau, & Narayan, p. 1). Likewise, literature on adult learning tells us that adults need to be part of the learning process—that knowledge is not enough. We should be asking: "How can we approach adult learning in health settings and, in turn, enhance health learning in literacy practice to achieve a lasting impact with individuals and with the systems that are intended to serve them?"

This question is discussed in this article by first looking back at the rich history of adult literacy. Then, the lessons we learned through a health literacy study in Nova Scotia are presented as a possible "third way" for addressing health literacy issues.

LITERACY AS SCHOOL OR TOOL?

For almost two centuries, adult literacy education has been divided between those who believe literacy education is best delivered through programs using a schooling model and those who believe literacy education should be one of many learning tools for adults. In the literacy-as-schooling tradition, literacy education has typically been constructed with <u>pedagogical</u> curricula influenced by the host profession and/or the sponsoring organization. Conscious of it or not, literacy-as-schooling typically brings ideological goals with its content. These, in turn, are typically founded on assumptions about learners. Although such underlying ideologies have changed as the sponsors have changed through time, such deficit perspective assumptions have stayed about the same. On the other hand, literacy is approached as a learning tool for adults—a tool to achieve their goals and address life problems. While both approaches effectively seek three objectives, skills development, knowledge acquisition, and values "clarification," there is typically more learner input in the learning process with the literacy-as-tool model.

The differences between the two models have immediate, critical implications for how health literacy will find its way in the 21st century world of adult learning and health. Both models have strengths but, in this article, a third way based on the Nova Scotia experience will be suggested to gain the best from both.

LITERACY-AS-SCHOOL

The pattern for the classic literacy-as-schooling model was set as early as 1816, when Dr. Thomas Pole made his argument for the establishment of what became the first documented, sustained English language adult education literacy program in the Western world. In what is today known as *Pole's History* (1816), he argued that the many adults who were unable to read the Scriptures—and consequently were doomed to eternal damnation—needed to be taught to read using the Bible itself. As Pole argued, if illiterate adults could read the Scriptures, "Industry, frugality, and economy will be their possession. They will also have learned better to practice meekness, Christian Fortitude, and resignation" (Verner, 1812/1967, p. 19). In this first history of adult education, Pole pointed to the example of his Methodist brethren in Bristol, England. He recounted how, in an annual meeting in 1812, many of the faithful complained that many in Bristol were illiterate. The congregation was asking: "Why provide them with Bibles they can't read?" Seeing the injustice in this, in 1812, William Smith, "a poor, humble, and almost unlettered individual" (Hudson, 1851/1969, p. 2) decided to initiate an adult school to teach reading.

In just one year, adult schools were formed in Bath, Ipswich, Plymouth, Salisbury, and Yarmouth. By 1816, the Bristol records showed "schools in Ireland, New York, Philadelphia, and Sierra Leone" (Kelly, 1962, p. 150). In America, at the end of the Civil War, the Bible was used in South Carolina during one of America's first major literacy initiatives. In the 1863 Port Royal Experiment, thousands of freed slaves came forward for literacy instruction as offered by Giddeonite missionaries from New York (Rachal, 1986). In 1911, the first Moonlight School was created in Rowan County, Kentucky. Hundreds of adults would come to the local schoolhouses, if the moon was shining bright. The Kentucky Moonlight School movement soon swept the nation, and according to Cook (1977), became the official beginning of adult literacy education in America (Cook; Quigley, 2006).

From salvation and morality, to a focus on citizenship through the 1940s, and employment and work skills since World War II, the schooling model of programs for individuals has become well established. Today literacy and adult basic education programs include corrections literacy, family literacy, workplace literacy, Aboriginal literacy, literacy for the homeless, and variations of first and second language literacy But does history support the notion that programs in the schooling tradition are the only way—or even the best way—for our nascent health literacy movement to develop?

LITERACY-AS-TOOL

The second major approach seen in our history has had a very different starting place and has sought very different results. Rather than beginning with sponsors' goals or the implicit assumption that individuals are fully responsible for their own social, cultural, and educational condition, educators in the literacy-as-tool approach begin with the condition itself. Instead of assuming individuals will make "good choices" given the appropriate knowledge, it is believed that not all adults have a fair and equal chance; that problems such as low literacy derive from inequities in society not from deficits in individuals. In this view, learners are encouraged to think critically, participate in their own learning projects, and redress injustices affecting their lives.

The examples of this approach are many. In the developing South, the World Health Organization helped organize multiple government agencies, nongovernmental organizations, and educational institutions to work in partnership to eradicate or reduce diseases. There are many examples in the USA, including the remarkable story of the Wisconsin Idea. In the 1880s, University of Wisconsin researchers worked shoulder-to-shoulder with farmers and policymakers to address the rural dairy cattle disease issues that threatened the economy of the state (Cremin, 1961). The work of Highlander Folk School is another example. Since 1932, education and support have been given to poor and working people, fighting economic injustice, poverty, prejudice, and environmental destruction at the Highlander Folk School in New Market, Tennessee (Quigley 1997).

There are countless examples in adult literacy history. However, the lessons learned from, and by, Jane Addams and the women of Hull House are among the best for purposes of this discussion.

HULL HOUSE: LITERACY-AS-TOOL FOR CHANGE

On September 18, 1889, Jane Addams and Brenda Starr Gates took up residence on the first floor of a Chicago home that once belonged to the Hull family. This aging house stood in the centre of the worst Chicago slums. Later, joined by Julia Lathrop and Florence Kelley the women worked with the thousands of disenfranchised immigrants seeking the American Dream only to find appallingly poor health, chronic unemployment, and conditions so squalid the children played with rats as pets (Linn, 1935). The Hull House mission was: "To provide a center for a higher civic and social life; to institute and maintain educational and philanthropic enterprises, and to investigate and improve the conditions in the industrial districts of Chicago" (Linn, p. 110).

The women began with the type of education they had been exposed to earlier. They offered classes on literature and drama, they loaned art to hang on tenement house walls, and they invited speakers such as Susan B. Anthony and John Dewey to address the immigrant audiences. However, they soon found themselves helping with birthing, washing and preparing the dead, and attempting to alleviate the illnesses and suffering around them. They began to organize occupational and health-oriented programs, including woodworking, iron and brass work, commercial photography, printing and telegraphy, and cooking nutritional American meals, but this still was not enough.

The transformation of the women—Jane Addams in particular—is instructive for us in health literacy. As Davis (1973) explains:

> Jane Addams never became a radical in religion, in economics or in politics, but she did become a social reformer, a defender of organized labor, and she did

come to believe that *her main task was to eliminate poverty rather than to comfort the poor* [emphasis added]. (p. 74)

Moving from discussions of poetry to literacy-as-a-tool for change, Addams marched for union rights with her learners. The women shifted literacy and ESL courses to social awareness issues, and worked to redress the injustices of health systems that were failing the poor. Addams was ultimately awarded the Nobel Peace Prize in 1931 for her life's work. The Settlement House Movement went on to help eliminate child labor in America and contributed to the establishment of a social welfare system.

What began as a movement to "uplift and educate" evolved into a movement that "educated the educators" and challenged the systemic injustices that contributed to poverty, disease, and illiteracy itself. With such remarkable experiences to draw upon, we today ask how best to develop health literacy?

NOVA SCOTIA AND REFLECTIONS ON A THIRD WAY

In this issue *of Adult Learning,* Doris Gillis discusses a participatory action research health literacy study we conducted in Nova Scotia, Canada. It arose out of literacy and health questions raised within the community, and was built on community partnerships. The voice of adults with low literacy, that of health and literacy practitioners, and input from key informants lead to dozens of recommendations on how health provision could be improved and made more accessible to adults with low literacy skills. Following two roundtable discussions to prioritize the recommendations, the findings lead communities and the government of Nova Scotia to act. Today, change is still going on through the advocacy of the regional Health Literacy Network.

As the co-investigator for the study it seems to me that four critical decisions were made that are of particular importance for the health literacy discourse. First, when faced with questions on adult low literacy and health in our community the local community health board did not launch their own set of programs based on assumptions. They sought to understand the complexities of the issue, and came to the university to enter a research partnership. Second, recognizing the importance of including a literacy perspective, Doris Gillis of the Department of Human Nutrition, with members of the Nursing Department, contacted me in the Department of Adult Education. Third, through continuous input from community meetings, community partners, and our working advisory panel, it was clear that our study should focus on ways adults with low literacy experience our health systems and what they need to make it more effective. The fourth major decision was really a group commitment to seek change. Our findings, as prioritized by participants and stakeholders, sought systemic and practice change. And, much has happened since, including ongoing advocacy.

Examined from an historical perspective, the starting point was not an assumption that adults with low literacy skills needed to be "educated," so they might make better use of existing systems. The starting place was the need to see the world through the eyes of those whose lives were to be affected. Like the Hull House workers, we came to the decision that our study was not to be based on what *we perceived* about adults with low literacy skills, but what they articulated *out of their own lived experiences.* Like so many historically successful movements in adult education, we began with partnerships. And, through ongoing partnerships, today's changes hold promise for further systemic change and improved health across our region as a result. We have the experience of two established literacy models and two centuries of history. Today, many adult literacy practitioners insist on having learners as partners. Why not build on this history for advancing health literacy?

References

Cook, W. D. (1977). *Adult literacy education in the United States.* Newark, DE: International Reading Association.

Cremin, L. (1961). *The transformation of the school.* New York: Random House.

Davis, A. F. (1973). *American heroine: The life and legend of Jane Addams.* New York: Oxford University Press.

Hudson, J. W. (1851/1969). *The history of adult education.* London: Wobuni.

Kelly, T. (1962). *A history of adult education in Great Britain.* Liverpool, U.K.: Liverpool University Press.

Linn, J. W. (1935). *Jane Addams: A biography.* New York: D. Appleton-Century Co.

Norris, S. L., Engelgau, M. M., & Narayan, K. M. (2001). Effectiveness of self-management training in Type 2 diabetes: A systematic review of randomized controlled trials. *Diabetes Care 24*(3), 561–587.

Quigley, B. A. (1997). *Rethinking adult education: The critical need for practice-based change.* San Francisco: Jossey-Bass.

Quigley, B. A. (2006). *Building professional pride in literacy: A dialogical guide for teachers and tutors of adult literacy.* Malabar, FL: Krieger Press.

Rachal, J. R. (1986). Freedom's crucible: William T. Richardson and the schooling of freed men. *Adult Education Quarterly, 3*(37), 14–22.

Verner, C. (1812/1967). *Pole's history of adult schools.* Washington, D.C.: Adult Education Associates of the U.S.A.

Source: B. Allan Quigley, "Knowledge Is Not Enough: Advancing Health Literacy Through Lessons from History," Adult Learning *Vol 15, Issue 1/2, 2004: 10–12. Reprinted by permission of B. Allan Quigley, Professor of Adult Education at St. Francis Xavier University in Nova Scotia.*

Comprehension Questions

1. What is "health literacy"?
2. How do the two schools of thought in literacy education differ?
3. What does the underlined word *pedagogical* in paragraph 4 mean?
4. Why did Dr. Thomas Pole believe adults need to learn to read? What were his suppositions?

5. What are the assumptions of the Literacy-As-Tool model?
6. What were the purposes of Hull House, and why was Jane Addams's work significant?

Critical Comprehension

1. Whose interests does literacy education serve?
2. Discuss Quigley's statement: "Examined from an historical perspective, the starting point was not an assumption that adults with low literacy skills needed to be 'educated,' so they might make better use of existing systems."

Assignment

Summarize Quigley's article in 300 words.

CHECKOUT

Here are some of the ideas you will take away with you after you have completed the chapter:

1. Summarizing and paraphrasing are critical skills for post-secondary academic work.
2. Paraphrases are longer than summaries.
3. Summaries and paraphrases have similar purposes.
4. A critical reader will think beyond the facts by trying to interpret them.
5. When you put research material into your essay, you must cite sources.
6. Never plagiarize; it could result in academic penalty or dismissal from your school.

Mastering the concepts in this chapter will also help you develop and apply the following employability skills highlighted by the Conference Board of Canada in *Employability Skills 2000+*:

Communicate

- read and understand information presented in a variety of forms (e.g., words, graphs, charts, diagrams)

Manage Information

- locate, gather and organize information using appropriate technology and information systems

Source: Adapted from *Employability Skills 2000+* Brochure E/F (Ottawa: The Conference Board of Canada, 2000).

chapter 7

Critical Skills: Evaluating

Chapter Objectives

After completing this chapter you will be able to

1. practise and develop critical thinking skills;
2. evaluate source materials for your research essays;
3. endeavour to be principled in your approach to evaluating;
4. measure evaluations using a set of criteria;
5. uncover arguments based on false assumptions;
6. prepare better-quality research questions.

INTRODUCTION

Frequently people find themselves in situations in which they must make decisions or choices. Sometimes the answers are simple because they require very little complicated thinking: what to make for lunch, what route to take to the campus, what brand of milk to buy at the store, and so on. However, sometimes decisions are tough. Selecting the best answer is not an easy task. Choices may have far-reaching impacts: what school to choose, what financial plans for the future, what person to have a personal relationship with, and so on. Although you cannot always be sure you have chosen wisely, you can prepare yourself in a number of ways to become better informed so that you can fairly judge your own thinking and actions. An important critical thinking skill is **evaluating**. This skill is complex and requires careful consideration and practice. Almost all of your coursework will require you to evaluate some issue or topic. Often you will be asked to write an evaluation of something or prepare a piece of research writing, including evaluation.

Thinkers and writers can develop their abilities to analyze and evaluate; they can also train themselves to be more open-minded and fair as they think critically about important issues. To become more principled in your approach to evaluating, you must learn about and practise some evaluation skills.

WHAT IS EVALUATION?

Many experts believe that critical thinking is the most important of all skill sets for any individual to have in the 21st century. Critical thinking comprises various subsets, and a very important one is evaluation. Training in order to evaluate an argument, a discussion, a film, a webpage, or anything else that may be significant in life will take particular focus, specific time, and some mental exertion. This critical thinking skill is an accumulation of other strategies you will use as you begin to analyze, consider assumptions, question, map arguments, and reach conclusions. Critical skill development is about making connections in new ways.

You probably associate the term *evaluation* with negative events from your earlier days in school: exams, report cards, grades, tests, and so forth. However, as a student in higher education, it is important to consider evaluation from a different perspective: a positive experience that can make you a better informed and more independent learner. Bear in mind: high-quality evaluations lead to enriched thinking and improvement.

Evaluation does not simply include likes, dislikes, or preference. It is not just a matter of personal taste. Instead, evaluation is the process of determining the worth of something by collecting information and assigning values in order to make effective decisions. Because evaluation is a process, it involves steps. Not everyone follows the same steps or uses the same method in evaluation, but as a student, you will find the following steps useful in your approach to evaluation.

First, you must determine the purpose of your evaluation: why you are doing it and what you hope to achieve. Are you trying to decide whether something has worked or not? Are you trying to evaluate how something compares to something else? Are you evaluating so that you can improve something? (Purposes of evaluation are outlined later in this chapter.)

Next, you should decide the type of evaluation you want to use. Perhaps your evaluation will concentrate on someone's performance. If so, you must develop a simple set of criteria you want to employ. If the performance you are evaluating is a speech, you might want to include as criteria such items as clarity of voice, the speaker's tone, his confidence when speaking, the organization of the speech, and the attention of the audience.

Steps for Completing an Evaluation

1. Determine purpose.
   ↓
2. Determine type of evaluation.
   ↓
3. Develop criteria.
   ↓
4. Apply and carry out the evaluation.
   ↓
5. Assess results.

Exercise 1 Applying the Steps for Completing an Evaluation

Suppose you are going to buy a new computer. How would you go about deciding among all of the choices available in the marketplace and online? Use the Steps for Completing an Evaluation. Jot down your answers for each step. Be prepared to share your answers with the rest of the class.

WHAT ARE SOME TERMS TO KNOW WHEN EVALUATING?

It is helpful to familiarize yourself with new vocabulary terms as you are learning new information. This section presents you with some terms you are likely to see when you are thinking about evaluation. Of course, evaluation itself is a very complex subject or discipline, a study in itself, and this chapter is not meant to provide you with a complete list of terms. However, it is intended to give you a nodding acquaintance with some of the terms used most frequently in the process of evaluation.

1. A **fact** is a piece of information that can be verified to be true; it has been proven to be true. For instance, it is a *fact* that people need food to survive.
2. An **opinion** is a personal belief not established on proof but on a personal idea or taste. For example, "People need chocolate to survive" is an *opinion*, not a fact.
3. An **assumption** is a statement that is taken for granted as being true. For instance, "All young men love beer" is an assumption. Many arguments are based on false assumptions. As a thinker, you must uncover assumptions in arguments and test whether they are true or false, fact, or merely someone's opinion.
4. **Analysis** is the investigation of the component parts in relation to the whole of something in order to understand how it is organized. For example, if you want to use *analysis* to explore family life in the far north, you would look at what parts make up family life—kinships, roles, values, societal structures—and then you would consider each part in relation to the others.
5. **Criteria** are the standards, measures, or guidelines used when you are making an evaluation. In your university studies, for example, the *criteria* for passing a course may be receiving a C+ or better on all major assignments, passing two exams with C or better, and participating in two group projects. The *criteria* you set up for evaluation must be clear and workable; otherwise, the evaluation will fail.
6. **Accountability** means the obligation for responsibility or being answerable for the results of something. In a job situation, for instance, you are *accountable* to your supervisor. Your supervisor, in turn, is *accountable* to another person higher on the management ladder. *Accountability* is a tremendously important term. To illustrate, *accountability* is the basis of democracy: democratic governments are responsible to their people.
7. **Feedback** is the response received from groups of users about products, services, ideas, policies, practices, and so forth. *Feedback* usually offers what was liked and disliked, along with suggestions for improvement. As a student, you may have been asked for *feedback* from other students on their papers, reports, or presentations.
8. An **argument** is a discussion that has a set of statements made up of premises: it ends with a conclusion supported by those premises.
9. A **valid argument** is one that has a true conclusion that flows from true premises. In this example, "I think Bailey will love this puppy because she loves dogs and always takes good care of them" is a *valid argument*. The two premises—"She loves dogs"

and "always takes care of them"—are true, and the conclusion—"Bailey will love this puppy"—flows logically from them. However, an argument may contain true premises but a false conclusion; in this case, the argument is not valid. For example, "Bailey loves horses. She takes good care of them and, therefore, she will love this puppy" is not a valid argument.

10. A **sound argument** is one that has a valid argument and all true premises. The first example above is a valid and *sound argument*.

Exercise 2 Providing Examples

Work in pairs. Provide examples for each of the following terms. Be prepared to share and discuss your answers.

1. A fact

 ____

 ____

2. An opinion

 ____

 ____

3. An assumption

 ____

 ____

4. A valid argument

 ____

 ____

5. A sound argument

 ____

 ____

6. An invalid argument

 ____

 ____

7. An unsound argument

 ____

 ____

WHAT ARE THE PURPOSES OF EVALUATION?

Why should we evaluate? We evaluate according to specific purposes. We do not evaluate everything in exactly the same way all the time. The following lists a variety of possible purposes for evaluating. Read over the list, and think about the examples. Then do the exercise that follows; the list is in no particular order of importance.

Purpose 1: To Improve Something

A manufacturer may be seriously concerned that sales of one of its key products are dropping off dramatically. The manufacturer may decide to improve the product to boost sales; however, in order to know if the new product is actually better than the original, the company has to evaluate if it really is better. The company may have a number of strategies to check out the improved product with the consumer, but it knows it must evaluate, using criteria to compare the new, improved product to the original. In another example, think of some of the evaluations you have received for assignments you are asked to do in your courses. Aren't some of them based on the idea of improvement?

Purpose 2: To Make an Individual, Group, or Organization Accountable

Some individuals or organizations have heavy social responsibilities. Often they are funded publicly and must report in a responsible way to the government or to the citizenry. Democratic governments are said to be democratic because they are answerable or responsible to the people. Groups hired by government to do specific tasks are also accountable for their performance, service, products, or actions. Voting may be considered the ultimate form of evaluation of a democratic government's tenure: if people have liked the job government has done during its term, then they vote for a second term of that government. If they do not agree that government has done an effective job, then they "vote it out." Civil servants are evaluated according to the service they have given government. For example, teachers are evaluated by provincial governments according to whether they have met the evaluation criteria for effective teaching based on learning outcomes, student evaluations, supervisors' reports, and the performance of their students.

Purpose 3: To Check Progress and Assist Planning

It is sometimes difficult to know how someone or some organization is getting along with a project or task. In order to determine their progress, a supervising or managing agency will do evaluations as part of project planning. For example, if a city is funding the building of a new convention centre using tax dollars, the city has a responsibility to meet its obligations. The convention centre project may have several evaluations along the way to be sure it is running according to plan. In this way, the city is being responsible in the management of its projects and expenditures. Planning and budgeting will then be adjusted according to the results of the evaluations.

Purpose 4: To Check If an Argument Is Sound and Valid

Thinkers may be hired to evaluate whether or not an argument being presented is sound and valid. (You will learn more about soundness and validity of arguments in Chapter 10:

Critical Skills: Argumentation.) An argument is sound if all its components and its conclusion are true; an argument is valid if it has been shown to be true and if the argument follows from its parts. Judges, for example, must decide if arguments presented in court are admissible according to law and to the structure of arguments provided.

Purpose 5: To Measure Outcomes or Success

Products or services may be provided, but in order to know whether they have met their objectives and are successful or not, they must be evaluated. A course or program you take in post-secondary studies is evaluated according to learning outcomes and according to whether or not students have satisfied the evaluation criteria and have completed the course successfully. In some programs, student follow-up evaluations may take several years to determine if graduates have been adequately prepared in various professions. Universities want to know how successful their graduates are as doctors, lawyers, engineers, teachers, government workers, and so on.

Purpose 6: To Check How Appropriate Something Is

Industry often tries out new products in new situations. In order to determine if products are appropriate in new situations or to test a new product in a traditional situation, companies must evaluate. For example, a company might have a new design for a baby stroller that can be used on the beach or on rough terrain. It tests the product but then must evaluate whether consumers find the new use appropriate or not.

Purpose 7: To Maintain Standards

Professional organizations may certify if a professional's performance is up to the standards set or not. Manufacturers may also have to produce and test products that meet industry and government standards.

Purpose 8: To Make a Purchase

Consumers always want to get the best buy possible, so they do their own homegrown research: they investigate consumer information on products, read manufacturers' brochures, do internet searches, talk to salespeople, and get opinions from other consumers. After they have collected all their data, they evaluate it, often by comparing and contrasting the information.

Purpose 9: To Determine the Authenticity of a Source

A critical skill in life is to be able to estimate what kind of information is being provided and determine if it is reliable. For example, most people use the internet to do personal or academic research, but it is not always easy to judge if the information is accurate or if the person providing it is really the expert he claims to be. Students must pay close attention to the sources they use for their research. Bad sources lead to misinformation.

In all circumstances, effective evaluation on an important issue is not simply a case of whether someone likes it or not. Extremely useful for evaluating is having a set of criteria by which evaluation is referenced and measured.

Exercise 3 Recognizing the Purposes of Evaluation

Work in pairs for this exercise. Read each of the scenario statements that follow. Use the purposes for evaluation outlined in the previous section as your guide, and decide which purpose for evaluation bests suits each situation. Then write the number after each statement. Be prepared to explain and defend your selection.

1. A large engineering firm has been hired to construct a floodway system for a small prairie city. It is now one month into the project.
2. Several English students are doing an assignment together on the Canadian poet George Bowering. They have come across some copies of letters purportedly written by one of his acquaintances. The group wants to include some of the information found in the letters.
3. A new employee is being considered for a permanent position as a system information technologist.
4. Two sisters are planning to buy a used car together. They have never owned a car before and are uncertain what to look for.
5. A student lawyer is just about to take her final exams; after this, if she passes, she will be accepted into "the bar."
6. A tenant is complaining to his landlord about the condition of the small, expensive apartment he rents. He has provided the landlord with a document outlining his concerns.
7. The board of governors at the University of Prestige is wanting to adopt a set of policies from another university to be applied to its three new on-campus daycare centres.
8. The professor who teaches English 200, Advanced Composition, regularly asks students to do peer reviews of their working drafts before they hand in assignments.
9. A new program offered by the local municipality through its Continuing Studies Branch is under threat of being cut. The program called "Teenagers as Coaches" has been extremely popular. Many community members do not want to see the program deleted from Continuing Studies.
10. A young police officer, only on the job for three weeks, meets an aggressive driver whom the officer has asked to pull over. The driver claims he does not need to provide information on a form the officer has handed him.
11. The town council of a small Ontario town wants to know if the new information retrieval system it has purchased is working effectively.
12. The president of a large Canadian university is in her third year of a five-year appointment. Some faculty members claim the president is not doing a very good job. Others suggest she has been very effective.

WHAT ARE THE TYPES OF EVALUATION?

Many forms and types of evaluation exist in different fields of study, governments, organizations, companies, and industries. Companies are interested in measuring the quality of their goods and services. Fields of study are interested in reviewing the quality of their research and the state of their combined knowledge. Organizations want to measure their performance in terms of the outcomes they have set for themselves. Good governments aim for accountability and must measure objectives and commitments on a continuous basis.

As an individual, you, too, are deeply involved in different types of evaluations. As a worker, you will probably have experienced a performance evaluation that looks at the quality of your work. As a student, you will have had to write tests and exams, do assignments, write term papers, prepare speeches, and work on various other projects related to your coursework. As a student in a professional program, such as nursing or dentistry, your evaluation will also include measures of your performance as a professional in your field. As a patient, you may have had to go through a series of diagnostic tests to evaluate the function of an organ, injured limb, or course of a disease or ailment. Indeed, in many aspects and roles in your life, you will encounter evaluation of some sort.

The form of evaluation you select will relate to your purpose, so once you have established your purpose for evaluating something, it will be much easier to select the type or form of evaluation you want to use. Although there are many types and forms of evaluation, the following are common.

Evaluations That Measure How a Person, Program, or Organization Has Behaved

1. *Performance evaluation*: As an employee of a company or organization, you may have experienced this form of evaluation. Your employer wants to evaluate you as an employee, using some sort of rating scale with performance criteria. Some performance criteria may include how well you work without supervision, how you get along with others, what kinds of initiative you take in your position, if you are co-operative, if you are helpful to customers, if you strive to be the best you can be in the position, and so forth. Students in medical training programs, dental hygiene, social work, engineering, theatre arts, visual arts, and education will find performance evaluations are commonly carried out. Their professional skills will be evaluated throughout their programs and will become part of their graduation criteria. There are different levels of performance evaluations that can take place, from the trainee up to senior management.

   The Conference Board of Canada has developed its *Employability Skills 2000+* for the modern workplace. One section, "Work with Others," is particularly relevant to evaluation and performance on the job. Fundamental skills, such as "ensure that a team's purpose and objectives are clear" and "understand and work within the dynamics of a group" are particularly important workplace skills. The section "Participate in Projects & Tasks" relates directly to evaluation, with skills such as being able to "work to agreed quality standards and specifications," "select and use appropriate tools and technology for a task or project," and "continuously monitor the success of a project or task and identify ways to improve." All attest to workers' having evaluation knowledge and capability.

2. *Developmental evaluation*: This type of evaluation occurs as a project is in progress, so as learning takes place, goals and outcomes emerge and are assessed.

3. *Efficiency evaluation*: This evaluation looks at how well resources are being used or how cost-effective something is.

4. *Program evaluation*: Educators evaluate how well a program performs: if programs meet program outcomes, if participants are satisfied, if graduates are successful, and so forth. Student evaluations are often part of program evaluations.

5. *Self-assessment*: You evaluate your own performance according to a set of predetermined criteria or ones you have developed for the task. Sometimes you will be asked to do a self-assessment of your work in a course or on the job. This self-assessment is used along with other evaluations from supervisors, colleagues, or, in the case of colleges or universities, your instructors or professors, to determine your overall performance evaluation.

Evaluations That Provide Written Feedback

1. *Reviews*: After reviewers attend performances, events, or films, they write evaluations about them: these can be positive or negative. Reviewers often use criteria they develop themselves.

2. *Critical reviews*: Reviewers evaluate the quality of text: books, plays, articles, or studies.

3. *Source evaluations*: Students and scholars want to assess the quality of sources, often written, for including in research work. As a student, you will be most interested in source evaluations as you become involved in writing a research paper. You will practise evaluating sources in Chapter 12: Critical Skills: Researching.

Exercise 4 Finding Examples

Bring an example of an evaluation to class. The evaluation can come from a book, magazine, internet site, report, film, or broadcast. Be prepared to answer two questions in connection with your evaluation:

1. What is the purpose of the evaluation?

2. What type of evaluation is it?

Be prepared to share your answers with the rest of the class.

HOW DO THINKERS EVALUATE? A TOOL KIT

As a thinking reader, you want to develop your powers to analyze and evaluate what you read. Here are some tools to help you. You must be able to distinguish fact from opinion, pay attention to underlying assumptions the writer makes, ask creative questions, and establish some criteria for evaluating ideas and arguments. You will also pick up tips and strategies as you experience more and different learning situations in your studies. These tactics will make up your critical thinking tool kit.

As you work through the following section, think over what other critical strategies you have found useful when you analyze and evaluate. How do they fit with new or different applications? Can you adapt old strategies to new situations easily? What new ideas might you be able to share with your peers?

Critical thinking skills must be practised and developed over time. The skills you learn in one area of your education or work can often be adapted to another. As an adaptable thinker, begin to add new strategies to your tool kit and get rid of ones that clutter or get in your way.

Check Facts and Opinions

As mentioned previously, facts are based on evidence and proof, but opinions are based on personal beliefs or tastes. Sometimes it can be difficult to tell them apart, particularly if a writer or speaker seems to be presenting compelling arguments.

Examples:

Statement 1:
My friend Toni has a delightful Jack Russell terrier; it's the best breed in the world because it is so much fun.

Statement 2:
Toni says Jack Russells make wonderful pets because they are curious, playful, and faithful.

Which statement is a fact, and which is an opinion? Why?

Statement 1:
My friend Toni has a delightful Jack Russell terrier; it's the best breed in the world because it is so much fun. (opinion)

Statement 2:
Toni says Jack Russells make wonderful pets because they are curious, playful, and faithful. (fact)

Read the following paragraph. Which statements are facts? Which are opinions?

Many collectors who have an interest in fashion have recently discovered a hidden treasure most have overlooked—the beaded purse, once a popular fashion accessory for discerning consumers of Europe and North America. Various fine examples are still available to the collector looking for entry-level items. Many are still available at a cheap price, from $150–$200. What a bargain that is! Of course, nothing is as beautiful as these old pieces, especially the ones with landscapes, portraits, or floral motifs, all crafted in various colours, sizes, and shapes of glass beads. One from 1910 shows a scene that depicts Count Ludwig's castle in Bavaria. As movies and movie stars rose to fame in North America in the early 20th century, fashion items were manufactured to meet the growing demand of fans. A celebrity series of mesh and beaded bags was produced: one displays Clark Gable on its front. Bags like these celebrity bags are very garish and should be avoided since they are not in good taste.

Which statements did you choose as facts? Which did you think were opinions? Sometimes writers will slip opinions into a discussion but will present them as facts.

Notice that the opinions in the piece are hidden in a small crowd of facts. How could the opinion statements be changed to indicate they are just opinions?

Exercise 5 Facts and Opinions

Work in a group of three to five people. Together, decide whether each of the following statements is a fact or an opinion. Explain the reasons for your choices.

1. Cephalopods have three hearts, can change colour, and are jet powered.

 ____

 ____

2. Brad Pitt is not as handsome as Cary Grant.

 ____

 ____

3. Because most parts of Canada have such cold winters, people from other countries do not want to visit here.

 ____

 ____

4. The legal blood-alcohol limit of 80 milligrams of alcohol for every 100 millilitres of blood in a driver's body is ludicrous; the legal limit should be lowered.

 ____

 ____

5. The world's most popular tourist attraction is Disneyland in California.

 ____

 ____

6. I am in favour of a four-day workweek because it helps people become better parents.

 ____

 ____

7. Professional hockey players playing for the NHL and basketball players playing for the NBA are overpaid.

 ____

 ____

8. The reason Tina's eight-year-old is such a brat is that Tina and Bob spoil her rotten.

 ____

 ____

9. The longest highway in Canada is the Trans-Canada Highway.

____

____

10. If you eat a lot of fish when you are pregnant, you will have a boy.

____

____

11. Alfred's Noodle House is a far better restaurant than Lon's Northern Cuisine.

____

____

12. Ontario has the best sport fishing in the entire country.

____

____

13. Magnesium and calcium are important to building strong bones in children and assisting bone density in the elderly.

____

____

14. Owning a cellphone is absolutely critical for everyone today.

____

____

15. Chamomile tea can soothe upset stomachs and can ease tension.

____

____

Exercise 6 Writing an Opinion

Write a short paragraph of about 100 words on your opinions about driving. Include three factual statements in your paragraph, and underline them. Bring a word-processed copy of your paragraph to class in order to share it with someone else. Your instructor will ask you to work in pairs to share your work.

Uncover Assumptions

You will recall that an *assumption* is a statement that is taken for granted as being true. Many arguments are based on false assumptions. As a thinker, you must uncover assumptions in arguments and test whether they are true or false, fact, or merely someone's opinion.

Examples:

1. Rodney won't want to work for that company when he hears about the recent cutting of employee benefits.
2. Voyageurs of the 17th and 18th centuries in Canada are the real heroes of the fur trade.
3. The brisk rise in housing starts, together with the real estate boom, helps to bring prosperity to the province.

First of all, why are these statements assumptions? Read each one carefully, and try to uncover what each is claiming as a "truth." Also, consider from whose point of view the statement is written.

1. Rodney won't want to work for that company when he hears about the recent cutting of employee benefits.

   What "truth" is being claimed? ______________________

   Whose point of view is this? ______________________

   Is someone being served by this point of view? ______________________

   Who? ______________________

   Who is being left out? ______________________

   How could this statement be changed to make it clearly an opinion?

   ____

   ____

2. Voyageurs of the 17th and 18th centuries in Canada are the real heroes of the fur trade.

   What "truth" is being claimed? ______________________

   Whose point of view is this? ______________________

   Is someone being served by this point of view? ______________________

   Who? ______________________

   Who is being left out? ______________________

   How could this statement be changed to make it clearly an opinion?

   ____

   ____

3. The brisk rise in housing starts, together with the real estate boom, helps to bring prosperity to the province.

   What "truth" is being claimed? ______________________

   Whose point of view is this? ______________________

   Is someone being served by this point of view? ______________________

Who? ____

Who is being left out? ______________________________

How could this statement be changed to make it clearly an opinion?

____

____

As you read in order to evaluate someone's claims, it is important to check out assumptions. Often writers may be unaware that their assumption sits on questionable ground, but some writers knowingly employ assumptions because they recognize that these statements are not so easy to spot. In addition, they also know that if readers are not reading and thinking critically, the assumptions will remain unchallenged. Some marketing and advertising firms are aware of this fact and take full advantage.

Examples:

From advertising pages in national women's magazines:

- Beautifully crafted for those people who've acquired both the taste and the means for the finer things in life.
- The gorgeous YOU you've always wanted to be!
- Create a true spa experience—right in your own home!
- Have a perfect smile in only 12 days!
- Turn heads with your sense of style.
- Along with your body, get your skin in shape!

What underlying assumptions do you see in these statements?
What comments do the statements make about women in general?
Who is being served by these statements?
Who is being left out of the picture in these statements?

Exercise 7 *Looking for Assumptions*

Select an advertisement from a newspaper, magazine, or webpage. Study it for a few minutes, paying attention to the language used in the ad. Evaluate the piece of advertising from the standpoint of the assumptions it is making. Write about 100 words about the piece and its assumptions. Respond to questions such as the following:

- What assumptions are made?
- Which statements are assumptions?
- Why?
- Whose point of view is this?
- Who is being left out?
- Why are these assumptions being made, in your opinion?

Bring your ad and your 100-word piece to class to share. The instructor may post everyone's pieces or may ask you to talk about your work.

Ask Creative Questions

In the previous sections on facts, opinions, and assumptions, you have been introduced to the importance of asking effective questions. Thinkers learn to ask the "right" questions—the ones that will help tease out needed information. These people have trained themselves to pay attention to the claims and assumptions within other people's arguments, whether verbal or written.

You know how important questions are in your classes. Professors or instructors often ask questions of classes, groups, or individuals, and most encourage creative questioning from their students.

Sometimes students ask questions. Have you ever noticed yourself thinking, "Wow! That was a good question!" after someone in a class asks it? You might have felt shy or uncomfortable asking questions yourself because sometimes you may not be sure what questions to ask. Everyone has been in a course where someone continually asks questions, many of them annoying because they are procedural questions that could be answered after class. Some questions can be helpful while others are simply time-wasters or attention-getters. As a student, you should ask questions on three levels: in your courses, in small group project work, or in independent study or work.

Different questions suit different purposes. Guiding questions are appealing because they can lead discussion or help participants navigate, while reflective questioning can help you gain more understanding of an issue or point. A guiding question is useful in small group work when you want to assist the group in meeting its discussion goals for the session. On the other hand, if you are reading a work of fiction, a difficult article, theory, or study, you will want to use reflective thinking, which means asking questions that will cause you to think more deeply about what you are reading and about how the reading relates to other reading you have done or experiences you have had.

Remember: good questions are really valuable because they deepen discussion and thinking.

General Guidelines to Asking Creative Questions

In classes:

- Will the answer to this question add new information to the discussion?
- Is my question clear and on the topic?
- Does my question show a different perspective on the topic?
- Does my question lead to more discussion?
- Do I think my question will be of interest to others in the class?
- Do I need clarification on a point?
- Is there something else I have read or experienced that I want to compare with the point or discussion, but I am not sure how the two might relate? How could I frame my question so that the two points relate? (Try something like this: "I was reading an article by Prof. X. In it, he suggested Y. Does this fit with what we are discussing here?")

In small group projects:

- How should we organize this or that?
- Does anyone in the group want to do this or that?
- Does anyone in the group have this or that special skill?
- Did anyone have any problems with this or that? What were they?
- I seemed to be having problems with this or that. Did anyone else have that problem?
- Do we want some guidelines for working together?
- What should those guidelines be?

In independent study and work:

- Do I understand what I am being asked to do in the assignment?
- Do I really understand what the author is saying in this passage or article?
- Is this the author's opinion?
- Where are the assumptions in this passage or article?
- What else have I read or experienced that relates to this?
- How does it relate?
- What conclusions has the writer reached?
- What evidence or proof has he or she provided to convince me?
- How are these conclusions different from anything else I have read?
- Is this a reliable source?
- Whose point of view does this represent?
- Who is being left out of the picture?

Certainly, there are many more questions you can ask, but these will start you thinking more creatively about the kinds of questions you pose. The idea is to learn to focus your questions, make them more precise, and use them as a tool to enrich your thinking life and your learning experiences.

Finally, start to pay attention not just to who asks questions in your courses but also to what types of questions are being asked. If you like the kinds of questions someone asks because the questions lead to interesting discussion, then jot down the person's questions. Consider:

- Are the questions open-ended? That is, do they open discussion and not have a yes or no response?
- Do the questions begin with *how*, *why*, *what*, or *when*? These interrogative pronouns lead to open responses, rather than to yes or no answers.

Exercise 8 Practice in Creative Questioning

Read the following article. Then think of three questions you might ask that will lead to further discussion or understanding. Work in pairs. Try to think of open-ended questions, not ones that will lead to yes or no answers. Each person in the pair will ask the other each of the prepared questions. Then you will discuss possible answers together. After your discussion, talk about whether the questions helped discussion or not. In what ways was discussion helped? Be prepared to share your questions and responses with the rest of the class.

Video Game Violence Linked to Aggression in Real Life

by Tom Spears

Your heart pumps and your knuckles are white as you aim your weapon, waiting for the video game's antagonists to leap at you from ambush.

Just a game? Your brain doesn't think so.

Scientists suspect this may be why young men who spend hours a day playing violent video games show high levels of aggression in real life.

"This is not just a game," German scientist Klaus Mathiak concludes. The University of Tubingen neuroscientist analysed the brains of men aged 18 to 26 who are avid players of "first-person shooter" games.

It was a small study: Just 13 men who play video games for 20 hours a week on average.

Mathiak put the men in an MRI. They lay on their backs with their heads in the scanning device and their hands free to work the controls of a violent video game.

As they played, the machine recorded what parts of their brains were active.

As each player entered a dangerous part of the game, his brain "lit up" with activity in a brain area associated with aggression, called the dorsal portion of the anterior cingulate cortex.

This high level of activity shows the players had a feeling of reality and "being there," says a summary of the research by the University of Southern California, which worked with the German team.

And as the fighting began, there was a drop in activity in another part of the brain, the amygdala. This is an emotion centre, where a person feels empathy with others, among other things.

Mathiak's conclusion: It's possible that reinforcing the circuits the brain uses to respond to a crisis with aggression, even violence, may prime the brain to act the same way in real life. After all, to the brain, the video game itself seems to be real.

REVIEW TEST

Try the following review test. It will help you assess what you have learned from the chapter. Be prepared to share your responses with others in the class.

1. Provide a clear definition of *evaluation*.

____

____

____

2. What five steps should you use to complete an evaluation?

____

____

____

3. Define the following terms:

- a fact ______________________________________
- an opinion __________________________________
- an assumption _______________________________
- analysis ____________________________________
- criteria ____________________________________
- accountability ______________________________
- feedback ____________________________________
- a valid argument ____________________________
- a sound argument ____________________________

____

____

____

4. Name five purposes of evaluation.

____

____

____

5. What types of evaluations are there? How do purpose and type of evaluation relate?

____

____

____

6. Below, write *O* after each statement that is an opinion and *F* after each statement that is a fact:

- Prince Edward Island is Canada's most beautiful province. ______
- A player should be at least 180 cm tall and 80 kg if she is going to play competitive basketball. ______
- A neuron is a cell in the nervous system of mammals specialized in its capability to conduct and generate electrical impulses. ______
- Sharks are the most feared creatures on earth. ______

- To ensure thermal comfort, building engineers should hold office temperatures at a constant range of 21–23 degrees Celsius. ______

7. What is a creative question? Write one about this chapter.

____

____

____

8. In a paragraph of 200 words, describe what evaluation is and what its purposes are. Double-space your work. Be prepared: your instructor may ask you to write this assignment in class in 20–25 minutes.

Assignment 1

With another person from the class, find two different movie reviews about the same movie. Develop a set of criteria for evaluating the two reviews. Evaluate the two reviews using the criteria. Bring the reviews, your criteria, and your evaluation to class to share with others.

Assignment 2

Using the same two reviews, your criteria, and your evaluation, write an essay of 700 words. Have your partner peer-review your essay, and, in turn, review your partner's essay.

Bonus Exercise The Subjunctive Tense

Occasionally you write something describing a wish, hypothesis, or condition that seems to go against the facts. In such a situation, you may use an unusual verb tense or mood called the subjunctive tense. Usually subjunctives are used with clauses beginning with *if* or *that*. Sometimes subjunctive mood relates to command or authority.

In the subjunctive mood, use *be* for the verb *to be* in the present tense. Use *were* in the past. Drop the *s* or *es* in the third person, present when using the subjunctive.

Examples:

If I <u>were</u> Uncle Squibb, I would grow wings and fly away!

The government's requirement is that everyone wear a seatbelt.

The governess commanded that the children be silent.

Form the subjunctive tense for each of the following situations. Check your answers with the Answer Key.

1. Doris is not kind to you. You want Doris to be kinder.

____

____

2. The supervisor of parking, J.K. Ruck, requests Bettina to move her car to another parking spot.

____

____

3. The health authority warns all new parents to have their infants immunized.

____

____

4. You make a wish. You want the moon to be made of green cheese.

____

____

5. The municipality requires new licences for farms under one hectare.

____

____

READING

Where Are Students Learning the Most?

A study of 610 universities suggests that smaller schools are best—and finds Canadian universities falling short of their U.S. peers

by Sandy Farran and Tony Keller

Sandy Farran is a journalist who writes for *Maclean's* and *The Globe and Mail.* Tony Keller is managing editor, special projects, for *Maclean's*.

It's mid-January, a couple of weeks after the Christmas break, and Mark Woodcroft, a fourth-year biochemistry major at Trent University, is hanging out in the lab with professor Steven Rafferty, his research supervisor and chair of Trent's chemistry department. Woodcroft is doing what many Canadian undergraduates never get a chance to do: an independent research project under faculty supervision.

So, a reporter asks, what's your research project about? Woodcroft casts a sly smile at his prof and then launches deadpan into an explanation of the "bioaccumulation of perfluorinated carboxylic acids." His audience predictably befuddled, Woodcroft stops mid-sentence. He and Rafferty chuckle in unison. It sounds like a well-rehearsed routine. Not something many 22-year-olds get to cook up with a professor.

"In upper-year courses, the class size is small enough for a professor to know each student by name," says Woodcroft. "I also know everyone in my program by name. I doubt many students at a larger school can say that."

Personal contact with faculty members, a sense of community among undergrads and classes that push students to their intellectual limits—these are all things that many undergraduate students desire. Research suggests that these also promote learning; in the language of the National Survey of Student Engagement, these and other aspects of student engagement are "correlates of quality." And according to the NSSE Benchmarks of Effective Educational Practice results appearing on the following pages . . . undergraduate educational quality at Canadian universities—with only a few exceptions—is below that of American universities.

On the following pages, you will also find results from the Canadian Undergraduate Survey Consortium, or CUSC, a Canada-only survey that is much more tilted toward assessing student satisfaction. In 2007, CUSC surveyed first-year students at 32 universities. The answers to two key CUSC student satisfaction questions are featured on page 46. NSSE asked two student satisfaction questions as well; the results for those questions are also published here.

While undergraduate student satisfaction remains relatively high at Canadian institutions, the NSSE benchmark results suggest a different story: satisfied or not, many Canadian university campuses are not as engaging and may not be offering as good an educational experience as their American peers. And the problem is particularly pronounced at Canada's large research universities—the schools educating the overwhelming majority of Canadian undergraduates.

The American-based NSSE (pronounced "Nessie") has been conducting its survey on a growing number of campuses, and calculating its Benchmarks of Effective Educational Practice for each participating school. Beginning in 2004, a growing number of Canadian universities began to take part in NSSE. The biggest push came from Bob Rae's 2005 review of post-secondary education in Ontario. Rae called on the province to establish measures for evaluating quality and publicly reporting on system performance. In his review, Rae asked, "How are we doing? How are others doing? Is there a jurisdiction that does it better?" His conclusion: "We simply don't know enough about how we are doing or how others are doing." To this end, Rae recommended that all Ontario universities participate in NSSE. All Ontario universities have done so over the past two years, and most universities in the rest of the country have joined them. Several of the 47 universities that *Maclean's* surveys in its annual rankings of Canadian universities have never participated in NSSE; they include Bishop's University, Cape Breton University, St. Francis Xavier University, Memorial University, Université de Moncton and Université de Sherbrooke.

Most universities on both sides of the border initially kept their NSSE and CUSC reports confidential or only released selected bits of information; it was only after *Maclean's*, backed by the power of provincial access to information laws, began asking for NSSE and CUSC results that the majority of Canadian universities began to go public. We began asking for the latest survey results four months ago; the only ranked university that failed to make public all of its NSSE and CUSC information in time for publication was the University of Manitoba.

On the following pages, you will find results for 41 Canadian institutions that participated in NSSE in 2005, 2006 or 2007. NSSE asks first-year and fourth-year undergraduates at participating schools nearly 100 questions about what they have been doing during their university careers. It is not a student satisfaction survey; it asks students to report on the mechanics of their classes, student habits and life at university. The questions—from how often they met outside of class with faculty members to how often they were involved in group work with other students—cover aspects of educational practice that have been shown to promote student engagement, which itself has been shown to promote more and better learning.

For example, faculty-supervised, independent research projects like the one undertaken by Woodcroft would have helped to boost a university's Student-Faculty Interaction, Enriching Educational Experiences and Level of Academic Challenge benchmark scores.

"What's important to stress is that NSSE doesn't directly measure learning outcomes. It measures engagement," says Ken Norrie of the Higher Education Quality Council of Ontario (HEQCO), which advises government on improving all aspects of post-secondary education, including quality, access and accountability. "If you believe in years of research that engagement is consistently highly correlated with learning outcomes, and we can measure engagement through something like the NSSE survey, then we have a proxy for learning outcomes which you can roughly associate with learning quality."

So what do the NSSE benchmarks tell us about the undergraduate learning experience at Canadian universities? A good number of Canadian universities—mostly smaller, primarily undergraduate institutions, but including larger institutions such as Ryerson, Queen's and McMaster—met or exceeded the 2007 NSSE Level of Academic Challenge benchmark average of the results from 610 mostly American universities. The academic challenge benchmark is made up of questions covering areas such as how much time students spent preparing for class, the number of textbooks assigned, number of written papers assigned, and coursework that emphasizes analyzing and synthesizing ideas.

A fair number of Canadian universities—again, mostly smaller institutions—also exceeded the NSSE benchmark for Supportive Campus Environment. The supportive campus environment benchmark focuses on whether the campus provides the support students need to succeed academically and thrive socially, and assesses the quality of students' relationships with their peers, professors and the administration.

But on the remaining three benchmarks, few Canadian universities met the American standard. A handful of small, primarily undergraduate schools, led by Mount Allison University and Acadia University, are among those that consistently exceeded their American peers. Interestingly, while the University of Western Ontario did not register above-average scores, two of Western's affiliated colleges—Huron and Brescia—scored highly in all areas.

The Student-Faculty Interaction benchmark—where no Canadian university exceeded the NSSE first-year benchmark and only three surpassed the fourth-year average—focuses on the different ways that students interact with faculty members inside and outside of the classroom. Students are asked, for example, whether they have worked with a professor on activities outside of coursework, talked about career plans with a faculty member, received prompt feedback from faculty on their academic performance and worked with a faculty member on a research project.

The overwhelming majority of Canadians students attend large, research-focused universities. Can institutions of such size offer top-level undergraduate experiences, as defined by NSSE? Results from the University of Michigan, a giant public university that is also one of America's leading research powerhouses, suggests that it is possible.

What is Michigan doing right in undergraduate education? Earlier this decade, Michigan was one of 20 American universities identified by NSSE as having outperformed on the NSSE benchmarks. A NSSE commissioned study visited each of the outperforming campuses to find out what practices were leading to those high NSSE benchmark scores. For example, explaining Michigan's success on the Student-Faculty Interaction benchmark, the study cited Michigan's small classes and research opportunities in the first-year; programs that encourage students and faculty to eat meals together; mentorship programs; extensive email contact between students and faculty and professors' offices that are located in residences. On the Level of Academic Challenge benchmark, the study pointed to a commitment to excellence that permeates the entire Michigan campus; faculty resistance to grade inflation, introductory courses designed to challenge students' ability to problem solve, and small classes that encourage active learning and challenge students to develop critical thinking and independence in carrying out research projects.

NSSE director Alex McCormick says while universities can use NSSE to improve, "these are things that take some intentional effort to move the needle on. It's not quite as simple as stepping on the accelerator in your car." And while he believes that universities can learn a lot about best practices from one another, he cautions that it's not always easy to make direct comparisons. Schools that enrol a large number of adults or commuters, for example, are likely to have lower scores because students have less time to spend on campus and, as a result, tend to be less engaged than traditional undergrads living on campus. Yet the same school's more traditional undergraduate population may be just as engaged as undergrads at other campuses. "There is a robust body of evidence that shows that the vast majority of the variation in individual student scores is within institutions, not between institutions," says McCormick. "So if you look at all the individual students that are surveyed and look at the variation in their responses to the NSSE items, about 90 per cent of that variation occurs within institutions and only about 10 per cent is between institutions." As a result, says McCormick, "distilling it down to a number or set of numbers for an institution" may mask variations among departments or faculties at the same university. McCormick says that NSSE needs to find ways "to help institutional leaders look more deeply into variations within their walls." In other words, the really interesting story may be one like that of the benchmark scores from Western's affiliate colleges, which are above those of Western itself.

Norrie of Ontario's HEQCO sees a similar promise in NSSE. Canadian universities are mostly still in the early stages of drilling down to examine variations among faculties, departments, courses and even gender and ethnic background. But Norrie says he regularly hears from university administrators who have hit on revealing findings. "When you start doing variations in NSSE results across faculties or departments, and you find some interesting variations, you say, 'Okay, what's going on?'" says Norrie. "And that gets you into a conversation about what explains the variation and the different ways of teaching and learning."

Phil Wood, associate vice-president of student affairs at McMaster University, has established his own mini-benchmark from a set of 16 NSSE questions that zero in on an area of particular interest to him: student growth and development. Because Wood oversees student services, he's interested in figuring out things like: is it beneficial for a student to live in residence? Do students living in residence report higher NSSE engagement scores and higher score on his mini-benchmark?

In 2005, the University of Toronto—an institution that is in many ways similar to the University of Michigan in terms of its vast size and the quality and breadth of the graduate and research programs it offers—hired American Tony Chambers to fill a newly created position, associate vice-provost of students. Having worked at post-secondary institutions in both countries, Chambers is often called upon to discuss the uses, and limits of NSSE, particularly in the Canadian context.

"The systems are considerably and extremely nuanced and I think for us to compare what happens in the States to what happens in Canada is sort of a worthless analysis, to be quite honest," says Chambers. "It gives us a sense of what institutions are doing for sure, where we can make some decisions at an institutional level, but in terms of systems of education, I don't think the analysis is worth a whole lot, quite honestly."

Chambers says that some NSSE questions use terms not in wide currency in Canada, or terms that some students may interpret differently than their American peers. This could affect the answers offered by Canadians.

Despite its limitations, NSSE is proving to be a valuable diagnostic tool for Canadian universities. Back at Trent, president Bonnie Patterson says NSSE has helped to validate what she and her colleagues already knew: that Trent is a smaller, tighter-knit campus, where students experience a good number of small classes, with professors who will probably know them by their first name, and opportunities to do research or independent study with a faculty member.

For Patterson, NSSE's value-added is that it offers comparisons among institutions, and highlights areas needing improvement. Partly in response to its findings, Patterson says that Trent has channelled resources into five key areas, including library resources and technology in the classroom. There is always a much longer list of what you can't do than the list of what you can do," she says. "Would I have loved to put money into hiring another 15 or 20 faculty members? You bet. You have to find the balance of what makes you successful in student opinion and in satisfaction and what makes you successful in learning outcomes, but at the same time trying to be responsive to them almost from a consumer perspective."

All Canadian universities struggle with trade-offs: whether to hire more professors or build an athletic complex; upgrade labs; fund new research or offer more undergrad course selection. Like Patterson, university administrators say that surveys such as NSSE and CUSC have helped in that process. "It validates, it informs, it gives us a better insight into the detail of issues," says Patterson. "Rather than our own serendipitous, ad hoc examples of anecdotes, it gives you large opinion pieces that we didn't have before we got into these surveys."

THE SURVEYS: WHAT THEY ARE, AND HOW THEY WERE DONE

The following pages contain the results from two major study surveys: the National Survey of Student Engagement (NSSE) and the Canadian Undergraduate Survey Consortium (CUSC). The NSSE and CUSC surveys, which were commissioned by the universities, ask more than 150 questions about specific aspects of the undergraduate experience—inside the classroom and beyond—designed to provide universities with data to help them assess programs and services.

The U.S.-based NSSE began in 1999 and is distributed to first- and second-year students. NSSE is not primarily a student satisfaction survey, but is rather a study of best-educational practices, and an assessment of the degree to which each university follows those best practices. In 2004, 11 Canadian universities participated for the first time in NSSE, with 14,267 students completing the survey. By 2006, that number had grown to approximately 60,000 students at 31 Canadian institutions. Seventeen universities or their affiliates participated in the 2007 NSSE, representing roughly 14,000 students—fewer than in 2006 because most institutions conduct the NSSE survey every two years.

The NSSE results are headlined by the Benchmarks of Effective Educational Practice, created by NSSE to compare performance across all universities—American and Canadian—in five key areas: Level of Academic Challenge, Student-Faculty Interaction, Active and Collaborative Learning, Enriching Educational Experience, and Supportive Campus Environment. Each school's benchmark result was calculated by NSSE, based on student responses to a variety of questions. NSSE also asked two important student satisfaction questions: school-by-school results appear on the following pages.

CUSC was created in 1994; it is a Canada-only survey, and unlike NSSE, it is in large part a student satisfaction survey. In 2007, 32 universities took part, including two institutions—UBC and the University of New Brunswick—that surveyed multiple campuses. Surveys were sent to a random sample of approximately 1,000 first-year undergrads at each university. Institutions with fewer than 1,000 first-years surveyed the entire cohort. More than 12,700 students responded.

READING THE CHARTS

The charts published on the accompanying pages list 41 universities, including affiliates, that participated in recent NSSE surveys, as well as 31 university campuses surveyed for the 2007 CSUC. In each chart, universities are listed in descending order. When displaying the NSSE benchmark charts, universities are listed according to the benchmark scores associated with their senior-year students; for student satisfaction questions, order was determined by the percentage of survey participants who chose the highest level of satisfaction when responding, for example, "excellent."

The NSSE and CUSC surveys include more than 150 questions; we have published those—the five key NSSE benchmarks, plus two satisfaction questions each from NSSE and CUSC—that are the most broad and summative of student experience. NSSE charts include universities taking part in the 2006 or 2007 survey—or both, as well as one institution (Regina) that last conducted the survey in 2005. In each case, we display results from the most recent survey year. No data from the first-year students are displayed for Royal Roads University as this institution does not offer first-year courses. Data displayed for the University of Western Ontario do not include results from the three Western affiliates, each of which conducted its own survey.

NATIONAL SURVEY OF STUDENT ENGAGEMENT (NSSE)

Benchmarks of Effective Educational Practice The NSSE survey asks undergrads nearly 1,000 questions to assess how engaged they are with their schools, their professors and their peers. Student engagement has been shown to be highly correlated with learning. The benchmarks compare engagement at all universities—American and Canadian—in five key areas. "Level of Academic Challenge" assesses the intellectual demands on students, measuring such things as the number of assigned readings and written reports, as well as coursework that emphasizes judgment and transforming information into more complex interpretations. "Student-Faculty Interaction" gauges professors as mentors, measuring how often students meet with faculty to discuss career plans or ideas, or work with them on research projects or other activities outside of class.

Level of Academic Challenge

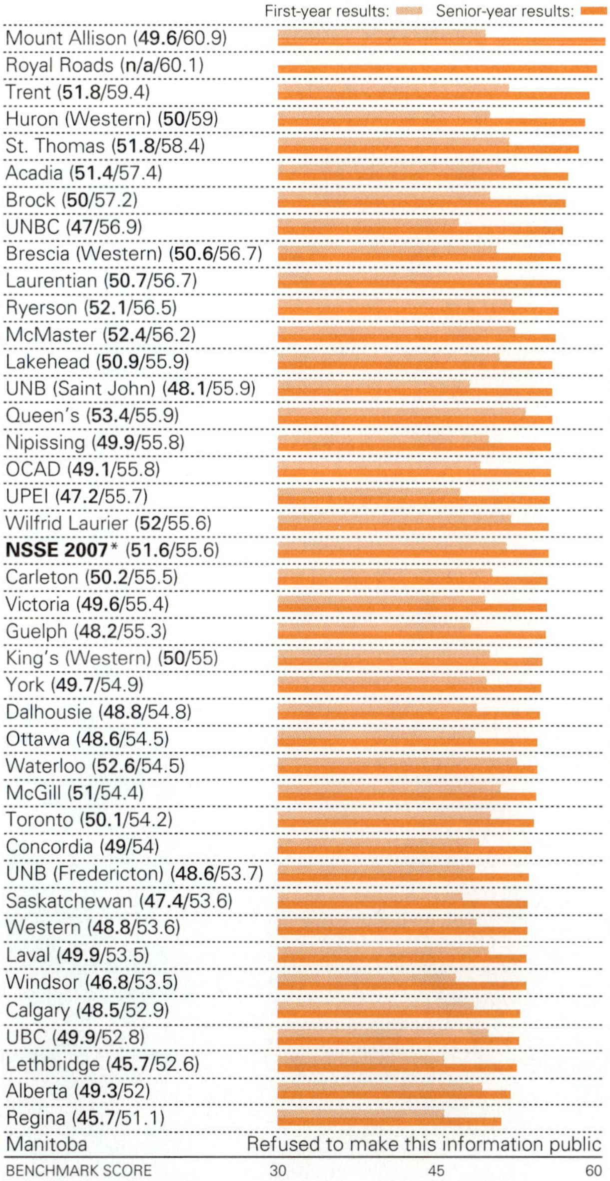

*NSSE 2007 represents results from 610 Canadian and American Universities

Student-Faculty Interaction

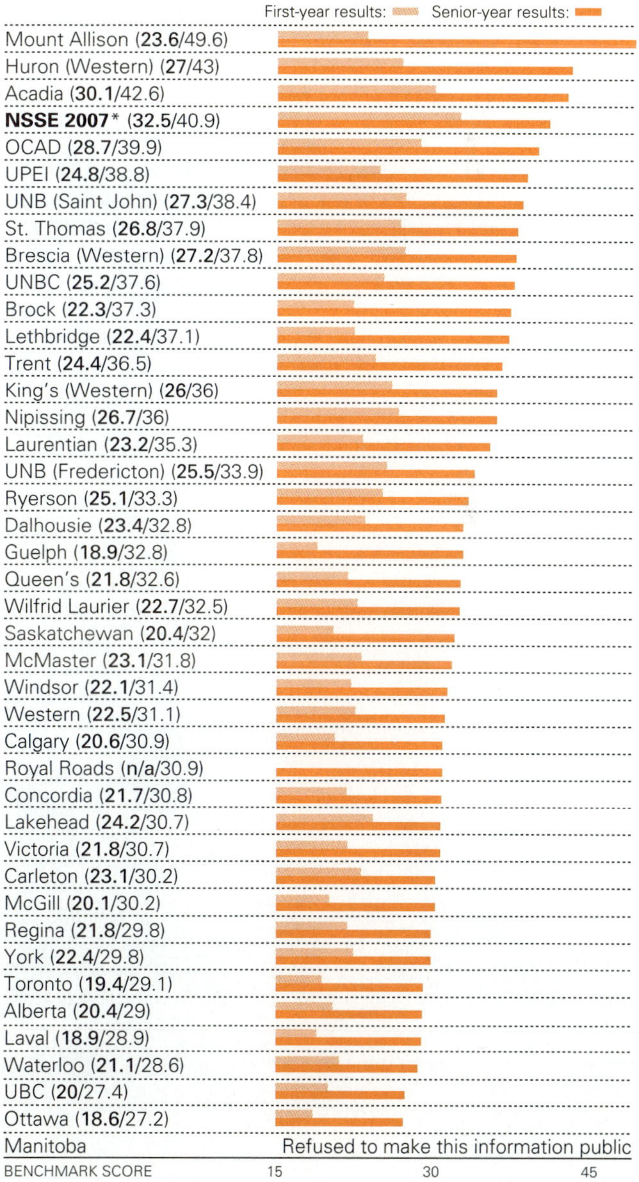

NATIONAL SURVEY OF STUDENT ENGAGEMENT (NSSE)

Benchmarks of Effective Educational Practice The Supportive Campus Environment benchmark recognizes that students perform better at schools that support academic and non-academic endeavours, and that cultivate positive relationships among students, faculty and staff. Surprisingly, scores at many schools decline between first and fourth year.

Supportive Campus Environment

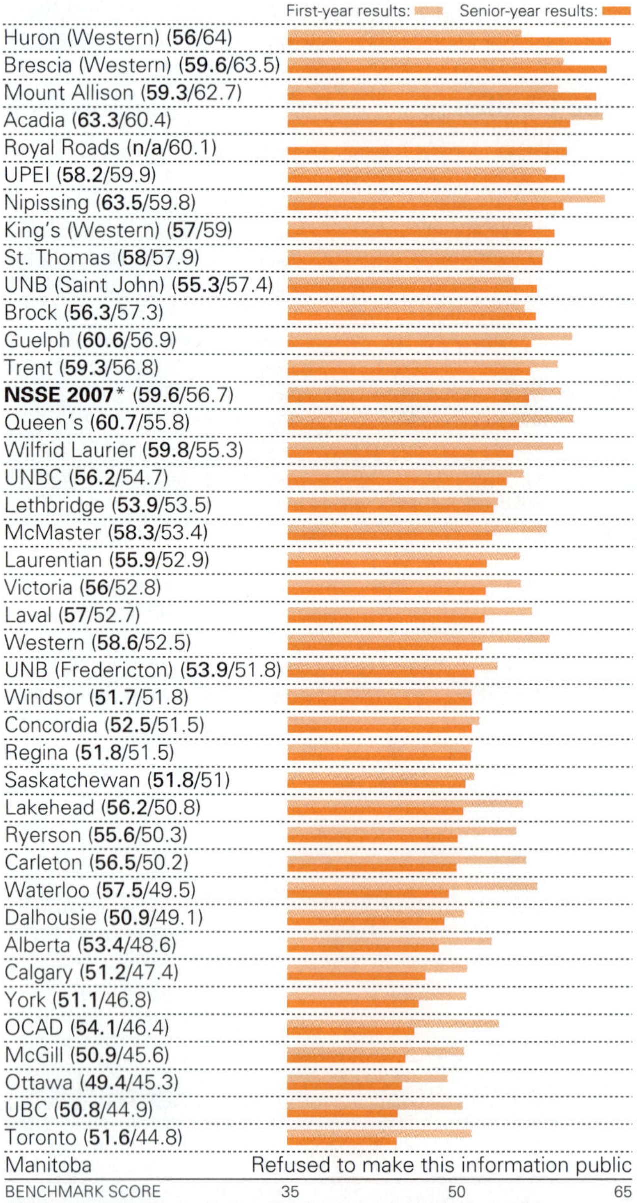

*NSSE 2007 represents results from 610 Canadian and American universities

CANADIAN UNDERGRADUATE SURVEY CONSORTIUM (CUSC)

Student Satisfaction Results The CUSC survey is an annual study, with a focus on student satisfaction. The 2007 survey, whose results are featured below, canvassed first-year students for their opinions. Participating universities sent an extensive questionnaire to a random sampling of up to 1,000 students, asking questions about everything from academics to support services. In 2007, nearly 13,000 students responded.

Generally, I am satisfied with the quality of teaching I have received.

	Strongly Agree (%)	Agree (%)
Nipissing	33	60
Trent	33	62
Wilfrid Laurier	30	63
Brandon	29	64
UOIT	29	57
Winnipeg	29	60
Carleton	26	64
Lethbridge	26	66
Ryerson	26	62
Fraser Valley	25	67
Mount Saint Vincent	24	60
UNB (Fredericton)	24	66
McMaster	23	65
Saskatchewan	23	65
Concordia	22	63
UNB (Saint John)	22	69
Saint Mary's	22	67
Montréal	21	67
UNBC	21	70
UBC (Okanagan)	19	69
Brock	19	72
Victoria	19	70
Dalhousie	17	70
Regina	17	72
Alberta	15	70
Ottawa	15	72
Simon Fraser	15	71
Windsor	14	69
UBC (Vancouver)	13	68
Calgary	13	71
Manitoba	Refused to make this information public	

I am satisfied with my decision to attend this university.

	Strongly Agree (%)	Agree (%)
Nipissing	54	38
Trent	51	40
Wilfrid Laurier	51	42
McMaster	48	45
Mount Saint Vincent	48	42
Winnipeg	46	48
Saskatchewan	45	47
UOIT	44	46
Victoria	42	49
Carleton	41	50
UNB (Fredericton)	41	50
Lethbridge	40	54
Montréal	40	50
Ryerson	40	52
Saint Mary's	40	50
Brandon	39	56
Brock	38	53
Concordia	36	58
Alberta	35	57
Dalhousie	34	54
UNBC	34	58
Regina	34	61
Fraser Valley	33	59
UNB (Saint John)	32	58
Simon Fraser	31	59
UBC (Vancouver)	30	60
Ottawa	30	61
UBC (Okanagan)	28	67
Calgary	25	64
Windsor	22	63
Manitoba	20	70

NATIONAL SURVEY OF STUDENT ENGAGEMENT (NSSE)

Student Satisfaction Results The NSSE survey is not primarily a student satisfaction survey. The main purpose of NSSE is to assess what students are doing . . . not to ask for their opinion. However, NSSE includes some satisfaction questions, including one asking students to evaluate their educational experience. Most institutions' scores declined from first to fourth year.

How would you evaluate your entire educational experience at this institution?

FIRST-YEAR STUDENTS

	Excellent (%)	Good (%)
Queen's	53	38
Western	47	41
Nipissing	45	45
Guelph	43	47
Mount Allison	43	45
Waterloo	41	44
Wilfrid Laurier	40	49
Acadia	39	49
St. Thomas	38	51
McMaster	37	48
King's (Western)	36	49
NSSE 2007*	**34**	**52**
McGill	33	48
Huron (Western)	32	49
Trent	31	51
Victoria	31	55
Lakehead	29	52
OCAD	29	45
Alberta	28	53
Brock	28	53
Carleton	28	53
Laval	27	57
Lethbridge	27	57
Ryerson	27	52
UPEI	26	57
Laurentian	25	54
Brescia (Western)	24	66
UBC	24	50
Dalhousie	23	54
UNB (Fredericton)	23	57
UNBC	23	59
Saskatchewan	23	60
Toronto	22	48
York	20	55
Concordia	19	58
Ottawa	19	59
UNB (Saint John)	18	58
Calgary	17	58
Regina	16	64
Windsor	16	55
Manitoba	Refused to make this information public	

*NSSE 2007 benchmark reflects the overall result for 610 Canadian and American universities

SENIOR-YEAR STUDENTS

	Excellent (%)	Good (%)
Huron (Western)	63	29
Brescia (Western)	57	32
Mount Allison	53	40
King's (Western)	51	41
Guelph	43	46
Trent	43	43
UPEI	41	50
Queen's	41	45
St. Thomas	41	49
Acadia	40	50
Western	38	47
Brock	37	40
UNBC	37	47
Nipissing	36	53
Waterloo	36	47
Wilfrid Laurier	36	52
NSSE 2007*	**34**	**49**
McMaster	34	47
Lethbridge	32	52
Victoria	29	57
McGill	26	52
Royal Roads	26	49
Ryerson	24	51
Alberta	23	56
Windsor	23	53
Carleton	22	57
UNB (Fredericton)	22	56
Concordia	21	55
UNB (Saint John)	21	56
Saskatchewan	21	60
Toronto	21	48
Dalhousie	20	55
Lakehead	20	52
Laurentian	20	53
Laval	20	59
Regina	20	58
UBC	18	52
OCAD	18	59
York	18	53
Calgary	14	53
Ottawa	11	55
Manitoba	Refused to make this information public	

NATIONAL SURVEY OF STUDENT ENGAGEMENT (NSSE)

Student Satisfaction Results NSSE is primarily an objective look at life and learning on campus, but it also asks students to answer a few satisfaction questions. In general, senior students are more critical when evaluating their university experience. While the majority of students would choose to return to their alma mater, the number drops—in some cases sharply—for students in their final year as compared to freshmen.

If you could start over, would you go to the institution you are now attending?

FIRST-YEAR STUDENTS

	Definitely Yes (%)	Probably Yes (%)
Queen's	60	31
Western	60	30
Guelph	54	35
Nipissing	54	35
Mount Allison	53	33
Waterloo	53	36
Wilfrid Laurier	53	36
McGill	52	37
Laval	50	42
St. Thomas	49	37
OCAD	46	45
Huron (Western)	45	39
King's (Western)	45	39
McMaster	45	43
Victoria	45	43
Acadia	43	45
UBC	43	43
NSSE 2007*	**43**	**41**
Alberta	42	46
Trent	42	41
Ryerson	41	44
Laurentian	40	43
Saskatchewan	40	49
Carleton	39	46
Lakehead	39	41
Brock	38	45
Lethbridge	38	49
UPEI	38	46
Brescia (Western)	37	44
Concordia	37	48
UNB (Fredericton)	37	45
Dalhousie	34	45
Toronto	34	43
UNBC	33	54
York	32	51
Ottawa	30	50
Regina	29	57
UNB (Saint John)	27	50
Calgary	26	54
Windsor	26	49
Manitoba	Refused to make this information public	

*NSSE 2007 benchmark reflects the overall result for 610 Canadian and American universities

SENIOR-YEAR STUDENTS

	Definitely Yes (%)	Probably Yes (%)
Huron (Western)	63	23
King's (Western)	56	34
Brescia (Western)	53	32
Guelph	51	34
Mount Allison	51	34
Royal Roads	51	35
St. Thomas	50	37
Acadia	46	38
UPEI	46	41
Wilfrid Laurier	46	36
Brock	45	38
Queen's	45	38
Western	45	38
McGill	44	38
Trent	44	36
Waterloo	44	37
Nipissing	43	41
UNBC	43	43
NSSE 2007*	**42**	**39**
McMaster	41	39
Victoria	39	47
Laval	38	47
Lethbridge	36	45
Alberta	34	50
Saskatchewan	34	49
Concordia	33	48
OCAD	33	50
Ryerson	33	44
UBC	32	45
Carleton	30	46
Laurentian	30	42
Regina	29	49
Toronto	29	39
Lakehead	28	44
Windsor	28	45
UNB (Fredericton)	26	46
UNB (Saint John)	26	47
York	24	45
Dalhousie	21	49
Ottawa	19	47
Calgary	16	50
Manitoba	Refused to make this information public	

Source: Sandy Farran and Tony Keller, "Where Are Students Learning the Most?" Maclean's *Feb 18, 2008: 38–49.*

Comprehension Questions

1. The article suggests that undergraduate students want three things from their institutions of post-secondary education. What are they?
2. What does NSSE stand for?
3. What is a research university?
4. What is the survey evaluating overall, and what is the purpose of the survey?
5. What type of evaluation is involved here?
6. What is a benchmark score?
7. In about 100 words and in summary form, describe the results of the survey.

Critical Comprehension

1. What assumptions are made in the survey and in regard to the results?
2. In 150 words, evaluate the criteria used in the survey, and discuss whether all, some, or none of the criteria are valid.

Assignment

Find your school in the survey and evaluate the results. Write a short essay of 500 words about your evaluation. If your school is not in the survey, write an evaluation of it using the same criteria employed in the survey. Put your evaluation into a 500-word essay. Use a third-person point of view.

CHECKOUT

Here are some of the ideas you will take away with you after you have completed the chapter:

1. Evaluation is a critical thinking skill and a process involving steps.
2. To be a thinking reader, you must analyze and evaluate.
3. It can be difficult to tell fact and opinion apart.
4. Some sources on the internet appear authoritative but are not.
5. Creative research questions are really valuable because they deepen discussion.
6. The Employability Skills 2000+ suggest that all workers need to work with others, manage information, and think and solve problems: these skills are part of evaluation.

Mastering the concepts in this chapter will also help you develop and apply the following employability skills highlighted by the Conference Board of Canada in Employability Skills 2000+:

Communicate

- read and understand information presented in a variety of forms
- use relevant scientific, technological, and mathematical knowledge and skills to explain or clarify

Manage Information

- locate, gather, and organize information using appropriate technology and information systems

Think & Solve Problems

- assess situations and identify problems

Source: Adapted from *Employability Skills 2000+* Brochure E/F (Ottawa: The Conference Board of Canada, 2000).

chapter 8

Academic Writing: An Overview

Chapter Objectives

After completing this chapter you will be able to

1. specify what defines academic writing;
2. recognize the components of academic writing;
3. identify the purposes of academic writing;
4. recognize why documentation styles are important;
5. identify the types of academic writing;
6. define *plagiarism*;
7. describe ways to avoid plagiarism;
8. locate instances of plagiarism in your own writing.

INTRODUCTION

As a student, you will soon discover that academic writing is a major part of your writing life. It is unlike writing letters, blogs, simple book reports, journals, notes, or emails. Academic writing has its own set of demands and rules, so if you are going to be a successful academic writer, you must pay strict attention to what the requirements are. Your instructors and professors will expect you to understand the principles of academic writing and apply them to all of your work.

WHAT IS ACADEMIC WRITING?

You will notice when you are reading for courses that the writing in academic journals, textbooks, academic websites, and periodicals is at a much higher level than in popular magazines, newspapers, regular websites, and modern novels. That is because academic writing must meet scholarly standards in terms of format, language expression, and organization. For example, you may be interested in biology and read current magazines such as *Nature*, *Discover*, or *Science Magazine*. Then, when you take your first biology course in university, you begin to read scholarly biology journals, which are much more demanding to read. In fact, sometimes the difference in intellectual demand can be quite surprising.

This textbook, for example, contains several examples of academic writing from professional journals. In chapter 3, Mike Schmoker's article, "Reading, Writing, and Thinking for All," comes from an academic journal called *Educational Leadership*. Jan Charles Haluska's article in chapter 5, "In Defense of the Formula Essay," is found in another professional journal called *Academic Questions*. You will also see articles in chapters 6, 8, 11, 12, and 13 that come from other academic sources: *Adult Learning*, *Fashion Theory*, *Journal of Adolescent and Adult Literacy*, *Canadian Journal of Rural Medicine*, and *Biologist*. As you read these articles, you will also be learning what academic writing looks like.

Let's look at a working definition of *academic writing* and what sets it apart from other types of writing. Academic writing is structured writing whose purpose is to join scholarly discussion, using critical thinking, investigation, research, analysis, a developed argument, a specific style of discipline-specific documentation for citing research sources, concise and well-edited standard English, and a specified presentation format. Because academic writing is meant to be objective, most often writers use a third-person point of view in the writing.

In their article, "Developing Critical Analysis Skills in Academic Writing," Knowles and McGloin (2007) state that competent academic writing requires "critical analysis in academic assignments" (p. 35). Summarizing the definition of *academic writing* given in the previous passage will help you understand the component parts. Academic writing is (1) structured writing whose purpose is to (2) join scholarly discussion, using (3) critical thinking, (4) investigation, (5) research, (6) analysis, (7) a developed argument, (8) a specific style of discipline-specific documentation for citing research sources, (9) concise and well-edited standard English, and (10) a specified presentation format.

Let's now consider each part of the working definition of academic writing in order to understand how to distinguish this type of writing from any other.

WHAT ARE THE COMPONENTS OF ACADEMIC WRITING?

(1) Structured Writing and (2) Scholarly Discussion

A *scholarly discussion* means that everyone in the discussion has a background in the field of study and understands the critical concepts in the field. Therefore, you must learn how to enter such a discussion.

You should consider academic writing differently for three reasons:

- According to Lloyd (2007) in "Developing Academic Writing Skills: The PROCESS Framework," academic writing "helps demonstrate students' learning" (p. 50). In other words, you must treat all your assignments earnestly since they are the means by which you will show what you have learned and, by extension, what you will have "earned" in a course. In short, your writing will be demonstrating what you are learning in your field.

- You are entering a field of discourse with which you are unfamiliar. You must learn what it takes to be a writer in your discipline because academic writing is specialized for every field of study. You must show all of the sources you have used in your paper, and you have to use a particular style of doing so, called a documentation style. There are at least seven different styles, depending on disciplines. For example, if you plan to study biology, then you must learn to write like a biology major, using a style known as CSE (Council of Science Editors). Most students must also learn to use two other styles: MLA (Modern Language Association) documentation for English or language studies papers and APA (American Psychological Association) for social sciences, education, and nursing. Chicago Style (CM) is another style that is often used in the humanities, particularly history. You will learn more about APA and MLA styles in chapters 12–15 of this text.

- As mentioned, you are learning to participate in a scholarly discussion. Part of such learning includes understanding the guidelines: debates have rules; structured meetings often use Robert's Rules of Order; Talking Circles use traditional ways of conducting ceremonies; courts, parliaments, associations, and most other significant proceedings all have ways and means of operating and of processing their work. As a new scholar, you, too, will be expected to learn the rules and treat your work thoughtfully.

(3) Critical Thinking

You may recall some of the ideas about critical thinking from chapter 1. Critical thinking is one of the most important skills you can develop as a writer, thinker, worker, and citizen. *Employability Skills 2000+*, developed by The Conference Board of Canada, emphasizes critical skills you need to employ in the modern workplace. Many jobs will demand that you use your abilities to think and solve problems. Inherent in academic writing is the requirement to analyze information and critique conventions, which is more advanced than work you may have done previously. Unlike high school writing, where you may have put together information from a number of sources, including the internet, and bundled it together in a report or research essay form, academic writing includes thinking critically about an assignment and using your analytical skills to come up with answers that show you understand the material and can develop different ways of thinking about it. Interpreting text, summarizing major points, weighing arguments, and developing effective lines of reasoning are all part of critical thinking and must become part of your work as an academic writer.

(4) Investigation

As an academic writer, you must analyze what an assignment is asking you to do, and you must understand what you need to do to get a possible answer. Such work requires investigation in three ways:

1. *Being able to analyze an assignment.* Do you understand what the problem or question is in the assignment? Can you outline it? Do you understand what it is actually asking you to do?

2. *Being able to analyze what is needed to complete the assignment.* What things must you do to be able to answer the question? What tools will you need to be able to carry out the assignment? How much time is required to complete it? How will you manage the task?

3. *Being able to use the required tools.* Do you know how a paper in your discipline is to be set up (documentation style)? Do you know what the writing should look like (style and presentation)? Do you know how to use valuable information literacy tools: researching various databases online, recognizing the value of abstracts in research articles, understanding how research in your field is set up in professional journals, knowing where to find professional journals online and in your library, knowing how to reference data in your paper, and knowing how and where to find help with current information technology tools?

(5) Research

You must do academic research for academic papers; however, research does not mean cutting and pasting from the internet or finding a paper you can purchase online. Instead, research means a process of investigation that includes integrity and academic honesty. It means organizing and planning that will take quite a lot of time. It means deep reading and thinking about what you read, while taking meaningful notes that help to enrich thinking about your research question. Research also means being familiar with current information literacy tools, including computers, online databases, and referencing. Academic writing means that all ideas in the paper must be supported by authoritative sources. Chapters 12–15 of this text will give you more information on these topics.

(6) Analysis

Being able to analyze something means you can summarize its main points or characteristic features, you can check out assumptions an author is making, you can distinguish a writer's argument, and you can interpret and evaluate all of these things. For example, if you were researching embryonic stem cell research for an ethics class in philosophy, you would first have to find out what the research actually entails: What does the research actually look like? Who is conducting it? What methods are being used? Who funds the research? Then you would research the arguments for and against such research: Who stands to gain from the research? What benefits to humankind might emerge from the research? What moral questions about working on human fetuses might arise? What rights do human subjects have in experimentation, and who decides? Then you would have to look at challenges: Are some of the assumptions correct or justified? Are the assumptions valid? Does the writer support her arguments? What kind of evidence is being used? After that, you would analyze what you have read, weigh the assumptions, and evaluate your position based on the facts, arguments, or compelling evidence you have found.

Academic writing also means you must provide support for your points; and to be able to establish points and elaborate them means you have some ability to analyze. It is also important to remember that the underlying skills of academic writing are developmental: in other words, you will develop them over time and with practice. The first piece of academic writing you do will be less polished and pleasing than one you complete later on in your academic career or in your professional life. Simply put, you get better and better with more and more skilful practice. Chapters 6 and 7 of this text are designed to help you with your development of analytical skills.

(7) Developed Argument

Learning to structure an argument also takes critical thinking and reading, analysis, organization, and practice. Academic writing includes the development of an argument, and this process also includes some rules. Arguments must be supported with convincing pieces of evidence and explanation. Chapters 10 and 11 of this text will help you learn some rules and will help you practise developing a clear, effective argument. Setting up your argument in the example of a paper on embryonic stem cell research for a bioethics course, for instance, will take careful organization. How well you lay out your argument, your explanations, and your supporting evidence will determine how compelling your presentation will be.

(8) Discipline-Specific Documentation

The area of study will determine which style of documentation you will use to cite your research sources. In other words, every quotation, summary, or paraphrase you use must be documented in a particular way in your writing. You will learn more about documentation styles in chapters 12–15 of this text.

(9) Concise and Well-Edited Standard English and (10) A Specified Presentation Format

Academic writing means using the standard conventions of English grammar and editing. Your instructor or professor will provide you with specific presentation requirements for your paper, and you will be expected to follow them. You may be asked to present title pages for many of your papers, and instructors may have particular specifications you must follow. Know that most instructors take off marks if a paper is poorly presented or badly edited. However, all academic writers can improve their grammar, usage, spelling, and punctuation, so keep track of the kinds of errors you make, and work at eliminating them. Chapters 16 and 17 of this text will give you information about and practice with editing and grammar.

WHAT ARE THE TYPES OF ACADEMIC WRITING?

Perhaps the genre you are most used to writing is the essay. Academic essays use the principles of academic writing outlined in the preceding sections. They must be carefully planned, researched, organized, argued, documented, and edited. Of course, not all disciplines use essays as their main form of academic writing. In technologies and engineering, for example, academic writers use the report format. Technical writing also has its own set of rules and styles, so if you are a student intending to study information technology—such as computer engineering; computer science; software engineering; civil, mechanical, or electrical engineering—then you can expect to write technical reports, proposals, and research studies. Technologies such as architecture, civil engineering, construction, fire safety, and urban and regional planning also employ technical writing. Business programs use case studies, reports, and technical writing as part of their academic programming, and medical students must know how to write for medical science as well as for the humanities.

Therefore, when it comes to academic writing, you may be expected to learn a variety of genres and documentation styles as they relate to your course of studies. Do not expect to write essays only or technical reports only. Be prepared to be flexible because you will have to respond well to different expectations in different scholarly communities.

HOW CAN YOU AVOID PLAGIARISM IN RESEARCH?

With the advent of information technology has come a tide of plagiarism. Post-secondary institutes are aware that plagiarism is on the rise, and they have created new policies and educational programming to help students realize the sombre nature of this form of cheating. To set out someone else's words or ideas as your own and present them in an assignment is dishonest. The plagiarism policies in all academic institutes are unequivocal and punitive, so be aware of what plagiarism is and how to avoid it.

The following article discusses this growing problem. Read the article, and then be prepared to discuss the questions that follow it.

Give Plagiarism the Weight It Deserves

by William Badke

William Badke is associate librarian at Trinity Western University. He has a strong professional interest in teaching research strategies to undergraduate and graduate students.

Cut-and-paste plagiarism from the Internet is increasing, according to the 2005 study from The Center for Academic Integrity (www.academicintegrity.org/cai_research.asp). The research findings showed that 40 percent of almost 50,000 undergraduates questioned have plagiarized from the Net, up from only 10 percent in 1999. What is more, fully 77 percent did not view such activity as a serious issue. For educators, this is sufficient to put plagiarism near the top of the information crimes agenda. You might not think that this is a topic for an information literacy column, but most standards in this field include the ethical use of information, which puts plagiarism front and center.

Plagiarism is presenting someone else's words or ideas as one's own, thus constituting misrepresentation and fraud. If I were to try to convince the world that it was I, not Pablo Picasso, who painted *The Old Guitar Player*, I would be labeled a fraud. Similarly, if I let on that I was the author of information that was someone else's, I would, in effect, be guilty of stealing the credit for that which is not mine.

We know what to look for—uneven language styles, language styles that differ from other work that has been presented, and ideas that are more sophisticated than or different from the writer's normal work. The real challenge is to help students recognize plagiarism as a problem and to correct it.

THE PLAGIARISM OF IGNORANCE

To be charitable, many people have no idea they are committing plagiarism. They use sources carelessly or falsely believe that information can be appropriated at will. One person's plagiarism is another person's research, isn't it? If it's on the Net and it's free to use, why can't I just copy and paste it?

Fortunately, we can overcome ignorance with education, so this aspect of plagiarism finds a ready solution. We can explain the scope of what students need to cite (words, unique ideas), and we can show students how to present ideas effectively to minimize the use of a source's terminology. We can show students models of good academic writing that gives credit where it is due.

I caution students to avoid paraphrasing (sentence-by-sentence rewriting), because it usually leads to plagiarism. A much better method is to read the source material and summarize it in briefer form. This takes the researcher away from the actual language of the source and demonstrates understanding of the material.

There are many Web sites available to guide us in the basics, but some plagiarism is resistant to easy solutions.

THE PLAGIARISM OF THE EASY PATH

There are students and information workers who think the risk of getting caught is worth the benefit, preferring the broad way that might lead to destruction to the narrow road that leads to honest enlightenment. We've made things even easier by providing them with so much digital content. Cut and paste is so easy, and the result can look so good, that it's worth the chance of getting caught.

While some of these types of plagiarists are just plain sneaky, others are desperate. These are the people who believe they lack the skills to pull off their own research projects. Perhaps English is not their first language, or they have trouble expressing themselves in words, or their powers of critical thinking are not up to snuff. The temptation simply to let other (better?) writers do most of the muscle work is powerful, because the possibility of survival is a bigger draw than the fear of detection.

THE PLAGIARIST WHO DESPISES INTELLECTUAL PROPERTY

Other plagiarists don't see themselves as academic criminals at all. They argue that information, once published in any form, is theirs to use as they see fit. In their view, to say that people "own" their words or ideas, once they are released into print or electronic form, is ludicrous.

In fact, the whole concept of intellectual property is taking a beating in today's postmodern digital world. From the Napster wars to bootleg movies off the Net, today's generation believes in open, free access in a big way. A large part of the problem is that the Worldwide Web looks like a candy store without a checkout clerk. If so much information is free for the taking, then what, exactly, is the point of asserting intellectual property?

The growing move toward seeing information as communal property is not just a Western problem. In many non-Western societies, information has always been seen as much more the property of the society than of the individual. Thus, we have international students coming to us with the view that considering information to belong to one person is foolish, even arrogant. This creates an easy platform for plagiarism.

THE CHALLENGE OF ANTI-PLAGIARISM EDUCATION

Education is supposed to be a positive experience. That makes droning on to a room full of students or researchers about the evils of plagiarism essentially anti-educational, as important as the topic may be. It hearkens back to high school when we were shown films of automobile accidents and their victims to scare us into being safe drivers. I suppose we could just view anti-plagiarism instruction as a necessary evil, not particularly educational in the positive sense, but necessary. I'm hoping there's a better way.

Let's consider an approach that might work more effectively than the "thou shalt not" tactic we've so often used in the past. Let's try helping those we are instructing to understand why we are so opposed to plagiarism. Maybe we have an opportunity to improve understanding of the issue.

DIFFERENTIATING BETWEEN ACCESSIBILITY AND PERMISSION TO APPROPRIATE

Suppose I have a friend who is a comedian and has just done his first big show in front of a live, paying audience. I like what I hear, so I start relating his jokes to my co-workers. My friend, the comedian, finds out and goes ballistic. It's hard enough for him to make a go of it anyway without having someone steal his jokes.

I counter with, "What's the big deal? You told the joke in a public place so it's out there now. Does my telling it too make it any more public?"

He answers, "Sure, my joke is out there, but it's my joke. You can't take credit for it as if you thought it up all by yourself."

This is a key issue that many starting researchers do not grasp—easy access to information does not bring with it the permission to pretend it's your information. It doesn't give you permission to put your name on it. Access and appropriation are different rights entirely.

THE NEED TO ASSERT INTELLECTUAL PROPERTY RIGHTS

We have just endured the Napster era, leading to a more regulated approach to music downloading, but slippage is appearing all over, from illegal downloading of new movies from the Net to counterfeiting software to widespread cutting and pasting from Web sites for student papers and industry research projects. Making a case against all this on financial grounds might work in some arenas, but for plagiarism the argument is, "It's free, so who am I hurting?"

Intellectual property is a complex concept in today's digital world. The more accessible property becomes, the harder it is for its originator to assert ownership over it. And what, exactly, does "ownership" mean—beyond the right to make a buck for one's own intellectual product? Asserting that you "own" an idea or a paragraph or the content of an article or book seems increasingly arrogant in today's easy download culture.

I think here that we need to emphasize the value of the product that comes from the human mind. At the most fundamental level, the motivation to produce and to create is bound up with the ability to have my product recognized as mine. Societies that maintain intellectual property rights are societies marked by creative development.

THE CONNECTION BETWEEN CREATOR AND PRODUCT

Intellectual property has an element to it that's highly significant to the plagiarism issue—the ability to put my name on what I produce. We need to emphasize the value of information's connection to its creator. I don't mean monetary value, but the fact that information is only as reliable or significant as its connection to the one who created it.

Knowing who produces our information, and under what circumstances, remains a value to us precisely because it verifies the value of the information. By the same token, an anonymous Web site is suspect because it's impossible to check the qualifications of the author.

Thus, I could write, "To engage the populace, scientists have to go beyond their narrow roles as experts to become leaders who go public with their concerns." But if I make it appear to be my view, I cut it off from its source (which is the Canadian environmentalist David Suzuki; www.sciencemag.org/cgi/content/summary/301/5638/1289?ijkey=XV0VKsmdPEmKg). I substitute his considerable authority with my own and thus rob the quotation of most of its power. The strength of our information, if it is good information, is inextricably linked with being able to identify its creator.

Plagiarists need to recognize that they are working on a false assumption when they think that they gain power by using other people's words as their owm. The fact is that they cannot take the words or views of others and pass them off as their own without robbing those words or views of most of their authority. If you want to write powerfully, firmly associating an author with his or her own writing is one sure way to do so. Guarding intellectual property is all about maintaining the connection between words/ideas and their creators.

RESEARCH WRITING AS DISCUSSION

A lot of plagiarism comes from a fundamental misunderstanding about the task of research. Research is not a monologue but a discussion—a sharing of ideas and viewpoints that involves debate and possible consensus. When we do research, we engage in a dialogue with others regarding a problem or issue, in such a way that the collective wisdom generated leads us closer to a solution or to a decision among competing voices. If we pass off the words and ideas of others as our own, we miss the point of the research task, which is to dialogue: "Brown argues . . . that Smith has countered with the view of . . . There are several problems with Smith's approach, including . . . , etc."

Linking the names of authors to their words and ideas both maintains the power of what they have written and allows me, the researcher, to interact with them as peers—evaluating, challenging, and ultimately concluding which voice is most likely correct. Sometimes I even have the ability to show that none of them are right and assert my own voice (trusting that no one will plagiarize my own words). If I take others' words and ideas as my own, the discussion is lost and the only authority I have for what I've written is myself.

PLAGIARISM AND THE RESEARCH TASK

It is time to move beyond simply declaring plagiarism a crime, though my next column will deal with catching the criminals when our education efforts have failed. We need to start teaching those who need to know why plagiarism defeats the purpose of research. First, accessibility does not carry with it the right to appropriate. Second, intellectual property, for all the beating it is taking these days, is crucial to a creative society. Third, cutting the link between creator and creation robs the creation of its power. Fourth, research writing is a discussion among many voices. Plagiarizing those voices ends the discussion and makes our work a monologue of limited authority.

Instructing people about plagiarism in today's world of easy access does not have to be a futile task. Those we instruct need to understand why plagiarism is so destructive so that they can learn to do genuine research.

Source: William Badke, "Give Plagiarism the Weight It Deserves," Online *Sept./Oct. 2007: www.onlinemag.net (Property of* Information Today, *pp. 58–60).*

Comprehension Questions

1. What does Badke mean by the underlined term "the plagiarism of ignorance"?
2. What is "intellectual property"?
3. Why does Badke discourage paraphrasing?
4. How does plagiarism "hurt" creativity, according to Badke?
5. What are the reasons Badke gives for treating plagiarism seriously?

Critical Comprehension

1. Are there circumstances in which copying is permitted? How do you distinguish these circumstances from plagiarism?
2. When is copying harmful to the academic process?
3. In his online paper, "Plagiarism by Academics—A More Complex Issue than It Seemed," Roger Clarke stated the following:

   A further consideration that blurs the concept of plagiarism is the considerable extent to which artists of all kinds are applying modern technologies to allude to earlier creative works. Cartoonists self-plagiarise their previous depictions of individuals, and their and others' symbols for events, attitudes and values. Digitised and originally-digital photographic images are manipulated with a level of professionalism that was seldom attainable with "air-brushing" techniques applied to silver chloride prints. The "sampling" of music has rapidly moved from oddity to established art-form. Recorded video is being manipulated to create surrealism and super-realism, which relies for its impact on being at once close to and distant from the original depiction of human experience. (www.anu.edu.au/people/Roger.Clarke/SOS/ Plag0410.html, retrieved April 8, 2008.)

   Do you agree that plagiarism can actually be a part of the artistic process? If so, do you believe that "some copying is fine"? How then can you make a case that plagiarism in academic writing is unacceptable?

TIPS FOR ACADEMIC WRITING

Although you will gain information about academic writing throughout *Spotlight on Critical Skills in Essay Writing*, Second Edition, following are a few quick tips to help you develop an overview of academic writing.

Tip 1: Keep a Writing Log

Many students find getting started and then staying on task are the most difficult things to do when it comes to writing. To make yourself more productive as a writer, you need to track your own activities, and you must write every day, even if it is only for a few minutes. Some experts claim that these "incremental writing" activities are more effective than anything else in developing students as writers. Become a writer by choice and not by chance. Keep a log of when you write, a summary of what you write, and how long you write. Make comments on what happens to you as you write. These comments can be really valuable because when you re-read them you will begin to notice patterns, strengths, difficulties, or other "truths" about yourself as a writer. If you write incrementally, you will begin to develop confidence in yourself as a writer. And with greater confidence comes greater productivity.

Tip 2: Get a Feedback Buddy

Try to find another person who also wants to improve his or her academic writing. Agree to meet at least once a week to discuss how your writing is going. Talk over assignments. Share strategies. If you feel comfortable with the idea, you can even share writing logs. Share writing, but be cautious: do not write for the other person or become the other person's editor. Be sure to share information about the writing itself and talk about the process. If you have developed a new strategy, share it with your feedback buddy. She will be willing to share with you, in turn.

Tip 3: Increase Confidence

Writing incrementally, writing every day, and sharing your writing with a feedback buddy will all increase your confidence. Think about what else will help you to increase your confidence in academic writing. Here are some ideas:

- *Improve your knowledge of grammar, mechanics, and usage.* Spend a little time each week developing your weak areas by investigating excellent online writing and learning centre sites. Your confidence in your academic writing may have to do with how well you think you write.
- *Read about writing and improving writing.* Online writing and learning centres have valuable information. You cannot read too much on the topic.
- *Read as a writer.* As you read articles, papers, chapters from textbooks, think about how writers have organized their work, what ideas they highlight, what arguments writers have presented, what evidence writers have provided, and how writers express themselves. You will learn to be a better academic writer by becoming a writing apprentice. In their "Researching Academic Writing within a Structured Programme: Insights and Outcomes" from *Studies in Higher Education*, March 2001, Morss and Murray suggested the following:

> *Confidence grows through a combination of a number of quite different activities: goal setting and deadlines, peer support, structured approach to writing, strategies for regular writing, strategies for making time for writing and protecting it. Poor goal setting for writing appears to lead to a misconception of the scale of the task. This, in turn, leads to a breakdown of the writing process. In fact, in discussions, it emerges that writing is not really conceived as a process by many writers. Perhaps this misconception is the cause of the dominant "binge" model of writing, i.e. if writing is seen as an enormous task, only large amounts of time will work. Over many*

> *discussions with writers, it is clear that this misconception creates a writing block and undermines writers' confidence. For writers to change their perceptions and habits requires thinking time, active practice of alternative strategies, and follow-up which enables them to embed it in, or adapt it to, their own practice. Once text has been generated, however much or little there is, confidence and motivation grow through the sense of achievement. We have found that it is essential, and fascinating, to have discussions about writers' experience of this perception shift. (p. 51)*

Tip 4: Learn to Become a Good Researcher

All academic writing is based on research, so the better researcher you become, the better papers you will produce. You will also be developing an essential *Employability Skill*, an absolute requirement in every professional workplace. In "Developing Academic Writing Skills: The Process Framework," *Nursing Standard*, vol. 21, no. 40, 2007, Lloyd sums up the importance of referencing in her remarks:

> *When an assignment is well referenced, it demonstrates the student's commitment to a good standard of academic writing and provides information required by the tutor. A well-referenced work will also provide evidence of where writers have obtained their ideas and how they have expanded on the work of others, which is a good indicator for overall marks awarded. Good referencing therefore provides evidence that students are working towards the required level for their award, and demonstrate their improved knowledge. (pp. 52–53).*

REVIEW TEST

Try the following review test. It will help you assess what you have learned from the chapter. Be prepared to share your responses with others in the class.

1. What is academic writing?
2. What is "scholarly discussion"?
3. What is research?
4. What is plagiarism? How can you avoid it?
5. As an academic writer, how should you approach an assignment?
6. How do you learn to be a good researcher? Why is being a good researcher important?

READING

The following reading is an example of academic writing. It comes from fashion research. Although the article is rather long, it is typical in length of many research articles you will come across in the professional journals online and in your academic library. As you read the article, think about what you have just read about academic writing. An abstract or summary begins the study.

Sizing Up the Wardrobe—Why We Keep Clothes That Do Not Fit

by Elizabeth Bye and Ellen McKinney

Dr. Elizabeth Bye is an associate professor in the College of Design at the University of Minnesota. Ellen McKinney is a graduate student in the Department of Design, Housing and Apparel at the University of Minnesota.

Abstract

A wardrobe is the sum of clothing, both worn and unworn, that women consider each day to construct their visual self. While there is little practical reason to keep clothes that are physically impossible to wear, there may be other connections that prevent their discard. This study investigated reasons for keeping clothes that do not fit the current body and women's feelings about these clothes. Responses from forty-six women, 35 to 65 years in age, were collected using a web-based questionnaire. The women were clients of image consultants and contacted because of their interest in clothing and appearance. Participants described up to four garments in their closets that no longer fit, the reasons they did not fit, and their reasons for keeping them. Open coding was used to examine the responses, and generated four themes for keeping clothing that do not fit: Weight Management, Investment Value, Sentimental Value, and Aesthetic Object. The results suggest a process for separating the self from the garment and the garment from the closet. This process occurs over a variable period, may not be linear, and may skip stages. A model for the separation process from garments that no longer fit is proposed.

KEYWORDS: wardrobe, fit, divestment, identity

A well-organized closet is the new status symbol in the home. Media mavens on shows such as *Clean Sweep* and *What Not to Wear* provide a weekly flow of advice to "Give your old wardrobe new life by purging the clothes you no longer look and feel great wearing" (*Clean Sweep* 2006). Could the dream of more closet space be realized by releasing our grip on what is in our closets? Or do women have good reasons for keeping clothes they can no longer wear? According to Cwerner, "The wardrobe articulates, both spatially and temporally, a set of material and symbolic practices that are fundamental for the constitution of selfhood, identity, and well-being" (2001: 1).

Through a daily process of wardrobe selection, we control presentation of our identity (Kaiser 1990). Although most fashion theories concentrate on worn clothes in the identity-formation process, it is important to recognize the role of stored clothes in self-definition (Cwerner 2001). From the garments in their closets, women piece together their visual self-representation to the world while meeting their functional, emotional, and aesthetic needs (Lamb and Kallal 1992). Cwerner (2001) envisions the closet as a library, depository, or stockpile of the symbols individuals have to select from to create their presentation to the world. Depending on its contents, the wardrobe may serve as a limiter or enabler in creative self-presentation. Furthermore, the wardrobe may serve as an archive of past selves or a hope chest for future selves.

For clothes to be part of the active wardrobe, they must fit the physical dimensions of the body and be in good repair. While this may seem like a common-sense statement, the abundance of popular culture magazines and television shows that direct women to discard garments that are worn, out-of-style, or do not fit (Beating Clutter 2005; Dunleavey 2005) might reveal that it is not commonly followed. Popular culture advises women that there is little practical reason to keep clothing that is physically impossible to wear. However, many women find this advice difficult to follow. It seems that discarding unwearable garments is not a completely logical process. Perhaps, sentimental or emotional reasons may lead women to keep clothing that does not fit. The personal connections to the clothing or the bodies that once wore them may guide their wardrobe behaviors. This study took a deeper look at why women choose to keep clothing that cannot be part of their self-presentation, because it does not fit their current bodies.

THEORETICAL UNDERPINNINGS

Wardrobe management behaviors are related to the larger theoretical realms of consumer consumption models and clothing as a communication tool. Consumer behavior related to how garments are used, stored, and eventually discarded after purchase is little studied. However, as the wardrobe is a basis for self-presentation, it is important to understand the individual connection between self and the pieces stored in the closet. Deeper examination of this connection may lead to greater understanding of this seemingly illogical behavior of keeping currently unwearable clothing.

Clothing as Objects of Consumption The consumption process requires multiple decisions by individuals based on both logic and emotion. These include: (1) Need Recognition, (2) Search for Information, (3) Pre-Purchase Evaluation of Alternatives, (4) Purchase, (5) Consumption, (6) Post-Consumption Evaluation, and (7) Divestment (Blackwell et al. 2001). Most apparel consumption research has focused on purchasing (May-Plumlee and Little 2001; Seo et al. 2001) and post-purchase evaluation of clothing (Chen-Yu and Kincade 2001; Kincade et al. 1998) with the goal of increasing consumer satisfaction and repurchase behavior. Clothing fit and sizing are critical to the consumer purchasing process (Eckman et al. 1990) and have been shown to be one of the top three evaluative criteria for both US and Asian consumers (DeLong et al. 2002; Hsu and Burns 2002). Women have reported difficulty in finding clothing that fits to purchase (Langer 2004). In the dressing room, women often blame themselves when garments do not fit (LaBat and DeLong 1990). The blaming behavior points to an emotional connection between the individual and garment before the garment even is purchased. We believe that sentimental connections between the self and wardrobe can deepen over time. This creates an emotional conflict when the garment needs to be discarded because it no longer fits or is beyond repair. However, there has been little research regarding the motivation and process of divestment decisions for this unwearable clothing. This study focused on the reasons women keep clothing that does not fit. Understanding the role of fit in the process of divestment expands our understanding of the consumption process.

Clothing as a Carrier of Personal Meaning McCracken (1986) briefly addresses separation from self as a ritual process in his study of the cultural meaning of consumer goods. He believes that meaning is transferred from objects to individuals. In order for separation from self to occur, an individual must remove the meaning attached to the clothing before it can be passed along. McCracken gives little insight as to how this process occurs or how individuals erase meaning contained in goods that are no longer useful. Banim and Guy (2001) explored the reasons women keep clothing they are not actively wearing. These included reminders of past feelings and ties to identity. In their interviews with fifteen women, they categorized the functions and roles that kept clothes play for their owners in terms of the self. These included (1) Continuing Identities, (2) Discontinued Identities, and (3) Transitional Identities. They found that clothing was not kept solely for positive associations but garments with problematic connections were also kept as part of their wardrobe. These women acknowledged that though irrational, they wanted their wardrobe to extend beyond what was currently wearable as a means of maintaining identity. One problematic connection they identified was clothing that no longer fit. This study focused on kept clothing that do [sic] not fit in contrast to the broader view taken by Banim and Guy (2001) of any kept garment that was not actively being worn.

Clothing as a Storage Unit of Self Cwerner (2001) defines the wardrobe not only as the set of clothes that one has, but also the space where clothes are stored and the complex set of practices surrounding the use, care, and storage of these clothes. Cwerner (2001) criticizes the lack of research on stored clothes and proposes five categories of wardrobe practices for investigation: (1) consumption, (2) organization, (3) individualization, (4) care, and (5) imagination. In a modern society, where most consumers possess far more clothes than they can wear at once, the wardrobe is a central part of the consumption cycle. The need to store clothes has led to an industry of closet organization experts and storage tools. Despite the abundance of advice and available storage devices, closets often become chaotic spaces of forgetfulness. Nonetheless, closets are the underpinning of appearance individualization. From the collection of garments, an infinite number of appearances can be mix-and-matched. The individual decides each day how much they will affirm or deny the impulses of fashion. To maximize these individualization choices, a range of care practices are necessary to keep the clothes in good repair. Lastly, Cwerner (2001) identifies the wardrobe as a place of imagination. The wardrobe stores all the potential selves—past, present, and future. The individual is limited in their appearance choices only by the garments in their wardrobe. While much fashion theory has focused on the dressed self, Cwerner (2001) encourages a research focus on the wardrobe as the vocabulary that affords the communication of the dressed body.

ASKING WOMEN ABOUT THE CLOTHES BEHIND CLOSED DOORS

The purpose of this research was to explore the reasons women keep clothing that do [sic] not fit their current bodies. A web-based questionnaire was used to collect information about sizes currently in the closet, number of garments that cannot be worn due to misfit, and current clothing sizes worn for tops, bottoms, and dresses. Participants also described up to four garments, the reasons these garments did not fit, and their reasons for keeping them. The sample of 300 participants was randomly selected from a mailing list of 2,000 of a nationally known image consultant located in the southwestern United States. Participants were invited by the image consultant through e-mail to complete the online questionnaire and were sent a reminder two weeks later. The survey was available for 60 days. Participant anonymity was insured with the use of an online survey service and direct participant contact through the image consultant. This anonymity may be one reason why women were so candid in their responses. Forty-six usable questionnaires were returned.

Participating women were 18–65 years old with the greatest number (39.5%) in the 36 to 45 age group, followed by 46–55 year olds (23.7%), and 26–35 year olds (15.8%). The majority reported annual household income of over $100,000.00 (56.8%) and had professional occupations.

WHAT I DON'T WEAR (AND WHY)

These women revealed a relationship with their kept clothing that goes beyond whether or not the garment fits the body. They were indeed storing clothing that they could not wear—often in multiple sizes. Their explanations for this behavior yields deeper insight into the intimate relationship of clothing to self.

The State of My Closet To the open-response question, "How many garments do you have in your closet right now that you CANNOT wear because they do not fit?" approximately 15% reported zero non-fitting garments, 37% reported one to ten garments, 17% reported eleven to twenty garments, and 15% reported twenty-one to fifty garments. The remaining 16% of participants gave a non-numerical response such as: "25 percent" (of what she had in her closet), "don't know," or "You want me to count????" Given these numbers of unwearable clothes in the closet, it was surprising to find that the majority (85%) reported following the media advice to clean out their closets once a year. How were these nonfitting clothes getting through the annual wardrobe purge?

Participants were also asked about their use of professional consultation on appearance. Half of the participants had sought advice from a wardrobe/image consultant. The most popular services were clothing style selection (97.5%) and clothing color selection (82.6%). Only 17.4% of the participants had used a consultant for help with closet organizing. Perhaps this relates to the intimate and personal nature of the wardrobe suggested by Cwerner (2001).

Some participants kept a range of labeled garment sizes in their closets. In general, participants reported having from two to six different labeled sizes of clothing in their closets with an average of three different labeled sizes. Most reported a three-size range, for example "8, 10, 12," which could be explained due to the practice of vanity sizing or perhaps a more modest fluctuation in weight. Roth says that most women keep at least three sizes of clothing in their closet—"thin, thinner, and fat" (2004: 77). One woman reported "from 7 junior to 18W," perhaps an individual whose weight fluctuates a great deal. The following quotes illustrate the range of responses:

> *Misses 14–16 primarily, but depends on fit rather than size.*
>
> *Size 7 all the way to 18W.*
>
> *4 to 8—but I'm the same size I have been for years. Some 4's fit like a 6 and some 8's fit like a 6.*

I Have My Reasons for Keeping These Clothes From the media's view of sensible behavior, the only reason to have a garment in one's closet would be that it is useful for wearing. However, participants made it clear that garments hold value well beyond their ability to be worn. Participants described up to four non-fitting garments, the reasons these garments did not fit, and their rationale for keeping them. Examination of these open-ended responses, guided by open-coding methods (Strauss and Corbin 1998), generated initial themes for keeping clothing that do not fit. The themes were then subdivided and links were explored through axial coding. Discussions led to deeper understanding of the integrated nature of the responses. Weight Management, Investment Value, Sentimental Value, and Aesthetic Object were the final categories that emerged. Most of the participants cited at least two of these reasons for keeping a garment and these were most often a combination of Weight Management and Investment Value. Garments described as an Investment Value were the greatest in number, followed by Weight Management, Sentimental Value, and Aesthetic Object. These categories seemed to comprise a process for separating the self from the garment and the garment from the closet. This process occurs over a variable period, may not be linear, and may skip stages. The typical process that emerged from the data is described.

While the move of a garment from active use to just being stored is seldom a conscious decision (Banim and Guy 2001), those garments that no longer fit are forced into inactivity. This forced decision may be positive or negative for the owner of the garment. Discovering that a favorite pair of pants or top no longer fits can be frustrating when the garment is too tight or satisfying if the garment is too big. Most women will put the garment back in the closet and wait, ever hopeful that diet, exercise, or time will allow the garment to fit again or that their smaller body will be maintained. As time progresses and the body does not change, there appears to be a second step in the process. The garments become an investment, too expensive or not worn enough to justify divestment, despite the inability of the owner to wear them. At this point, the women still seemed hopeful that their bodies would change, but there appeared to be a need for additional justification for keeping the garment that did not fit. Over half of the investment descriptions also included mention of weight management. We believe these garments were in divestment transition moving from Weight Management to Investment Value. Other investment descriptions made no mention of hopeful body change, and thus were further along in the separation process. Finally, the woman accepts that the garment no longer fits and investment is no longer justification for keeping it part of her wardrobe. At this point, many garments are divested, some are kept and put in storage because they hold sentimental meaning, and others are kept because they are viewed as aesthetic objects. The following model for the separation process from garments that no longer fit (Figure 1) is proposed.

The following quotes illustrate this process.

Weight Management: Tan cropped pants. A little too tight, it is so close on a thin day it might and it is my only pair.

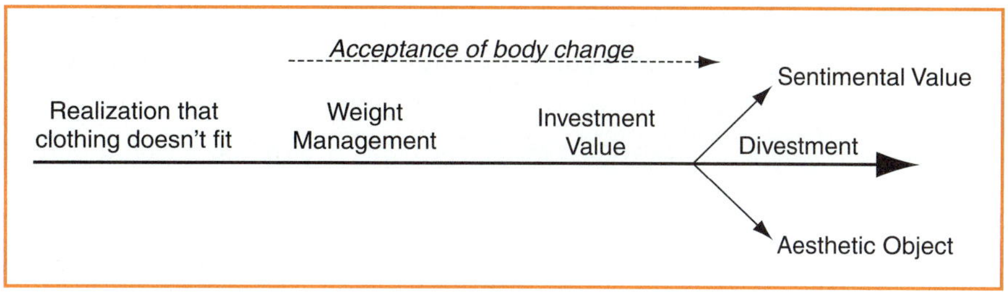

Figure 1 Model for the separation process from garments that no longer fit.

Weight Management and Investment Value: Silk purple button down, V-neck dress, size 16. The dress is too tight in the bust but, once again great color for me and have not had in my closet as long as the grey suit. I feel that someday I will be able to fit into again!

Investment Value: Tan slacks—too small. Paid good money.

Sentimental Value: Dress I wore for my engagement party sentimental value.

Aesthetic Object: Green suede bomber jacket. Too small. One of a kind item.

Discussion of each category follows.

Weight Management—I Keep Thinking I'll Lose the Weight Many women in this study mentioned weight gain or loss as a reason why the garment did not fit and was being kept. Some participants described their body changes in terms of a specific amount of weight they had gained or lost, some used the garments as a guide to the amount of weight they needed to lose, while others were more focused on getting into a specific size. One woman sent a separate e-mail explaining that she had kept two sheath dresses and a pair of slacks that have fit her for many years and used them as a guide to control her weight and exercise habits. She did not complete the questionnaire because all her clothing fit. Clothes that were both too large and too small were kept for reasons related to weight management. Only one participant mentioned a garment that no longer fit due to shrinkage. Perhaps these garments were not kept because individuals viewed the failure of the garment as being beyond their control and thus it may have been easier to divest the garment. This is in contrast to women taking the blame when garments do not fit in the dressing room (LaBat and DeLong 1990).

Many participants cited the need to reduce their weight in order to wear the garments they were saving and were strong in their hope that they would lose weight. Too small garments that were kept seemed to provide some incentive in hopes of losing weight. These garments seem to relate to Banim and Guy's concept of Transitional Identities. There is a desire to "revisit the images that these clothes achieve" (2001: 212).

Brown animal print pants too small very cute and I will get back in them soon!

I've gained 15 pounds since I bought them, but keep HOPING I will lose the weight.

Size 10 jeans . . . they are too small. Someday I want to fit back into them.

Pants outfit—too tight in thighs—love it and will lose enough weight to wear it again.

Several slacks. They are a size too small around the waist. Hope to lose weight to fit into them again. The slacks are still in style.

For some participants, keeping too small garments was an insurance policy if their weight loss efforts were successful, as in these comments:

Grey striped wool suit . . . does not fit because of the size 12/13 . . . cannot bear to get rid of it in case I ever get down to that size again.

I hope to lose some weight and would like to have a few pieces of clothing a couple of sizes under my current size so I don't have to run out and buy a whole new wardrobe immediately.

Don't want to have to buy a whole new wardrobe if I lose weight.

Several women held on to garments that were currently too big, just in case of a future unintended weight gain.

Black pleated trousers . . . too big. Wore them when I was a little heavier—I guess I keep them just in case—though even if I gained weight I probably wouldn't wear them with the pleats!

Misses size 16, off white shorts. Too large. May need bigger size in the future/ would not want to buy the same size again.

In addition, others who had successfully lost weight were either planning to have a garment altered, "but haven't gotten around to it" or wear the garment a little big because, "they are quality and great colors for me."

While most women kept garments to wear again at some indefinite time "when I lose the weight," others were more concerned with a definite time period. Some women hoped that by the time the season or event to wear the garment occurred again, their body would have changed to fit into the garment.

A short sleeve fitted denim shirt. It is too tight . . . doesn't look good when buttoned. I keep it because I am just switching into my spring/summer stuff and had hoped I would have lost some inches this winter to be able to wear it again.

Turquoise blue sheath dress with jacket. It is slightly tight through the hips. I keep it because it is SLIGHTLY tight, and I hope to lose enough to wear it this summer—it is a summery, "we're on vacation" dress.

Roth cautions against keeping "thin clothes" or "fat clothes" because they are like "a shrieking voice in your closet that automatically turns on when you open the door" (2004: 77). In her practice of counseling women, she finds that people are "afraid to give away [their] thin clothes, because [they] feel like [they] are giving away hope" (2004: 77). The women in this study seemed indirectly to echo this sentiment. It was clear that the majority of the sample perceived a smaller body size to be desirable. One woman was very clear about this.

Jeans. Too tight. I don't want to wear my current size. I want to fit into the jeans.

Investment Value—I Paid Good Money for it Many women cited the value of the garment as a reason to keep it even though it did not fit. Some kept garments that had not been worn enough to justify the monetary investment, other garments were an expensive purchase, and some garments just were not old enough to be discarded. The garment itself still had value, even though it did not fit the owner.

It seemed that there was some guilt associated with getting rid of garments which had received little use or were fairly new. So they were kept instead. Usually this was seen in combination with some hope of being able to use the garment again in the future. This was sometimes seen in combination with having spent a substantial amount of money on the garment. This concurs with a recurring theme in Banim and Guy's (2001) of women feeling the need to get enough use out of something to justify its price.

As the women described garments that no longer fit but were still kept in their closet, a majority included the concepts of quality, cost, length of ownership, or the effort required to shop for the garment. In some cases, perhaps the investment is a more tolerable justification for keeping something that does not fit rather than accepting that the weight they had hoped to lose has not disappeared. We believe this is part of the process of divesting garments that do not fit the physical body but still have value in the eyes of the owner. McCracken (1986) says that there is a process individuals must follow in order to remove the meaning from the clothing that they own, before it can be discarded. Banim and Guy (2001) might classify these garments, held for their investment value, as part of a transitional identity representing a value to the owner's self image, but one that is not yet resolved. In this sample, the women were focused more on the value of the garment than the meaning of the garment.

Sentimental Value—It Reminds me of a Lovely Time Sentiment related to an event or memory provided reasoning for keeping a garment that does not fit. This category had the fewest responses, which contrasts with the results presented by Banim and Guy (2001) in which the majority of their participants tied some meaning of an earlier life or event to the kept, but not actively worn, garment.

Participants described sentimental garments that did not fit, but the reason the garment was being kept was clearly related to the sentimental value it held and not to investment value or as incentive for losing weight. Many sentimental garments that no longer fit were kept because they reminded the wearer of a favorite event or occasion. Blackwell et al. (2001: 456) states that possessions can be "anchors for our identities" and Cwerner (2001) thinks of clothes as having biographies including the making, purchase, and wearing of a garment. Banim and Guy (2001) found that some women kept clothes because they wanted to remember a story that was associated with the clothing.

We believe sentimental reasons for keeping garments that do not fit are valid and enable the owner to hold onto an important piece of their personal history, much the same way historic costume collections hold our collective history. These garments deserve careful storage separate from the everyday wardrobe.

Aesthetic Object—I Just Really Love it Beyond sentiment, a category emerged in which the participants described their kept garments as beautiful objects. These women kept clothing primarily for its aesthetic value. Participants that described garments that did not fit when purchased were most likely to view the clothing as an object.

[. . .]

Responses categorized as Aesthetic Object were singular in their reasoning, and void of any reference to sentimental attachment or an actual desire to wear the garment. Participants had objectified the kept clothing with attention focused on the beauty of the garment. Clothing kept as an aesthetic object should also be viewed as separate from the active wardrobe and stored or displayed so that the owner benefits from its full aesthetic value.

CONCLUSIONS AND IMPLICATIONS

It is clear from the data that a woman's relationship with her clothing that does not fit is complex. Though discarding garments that no longer fit may seem like a relatively practical matter, these women revealed that there are other issues that must be examined before the reality of letting a garment go can take place. These garments do hold meaning for the owner as suggested by McCracken (1986) and Banim and Guy (2001). In addition, in this sample, it appears that the women needed to go through a process of divesting garments that no longer fit. McCracken (1986) does suggest that a ritual process is necessary to remove meaning from the garment; however, the results of this study reveal more details about this process.

The proposed model of divestment of garments that no longer fit expands on the current consumer consumption process model (Blackwell et al. 2001). It provides details about the process that reveal the relationship individuals have with their clothing. The model may serve as a basis for future research on the way individuals manage clothing after purchase, as suggested by Cwerner (2001). Continued research is needed to expand the model to include other motivations for divesting garments from the wardrobe. How a garment was purchased or acquired may relate to the process of divestment. In addition, divestment behavior is influenced by culture (Blackwell et al. 2001), so clothing divestment behavior in other countries may be compared to that of this study's sample.

Few individuals or manufacturers think about divestment during purchase. Divestment of clothing is considered when an item is no longer needed due to changes in fashion, fit, lifestyle, or perhaps is worn out. Consumers may feel guilt or frustration with the process of divestment. Validation of the process may support individuals as they work to maintain a functional wardrobe. Valuing a garment for sentimental or aesthetic reasons should be viewed as a valid alternative to divestment. Such a view would give women permission to remove these garments from the active wardrobe, resulting in a more functional and less emotionally charged closet. Education for consumers regarding proper fit, regardless of size or weight, may also help consumers to make better purchase, consumption, and divestment decisions in the future.

References

Banim, M. and A. Guy. 2001. "Dis/continued Selves: Why Do Women Keep Clothes They No Longer Wear?" In Ali Guy, Maura Banim, and Eileen Green (eds). *Through the Wardrobe: Women's Relationships with Their Clothes,* pp. 203–19. Oxford: Berg.

Beating Clutter. 2005. *U.S. News and World Report* 3 January: 39.

Blackwell, R. D., P. W. Miniard and J. E Engel. 2001. *Consumer Behavior.* 9th edn. Fort Worth, TX: Harcourt.

Chen-Yu, H. J. and D. H. Kincade. 2001. "Effects of Product Image at Three Stages of the Consumer Decision Process for Apparel Products: Alternative Evaluation, Purchase and Post-purchase." *Journal of Fashion Marketing and Management* 5: 29–43.

Clean Sweep, Tips & Tricks from episode 230, "Clothes Make the Mess." Retrieved 10/17/06 from http://tlc.discovery.com/fansites/cleansweep/tips/episode230.html.

Cwerner, S. B. 2001. "Clothes at Rest: Elements for a Sociology of the Wardrobe." *Fashion Theory* 5(1): 79–92.

DeLong, M., K. Labat, N. Nelson, A. Koh and Y. Kim. 2002. "Global Products, Global Markets: Jeans in Korea and the United States." *Clothing and Textiles Research Journal* 20: 238–45.

Dunleavey, M. P. 2005. "Conquer Clutter." *Good Housekeeping* March: 113–22.

Eckman, M., M. L. Damhorst and S. J. Kadolph. 1990. "Toward a Model of the In-store Purchase Decision Process: Consumer Use of Criteria for Evaluating Women's Apparel." Clothing and Textiles Research Journal 8: 13–22.

Hsu, H. J. and L. D. Burns. 2002. "Clothing Evaluative Criteria: A Cross-national Comparison of Taiwanese and United States Consumers." *Clothing and Textiles Research Journal* 20: 246–52.

Kaiser, S. B. 1990. *The Social Psychology of Clothing: Symbolic Appearances in Context,* 2nd edn. New York: Macmillan.

Kincade, D. H., V. L. Giddings and H. J. Chen-Yu. 1998. "Impact of Product-specific Variables on Consumers' Post-consumption Behavior for Apparel Products: USA." *International Journal of Consumer Studies* 22: 81–90.

LaBat, K. L. and M. R. DeLong. 1990. "Body Cathexis and Satisfaction with Fit of Apparel." *Clothing and Textiles Research Journal* 8: 43–8.

Lamb, J. M. and J. M. Kallal. 1992. "Conceptual Framework for Apparel Design." *Clothing and Textiles Research Journal* 10: 42–7.

Langer, W. 2004. "Poor Size, Fit Drain Profits for Catalogs, Web Retailers." *Apparel Magazine* March. [WWW document]. http://www.apparelmag.com/bobbin/headlines/viewpoints_display.jsp?vnu_content_id=1000475612.

May-Plumlee, T. and T. J. Little. 2001. "Consumer Purchase Data as a Strategic Product Development Tool." *Journal of Textile and Apparel Technology and Management* 1: 1–10. http://www.tx.ncsu.edu/jtatm/volumelissue3/issue3_abstracts.htm.

McCracken, G. 1986. "Culture and Consumption: A Theoretical Account of the Structure and Movement of the Cultural Meaning of Consumer Goods. *Journal of Consumer Research* 13: 71–84.

Roth, G. 2004. "Throw away Your Thin Clothes." *Prevention* April: 77–82.

Seo, J.-L, J. M. Hathcote and A. L. Sweaney. 2001. "Casualwear Shopping Behavior of College Men in Georgia, USA." *Journal of Fashion Marketing and Management* 5: 208–22.

Strauss, A. L. and J. M. Corbin. 1998. *Basics of Qualitative Research: Techniques and Procedures for Developing Grounded Theory*, 2nd edn. Thousand Oaks, CA: Sage Publications.

Comprehension Questions

1. How do Bye and McKinney define a wardrobe?
2. How does Cwerner (2001) envision the closet?
3. What is "self-presentation" (underlined on page 213)?
4. What do Banim and Guy (2001) say about why women keep clothing they do not actively wear?

Critical Comprehension

You will recall that academic writing is (1) structured writing whose purpose is to (2) join scholarly discussion, using (3) critical thinking, (4) investigation, (5) research, (6) analysis, (7) a developed argument, (8) a specific style of discipline-specific documentation for citing research sources, (9) concise and well-edited standard English, and (10) a specified presentation format.

After you have read the article, analyze its various parts. Be prepared to analyze the article in a small-group discussion. Then answer the following questions together.

1. What new scholarly knowledge have Bye and McKinney brought to the discussion table?
2. What questions are critical questions in the research article?
3. What arguments appear to be the most compelling? Why?

Assignment

In a paragraph of 300 words, summarize the article. Your instructor may ask you to turn in your summary for marking. Review the ideas on summarizing and summary writing in chapter 6 before you do your summary.

CHECKOUT

Here are some of the ideas you will take away with you after you have completed the chapter:

- Academic writing involves structured research.
- Academic writing means using analysis and required tools.
- As an academic writer, you must use a specified form of documentation in your papers.
- As an academic writer, you must maintain academic honesty by not plagiarizing.
- Use tools such as writing logs to help you in the academic writing process.

Mastering the concepts in this chapter will also help you develop and apply the following employability skills highlighted by the Conference Board of Canada in *Employability Skills 2000+*:

Communicate

- use relevant scientific, technological and mathematical knowledge and skills to explain or clarify ideas

Manage Information

- locate, gather and organize information using appropriate technology and information systems
- access, analyze and apply knowledge and skills from various disciplines (e.g., the arts, languages, science, technology, mathematics, social sciences, and the humanities)

Think & Solve Problems

- seek different points of view and evaluate them based on facts

Participate in Projects & Tasks

- plan, design or carry out a project or task from start to finish with well-defined objectives and outcomes
- work to agreed quality standards and specifications
- select and use appropriate tools and technology for a task or project

Source: Adapted from *Employability Skills 2000+* Brochure E/F (Ottawa: The Conference Board of Canada, 2000).

chapter 9

Expository Writing

Chapter Objectives

After completing this chapter you will be able to

1. take advantage of rhetorical modes to shape ideas in expository writing;
2. write an expository essay informing readers about an academic subject;
3. provide reasoned support for your opinions in an expository essay;
4. draw a timeline to help you in developing your thesis statement;
5. improve your writing by appropriate placement of transitional words and phrases.

INTRODUCTION

Expository writing informs readers by explaining ideas. The writer may choose to write using opinions, but they must be reasoned out and supported. As a student, most of the writing you will do for courses will be expository. A nursing student may be asked to write an essay about nursing principles; a biology student may be asked to write an essay about ecosystems; a history student may be asked to write about the first administrator of British Columbia.

As a student using expository writing for many of your course assignments, you want to know about the rules and guidelines, or the **conventions of writing**, connected to this kind of writing. This chapter will help you focus on the conventions of expository essay writing.

USING COMMON RHETORICAL MODES IN EXPOSITORY WRITING

Rhetoric is a term originally used by the ancient Romans and Greeks to refer to the powers of oration. The ancient Greek orators, known for their eloquent use of language, gave moving, persuasive speeches about important themes many centuries before text was widely available. To be a brilliant orator in those times meant a life of study of rhetoric, dialectics, and grammar. Today rhetoric has just as much to do with argumentative and persuasive writing as with great speeches.

Rhetoric is the effective use of persuasive language. Some of the tools used in rhetoric to organize ideas are still valuable today. These tools, often referred to as rhetorical modes, develop ideas by arranging them into patterns: by time, definition, cause and effect, comparison and contrast, classification and division, and so forth. Rhetorical modes are also discussed in chapter 5.

Expository writing also takes advantage of rhetorical modes to shape ideas in a variety of ways, depending on the writer's purpose. For example, if you wanted to write about child care in Canada, you could organize your ideas with the use of different rhetorical modes: a historical view of child care in Canada, for example, employs a time order or process approach. But if you look for similarities and differences between traditional Aboriginal child care and 18th century European child care, then you are using a comparison and contrast mode. If, on the other hand, you want to consider the range of child care in Canada in 2009, you might put the services into groupings; in other words, you would be using a classification approach. Should you wish to define what child care is, then your approach would use a definition rhetorical mode. You might also decide to use a blended approach in which you mix two modes, perhaps historical (time or chronological) and contrast. Whichever mode you choose will depend on your purpose and sometimes the nature of the assignment.

Process Analysis

A process analysis is a piece of writing that describes something that happens over time. It deals with the stages of something or the sequence of events that take place in an activity of some sort. Process analysis writing is used in many subject areas. For example, much writing within a course in one of the technologies will include how to do something: how to program a computer using a special new computer language, how to measure something, or how to design something. Many science courses and health courses also use the process pattern. In a nursing course, students might read how to change a dressing, how to give an injection, how to chart, or how to communicate with a worried patient. In chemistry, much of the writing within the texts and the writing done by students will involve some sort of process design. Your process pattern could be made up of

- stages,
- a sequence or set of sequences,
- steps,
- dates,
- points of separation.

TIPS FOR WRITING PROCESS PIECES

Tip 1. *Have a clear purpose in mind.* To use a process pattern in an essay, you must have a clear idea of the process, how it is arranged or how you want to arrange it, and why you want to talk about it. The thesis statement plays a key role in the construction of an essay by rhetorical mode. If you choose to use the process pattern, you must let the reader know in the thesis statement the point of telling the reader about the process in the first place. Are you trying to be interesting? Are you trying to compare one process with another? Are you attempting to help the reader understand something by analyzing a process? Keep this in mind when you write an essay that is going to describe a process. There must be some angle of interest in the thesis statement; otherwise, the reader could simply look up the information in a reference book. Ask yourself, "Why am I telling the reader this? Am I merely stating the obvious?"

Examples:

1. Here's how I make my own clothes!

(Poor thesis statement. True, it shows process analysis. But there is no angle of interest. Why would anyone want to bother reading this?)

2. Any woman can make herself a dress that is glamorous and trendy yet relatively inexpensive compared to designer labels.

(Better: Now there is a point to writing the essay. The writer will talk about making a garment and show through the description of the process how the dress will save the maker money without sacrificing style.).

Tip 2. *Use a timeline.* You may choose to employ a timeline, used for arranging stages over a duration. As you do your thinking or arranging, you will have some sort of framework in which to put your ideas. The arrangement may be a sequence of events, so the events themselves can be charted out on a line. However, not all events are clear when trying to describe something, so often you are forced to cluster smaller sets of events into stages, which is, in effect, categorizing ideas. We cluster small steps into larger stages, and we may then choose to chart these stages on a timeline. Timelines help us to arrange our ideas clearly.

Another advantage of drawing a timeline is that it can also help you to develop your thesis statement. For example, if you drew a timeline with four stages shown by four important dates in Canadian history, you might then develop the following thesis: *Canada has gone through four distinct stages during its journey from colony to independent nation.* After you have charted the sequence on the timeline and developed a good working thesis, you might start thinking about other keywords or phrases that you would want to include in your essay.

Tip 3. *Use key words and phrases.* Key words and phrases help the reader follow the passage of time throughout the essay. You might choose actual dates to mark the time, but if you are simply putting forth phases, you will probably use transitions, such as *next*, *later*, *after that*, *soon*, *by this time*, and so forth. (Refer to the detailed list of transitions in chapter 4 for a more complete listing of process or time-order transitions.) In addition, you may want to repeat key phrases in the process itself. This repetition not only reminds the reader of your thesis, but also lets the reader follow the overall process more easily. A caution, though: do not make your writing sound *too* repetitive. Sometimes you can use synonyms for terms rather than using the same word over and over again. Using synonyms can help keep the reader's interest and will also help you expand your written expression and style.

Comparison and Contrast

Throughout your life you have learned by comparing and contrasting things. You might have discovered more about apartments by comparing them to houses; you might also have known which dogs on your street to pet and which ones to leave alone through the use of comparison/contrast; you may have decided important life choices based on this mode.

TIPS FOR WRITING COMPARISON AND CONTRAST PIECES

Tip 1. *Choosing the items.* The first stage of carrying out a comparison could not be more straightforward. Take two people, events, ideas, books, works of art, or two of anything, and ask yourself, "How are these two things the same? How are they different?" By so doing, you are conducting a comparative analysis.

A well-planned comparison/contrast essay will almost write itself, but its initial construction takes some thought. Deciding which two things to compare broadly is quite an easy task. But then you must decide how to compare them. A point of comparison is a characteristic that you choose that is common to both items being compared, and to be effective it must be clear and logical. For example, let's suppose you wanted to compare children living in Canada with children living in China. One point of comparison might be education because both groups of children attend school. Another point of comparison might be entertainment because children all over the world love to play. Finally, the last point of comparison you might choose is responsibility in the family. Most children are responsible for helping out the family to lesser or greater degrees.

Tip 2. *Make the items relate.* It is unproductive and confusing to talk about points that do not relate in some way to the two broad categories you are writing about, and so well-thought-out points are critical to a good essay using a comparison/contrast pattern. Also remember that each point of comparison must be distinct; do not overlap these major points because your writing will become repetitious.

Here is a further example. Suppose you want to discuss Calgary and Vancouver in relation to one another because you want to determine which place to live. Perhaps you have decided on four points of comparison:

1. population
2. industry
3. climate
4. architecture

Thus you would not include harbours in your discussion because Calgary has none. If you added a point of comparison like annual rainfall, you would find it overlaps with climate. However, if you did decide to discuss Vancouver's harbour because you believed it to be a very important feature, then you might invent a point of comparison like transportation systems. Similarly, if annual rainfall seemed vital to your discussion, then you could include it in the discussion of climate.

Tip 3. *Develop a clear framework for discussing the items.* Once you have thought out your points of comparison and sketched out a few notes for each point or planned some of the discussion, then you must decide the actual structure of the comparison/contrast essay. Will you discuss each city separately? Will you use the points of comparison for each paragraph and include both cities under each point? The choice is yours: block format or point-by-point. Sometimes it is good practice to include both cities in the discussion throughout the essay because the points of comparison become the feature of the paper. But at the same time this type of set-up can become rather tedious to read if the writer is not paying attention to style. Here are two possible models of the structure of the essay:

Model 1: Block Format

Introductory paragraph

Body paragraph 1: Calgary

- population
- industry
- climate
- architecture

Body paragraph 2: Vancouver

- population
- industry
- climate
- architecture

Concluding paragraph

Model 2: Point-by-Point

Introductory paragraph

Body paragraph 1: population

- Calgary
- Vancouver

Body paragraph 2: industry

- Calgary
- Vancouver

Body paragraph 3: climate

- Calgary
- Vancouver

Body paragraph 4: architecture

- Calgary
- Vancouver

Concluding paragraph

Both of these models will work; however, each has different characteristics. Model 1 contains only two large body paragraphs and so would be structurally awkward. It would not really be a conventional essay because it would not fit the expected number of body paragraphs. Besides that, it requires the reader to remember the points made in the first half of the essay in order to compare them to the information given in the second portion. Obviously, the longer an essay is, the more difficult it will be for the reader to hold pertinent ideas in mind. The writer could add body paragraph 3 to discuss differences.

In Model 2, points of comparison are arranged by paragraph so that they are emphasized and are easier for the reader to retain. Its structure seems to balance points, so the discussion itself "feels" more balanced upon reading. To help make ideas cohere, use transitions. Keywords to use in comparison/contrast essays are words like *similarly*, *same*, *different*, *on the other hand*, *conversely*, and so forth.

Tip 4. *Use comparison and contrast to help develop your critical thinking and reading.* Most experts agree that comparing and contrasting are two of the most important of the critical skills. One composition professor observes just how relational this skill is: "I ask my students to think about people, places, and things, as well as ideas. I ask them to explore the connections between time and space, between global and local concerns, between divergent lifestyles and cultures, between events and ideas, between individualism and independence" (V.P. Stephen, "Hello, out there . . . Is anybody thinking?" *Teaching* Fall 2004: 54).

The following example shows how one student wrote about an important event in his life—whether to buy or to rent.

To Buy or to Rent?

Recently couples have been having a hard time deciding whether to own or rent a home. Because interest rates have risen, potential homeowners have had to weigh the benefits of owning against those of renting. This problem is even more confusing because of the high rents that are now being charged. In some aspects renting may seem more secure, but owning has far more benefits.

First, the investment in land has always been the safest. A mortgage may seem like a large debt, but property value does increase, and the opportunity of selling can mean receiving more money than has been paid. For example, homes in 2004 have increased in value by at least 150% since 1984. In fact, paying rent is paying someone else's mortgage, and receiving no investment or property in return. Also, owners can borrow money on their equity, the value of their home less the debt still owing, for emergencies or new investments.

Subsequently, owners can use the money made available through these loans toward renovations, increasing the value of their home. Renovation is sometimes necessary when there is a new member in the family and an extra room is needed. On the other hand, renters have no alternative but to move. Along with renovations, owners can paint or wallpaper without having to ask permission. Renters must, and are usually denied permission because landlords (owners) do not trust the quality of work or the taste of the renter. If landlords do agree, usually renters are not reimbursed for the supplies and work they have put in. Additionally, this increases the value of the home or property for the owners, but it does nothing for renters except perhaps make a difficult situation a little more liveable.

With the threat of having to move at the request of the landlord, renters must consider many problems that can arise from moving often. First, moving is expensive: truck rental and connection fees for hydro, telephone, and cable add up to a great deal of money, not including the damage deposit. If renters have children, they must also think about the adjustments they will have to make. Moving from school and friends can be quite a psychological trauma for children, and they may become shy and evasive. Children who do not have this threat can feel secure, making good, long-lasting friendships.

Is owning a home better than renting? Owning allows people to renovate, invest, and feel secure in the family's well being, whereas renting means moving, having to ask permission to paint or wallpaper, and possibly causing anxiety in children. With all this taken into account, the benefits of owning far outweigh those of renting.

Definition

The definition rhetorical pattern explores what something is or what the nature of something is. Definitions look at what characteristics define something. Many writing assignments are based on conceptualizing some idea or quality through definition. Read the following to get an idea of how definition works.

TIPS FOR WRITING A DEFINITION PIECE

Tip 1. *Choose the concept wisely.* Try to select a topic, idea, or concept with some depth. An abstract idea generally offers the potential for a richer discussion. For example, talking about the nature of something can lead to interesting deliberation. Think of the nature of violence, the nature of family kinships, the nature of a contest, or the nature of research. Aren't you really thinking of what could constitute each of them?

Tip 2. *Use a technique that gets at your purpose.* You can structure your definition using one of the following techniques:

- Define by how something works.
- Define by how something is put together.
- Define by what distinguishes the term or idea.
- Define by how something is different from something else.
- Define by what something is not.
- Define by where something comes from.

Examples:

- How something works: A defibrillator is a device that actually uses the body's energy in an unusual way.
- How something is put together: An ideology is a theory organized around a single common purpose.

- What distinguishes the term or idea: Space travel is unlike ground or sea transport.
- What something is not: Desire is not love.
- Where something comes from: Canadian social democracy has its roots in the Prairies and in the region's work ethic.

Tip 3. *Plan carefully.* When defining a quality, issue, idea, or object, be sure your definition essay has the following elements:

In the introduction:

- the term or idea you are defining
- a sentence that contains your definition
- a clear thesis with definition as a clear rhetorical mode

In the body:

- paragraphs that explore distinguishing features
- clarification, using supporting examples or anecdotes

In the conclusion:

- a renaming of your term or idea
- your summary definition

Examples:

What is a friend?

A friend is a person who trusts you to tell the truth, laughs at your jokes, and helps you build the new porch you need.

For the writer, a friend has three characteristics that distinguish friendship from non-friendship.

In the following paragraph, the writer gets at the idea of a pessimist by attempting to define one.

Pessimists are people with a problem. Their negative attitudes towards most things follow them everywhere they go; they see shadows instead of light, sadness instead of joy, and anger instead of laughter. Convinced that they have been born with "bad karma," they journey through life as if a permanent black cloud were over their heads. Scornful, self-pitying, sarcastic, they surround themselves with others who share their doom-and-gloom philosophy. Together, they revel in the misfortunes of others, natural catastrophes, and destruction wrought by humans, using these events to reinforce their belief that life is a cruel trick invented by a sadistic deity for its own amusement. As self-proclaimed experts, pessimists recount utopian visions of living, absent from the "real" world. Their cynical nature prevents them from feeling enjoyment and relaxation. Their credo is Murphy's Law—what can go wrong will go wrong—and they await the next misfortune. They have little ambition because ambition prefigures hope, and hope is for optimists—fools who live to try to find happiness in their days. Bitterness and resentment become pessimists' constant companions, and sadly, their predictions come true—loneliness follows.

What characteristics define a pessimist in this writer's view? How is a pessimist distinguished from an optimist? Has definition helped you to think through some ideas about pessimism?

Cause and Effect

Cause and effect are relational. When you write an essay using this rhetorical mode, you must show how something influences or is influenced by something else. You consider impact, results, consequences, and outcomes in thinking through a cause-and-effect relationship.

TIPS FOR WRITING A CAUSE-AND-EFFECT PIECE

Tip 1. *Choose two items that relate.* When you select the items for discussion, be sure that you are able to discuss how they relate. You can find the relationship between ideas, but the connections may not always be visible. Try to find something interesting to say about the relationship. Do not simply state what is obvious. Sometimes you may have to do some research to determine the nature of the relationship.

Tip 2. *Use creative questioning.* Ask questions about the nature of the relationship in order to generate and deepen discussion. Here are some examples:

- Do children view depictions of violence as real?
- How do small children view such representations on television?
- Do children copy what they see?
- Do depictions of violence in television programming influence children? How?
- What effects does television watching have on young viewers?

Tip 3. *Select items of interest.* If possible, choose something that interests you. Read the following examples. In the paragraph about walking, the writer was interested in finding connections between wellness and fitness. In the paragraph about stress, the writer wanted to establish what kind of impact it has. There may be more to these relational ideas than is first obvious. Also, ongoing research on topics of interest often changes what people once believed about them. Assumptions are challenged by the research, and new knowledge emerges.

- Moderate exercise improves wellness.
  (Something influences something else.)
- Cheating on exams results in failure.
  (Something is a result of something else.)
- Good advertising brings in business.
  (Something is the consequence of something else.)

In the following paragraph, the writer explores the benefits of walking by relating walking to its positive effects.

Walking can have positive effects on the body, mind, and spirit. Beginners can start easily and feel the benefits quickly. Fitness levels can be improved by just walking around the block a few times a week. Walking helps to encourage the strengthening of bones and to reduce bone porosity, especially important to women in later life because the loss of bone density results in bone breaks. In fact, walking stimulates bone cells to build more bone. Walking on a regular basis can also decrease the need for some medications, and it can help people who have just had heart surgery with their recovery. Moreover, circulation is improved by walking, and pumping more blood through the body benefits energy levels, improves muscle tone, and generates a feeling of well-being that radiates into other aspects of a person's life. Furthermore, a powerful benefit is an increase of energy, which brings on a feeling of well-being. In a study carried out in 2007 at the University of Eastern Ontario, people reported that, after taking walks after supper, they felt more relaxed and happy than they did before the walk. Serotonin builds up in the blood and is carried to the brain; this natural chemical makes people feel happier. Also, walking promotes safe and healthy weight loss which, in turn, makes walkers feel better about themselves. When people feel discouraged or overwhelmed by life, they feel their spirits lifted as they walk, and they seem to find solutions to many problems. The link between walking and improved health is clear; people simply have to take responsibility for their own fitness and get started.

What cause-and-effect connections does the writer make? What examples are used? Is the relationship between walking and health clearly established? Is it convincing? Why or why not?

In the following essay, the writer examines the relationship between stress and its results. Notice her clear thesis statement, which establishes a cause-and-effect mode and three distinct areas of effect.

The Effects of Stress on Everyday Living

Modern life has made people more anxious and rushed. Getting to work on time or finishing a paper can leave a person frustrated. Stress, the adjustment period to any change in life, physically, mentally, or spiritually, varies from day to day. If too many changes occur, and there is not enough time to absorb these alterations, a person will suffer from chronic stress. Stress will eventually affect family life, work capabilities, and health.

When parents are pressured to get a job done, whether it be at school, work, or even at home, their actions affect those around them. While parents are at their busiest, the children are vying for attention, negative or positive. Caught in this vicious circle, the parents become angry and impatient, which then causes the children to become more upset and erratic. For teenagers, drugs and vandalism can become their way of coping with the lack of attention and understanding. Studies done on the reasons why teenagers became delinquent found that, in most cases, it was because of a bad family situation. Rheinhold (2008) suggests that family break-up was the cause of teenagers acting out against authority in 83.5% of the cases studied. Stress causes people to say things and act differently. Husbands and wives lose communication, and the home becomes a place of tensions rather than relaxation.

Because stress affects sleep, it also affects how alert and energetic people are. If individuals are tired and lack motivation, the quality of work will deteriorate. In the report, "On the Job: Workers, Employers, and the Cost of Stress," the Canadian Association of Workplace Safety claims that absenteeism and safety on the job cost Canadian companies about $3.4 billion annually (2007, p. 27.) In addition, production slows down. Jobs that were once completed easily now take days to finish. Fellow workers also notice changes. Where they once saw a good-natured person, they now see a tired and irritable ogre. Eventually, with the lack of contact from fellow workers, the workload seems greater and becomes a burden for the employee until he or she does not care anymore.

The relationship between stress and health has also been chronicled since the beginning of the twentieth century. Hans Selye (1974), a Canadian pioneer in stress research, called it "the new modern silent disease" (p. 12). Although researchers are still conducting studies on this relationship, most evidence has shown that when people are mentally worn down they are more susceptible to disease and illness. Stress can cause a loss of appetite or an increase, and the effect on the body can be hazardous. Obesity is one of the major causes of strokes. In contrast, if a person is not eating, he or she begins to lack the essential vitamins and minerals that are necessary to fight off illness. Terminally ill patients have found that exercising regularly releases stress, improves their tolerance for pain, and for some, extends their lives.

The family, the workplace, and the individual are all susceptible to the serious effects of stress. Whatever the causes of stress are, be it a death in the family, a heavy workload, or a lack of money, people should find positive ways of releasing it. Taking walks, exercising, or working on a relaxing hobby are very essential and should be done every day so that stress is kept to a minimum. Learning to cope with stress will not only improve people's lives but also the lives of those around them.

Classification and Division

This rhetorical mode groups ideas. A classification pattern puts things into groups, categories, or types. A division pattern describes what parts or elements make up something. For example, you may want to discuss parenthood. If you ask, "What types of parents are there?" you would be using a classification pattern. If you ask, "What makes up a good parent?" you would be using a division type of pattern. This rhetorical mode is a useful one in the natural sciences, in social sciences, and in philosophy discussions.

TIPS FOR WRITING A CLASSIFICATION AND DIVISION PIECE

Tip 1. *Consider your specific purpose.* This rhetorical mode may suit various purposes. You might be trying to consider ideas in a new way, perhaps to create new classifications of things. By the same token, you may find that you are asked to consider the components of something. For example, in a literature essay you may decide to define a hero as someone who is loyal, stands up for his own convictions, and sacrifices for others. Then, you might consider the main character of a novel and attempt to fit him into your definition. This division pattern is commonly used because it asks a writer, thinker, or reader to consider what constitutes something. This is a fairly straightforward pattern to use and is effective because once your categories or parts have been decided, most of the organization of the essay has been taken care of.

Tip 2. *Do not overgeneralize or stereotype.* When using this type of pattern, be careful of grouping people into categories and then making sweeping definite statements about their characteristics. This is a form of stereotyping that can be racist or sexist. Be sure your statements about people are fair and well supported.

Tip 3. *Try to classify in an interesting way.* If you choose classification, try to think of new and engaging ways of grouping your ideas. Do not simply state the obvious. Instead of re-hashing categories, try to invent new ones. For example, could you devise new categories for fashion? Could you invent another way of looking at the movies?

Tip 4. *Use transitions that indicate a classification and division mode.* These transitions will reinforce the mode for the reader and will help to unify your piece of writing. Use keywords and phrases like *type*, *division*, *group*, *kind*, etc. Review chapter 4 for more transitions.

Read the following essay example based on classification and division. Look over the thesis statement, the categories the writer invents, and the support for each category. What do you think the writer's purpose was in writing the piece?

Example: Classification and Division

Three Kinds of Drivers

Since cars were invented, western society deals with the problems and harm stemming from a variety of driving habits. Most drivers seem unaware of the potentially damaging power of the ordinary automobile. Others drive by the rules. Three types of drivers—the reckless, who is a danger; the inconsistent, who is a menace; and the circumspect, who is an exemplar of safe driving—dominate Canadian roadways.

The first type, the reckless driver, causes harm. Since most drivers in this category are male and 18–35 years of age, according to accident data, this type of driver will be referred to as "he." Largely, he does not obey posted signs and speed limits. He is caught speeding more than drivers in any other age group. He speeds while ignoring road conditions and drives according to how he feels. Secondly, this driver respects neither drivers nor pedestrians. He is seldom aware of pedestrian crosswalks or walkers, bikers, or joggers on the road. According to a 2008 Alberta Council for Road Safety report, pedestrian deaths in crosswalks is on the rise. The Insurance Alliance of British Columbia also confirms this evidence in a 2007 study of fatal accidents. Property is also damaged by this driver. Some estimates claim insurance rates increase by 10 percent a year due to damage to vehicles and real property. The reckless driver causes the most harm, but another type is also dangerous.

The inconsistent driver is unpredictable. Driving habits change, depending on the driver's stress levels. Most of the time, this person obeys the road signs and the speed limits, but sometimes, he or she will take undue chances. He or she may run an amber light because he or she is late. This driver may carelessly ignore speed limits because of inattention. The inconsistent driver may suddenly change lanes without giving other drivers proper signals. He or she may weave all over the lane as the individual fumbles with a coffee cup, a cigarette, or the stereo system. This driver may like to socialize as he or she is driving down the road, paying more attention to the conversation than the road conditions. Moreover, this driving type is totally distractible. If there is a scene alongside the road, this driver will "rubberneck" in order to get a glimpse, completely unaware that by doing so, he or she has slowed traffic or made the driver behind come to a screeching halt. This driver does not intend to drive recklessly; he or she is simply unmindful, in contrast to the third type of driver.

The circumspect driver is the most reliable and is generally accident-free. This driver obeys signs, attends to speed limits, and is attentive of the road conditions. He or she drives defensively, taking in the "big picture" on the road, including construction zone speed limits, school zones, dangerous drivers in other lanes, black ice, detours, and other roadway hazards. This driver respects the road rights of others and pays close attention to pedestrians. He or she drives for safety: In rush hour traffic, this is the driver who will allow another driver to access a lane or make a lane change. He or she also respects the need to give opportunities to commercial drivers like bus or cab drivers, or truckers who drive as their livelihood. Because the circumspect driver is so expert, he or she rarely gets into collisions or causes harm on the road.

These three types of drivers are on Canadian roadways night and day. Two types create problems and harm, while the last makes driving pleasant and safe. All in all, some drivers are uneducated as to the potential damage of careless driving, and as NRW news reports, 72 percent of people killed on the roads were killed by reckless, ruthless drivers. Each driver on the road chooses the type of driver to be. With more consideration and thought, every driver could become the circumspect one.

USING A BLENDED APPROACH IN EXPOSITORY WRITING

Generally speaking, you will find that writers use a combination of rhetorical modes when they write, although one mode may dominate. Different modes are better suited to different purposes, so it is not unusual to see body paragraphs in different modes.

Sometimes your topic requires this flexibility. It will depend on your purpose, your audience, and your tone to some extent. For example, if your audience is a group who might require further explanation, then you may decide to define some key ideas in your first body paragraph. In the second and third body paragraphs, you might decide to compare and contrast your definitions to other popular ones, considering what is different and what is the same about them. In the paragraphs following, you might decide to discuss the impact of certain ways of representing something through the definitions—a cause-and-effect rhetorical mode.

Sometimes you will be assigned one particular mode to work with, but in many other writing situations, you will decide the design of your paper. A history course, for instance, may have three or four written assignments in it. Your professor or instructor will be interested in how you make your ideas relate. You may choose cause and effect, classification, and process analysis as tools to organize and design one paper. You may choose another set for another paper, depending on your purpose. If you wish to explore how ideas contrast in two different periods of Canadian social history—ideas of marriage, for example—then you will use this tool mainly, but you may also want to bring in definitions of marriage as part of your paper's discussion. You may also want to divide the idea of marriage into the component parts that have traditionally comprised it. Therefore, as a matter of critical thinking and writing, you will choose the appropriate rhetorical modes and thinking tools to develop your topic and to suit your specific purpose in writing.

The following article comes from a popular Canadian magazine. The writer uses a blended approach in the organization of the piece. Read the article, paying attention to the rhetorical modes Jennifer Quist uses. Since the piece is written for a magazine, you will notice some differences in paragraphing style between this article and academic writing. For example, the last part of the article is a single sentence only. In academic writing, you must use complete paragraphs in all sections of your paper.

Example: Blended Approach

It's All in the Bag

by Jennifer Quist

Jennifer Quist, her husband, and three young sons live in Fort McMurray, Alta., where she writes a weekly newspaper column.

It looks like a shrunken, leather Noah's ark with a long shoulder strap sewn onto its ends. It can still be found slumped on the third step up to the second floor of my parents' house. Inside, it's crammed with credit cards, hand lotions, tissues, gum, makeup, half a dozen pens (some that actually work), a cellophane rain hat from decades past, and a cellular phone from the cutting edge of technology. It's always been an institution of motherhood in our family—the Big Purse.

My mother isn't a cruel woman, but she is merciless when it comes to the primacy of the Purse. She has forced her own children to fetch it for her, sit crowded in shopping carts with it, and feel it tossed heavily onto our feet in the front seat of her car. She has even made us carry it in public. The loss-prevention sentinels that "greet" shoppers at discount stores bristle with even greater suspicion than usual when a teenager skulks sheepishly through the automatic doors with a behemoth handbag half-tucked under her jacket. I could almost hear the surveillance cameras zooming in to see that the bulging purse stayed shut. It was with us everywhere—the Big Purse.

It was one of those mothering institutions that I dreaded as a young girl, like varicose veins and zippered housecoats. In my younger days, as I peered at it over the tops of my sociology textbooks, the Big Purse looked exactly like a shackle of male oppression. It slouched on the stairs embodying the injustices of a society where women must be weighed down by huge, ugly sacs in order to maintain social order. In those early days, I assured myself that it must be possible for me to someday have a family of my own and at the same time resist the powerful gravity of the Big Purse.

It was also in the midst of my liberal feminist education that I decided that male power in modern society has a major seat that has been overlooked in all the excitement over pay equity and patrilineal nomenclature: the unfair allocation of pockets between the sexes.

Even in an age that has seen practical fashion movements like "cargo" clothing, there are still times when women are expected to dress in clothes that are completely devoid of pockets. This is especially true when women need to dress in formal wear or maternity clothing. Women are consistently deprived of pockets in the clothes that are designed and merchandised for us. Maybe someone is afraid that a pregnant woman with pockets would be too socially powerful. After all, a fruitful womb is the ultimate pocket known to humankind.

Regardless, most women, pregnant or not, find themselves often relying on the charity of the many-pocketed opposite sex to carry our car keys and bank cards. Men's clothing is slathered in pockets. While women teeter around dress-up affairs juggling ridiculous, shiny clutch purses and glorified wallets on strings, men tuck what they need into the nine pockets sewn into most of their suits.

Growing up is full of surprises. As my life unfolded, it turned out that things aren't quite as unfair as I had once thought. I didn't find this out all at once. It crept up on me little by little as I started having my own children. It seems that with every new phase my kids pass through, I find myself back in the accessories sections of cheap department stores rifling through tables full of cavernous, discount purses. Every time I visit the sales racks I come away with a bigger purse than the I one I brought in with me.

Now it sits in a corner of my bedroom—my very own Big Purse. It holds water bottles, baby wipes, diapers of two different sizes, Aspirin, toddler-bribing treats, half a dollar in pennies, and even something my own mother was never neurotic enough to carry herself: a coupon file.

I admit that I was wrong about the Big Purse. With my Big Purse at my side I'm almost completely self-sufficient. I can blow my nose whenever I want to because I always have a tissue. I'm the only one at noisy amusement parks with access to Aspirin. And when the baby spits up I'm the heroine, with a perpetual stash of baby wipes within arms' reach.

The Big Purse is probably not a symptom of male oppression. Instead, it might just be part of the cure for it. In the lives of women like myself and my mother, the Big Purse makes it possible for us to be independent, adaptable, in control and functional in a world that is more focussed on meeting the needs of the many-pocketed. The Big Purse doesn't embody the whimper of a defeated sex but the war cry of a resourceful gender with a workable alternative to simply mimicking its oppressors.

I lug my Big Purse with pride. It doesn't weigh me down. It helps to set me free.

Source: Jennifer Quist, "It's All in the Bag," Maclean's *1 Apr. 2002: 12. By permission of Jennifer Quist.*

Assignment In-Class Writing

Your instructor will ask you to write a short (500- to 600-word) essay in class, using one of the rhetorical modes or a blended approach. The instructor may select one of the two readings from this chapter or from another. You will read the selection in class, and then have the class develop topics. You will choose one of the topics and write your essay during class time, using about 40–45 minutes.

Tips for Timed Writing

Timed writing is unlike writing for take-home assignments. In-class assignments or exams are part of most post-secondary courses. In timed writing, you will have to "think on your feet." You will not have much time to generate ideas, to organize, to reflect, to revise, to edit, and to proof-read. Follow these tips.

Tip 1. *Prepare a good writing plan.* This is the most important part of in-class or timed writing. Plan for at least five minutes. Make your plan a visual one wherein you sketch ideas clearly. A good plan will give you the confidence to write better.

Tip 2. *Have an overall plan for managing the whole writing task.* Here is an example:

- writing plan for five minutes
- composing for 30 minutes
- revising, editing, and proofreading for 10 minutes

total: 45 minutes

Tip 3. *Switch topics quickly.* If, after two minutes, you find you cannot think of enough to say on your first selection and your sketch outline is weak, switch topics.

Assignment Writing an Essay

Write an essay of about 700 words on one of the following topics. Double-space your writing. Use APA or MLA style if you do research and want to include it. (See chapters 14 and 15 for more information.) Use a third-person point of view.

Topics:

- cheap recreation
- responsibilities of parenthood
- what it means to be a Canadian
- philosophy for kids
- differences between charities and corporations
- how to make a time machine
- drivers' habits
- remodelling your home
- fashion disasters
- family dinners
- the best pets
- weekend projects
- athletics and competition

REVIEW TEST

Try the following review test. It will help you assess what you have learned from the chapter. Be prepared to share your responses with others in the class.

1. What is a rhetorical mode in writing?

____

____

____

____

2. What is a classification mode?

____

____

____

____

3. What is a process analysis mode?

____

____

____

____

4. What is a blended approach?

____

____

____

____

5. What is the purpose of rhetorical modes in writing?

____

____

____

____

Bonus Exercise *Avoiding Double Negatives*

Using double negatives means placing two negative words or phrases together. This phrasing is considered incorrect. Double negatives are confusing because it is not clear if the writer wants the sentence to be positive by having one negative cancelling out the other or if the writer wants to be emphatic. The Brian's Errors website **(www.wsu.edu/~brians/errors/double.html)** provides a fun example of a double negative: "Douglas Adams' description of a machine dispensing 'a substance almost, but not quite, entirely unlike tea'."

In any case, avoid writing in double negatives. Check your answers with the answer Key.

Examples:2

Error: Rochelle doesn't have none. (negative + negative)

Correction: Rochelle doesn't have any. (negative + positive)

Correct each of the following by eliminating the double negatives. Check your answers with the Answer Key.

1. Nick doesn't want nothing for lunch.

____

____

2. I can't share my pizza with you because I don't have hardly any.

____

____

3. The dog couldn't scarcely walk after the accident.

____

____

4. Mr. Mueller, the new manager, has not been here barely a year.

____

____

5. The shopper could not find nowhere to buy new shoes.

____

____

READINGS

Read carefully the following two articles. Pay attention to the rhetorical patterns the writers have chosen. Be prepared to answer the questions that follow.

Sea Urchins and Sand Dollars—No Brains but Lots of Sense

by Julie Johnston, Pat Haugh, and Susan Taylor

This article is one of a series about the species you might find on Gulf Island beaches. Julie Johnston (writer), Pat Haugh (researcher), and Susan Taylor (illustrator) are members of the Georgia Strait Alliance Straitkeepers, a volunteer group supported by the Pender Islands Conservancy Association (PICA). They conduct surveys of shore life between high and low tide, to encourage ongoing intertidal stewardship in the community.

Sea urchins and sand dollars are intriguing marine animals. Even with no brains, they've prospered for over 500 million years. By comparison, we humans have only been here one or two million years.

There are about 700 species of sea urchins and 150 species of sand dollars worldwide. In fact, sand dollars are found in oceans throughout the world, except off Europe and Antarctica, and are among the most highly populated species of marine life.

Both sea urchins and sand dollars are echinoderms ("spiny-skinned" invertebrates) that live on the ocean floor. All echinoderms have calcareous plates covered with a soft layer of skin. Like their relatives, the sea stars and sea cucumbers, the sea urchins and sand dollars show five-fold radial symmetry—like spokes in a wheel.

Unlike sea stars, urchins have a hard round body and sand dollars a disk-like body (called the "test"). Sand dollars are essentially flattened sea urchins with reduced spines. Both have five sets of pores arranged in a petal-like pattern. The pores are used to move sea water into an internal water-vascular system (a rudimentary circulatory system).

Sand dollars live up to their name, burrowing into sandy bottoms in low tide areas or subtidally to 130 feet, in sheltered bays and along open coasts. They are typically found oriented to the currents, lying flat or standing vertically, with a third or more of the body buried. Young sand dollars swallow heavy sand grains to weigh themselves down, and adults fight the currents by growing heavier skeletons. Because sand dollars are unable to right themselves if upturned and will die, it's important not to disturb them. In subtidal areas, even shallow ones, the density of sand dollars can be staggering, more than 500 per square yard.

Sea urchins, sometimes in huge herds, live on the rocky sea floor or in larger tidepools, from the intertidal zone to depths of over 3500 feet. Purple sea urchins actually work themselves into hollows in the rock, to protect them from the pounding surf. The word "urchin" comes from the Greek for hedgehog. Sea urchins look like little hedgehogs with their movable calcareous spines, which can be long or short, blunt or sharp, and some times venomous. The spines point out in all directions, and are connected to the skeleton by ball-and-socket joints. Urchins also have five double rows of tube feet protruding from the skeleton, which together with the spines, provide a surprising range of movement. Sea urchins have an anus in the centre of the upper surface, and a mouth in the centre of the lower surface surrounded by five sharp-toothed jaws, which are moved by 60 muscles. The mouth's complex structure is called Aristotle's lantern because the Greek philosopher described it as being similar to an ancient lamp.

Sea urchins use their spines for protection, moving, and trapping food. They eat plant and animal matter, including kelp and other algae, dead fish, sponges, mussels, and barnacles. They use their Aristotle's lantern to chop the food into tiny fragments that can be swallowed and digested. Sea urchins consume so much algae that heavily grazed areas are sometimes referred to as "sea urchin barrens." When the sea otter was hunted to the brink of extinction, sea urchins destroyed whole kelp forests by cutting away at the lower portions of the plants. In the Pacific Northwest, sea urchins are now cultivated for their roe, which is popular in sushi.

The most common sea urchins in our area are green sea urchins, with short, fine, crowded spines and a definite greenish tinge, sometimes found around docks and pilings; the red sea urchin, the giant of the three, up to almost five inches with spines more than two inches long; and the purple sea urchin, with short, stout spines, found mainly on wave-swept shores.

Sea urchins are also well-known to biology students for their laboratory role in teaching the wonder of fertilization and development. In both sea urchins and sand dollars, the sexes are separate. The females release several million tiny, jelly-coated, transparent eggs, while the males discharge sperm. Fertilized eggs develop into free-swimming larvae, which, unlike the adults, have bilateral symmetry (like us). The larvae travel many miles as they are swept along by ocean currents. The lucky ones eventually sink to the ocean floor and metamorphose into the adult form, a process that can take two to five years. Sea urchins can live up to 30 years; and sand dollars up to 50!

Sand dollars average three inches in diameter. The almost-velvety, black or purplish spines are flattened and smaller than the sea urchin's, allowing them to wiggle through sand, trapping food (organic waste) as they move. Fine, thin hairs cover the spines and, in combination with a sticky mucous, aid in moving food to the mouth. Tube feet stick out from the holes that form the five-petalled pattern on the top surface and are used as gills for breathing. Because of its off-centre petal pattern, our local species is called the eccentric sand dollar. Sand dollars have a modified Aristotle's lantern on the underside for processing small particles of food. Both sand dollars and sea urchins are eaten by sea otters, sea stars, fishes, crabs, snails, and some birds.

Sea urchin spines can sting, are difficult to extract, and can lead to abscessed wounds, so be careful. A popular French expression about someone's stinginess ("He has sea urchins in his pockets") serves as a reminder that they must be handled with care, if at all.

Children have been known to say that sand dollars are pressed sand, or mermaid coins washed up from the deep. Because what we mostly find on beaches are skeletons, it's easy to forget that sea urchins and sand dollars are not mere trinkets, but beautiful living creatures.

Source: Julie Johnston, Pat Haugh & Susan Taylor, "Sea Urchins and Sand Dollars—No Brains but Lots of Sense: Exploring Our Intertidal Zone," Island Tides *28 Aug. 2003: 8. Reprinted by permission of Christa Grace-Warrick, Island Tides Publishing Ltd.*

Comprehension Questions

1. How large do sand dollars grow on average?
2. Without using a dictionary and using context clues, what does the underlined term "intertidal zone" mean in the selection?
3. What two main purposes do spines in sea urchins serve?
4. Why is the kelp so important to the balance of life in coastal waters?
5. If sea urchins continue to be overfished for sushi, what will the impact be?
6. What predominant rhetorical mode do the authors use to develop their ideas in the article?

Critical Comprehension

1. How does symmetry in animals reveal something about their habitat and their way of making a living? Provide examples from the article.
2. How are echinoderms in balance with their surroundings?

Humpty Dumpty Can't Get Up

by Gina Mallet

Gina Mallet is a writer living in Toronto. Previously, she wrote for the *Toronto Star* as a theatre critic. Most recently she has been writing articles about food and the food industry for the *National Post.* In "Humpty Dumpty Can't Get Up," a section from "The Imperiled Egg" in *Last Chance to Eat: The Fate of Taste in a Fast Food World*, Mallet looks into egg production and marketing, providing some surprising information.

The egg producers had just got their heads above water when they were struck by another menace: *Salmonella enterides*, a pathogenic strain of the bacteria. *Salmonella E* produces a mild form of typhoid fever in humans, and most people don't notice it; but in susceptible people, it may be, and very occasionally has been, fatal. Before Healthism, people would have simply sniffed and gone on eating. Instead, after *Salmonella E* was first discovered in eggs in Europe and then in the United States in the 1980s, a major threat to life was perceived. One death is all it takes in a society scared witless about food safety to condemn a food. The idea that out there was a chicken Typhoid Mary laying infected eggs was bad enough; but the fact that nobody knew how *Salmonella E* got into the egg caused consternation.

An egg is a little fortress. Nature has provided it with a natural barrier, an inner skin that stalls any bacteria that may slip through the porous shell. You don't have to be a hen-hugger to suspect that nature was biting back with *Salmonella E.* Industrialized humans crammed together in slums with bad sanitation were prey to many diseases of close proximity, notably typhoid fever. Why shouldn't it be the same for hens? In Canada, where the industrial flocks are smaller, *Salmonella E* is practically nonexistent. The circumstances of an industrial hen's life seem guaranteed to weaken her. The hens are confined to battery cages crammed with other birds, deprived of fresh air, and forced to lay far too many eggs. Most of the calcium they need goes into the shells of the eggs, and so they develop osteoporosis. No wonder hens often break a leg. And the smell! Anyone who has had the misfortune to visit an egg factory wishes they'd taken along a gas mask. The hens themselves are made ill by the smell of their own excrement.

But the egg industry was less interested in finding the root cause of *Salmonella E* than in stopping it. In Europe, the hens were vaccinated. In North America, everything that could be cleansed was cleansed again, and warning bulletins about egg handling were broadcast widely. *Salmonella E* hasn't disappeared, but it has declined. According to the American Egg Board (AEB), the chance of anyone getting infected by an egg in America is about 1 in 20,000, and then if you're healthy, you probably won't get sick at all.

Even so, an industrial solution has to be found. In some parts of the United States, shell eggs are already being pasteurized. A computerized conveyor belt passes the eggs through successive baths of water, heated from 144°F to 162°F in order to destroy any pathogens. Pasteurization, of course, also wipes out any egg taste. The American Egg Board encourages the use of these eggs, even if they don't quite look right. The board advises: "The heating process may create cloudiness in the whites and increase the beating time for foam formation. When you separate pasteurized shell eggs for beating, allow up to about four times as much time for the full foam formation to occur, as you would in the whites of regular eggs."

The final solution is the irradiated egg. Irradiating eggs, or any food for that matter, is similar to radiation therapy. It is not likely to be good for an egg any more than a gamma ray is good for a human. But gamma rays, electrons, or X-rays that are beamed through the eggs will knock out all pathogens. The Food and Drug Administration admits that eggs lose 24 percent of their vitamin A when exposed to just one third of the approved level of radiation. The yolks of an irradiated egg are watery and dim, and the egg itself is no longer the cook's little helper. The irradiated egg is more difficult to cook, requires more time to whip, and yields angelfood cakes with half the volume.

Should you wish to order one of the old-fashioned natural eggs sunnyside up or over easy at your favorite diner—well, you may not be able to. In 2000, the U.S. Food and Drug Administration decreed that egg cartons must carry the warning that eggs should be cooked solid. An egg is only safe when cooked to 161°F. So over the side goes Caesar Salad and mayonnaise, just when the all-clear was sounded on eggs and cholesterol. Gone too is Thames Mud, Ulisse's classic chocolate mousse, made only from melted chocolate and raw eggs, and of course Carême's soufflés. I doubt whether a hot soufflé reaches more than 161°F in the middle, which must be creamy. Meringues are axed as well—egg whites and sugar, a dash of vanilla, baked overnight in a 100°F oven. The last straw was the FDA announcement that the venerable practice of the child licking the bowl and beaters used to make cake batter with raw eggs is a no-no. One of the most powerful and evocative memories of childhood has been obliterated, and a link to the past broken. Better safe than sorry, said the FDA spokesperson piously.

I stop right there. The future industrial egg is not going to be an egg at all. Those rows and rows of eggs in plastic packages in the supermarket are Andy Warhol eggs, clever facsimiles of the real thing. In the future, I see the end of the shell egg altogether; eggs will be shelled and repacked, six or twelve to a rectangular transparent plastic box. A whole variety of eggs will be packaged this way. We can have square hard-boiled eggs for instant picnics (if picnics have not been banned by the Food Police), and square scrambled eggs ready for nuking. One day not so far off, the properties of the egg will be synthesized in the lab and the real thing done away with altogether, along with the tiresome hens that lay them. So much cleaner and quicker.

But maybe not. The *Salmonella E* scare did something that the cholesterol scare had failed to do. For years, the Animal Rights movement had protested the cruel treatment of industrial hens, but the sight of grown men and women dressed as oversized Rock Island Reds accosting egg industry executives never moved the public. The idea of toxic eggs did. By the end of the nineties, public pressure forced the European Union to draw up a hen's bill of rights, including phasing out the ubiquitous battery cages. The great breakthrough came in 2000, when McDonald's, the global fast food giant, went further and declared that it would no longer buy chickens that hadn't been raised humanely. The cruel battery cages must be phased out in short order, and false molting (the practice of starving chickens to force them to come back to laying faster) and debeaking discontinued. Since McDonald's buys 1.5 billion eggs a year, the suppliers agreed. McDonald's followed this up with a ban on any hens being fed antibiotics—a common industrial practice to make the birds grow faster.

The American egg industry was rocked by the McDonald's announcement. If such stringent guidelines were adopted by the industry, mass egg production would cease. But consumers were now aroused, and supermarkets and fast food chains bowed to pressure and came up with their own voluntary guidelines. In 2002, the United Egg Producers followed suit with less stringent standards for hen welfare, which were also voluntary.

This turnaround in hens' fortunes was boosted by the growing organic movement. The industrial chicken was a limping disaster, and it cut a pathetic figure beside the hens raised on small farms and fed food uncontaminated by pesticides and antibiotics. As enthusiasm for organic food grew in the 1990s, so did the market for farm eggs, sold locally and over the Internet, which has become the gourmet's mail-order market.

Moreover, the farmers are proving canny marketers themselves. They now market new categories of eggs designed to appeal even more to healthists—vegetarian eggs laid by hens on strict vegetarian diets; Omega-3 eggs laid by hens fed flaxseed. Omega-3 is a death defier of a fatty acid, fending off thrombosis and cancer, among other killers. The latest super-egg in America is "Cage Free," the hen-hugger's darling. Cage Free hens stroll free, and their beaks are clipped, a process farmers insist is no more painful than a human person clipping her toenails. And the supermarkets are taking notice, so that more and more designer eggs, from the big egg producers, get space on the shelves.

There's just one niggling problem. "Organic" eggs are hot sellers because a growing number of people believe that organic is the healthiest of all seals of approval. But is it? A U.S. Department of Agriculture (USDA) certified organic egg has been laid by a hen raised on blameless organic food. Wait a minute. The hen is also guaranteed to have been allowed outdoors to take a dustbath. But the outdoors is where the hen is most likely to pick up *Salmonella E*, according to the same USDA . . .

Then there's the environmental objection. It's one thing to have a flock of a hundred or so hens pecking around a yard, and quite another to loose a vast commercial flock outdoors. The battery system handles one aspect very well: it removes excrement efficiently and uses it in cattle feed and garden fertilizer. But if a hundred thousand hens lived outside, in a constrained space, the excrement would be overwhelming, sinking into the earth and poisoning the groundwater.

Source: Gina Mallet, "The Imperiled Egg," Last Chance to Eat: The Fate of Taste in a Fast Food World *(Toronto: McClelland & Stewart, 2004) 87–92.* 2004. *Used by permission of McClelland & Stewart Ltd.*

Comprehension Questions

1. What changes to the normal qualities of yolks and whites result from irradiation of eggs?
2. Without using a dictionary and using context clues, what does the underlined term "pasteurization" mean in the selection?
3. According to the article, do the fast-food chains and supermarkets want to increase profits or please consumers? What evidence can you provide for your answer?
4. Do consumers care more about humanizing industrial food production methods or product availability and cost at the checkout? How?
5. Will strict government regulation and inspection of chicken products be needed to protect Canadian consumers from *Salmonella E* infections?
6. What predominant rhetorical mode does Mallet use to develop her ideas?

Critical Comprehension

1. Define what you think Mallet means by "healthism"?
2. What are some of the harmful effects of irradiating foods?
3. How do "food scares" affect product and production?

CHECKOUT

Here are some of the ideas you will take away with you after you have completed the chapter:

1. Rhetorical modes shape ideas by arranging them into patterns.
2. Expository writing informs readers and provides explanation.
3. Transitions help your essay stick together.
4. There must be some angle of interest in the thesis statement; otherwise, the reader could simply look up the information in a reference book.
5. A thesis statement should show a clear rhetorical pattern of development.
6. The rhetorical pattern you choose will depend on your purpose in writing.
7. Timed writing takes practice and a plan.

Mastering the concepts in this chapter will also help you develop and apply the following employability skills highlighted by the Conference Board of Canada in *Employability Skills 2000+*:

Communicate

- read and understand information presented in a variety of forms (e.g., words, graphs, charts, diagrams)
- use relevant scientific, technological and mathematical knowledge and skills to explain or clarify ideas

Manage Information

- locate, gather and organize information using appropriate technology and information systems

Source: Adapted from *Employability Skills 2000+* Brochure E/F (Ottawa: The Conference Board of Canada, 2000).

chapter 10

Critical Skills: Argumentation

Chapter Objectives

After completing this chapter you will be able to

1. contrast persuasion and argument as they relate to academic writing;
2. read text, evaluate it, and then argue a position on the topic;
3. provide sound arguments in your writing rather than emotional appeals;
4. study the structure of someone else's argument to help you frame your own;
5. improve your arguments by getting the "reader profile" right;
6. vary your tone, attitude, words, writer's voice, and arguments as a writer.

INTRODUCTION

Has your opinion ever been swayed because of something you read or heard? Have you found your point of view suddenly shifting because a writer or speaker has presented new, compelling facts or examples? If you were undecided in a choice of a purchase, have you changed your mind because a salesperson has convinced you? If you answer "yes" to these questions, then you know about the powers of persuasion in the everyday world. A famous expression is that persuasion is more an art than a science. However, to persuade means to provide a compelling argument, based on sound principles of critical thinking and reading.

You may believe that learning to construct a written argument is not a particularly important skill, but Nussbaum and Schraw (2007) counter this in their article, "Promoting Argument-Counterargument Integration in Students' Writing":

> *Researchers have found that good argumentation skills promote learning and conceptual change in science (Alexopoulou & Driver, 1996; Baker, 1999), understanding of mathematical concepts (Lampert, Rittenhouse, & Crumbaugh, 1996; Schwarz, Neuman, & Biezuner, 2000), better mathematical problem solving (Vye et al., 1997), and comprehension of issues in history and social studies (De La Paz, 2005; Wiley & Voss, 1999). Argumentation can also enhance intrinsic motivation and problem-solving performance (Chinn, 2006). (p.60)*

Currently the most recognizable form of argument is found in advertising. In a business-driven, consumerist economy, you are bombarded by an enormous amount of persuasive advertising every day, so experts have got to get their messages out quickly and effectively. Most magazine ads contain few words—sometimes as few as one or two—together with plenty of visuals. Therefore, most advertising copy has to convince you fast that you should buy a product or service. Your attention is itself a precious commodity that every advertisement is attempting to obtain.

However, argument, its techniques, and its purposes have been part of human discourse for a very long time. Even the early Greeks examined the topic thoroughly. Aristotle wrote about it extensively. Today anyone interested in human communication examines argument because of its significance in both the intellectual and real-life world. Attempting to argue your point of view convincingly can be a very real and complex challenge. To study argument and persuasion in depth would take much more time and resources than *Spotlight on Critical Skills in Essay Writing*, Second Edition, can offer. However, this text will help you examine important aspects of persuasion and argumentation as they relate to academic writing.

One of the most common writing assignments at college or university is to read text, evaluate it, and then effectively argue a position on the topic. A major part of argumentation is how you think critically about points and ideas. As you have seen in previous chapters, critical thinking comprises a number of skills and steps:

1. Summarize or paraphrase a writer's ideas to be sure you have recognized and understood the most significant major ideas, premises, and facts.
2. Then compare and contrast these ideas with those of different writers and with your own experiences.
3. Afterward, analyze the text or argument specifically to understand its particular construction and find the writer's reasons, proof, and conclusions.
4. Evaluate the data.
5. Develop your own position and argue from it in order to present a clear line of reasoning.

The sequence of these steps may change as you work through different projects. The level of difficulty will determine how deeply you will drill into these skills. The next chapter provides you with practice in applying all of the skills and steps in order to convince your reader, using some persuasive arguments.

DISTINCTIONS BETWEEN PERSUASION AND ARGUMENT

When you use *persuasion*, you take a position or stance on an issue in an attempt to change someone's mind about it. You try to appeal to her emotions, ethics, or reason. When as a writer you use *argumentation*, you engage in a process of using logical reasoning to arrive at some sort of truth. Your purpose is not necessarily to persuade your reader because you may, in fact, construct a sound argument, but your reader may not be persuaded by it. In argumentation, you are concentrating on the form of your argument rather than the appeals to emotion or character you might make in order to convince your reader of your point of view or opinion on a matter.

However, to write persuasively, you must provide sound arguments, too. You cannot simply rely on emotional appeals alone because your reader or listener will surely begin to figure out that you have little evidence. Of course, facts alone may or may not be convincing. Therefore, when you write persuasively, you look for an intelligent balance between the types of evidence you use (the appeals), the words you choose (connotation) that will convey your attitude (tone), and the construction and development of your presentation (the argument).

Persuasion and argument are often seen as distinctly different: in persuasion, you use emotional appeal in an attempt to change a reader's point of view; in argumentation, you use reason and logic to analyze the soundness and validity of an argument. However, the interplay between argument and persuasion is necessary. To convince a reader or listener, you must present a compelling case, and the more reasonably constructed it is, the more persuasive it will be. To build such constructions, you must be able to recognize what arguments others are making in their work, and you must be able to analyze how they have developed them. Your ability to recognize the structure of someone else's argument can help you frame your own when it comes time to think about issues and write about them. It will also help you to think of counter-arguments and effective pieces of evidence. All in all, analysis, critical reading and thinking as part of argumentation are really tools for deepening your understanding of topics and issues.

PURPOSES OF PERSUASION AND ARGUMENT

Have you ever been persuaded by a convincing argument? Describe in writing a situation in which you had been persuaded, either to buy or to do something. Free-write for 10 minutes. Then be prepared to share and discuss answers with others in the class. How were you persuaded? How were others in the class convinced? The **claims** or **warrants** others make are central to their arguments. What claims were made that helped persuade you? Having a clear purpose in mind helps you strengthen your position.

These purposes can be different, depending on the writer and the writer's context.:

1. For financial or political gain.

   Advertising wants you to change your mind in order to use a product or service. For example, if you have used a particular brand of laundry soap because it is relatively cheap and does a passable job, then it will be somewhat difficult to change your mind, so what can an advertiser do? Companies must find appeals that work, and these appeals must come in the form of reasons. Corporations might discuss environmental issues and declare their product more environmentally "safe" than your old brand. They might prove the efficiency of their product by showing you how many more wash loads you will get from their brand than from the competition's, or they might appeal to your parental pride by showing you how clean, tidy, and well cared for your family will look in clothes washed in their product. More appeals are available through a variety of techniques that advertising and marketing experts know well.

   Political parties also want you to change your mind on issues and policies. They are constantly looking for ways to make inroads into your personal political life. They want you to join their party, vote with them in particular ways on particular issues, and stand with them philosophically. Governments spend billions of dollars endeavouring to sway voters, but these appeals must be based on reasons.

2. For social equality and action.

   Most environmental groups work to change perspectives on issues and policies that have an impact on the natural world and people's lives. They use argumentation techniques that work on ethical and emotional grounds in order to persuade listeners or readers. They may draw attention to an issue such as global warming, for instance, and then provide examples of extreme, devastating weather changes that have occurred over the past decade. Through careful reasoning by looking at the cost of human lives and the penalty on other living things due to tsunamis, droughts, or floods, they can then argue successfully.

   Other public watchdog groups may be lobbying for changes in legislation related to drinking and driving, education, child safety, consumer protection, and so forth. These interest groups use a mixture of appeals, including statistics, reports, studies, and eye-witness accounts. For example, they may cite the number of deaths related to youngsters and recreational vehicles, such as all-terrain vehicles.

Read the following example involving snowmobile-related deaths, and then think about answers to the questions that follow.

The Cold Truth about Snowmobiling

by Laura Aiken

Snowmobiling is one of the most dangerous sports in Canada, a report from the Canadian Institute for Health Information (CIHI) indicates.

Major Injury in Canada 2002 indicates that 16% of severe sports and recreational injuries during 2000/2001 were caused by snowmobile accidents, a much higher rate than for winter sports such as downhill skiing (6%) and snowboarding (5%).

The data were collected from 30 trauma units in 7 provinces (facilities in Saskatchewan, Newfoundland and Labrador and Prince Edward Island did not participate). The study considered only the 92 most severe snowmobile-related injuries, which resulted in an average hospital stay of 2 weeks, including time in intensive care. Alcohol use was a factor in 26% of the cases. "[That] number . . . is way too high," says Julian Martalog, the study's lead analyst.

Most of those severely injured on snowmobiles were male (85%) and the average age was 33.

Overall, snowmobiling ranks second only to cycling (18%) in terms of severe injuries incurred through sports and recreational activities. More than 250,000 snowmobiles are registered across Canada. Most are in Ontario and Quebec, where 76% of the severe injuries occurred.

The study, which used an international index to rate severity, found that snowmobilers had more severe injuries than participants in other winter sports. CIHI does not know if the number of severe injuries is rising in the sport, but data indicate that over the last 5 years there has been a 20% decrease in the number of snowmobile-related injuries, regardless of severity.

Source: Laura Aiken, "The Cold Truth about Snowmobiling," CMAJ *168.6 (2003): 753. Reprinted by permission from the publisher.*

Exercise 1 Questions to Consider

1. Did you change your mind about safety in snowmobiling?
2. What changed for you?
3. What in the article helped to change your mind?
4. What type of evidence does the writer use?
5. What recommendations would you make to policy-makers?

PERSUASIVE APPEALS

In *Rhetoric*, Aristotle discusses how persuasion works through three appeals: character (ethos), emotion (pathos), and logic or reason (logos). First, persuasion works when it appeals on the grounds of a person's character: who the person is, along with the person's moral and ethical belief systems. The personal character of the speaker or writer helps to establish credibility. For example, a statement coming from the minister of finance like, "All parents should support their children financially" is just such an appeal. It convinces because the speaker is considered an authority on financial matters (appeal of character) and because it relates to a moral belief (appeal of character).

Next, emotional appeals can also influence readers or listeners. Aristotle believed that could be accomplished if a writer or speaker used appeals that would invoke anger, fear, indignation, shame, pity, or envy. In the example, if the minister of finance's statement had been, "All good and caring parents should support their children financially," then the appeal is fortified by emotion. After all, the implication is that people who do not support their children financially are not "good and caring parents."

Finally, the appeal to logic or reason is powerful. The speaker or writer can provide forceful reasons that have been carefully presented and argued. For instance, the minister of finance uses this appeal when she says, "Canadian parents contribute $18.2 billion dollars per year in the support and care of their children. These dollars directly fuel the economy, both locally and federally. Without this financial contribution, the Canadian government could not sustain the present standard of living its citizens so richly deserve."

Exercise 2 Three Appeals

Work in pairs. Read each of the following and tell which appeal the statements are based on: character, emotion, or reason. Be prepared to explain your answers.

1. Everyone deserves a better life.

   ____

2. The slaughter of 200 wild horses was witnessed by one of the officials of the Nightingale Society as she visited a field hospital.

   ____

3. Was it not our last great president of the board, Almo Y. Yardman, who said, "Good investment brings prosperity to all"?

____

4. Since 74 percent of the members were against the proposal in the Spring Survey 2006, why should we waste time and energy debating the issue at our annual general meeting?

____

5. The green variety, although excessively juicy and flavourful, did not pack as well and store as long as the orange type.

____

6. The Association of Better Accounting recommends the purchase of "HomeWorks Accounting for Small Business."

____

7. A world-famous soccer player is pictured on a poster for Fruiteeze Energy Drink. He is holding a bright green bottle of the liquid. The caption reads, "Go For It!"

____

8. Since Violet Pepperoni was not Parm Peppercorn's legal partner, she is not entitled to half of his restaurant business.

____

9. Use the minty fresh taste of Pumper's Toothpaste to get your day started!

____

10. No one, not even you, Mr. Queasley, has ever managed to make that particular policy stick here at Smart University.

____

11. We guarantee that our solar-powered ice-cream maker will last 10 years, or we promise to replace your unit at no extra cost to you!

____

12. Two studies by Collins and Short (1999 and 2005) failed to prove the connection between motivation and action.

____

13. Mr. Roy Gooze and his grandchildren reported seeing the Sasquatch on April 20, 2006, just outside their pond in the backwoods of their Merriam, British Columbia, home.

____

14. We cannot believe Koster is guilty; although he was not a leading citizen, he was a dedicated father and a skilled woodworker.

____

15. Community members are opposed to further development along the river since the single species of stickleback fish has disappeared from the local waters.

____

Exercise 3 *Which Appeal Works?*

Work in pairs for this exercise. Read each of the following. Decide together which appeal would fit in each scenario: emotion, character, or reason. Discuss how and why you made your selection. Be prepared to discuss your responses with the rest of the class.

1. Suppose you are a member of a school board. You want to see junk food removed from all of your school district's vending machines. You want to convince the school district's parent advisory groups, so you write a persuasive piece for distribution.

   ____

   ____

2. Suppose you have just gotten a new job at a small company that specializes in financial services to professional associations. You have a brilliant idea involving a special package to assist members from various professional associations who want extended health benefits. You must write to the board chair to convince her to try out your idea, despite the start-up costs involved.

   ____

   ____

3. Suppose you are going to write a letter to the editor of your favourite newspaper. The issue concerns a small area of wetland inhabited by a number of species of waterfowl. Since your city is growing rapidly, it has approved the development of the land for housing, declaring that the municipality has plenty of other wetlands available for wildlife. You disagree.

   ____

   ____

4. Your college or university has decided on a dress code for its students. The board of governors, along with the student society, has agreed to the new policy. You disagree and are about to write a letter to the board.

   ____

   ____

5. Suppose you are applying for a promotion at your place of employment. The new position is a supervisory one in information technology. You will be expected to travel quite a bit and to supervise a number of managers in three other cities in

Canada. You are very excited and want the job. You are about to write the most important cover letter of your life.

____

____

BACKGROUND ELEMENTS OF ARGUMENTATION AND PERSUASION

Certain key elements are important for effective argumentation and persuasion. Consider all of them as you think about what you want to include in your writing.

Element 1: Know Your Audience

You cannot argue or persuade effectively if you do not consider to whom you are making the appeal. A large part of effective persuasion is getting the "audience profile" right. Here is an amusing anecdote by Dr. D. Adam, former commissioner of Official Languages in Canada, in a speech given in 2003:

> *One day a zookeeper fell into the lions' pit. There he was, all of a sudden, surrounded by ten big cats with one thing on their mind: devouring him. To dissuade them, the keeper launched into a great harangue, with all the eloquence born of terror.*
>
> *He reminded them through various examples that all humans and animals are brothers and that, one day, the lion will lie down with the lamb . . . even though, as Woody Allen says, the lamb might not sleep very well.*
>
> *The lions listened very respectfully to the keeper's lecture. Some even had a tear in their eye. At the end, there was a warm round of applause.*
>
> *And then, with no further ado, they ate him up.*
>
> *The moral of this story is very simple: when it comes to strategy, preaching must not be confused with persuading. Fine speeches are no substitute for good strategies. The keeper's mistake was that he did not understand the organizational culture of the group he was addressing.*
>
> *Source: Dyane Adam, "Convincing: The Tightrope Walked by Ombudsmen," Notes for an address to the Third Statutory Conference of the Association des ombudsmans et médiateurs de la Francophonie, Yasmine Hammamet, Tunisia, 15 Oct. 2003. Office of the Commissioner of Official Languages website www.ocol-clo.gc.ca/html/speeches_discours_15102003_e.php. Reprinted with permission.*

The lesson here is clear: you must know your audience. You will write differently for different audiences, no doubt. The tone or attitude you choose, your word choices, your writer's voice, and the construction of your arguments will vary greatly. For example, suppose that two different writers want to write about the same issue, but each wants to address a different audience. If the issue is skateboarding on sidewalks, one writer decides to write from a skateboarder's perspective appealing to other skateboarders. The other writer intends to write from the point of view of a pedestrian speaking to other pedestrians.

Each writer must consider in general terms what the target audience is like. Each must formulate questions to help guide her writing. The writers might consider these background elements:

Would most skateboarders know the concerns of pedestrians?

What do pedestrians know about the skateboarders' concerns?

What do municipal or city bylaws say?

Have there been accidents?

What sort of accidents have occurred?

Are there any studies on the issue?

Who has sponsored the studies?

Was there bias?

Could the situation be resolved? How?

As you consider your audience, be cautious not to overgeneralize the facts or to stereotype who your audience is. Overgeneralizing and stereotyping are similar: both tend to base assumptions and arguments on single cases and misinformation. Here is an example. If a consumer buys a product from the Yippee Company but dislikes it, she might decide on the spot that any product from the Yippee Company will be inferior. The consumer could be right perhaps, but it is more likely that she has overgeneralized—that is, decided that all cases could be based on this one example.

Stereotyping is a form of overgeneralizing, except that people rather than products or ideas are framed in particular and inaccurate ways. Stereotyping can occur because of prejudice or overgeneralization. If, for instance you meet a person from the Yukon who happens to be a good hunter, and afterward you say, "People from the Yukon are all good hunters," you are stereotyping (and overgeneralizing).

Most of the time stereotypes are hurtful or harmful because they can be used to frame whole groups of people in negative ways. They can also lead to other false assumptions. Consider this example:

All women want to be mothers.

In what ways does this statement stereotype women? What assumptions underlie the statement? What implications are there for women who do not want to be mothers?

Exercise 4 Audience

Suppose you were asked to write about each of the following topics or issues. Name two audiences for whom the piece might be intended. Then tell how you would address each audience differently. Be prepared to share your answers.

1. Pet licensing

____

____

2. Grade inflation

____

____

3. Seatbelt regulations

____

____

4. Underwater safety

____

____

5. Gay divorce

____

____

6. Diet pills

____

____

7. Action heroes

____

____

8. Canadian national parks

____

____

9. Personal privacy issues

____

____

10. Internet security

____

____

11. Housing prices

____

____

12. Drinking on campus

____

____

13. Extreme sports

____

____

14. Editorial policies of newspapers

____

____

15. Genetically modified foods

____

____

Element 2: Develop Common Ground

Establishing a common ground means you look for factors between you and your audience that are common to both of you. In other words, you look for possible points of agreement. This common ground will help foster trust with your audience and begin bridging understanding between you. This includes having knowledge of your audience, knowing your own purpose, and understanding the levels of commitment of both. Trying to find common ground or shared knowledge is important if you want to establish open communication. Finding common ground means that your reader or listener is more apt to set aside doubt to listen to your point of view.

Establishing common ground helps you to maintain focus on the important issues. You will use "shared assumptions," or ideas, values, or beliefs on which you and your reader can agree. Once you have found these points of agreement, you are free to develop your ideas.

What might "points of agreement" mean? If you go back to the example in Exercise 1 of snowmobile-related accidents, you can probably develop a list of questions to help find common ground:

1. Start with a question like this: what areas of the issue could the writer and you agree on?
2. Could you both agree that preventing snowmobile-related injuries is a good thing?
3. Could you both agree, based on the article, that more training is needed?
4. Could you both agree, based on the data given in the article, that the training should be targeted to males in their 30s?
5. Could you both agree on what restrictions should be placed on operators of snowmobiles?

As you can see, using questions like these can help establish common ground. Although you make assumptions about the points of agreement, you are basing them on what you consider the shared knowledge between you and your reader will be. Thus, if you were to write about the dangers of outdoor recreational activities, such as snowmobiling, you might use some of the points of agreement early in your discussion: that although such outdoor activities are fun, most people (including your reader) will agree that related injuries must be decreased, perhaps through better training.

Finding common ground also means finding a common language and vocabulary. If you choose to use certain terms in your writing, you must be careful to define them clearly so that your reader understands what you mean by them. For example, if you talk about "severe" injuries, you might also include what *severe* means by defining it clearly, as the article did: "an injury resulting in a stay of two or more weeks in hospital, often in intensive care."

Element 3: Use the Appropriate Appeal

As mentioned earlier in this chapter, you should decide, based on your audience and your purpose, which appeals are going to work more effectively.

1. Choose statistics, expert testimony, reliable eyewitness reports, test results, studies, or surveys as your evidence if you want to make a logical appeal.

   Example:

   According to a 2001 study in persuasion theory by Jim Lyttle and reported in *The Journal of General Psychology,* people in education, advertising, and politics who want to use humour should consider that "ironic humor [sic] may be more effective than cartoon drawings" (214).

   Using an expert's study and his findings will be more convincing than simply saying, "Ironic humour works better than cartoons." Many audiences will want expert evidence to back up the claim. A presenter at a business conference, for example, knows convincing and logical evidence is what her audience will expect and accept.

2. If you want to appeal to character or ethics, then use moral standards and call on patriotism, the family, ideas of good citizenship, and so on.

   Example:

   Having worked in peacekeeping operations in Bosnia and Herzegovina, Afghanistan, and Sudan and having spent over 20 years in the Canadian military, I know that we should continue these missions in order to bring democracy to war-torn regions of the world by reducing the level of violence.

   The writer has established her credibility (character) for the reader by providing her background and training. In this way, the reader recognizes that the writer (or speaker) is knowledgeable about the subject. Therefore, it is more likely that the reader will listen to what the writer has to say.

3. To use an emotional appeal, evoke your reader's fears, needs, or desires. "Scare statistics" are often used by groups, particularly the media, to appeal to the listener's, viewer's, or reader's emotions.

   Example:

   DDT is a dangerously persistent chemical. Once it is absorbed by the fat cells of an organism, it cannot be removed. An early pioneer of the environmental movement, Rachael Carson, estimated that DDT, once used pervasively as a pesticide on food crops, will stay in the soil for thousands of years.

The facts and statistics given in the statement above are meant to alarm readers and change their perspective. These attention-grabbing pieces of information can be convincing if, for example, you are appealing to government groups and concerned citizens. However, this appeal will not work with all audiences. Groups representing chemical industries, for instance, would not be persuaded because they have a vested interest in the use of chemicals.

Element 4: Anticipate the Opposing Arguments

As you think through your argument, consider your best—that is, most convincing—points in terms of what your opponents will have to say about them. You try to anticipate what opposing arguments others may have in order to diffuse their points in favour of your own. Your anticipated responses are sometimes called *counter-arguments.* You may also try to think of reasons the opposition may have for their counter-arguments.

Remember that besides being prepared for the opposition by thinking of counter-arguments and reasons for counter-arguments, you are also trying to present as many points of view on an issue as possible. Your paper will then be unbiased and fair. It will present a balance of views, so that your position is a more examined one.

Example of Counter-Argument:

> Some concerned citizens believe the sentencing of criminals who commit violent acts is far too light. Although they support heavier sentences for dangerous offenders, they must recognize the high cost of maintaining a federal offender in a federal penitentiary is about $52 000 annually. They must also look at Canada's incarceration rate: it is the second-highest in the Western world.

In the example, the writer has acknowledged that critics (the opposing view) see our courts as being too lenient in the case of violent crime. To counter the point, the writer finds evidence to help refute the idea of adding to prison terms. In this case, a financial fact is useful. Tax dollars support the justice system, so the writer is countering with an emotional appeal to the reader, using a statistic.

Exercise 5 How to Counter Counter-Arguments

Form a group of three to five people. Use each of the following as your stance or position on a topic. Then think of what counter-argument your opponents might use to contest the position. Next, think of what you could use to defeat their counter-arguments—the rebuttal. Write your answers in the spaces provided. Be prepared to share your answers.

1. Your stance: The minimum wage needs to be increased in your province.

   The opposition's counter-argument:

   ____

   ____

   Your rebuttal:

   ____

   ____

2. Your stance: Organic produce is overpriced.

   The opposition's counter-argument:

   ____

   ____

   Your rebuttal:

   ____

   ____

3. Your stance: Large dogs should not be kept in a city environment.

   The opposition's counter-argument:

   ____

   ____

   Your rebuttal:

   ____

   ____

4. Your stance: All high school graduates should be technologically prepared for the work world.

   The opposition's counter-argument:

   ____

   ____

   Your rebuttal:

   ____

   ____

5. Your stance: Government should legislate mandatory retirement at age 65.

   The opposition's counter-argument:

   ____

   ____

   Your rebuttal:

   ____

   ____

Element 5: Use Humour

Some writers use humour as part of their persuasive technique, and you may choose to use it, too. By getting readers to laugh at some aspect of the issue, you have succeeded in building a bond and trust between you. You have also helped your reader to relax, and by relaxing a little, your reader may be more open-minded or accepting of your point of view.

Obviously, you must use humour appropriately. If your topic is a sensitive one and you use humour tastelessly, you will likely succeed in alienating your readers rather than engaging them. Although most readers will tolerate some jokes around serious issues, they are not likely to be persuaded to change their minds if they feel they have been insulted or offended by a writer's words.

Advertisers know that certain types of commercials work because viewers remember the humour in them. In fact, a popular television show is based on the world's funniest commercials. If listeners, readers, or viewers are paying attention to the humour in a message, they are also paying attention to other less visible features. Humour has a way of creating a positive feeling that is very useful in persuasion. You can use humorous anecdotes from your own experiences.

Your experiences or the stories you have heard from others may contain the examples you are looking for. After all, storytelling has a long and honoured tradition among all cultures of the world. Many stories from Aboriginal cultures, for instance, are very convincing, yet entertaining at the same time.

Example:

Stories to explain origins

In those days we lived beside the river. An utterly beautiful river, with its depths turned in our direction. My grandmother said that the river was a baby bottle for the whales and their children, formula which went to their heads and made them sing and snort out loud.

Source: Jovette Marchessault, "Song One: The Riverside," All My Relations: An Anthology of Contemporary Canadian Native Fiction, *ed. Thomas King (McClelland & Stewart, 1994): 176.*

Example:

Topic: Children should learn the value of money

Not every Canadian child automatically receives allowances. Some parents do not believe in simply handing out money because their children are too young to earn any for themselves. Some children had to be pretty inventive. For example, when I was eight years old, I began a money scheme in collaboration with the tooth fairy. Using the natural resources of the neighbourhood children—lost teeth—and my own powers of persuasion, I was able to garner enough pocket money for three successive summers by just applying a bit of planning and negotiating.

Element 6: Provide Evidence

The type of evidence you choose to use is very important. Weak or unreliable evidence will not do much to propel your argument. The following section discusses how you can go about finding proof for your arguments.

FACTS AND STATISTICS

You may use facts and statistics as evidence. You should show where you found the facts and statistics in your paper; otherwise, it might appear that you are making things up. If you are a known expert in a field, then your facts may not be doubted. However, as a student writer, you should cite all information you use in your paper because you want to avoid plagiarism at all costs.

When you select facts or statistics, try to choose information that will have an impact on your reader. In other words, the facts should help change your reader's mind. You might use a statistic that is an attention-getter.

Example:

It is never too late to quit smoking. According to Dr. Richard Peto in "Smoking and Smoking Cessation" in the British Medical Journal, August 5, 2000, "People who stop smoking, even well into middle age, avoid most of their subsequent risk of lung cancer, and stopping before middle age avoids more than 90% of the risk attributable to tobacco."

You might choose a fact or statistic that is meant to appeal to the reader's emotions.

Example:

According to a pamphlet distributed to students at the University of Waterloo, "University and college students make up 30% of all young adult smokers and 7% of all smokers in Canada." (www.ahs.uwaterloo.ca/~dhammond/Research/Appendix%20C_Health%20Pamphlet.eng.pdf)

The internet is a rich source of data. Many government websites offer helpful statistics on many topics. Organizations and associations also provide specific information on specialized topics. However, be cautious about which source you choose to use and cite. Some sources on the internet "look" authoritative but are not.

Some Tips for Checking How Trustworthy an Internet Source Is

1. Check the author's credentials. Usually each website provides a link to a "bio" on the author. Read about who the author is, the author's background, experience in the field, and education. If not much information is provided, be hesitant to use the source.
2. Check out the sponsor of the site. For example, if you are looking into tobacco-related health problems and you find a site sponsored by a large tobacco company, you will probably see a biased view.
3. Check the currency of the webpage. You will want to use up-to-date statistics and facts. For example, if you are writing about inner-city gang violence and whether or not it has increased or decreased, you will want to have the most recent information you can find.
4. Check the writing on the page. If there are quite a number of grammatical or spelling errors, you should be suspicious. Generally speaking, experts want their websites to reflect their professionalism, so their pages will reflect care and accuracy in good writing.

Element 7: Give Effective Reasons

Reasons are the justification for the position you take in an argument. Consider that some reasons are effective; others are not. Why?

Sometimes it is difficult to tell the difference. The reasons have to be specific, clear, and based on actual evidence. Look at the example below.

Example:

Your position: Children should not smoke.

Reason: It is bad for them.

What is wrong with this reason? First of all, it is not wrong. It is difficult to deny that smoking is bad for children, but does the reason—it is bad for them—convince you? What does the writer need to do in order to make the reason more compelling?

The reason as given is vague. "Bad" has no specific meaning. Suppose the writer tries to make the reason more convincing by making an addition:

Reason: Smoking is bad for children's health.

The writer has added the idea of health. Are you more convinced? The reason is still too generalized. The writer needs to add examples, statistics, or expert testimony.

Reason: Smoking is harmful to children's health. According to the Quebec Lung Association, bronchiolitis, bronchitis, pneumonia, rhino-pharyngitis, asthma, otitis, and other infections are directly linked to cigarette smoke exposure in children under the age of 10.

Now the writer has included a real example from an expert group. You are more likely to be persuaded because the reason given is based on scientific evidence.

INDUCTIVE AND DEDUCTIVE REASONING

Sometimes reasons take time to explain. If your reasons require an elaborated explanation, then you will have to construct your explanation carefully, using a variety of evidence. You might begin with a generalization and draw your reader to a specific conclusion based on that generalization. This type of thinking is called *deductive* reasoning. It is sometimes called a "top-down approach." Mathematics solutions are based on deductive thinking. The example of children and smoking has some elements of deductive thinking in it because the writer begins with a generalization that leads to a particular conclusion.

Examples:

All humans have language.

Yany is a human.

He has language.

Deductive reasoning is the process of concluding something must be true because it is a case based on a general principle known to be true. On the other hand, *inductive* thinking is the process of constructing a general principle from specific cases or observations made. For example, a detective might find a series of clues in a case and draw a general conclusion based on those clues.

Examples:

Jerry has patience and a steady hand.

He is a watchmaker.

Watchmakers need patience and a steady hand.

In your persuasive writing work, you might use either approach, depending on which one is more appropriate. The examples you choose to support your line of reasoning will depend on which approach you take. In other words, the examples you use in an inductive line of reasoning may be quite different from examples you might use in a deductive approach.

In inductive reasoning, you might want several specific examples that will help you establish a general principle or position of some sort. For instance, you could find statistics or examples from a number of studies that show smoking among children under 16 in the province of Ontario has increased rather than decreased from 2000 to 2006. You could use these examples to develop a general position: that campaigns against smoking are not working. If you wished to use a deductive approach to the same topic—young teens and smoking—you might begin with a general principle: advertising campaigns do not work the same way on all sectors of the population. You will choose effective reasons (specific, concrete, based on real examples or evidence) in order to lead to a specific conclusion.

Exercise 6 Inductive and Deductive Reasoning

Work in pairs. Read each of the following conclusions. Discuss if you think the conclusion was reached by deductive or inductive thinking. Be prepared to discuss your responses.

1. Skateboards made from fibreglass are the sturdiest.

 ____

2. The criminal was a woman who wore glasses and enjoyed poetry.

 ____

3. Ford produces sturdy and reliable pickup trucks.

 ____

4. The sum of the angles of a triangle is 180°.

 ____

5. The red-breasted nuthatch spreads pitch around the opening of its nesting cavity.

 ____

6. Eating trans fats can clog human arteries.

 ____

7. Email has replaced traditional letter writing.

 ____

8. Snigley detested musicians.

 ____

9. First-world countries are responsible for 92 percent of oil consumption.

 ____

10. The design of the Coke bottle reflects fashion trends.

 ____

Element 8: Avoid Logical Fallacies

As you are researching, collecting, and thinking your way through your evidence and constructing your paper, keep in mind logical fallacies or errors in thinking. The following section discusses five common logical fallacies student writers make in their written arguments. Study each type of logical fallacy; then try the exercise that follows.

1. **Hasty Generalizations**

 Overgeneralizations or hasty generalizations are unsupported conclusions. Basing a principle on one example is a case of overgeneralization. If you purchased grapes from Chile and they were delicious, and you claimed, "Grapes from Chile are delicious," then you would be making a hasty generalization. Not all grapes coming from Chile may be delicious.

Some overgeneralizations are actually stereotypes. For example, suppose a person visits Canada and meets three Canadians. Each Canadian confesses that she really enjoys the sport of hockey. The visitor might make a generalization like this:

Example: Hasty generalizations

Everyone in Canada loves hockey.

When you are providing evidence, be sure that you do not use a single case or too few cases to prove your point. You must be cautious, too, when you are using your own experience as evidence of something. If you say that your experience represents everyone else's, you are overgeneralizing.

2. **Ad Hominem**

Ad hominem arguments are aimed at a person's character; they attack the person, not the point. Avoid using this strategy because it usually fails in an academic argument.

Example: Ad hominem

Parents who allow their children to surf the internet freely without any adult guidance or monitoring are ignorant and neglectful.

The writer attacks the parents' characters but does not really address the point and does not add any convincing evidence or explanation. The writer also runs the risk of alienating her audience, particularly if the readers happen to be parents who do allow their children complete internet freedom. Rather than engaging in an ad hominem attack, you should concentrate on offering effective reasons for monitoring children's internet activities: convincing proof, opponent's counter-arguments, and your rebuttal.

3. **Bandwagon Thinking**

This type of thinking is based on "popularity rules." In other words, the writer asks the reader to "jump on the bandwagon" on a position because everyone else has. "If most people believe something, then it must be true" is what typifies bandwagon thinking.

Example: Popular vote rules

Eighty-five percent of the people surveyed say that Burpee Cola tastes better than Flagwort Cola, so Burpee Cola must be better.

A good deal of commercial advertising uses bandwagon thinking in order to attract consumers to products. Bandwagon thinking also works on snob appeal. If someone rich and famous uses a product and you want to associate yourself with the rich and famous, then you will buy the product or idea, too.

Example: Snob appeal

Who wouldn't want the elegance of a new XKE sitting in their driveway? Be the only one on your street to be the proud owner of a sleek XKE. Imagine your neighbours' amazement when they see your new purchase! Teddy Snert, world-famous NASCAR driver says, "It is the only vehicle on the road I trust."

Since Teddy Snert, a high-profile celebrity athlete who is very rich, recommends the product, the reader might be persuaded to purchase it. The ad is appealing to snobbery when it alludes to social class and envy. This approach works surprisingly well in advertising.

4. **Argument from Ignorance**

The writer maintains that a lack of evidence for some claim means it is proof that the claim is false.

Example: Argument from Ignorance

No one has ever proven that the human soul exists, so it must not exist.

This type of thinking seems to be a form of "seeing is believing." The lack of proof constitutes evidence that something doesn't exist.

5. **Drawing Illogical Conclusions**

The writer must show that a conclusion follows reasonably from the points or claims given in written argument. The writer jumps to a conclusion without having established clearly developed points and proof that would lead to the conclusion. Sometimes a writer might draw an illogical conclusion because he or she has made too many assumptions or has not bothered to supply substantive reasons. In other cases, the writer may seem to provide good points but then draws an irrelevant or sometimes specious conclusion from them.

Here is an illustration of how a writer could go about reaching a ridiculous conclusion.

Example: Illogical Conclusions

The Japanese eat very little fat and suffer fewer heart attacks than the British or Americans. The French eat a lot of fat, but they too suffer fewer heart attacks than the British or Americans. The Japanese do not drink much red wine yet they also suffer fewer heart attacks than the British or Americans. The Italians drink excessive amounts of red wine, yet suffer fewer heart attacks than the British or Americans. Conclusion: We can eat and drink what we like—it's speaking English that causes heart attacks!

Source: "Critical Thinking," Ardell Wellness Report, *Fall 2003: 2.*

Exercise 7 Identifying Logical Fallacies

Work in pairs. Read each of the following. Then tell what type of logical fallacy each passage represents. Be prepared to discuss your answers.

1. I roomed with a student from Malaysia. She had a university scholarship and came from rich parents. She was always shopping and buying things. Foreign students spend too much money.

   ____

2. The campaign for city council elections is not going well. My opponent, Mr. Chester Curly, has no right to be in the race because he has lived in the city for only two years, and he is a proven liar.

   ____

3. Many kids learn about money and the world very quickly today. Maybe it's television's fault. Children are independent in Canada by age 12.

   ____

4. All Canadian teenagers watch too much television.

____

5. Scientists have not proven the supernatural exists. Therefore, I believe that ghosts and spirits do not exist.

____

6. During September of this year, we received about 11 mm more rain than the average. I got two head colds in September, so my colds must have to do with the rain.

____

7. In a recent survey done by DataTex Corporation from Oshawa, Ontario, 71 percent of the people surveyed believed it was okay to cheat on your income tax returns. Therefore, cheating on income tax returns is a socially accepted practice.

____

8. I have two friends, Lulu and Bruno, who are left-handed. They are extremely gifted artists who spend most of their lives studying and working at their art. Another person at work was recently given a promotion. He is also left-handed. Left-handed people are more intelligent and creative than right-handed people.

____

9. People with sophisticated tastes will find that certain parts of the city will appeal to them more than others. Everyone appreciates tidy lawns, neatly maintained houses, and landscaped yards, so real estate should be more expensive in those locations, and people should expect to pay more.

____

10. Charlie is the worst boss I ever had. He was always telling me what to do and complained whenever I didn't get things done to his satisfaction. He was grumpy and wore bad suits. Charlie is the reason I got fired from my new job.

____

Exercise 8 Looking for Logical Fallacies in an Argument

Read the following passage. It contains several logical fallacies. Underline each one and identify what type of logical fallacy it is. Be prepared to discuss your choices.

> People should not purchase goods online or give out any personal information over the internet. Perhaps most buyers are ignorant of the dangers of doing so. Everyone ought to be terrified of identity theft today and should protect themselves against it. For example, Uncle Longshot experienced a break-in at his house; the thief took my uncle's computer with all his personal information on it. This example just proves how important it is to have good locks on your house or apartment. Another example can be found right in my own neighbourhood. A few of my neighbours are a bit stupid and leave their doors unlocked all the time. They deserve to be robbed! No one has ever been able to stop identity thieves, so therefore, identity theft is pretty much unavoidable. I think the most you can hope for is to limit the damage done.

REVIEW TEST

Try the following review test. It will help you assess what you have learned from the chapter. Be prepared to share your responses with others in the class.

1. What is the difference between persuasion and argumentation?

 ____

 ____

 ____

2. Name one important purpose of persuasion and argument.

 ____

 ____

 ____

3. Which appeal—character, emotion, or logic—is each statement based on?

 - Major-General Courier Davis who is the highest authority in the land on underwater speed craft states that Q-Z Cruisers are the fastest and most reliable on the market today.
 - Every mother will want to use Best Flour in family baking because it is nutritious and fortified with extra niacin.
 - Not everyone can afford to pay $250 for a pair of running shoes, so companies should be addressing the need for median-priced, stylish, and reliable alternatives.

 ____

 ____

 ____

4. What elements should you consider when you construct a written argument?

 ____

 ____

 ____

5. What is an overgeneralization? Give an example.

 ____

 ____

 ____

6. What is a stereotype? Give an example.

 ____

 ____

 ____

7. What is a counter-argument?

8. In each of the following conclusions, decide if each was reached by deductive or inductive thinking.

   - Young children should not eat Konjac mini-cup jelly products because of a potential choking hazard.
   - The e-coli inspection was spread by contaminated water used on two major produce farms.
   - The intruder wears size 10 shoes and is left-handed.

9. Identify the logical fallacy in each of the following statements:

   - No one has actually ever found any physical evidence of UFOs; therefore, they simply don't exist.
   - My niece Marlee who is seven is really influenced by the fashions she sees on television, so I don't think advertising should be allowed on children's programs.
   - Their marketing survey showed that 94% of customers loved getting free sample packets of dog biscuits, so our company should follow suit.

Assignment

Bring in a letter to the editor from a recent newspaper. Make three copies of the letter to share with others in a small group. Each person will take the other two group members' letters and evaluate the argument the writer presents.

1. List the points the writer presents.
2. Decide if the points are supported.
3. List the evidence the writer uses to support her claims.
4. Did the letter persuade you? Why or why not?

Be prepared to share your answers in the group. Choose one of the letters to present to the rest of the class. Your instructor may also ask you to present one of the letters to the editor and your evaluation of the letter to the rest of the class.

Bonus Exercise Reason and Definition Statements

Students often use two expressions when they are writing persuasively: "the reason is because" and "X is when." Avoid these two constructions. "The reason is because" is redundant. In the second expression, the writer is linking a definition to time. Correct the following sentences, eliminating the two expressions, and improving the sentence style by removing repetition.

1. The reason most people do not go out to the movies more often is because it is too expensive in terms of cost.

   ____

   ____

2. Cacophony is when harsh loud sounds come together to be disagreeable and unpleasant.

   ____

   ____

3. Jared and Kippy have not completed their research assignment, and the reason is because they have procrastinated and put off doing the initial research to begin with.

   ____

   ____

4. A soliloquy is when an actor gets on the stage by herself and talks to the audience all alone, and the reason is because the actor wants to let the audience in on some information.

   ____

   ____

READING

Carefully read the following article by John Ralston Saul, paying attention to the argument he builds. Answer the questions that follow.

In Defence of Public Education

by John Ralston Saul

John Ralston Saul received a Companion of the Order of Canada in 1999. He is author of five novels and many works of non-fiction, including essays and volumes on political, philosophical, and economic thought. He has twice received the prestigious Gordon Montador Award for Best Canadian Non-Fiction Book. He works tirelessly for Canadian education and freedom of speech. In the following selection, Saul argues against a class-based society and for citizens to take action in ensuring that good public education includes the elements of a civil society.

What is the tragedy of a class-based society? Quite simply, it is a society which has institutionalized selfishness. We all have selfishness within us. We all have our self-interest.

And we need it. But that is quite different from acting as if selfishness were the leitmotif of civilization. A healthy democracy is one which works to avoid that tragedy.

As for public education, it is a simile for civilized democracy. You could say that public education is the primary foundation in any civilized democracy. That was one of the great discoveries of western civilization in its modern form in the middle of the 19th century.

Any weakening of universal public education can only be a weakening of democracy.

I personally do not believe that citizens—Canadian citizens in particular—have any desire to abandon the true strengths of their society. I believe that there is a profound understanding in our society of the long-standing essential role universal public education plays in making us a civilized democracy.

Citizens live complex lives and have little free time. Yet they are obliged to deal with all of those fashions and ideologies which come along, grab hold of the mechanisms of public influence, and then set about undermining the fundamentals of civilization.

The ideologies of our day are comfortably ensconced in various schools of economics which have embraced late 19th century simplistic theories of inevitability. You can also find them in various schools of managerialism, which also are attached to a belief in the inevitability of events.

Floating around these economists and managers is a whole new class of what used to be called courtiers and are now called consultants. Some of them are operating out of what are called independent think tanks, financed in such a way that they are independent on behalf of those who finance them.

All of this represents a tidal wave of specialists who have drawn as their principal conclusion that inclusive systems which serve the public good are no longer viable. In other words, the ideologies and fashions of our day are devoted in good part to a return of the tragedy of the class-based society. They are devoted to weakening the universality of the very public education system which has made Canada such a remarkably successful society.

Let me point out something which is difficult to accept for many people who are themselves devoted to managing—and managing well—classes, schools and the school system. Managerialism encourages and rewards agreement among professionals. It admires discretion and conformity, it encourages us all to believe that through detailed work, we can rectify enormous problems.

Let me give you two examples of the contradictions this creates. We all agree on the need for small classrooms, particularly in this era of high immigration, ever more complex societies and ever more open borders. We need intense, personalized education. This seems to mean classes of twenty or less students.

Yet the managerial solutions of today are carrying us towards larger classrooms. Why? Because no matter how modern these managerial theories sound, they are usually rooted in the industrial theories of the late 19th century. And those theories are based upon a belief in economies of scale. What is more, we are consistently bombarded by statistics which assert that class sizes are not actually too big. This is where the business of discretion and conformity and attempting to solve problems behind the scenes comes in. In most cases, those statistics are a form of gerrymandering.

The statisticians take the total number of accredited teachers and administrators, and divide them into the total number of students. But many of those included in the calculation never go into a classroom because they are principals, vice-principals, counsellors and so on. And so the official statistics talk of 25 or 30 students per class, when parents—that is citizens—know that their children are in classes of thirty five.

Let me give you another example of what happens when we buy into the closed arguments of inevitability. In school after school around the country it seems that there is ever less money for what are now described as the soft edges of education. Many of these soft edges were included automatically in education until a few years ago. Schools find themselves short of books and of equipment. They find that certain advanced classes are suddenly too expensive. Certain special needs are too special. Many extracurricular activities suddenly are beyond their budgets.

Principals, teachers and parents find themselves obliged to go out and raise money—i.e., engage in private fundraising. This presents two very real problems. The first is that raising funds for a public school in a middle or upper middle class neighbourhood is not all that difficult. Raising funds in a working class or lower middle class neighbourhood—or indeed a neighbourhood with many new immigrants trying very hard to begin their lives in Canada—is a much more difficult undertaking. The whole idea of private fundraising for public schools is the first step towards introducing a class-based society into Canada. Private fundraising is, in and of itself, a form of exclusion.

Let me add a tougher comment. By going out and spending a great deal of their valuable time fundraising, principals, teachers and parents are actually collaborating in the gradual privatization of the public school system. They are making privatization easier for those who do not wish to take public responsibility for raising the necessary amounts of public money. I often feel we would do better to stand back and to say openly that this is a public system and that if society and its leaders are not willing to fund the system, then we collectively, and they specifically, must all take responsibility for the decline in the education of our own children and the children of our fellow citizens. Perhaps there is a need for citizens to stand back and say to the public authorities: It is your obligation to raise the funds and to deliver universal public education. It is not our responsibility to undermine that universality. Over to you.

Our country has been built, from the very beginnings of its democratic system 150 years ago, upon a happy linkage between democracy and public education. These are the basic principles of the Canadian democracy.

In the 19th century, we were a naturally poor country, working under the extremely difficult circumstances of our climate and geography. We constructed our prosperity consciously and intellectually. We constructed our success and we did so to a great extent through our public education system. Any move towards weakening that system will risk undermining not simply our society, but also our prosperity.

Our success as a country is built upon this system. It is only with great difficulty that I could imagine a greater betrayal of the principle of Canadian democracy than the piecemeal reduction of public education to private education.

There is one point on which there should be no misunderstanding. The concept of universality does not mean that everything must be the same. The strength of a public education system such as ours is that, being so large and serving so many different communities, it is capable of enormous diversities. We only have to look at the remarkable success story of French immersion over the last quarter century to see what our public system is capable of. Starting at zero, we have today over 320,000 students in French immersion.

Let me add to that the other large requirement of diversity in our society. This country has been built on a combination of its Aboriginal peoples and its immigrants. Most of those immigrants have come as reasonably poor people, very often illiterate or not speaking either of our official languages. The Saul's [***sic***], for example, came here in the middle of the 19th century as virtually illiterate stone masons. My family, like yours I'm sure, is a product of the public school system.

We citizens take the responsibility of inviting people from around the world to come to join us in Canada. We're the host. The primary obligation and responsibility is ours, as it is with any host. We offer these newcomers an open, inclusive society in which the citizens can act as citizens, can speak out, become involved in public life as they wish, and perhaps do well economically. We have three primary obligations when we invite immigrants to come to join us here. First, to ensure that our democratic system and its values are clearly understandable and accessible to them. Second, to ensure that our public systems work. Third, to provide an intense, inclusive public education system which will allow them and their children to adjust to Canadian society. All the state has to provide are public systems which work and a good education system. The immigrant or citizen does all the rest. My family, like yours, is the proof that this is a bargain which no self-respecting democracy can turn its back on.

One of the particularities of Canada is that we have many levels of government, as befits the second largest landmass in the world with a reasonably small population, two official languages and three founding peoples. The system is as it should be. And fundamentally it works well. After all, we are the second or third oldest democracy in the world.

One of the specific realities of this system is that the responsibility for education was given, from the beginning, to the provinces and territories. This ensures that the regional nature of Canada is not overwhelmed, as it was in most parts of Europe, by monolithic, centralizing theories of state and mythology. Our civilization is intended to be complicated and the regionalization of our education system allows it to maintain that complexity.

What this means is that the primary arm for the creation of citizens, whether children of people born in Canada or immigrants, lies in the hands of the provinces. It is their most important responsibility. And it is regional, national and international at the same time.

You may be for or against globalization. But at the end of the day, the ability of our young citizens to face the various effects of the opening of borders lies in the hands of the provincial and territorial governments. That is, it lies in their obligation to provide universal public education; to maintain the century and a half–old tradition of a middle class egalitarian inclusive society. And it means that we have to provide a very complex education: we need to produce kids who can read a minimum of two languages, probably English and French, but they probably should have three or four to go anywhere or to do anything internationally. They have to have in-depth education in thought, philosophy, history, the social-political economics of Asia and northern Europe, *literature*—a very complex education. Otherwise, they can't go out into a win-win situation.

Today we have a largely urban population. Our cities are filled with a highly mobile population, two job families, high divorce levels, single parent families, the return of long hours of work, the loss of community identification, high immigration levels, a new rise in the division between rich and poor and so on. All of these factors mean that the one—if not the only—public structure we have which is capable of reaching out to all citizens in all parts of the country and making them feel part of the extended family of citizenship is the public education system. In the classic sense of the inclusive democracy, those simple brick and mortar buildings, which we call the public schools, are in fact the one remaining open club house of citizenship. Not only is the public education system and its fundamental structure not old fashioned, it has found a new form of modernity. I would argue that we are more reliant on it today than we were through most of the 20th century.

We must turn away from the mediocre and tired management theories of efficiency through economies of scale. We must particularly be wary of their latest manifestation which preaches training rather than education. If you spend a lot of time training kids on machines, you know perfectly well that by the time they get out of school, the machines are going to be obsolete. In the meantime, they haven't learned how to dance on one foot and think of six things at once, which is what they'll need to do in an unstable, changing world economy, where they're going to have to move their career five or six times in different directions. Philosophy and literature are far more useful than turning a machine on and off.

We need more than ever to look at the public education system as the primary tool we have to ensure that children are able to grow up to become citizens.

Source: John Ralston Saul, "In Defence of Public Education," Read This! Why Books Matter, *ed. Karen Zoppa (Winnipeg: J. Gordon Shillingford Publishing 2003) 1–6. Reprinted by permission of J. Gordon Shillingford Publishing.*

Comprehension Questions

1. What are the components of a "healthy democracy" according to Saul?
2. Find the underlined word "leitmotif" in the early part of the selection. Without using a dictionary and using context clues, write down what you think "leitmotif" means.
3. According to the writer, why do specialists believe that "inclusive systems which serve the public good are no longer viable"?
4. What is the author's tone? What words support that tone, in your opinion?

Critical Comprehension Questions

1. What do you think the writer would have to say about private schools in public education?
2. With continued private interests influencing universal public education in Canada, what do you think schools will be like in 50 years?

Assignment Analyzing the Argument

1. Using the chart below, fill in what Ralston Saul's main claims are.
2. Using the chart below, fill in the evidence Ralston Saul provides for his claims.

Main Claim	Supporting Evidence or Explanation
______________________	______________________
______________________	______________________
______________________	______________________
______________________	______________________
______________________	______________________
______________________	______________________

CHECKOUT

Here are some of the ideas you will take away with you after you have completed the chapter:

1. Persuasion and argument are different.
2. To build an argument, a writer must anticipate counter-arguments.
3. Humour may unintentionally insult your reader.
4. Persuasion includes trying to change your reader's viewpoint.
5. Arguments must be carefully constructed and supported. Writers often present arguments objectively without attempting to appeal to a reader's emotions as in persuasion.

Mastering the concepts in this chapter will also help you develop and apply the following employability skills highlighted by the Conference Board of Canada in *Employability Skills 2000+*:

Communicate

- read and understand information presented in a variety of forms (e.g., words, graphs, charts, diagrams)
- use relevant scientific, technological and mathematical knowledge and skills to explain or clarify ideas

Think & Solve Problems

- seek different points of view and evaluate them based on facts

Source: Adapted from *Employability Skills 2000+* Brochure E/F (Ottawa: The Conference Board of Canada, 2000).

chapter 11

Structuring Argument

Chapter Objectives

After completing this chapter you will be able to

1. write a strong thesis statement for your argument paper;
2. follow steps in writing argumentation;
3. research using advanced internet search functions;
4. gather examples, facts, and statistics from your research;
5. construct arguments closely related to your audience's profile.

INTRODUCTION

Constructing a written argument will take careful planning. Follow the three-step process discussed in the next section. Remember that as you write, you can revisit this chapter as often as you require. Reviewing the key ideas in this chapter from time to time will help you develop your paper.

Writing an argument comprises a number of different steps. Bundling the steps into a three-step process will help you manage the task more effectively.

STEP 1: CHOOSE A POSITION AND PURPOSE

Choose a clear position on your topic. Are you in favour of something? Do you disagree with something? Do you think a certain stand on an issue needs to be re-examined? What is it that you hope to do in writing the paper? Do you wish to help change a policy of some sort? Do you want your reader to think about an issue in an entirely different way? Do you want your reader to understand another position that is usually seen as unpopular?

The thesis statement in the introduction should clearly show your stance or position. Use *should* in your thesis statement, and avoid using the word *I* in your paper; instead, use a third-person point of view. Most instructors prefer that you place the thesis statement at the end of the introductory paragraph.

Examples:

- Weak thesis statement: Independent films are underfunded.

This thesis is weak because it is not debatable. The writer has not shown a clear position and will have difficulty finding a direction for the paper and developing a clear line of reasoning that the reader can follow.

- Stronger thesis statement: Independent films should be funded through federal tax dollars.

This thesis shows the writer's position: independent films ought to get public funding. The writer can set out her argument using good evidence to convince the reader there has to be a change in public policy toward funding in the arts, specifically filmmaking.

Checklist for Setting Position and Purpose

After you have written your introduction, check each appropriate item.

I have a clear purpose in mind for my paper.	yes ______	no ______
I wish to see a policy change.	yes ______	no ______
I want to change popular opinion on an issue.	yes ______	no ______
I want my reader to see an issue in a new way.	yes ______	no ______
My thesis statement contains *should.*	yes ______	no ______
My thesis statement shows my position on an issue.	yes ______	no ______
My thesis statement shows I am in favour of something.	yes ______	no ______
My thesis statement shows I am opposed to something.	yes ______	no ______

STEP 2: CONSTRUCT THE ARGUMENTS

Once your position and purpose are firmly established, you can begin to develop your arguments. Use your thesis statement as a guide as you plan and build: it is like a light that shines on your writing path.

Do Some Research

You will not have to do research for every academic paper you write, but you will construct a more convincing argument with outside pieces of evidence. Your college or university library provides you with access to many different databases with many online scholarly journals. In addition, you can use reliable sources from the internet, reputable newspapers, and popular magazines.

Set aside a few hours to do the research.

Tips for Researching

- Use keyword searches.
- Use the advanced search functions on your browser and in databases.
- If your search shows too many sites on the first try, narrow your search terms, or use the advanced search functions.
- Keep accurate notes: be sure to copy the writer's or writers' names concisely. Write down where you found the article (the source) with the date of publication, the volume number (if pertinent), the page numbers of the article, and the page number on which you found the quotation. Writing down this type of bibliographic information is essential and will take you less than a minute to record. Also make this activity part of your research routine; you will never regret having information such as this. Even if you do not use all of the information all of the time, it will be there for you when you really do need it.

Provide Good Evidence

In order to argue your position effectively, you will need convincing evidence. Use outside sources (research), specific facts, your experience, clear explanations, and a variety of appeals as part of your evidence. If you use the internet for information, be sure your sources are reliable. You can review how to ascertain the reliability of internet sources in chapters 7, 10 and 12.

Include a Variety of Appeals

As you are collecting and developing evidence, think about the types of appeals you are making. Are you appealing to the reader's emotions? Are you establishing a moral, ethical, or character appeal? Are you trying to use reason or logic?

In a written argument, you may use your knowledge of appeals. However, avoid overusing emotional appeals because you may actually alienate your reader. Your arguments will be more persuasive if you blend the appeals throughout your paper.

Think about the Counter-Arguments

To show your fair-mindedness, you will anticipate your opponents' arguments. These are called *counter-arguments*. After you anticipate the counter-arguments, you should think about how to refute or dispute these claims. This part of the argument is called your *rebuttal*. In your rebuttal, you should use examples, facts, statistics, or information you have gathered from your research.

Establish Your Target Audience

Clearly, you must determine who your target audience is. What evidence you select, your tone and voice in the paper, and the construction of your arguments will relate closely to your audience's profile. Remember that what might seem appropriate for one audience may be completely unacceptable to another.

Establish Tone

Select the appropriate tone for the audience you are targeting. If you are being respectful to your audience, you will not

- discuss in a condescending tone ("talk down" to your audience);
- resort to insults, anger, sarcasm, or preaching;
- vent;
- bluster.

Avoid Logical Fallacies

Review the information on logical fallacies found in chapter 10. Remember that logical fallacies are errors in thinking, so you do not want to weaken your position by using them. Avoid

- making hasty generalizations,
- making ad hominem attacks,
- using bandwagon thinking,

- using argument from ignorance,
- drawing illogical conclusions.

Reread your draft, looking specifically at the arguments you have made. Ask yourself if you have made any errors in logic. Use the following checklist to assist you in the process.

Checklist for Constructing the Arguments

After you have developed your arguments, check each appropriate item.

I have completed some research for my paper.	yes _______	no _______
My research sources are reliable.	yes _______	no _______
I have bibliographic information for each source.	yes _______	no _______
I have used a variety of research sources.	yes _______	no _______
I have good evidence for each of the points I want to make.	yes _______	no _______
I have used a variety of appeals: character, emotional, logical.	yes _______	no _______
I have developed effective counter-arguments.	yes _______	no _______
I have written for a specific target audience.	yes _______	no _______
The tone I use is appropriate to the target audience.	yes _______	no _______
I have avoided these logical fallacies:		
I have made no hasty generalizations.	yes _______	no _______
I have avoided ad hominem attacks.	yes _______	no _______
I have not used bandwagon thinking.	yes _______	no _______
I have avoided the argument from ignorance.	yes _______	no _______
I have not drawn illogical conclusions.	yes _______	no _______

STEP 3: WRITE THE FIRST DRAFT

Now that you have done all the preparation for your paper, you are ready to write your first draft. The following section gives you some ideas for thinking through each part of your paper. Each part contains important elements that you should include in your paper. Read through the sections, and then prepare a sketch outline or formal outline based on your ideas and research.

The design of the argument is based on the following scheme:

1. Introduction with clear position stated in the thesis
2. First body paragraph with opponents' counter-arguments and your rebuttal
3. Two or more body paragraphs, each outlining major claims, points, or warrants in your argument and reasons for making each claim
4. A conclusion that is drawn logically from your argument

Begin with a Strong Introduction

- Begin with an attention-getter.
- Build a bridge between you and your reader (establish common ground).

- Establish argument—tell the story behind the argument (background).
- Clarify and define your terms if needed (part of background).
- Establish the appropriate tone for your audience.
- Clarify and stress the importance of the issue.
- State your position in the thesis at the end of the introduction: use a "should" statement and a third-person point of view.
- Ensure that your thesis statement is arguable.

Develop a Sketch Outline

Put your ideas together in a sketch outline for your introduction, body paragraphs, and conclusion, using the guidelines in the following sections. If you prefer a more detailed outline, use a formal outline.

Write an Effective Body

- Start with a sketch outline. Have at least three body paragraphs, but you may have as many as you need. The number of body paragraphs you develop will be dependent on your argument and the assignment length.

BODY PARAGRAPH 1

- Refute the opposition in body paragraph 1. Examine the counter-arguments your opponents might make to your position. (Check with your instructor or professor to see if she prefers a different organization.)
- Rebut opposing arguments, showing the faulty reasoning: tell why as clearly as you can.
- Provide examples, reasons, or other evidence in your rebuttal.
- Keep in mind who your target audience is. Write appropriately for the audience you have selected.
- Shape your topic sentence to the paragraph's purpose, and link it to the thesis.
- Check your assumptions.
- Use transitions that show logical flow of ideas.

BODY PARAGRAPHS 2 AND BEYOND

- Develop your argument, using good evidence: a variety of appeals and types of examples, facts, statistics, anecdotes, experience, outside sources (research).
- Shape each topic sentence around a major point that relates to the thesis.
- Provide two to three well-developed points to support each topic sentence.
- Place each point in the paragraph in a separate sentence.
- Follow each point by proof (good evidence).
- Use logical transitions between points.
- Use key terms more than once throughout the paper to add emphasis and coherence.
- Use correct in-text citations for any outside sources you include. See APA or MLA in chapters 14 and 15, respectively, of this text.

Write a Strong Conclusion

- Finish with a strong summary statement.
- Relate the issue to a larger, more global one.
- Suggest a course of action, or make a recommendation.
- Finish with a strong conclusion. Weak conclusions undermine your arguments and the paper overall. Check that your conclusion logically follows from the argument you have made in the body of your paper.

Begin the First Draft of Your Paper

Using your outline, start writing the first draft of your paper. Review the sections discussing drafting in the earlier chapters of *Spotlight on Critical Skills in Essay Writing*, Second Edition, if you need help. Write your first draft in one to three writing sessions. Then reread the first draft and get some feedback from a member of the class or a trusted friend or relative. You can start to revise the paper at any point in the process. Check your assignment instructions against your first draft to be sure you have followed directions and answered the assignment question.

USE USEFUL TRANSITIONS

Adding ideas to other ideas:

moreover	in addition
furthermore	also
besides this or that	

Showing relationship between ideas:

as a result	consequently
thus	therefore

Adding emphasis to ideas:

in addition	indeed
in fact	certainly
all in all	

Showing contrast between ideas:

however	on the contrary
nevertheless	on the other hand

Revise Your First Draft

Begin revising. Finally, proofread and edit. Be sure your final presentation is in the format requested by your instructor, according to line spacing, selection of font, font size, length of the paper, or special guidelines. Your instructor may ask you to use a particular documentation style, either MLA or APA. Chapters 14 and 15 of this text provide specific information about these two documentation styles.

Checklist for Constructing the Paper

Use this checklist after you have completed your first draft. Then use it to guide you in revising the next draft.

I begin with an attention-grabber.	yes ______	no ______
I provide some background in the introduction.	yes ______	no ______
I clarify or define my key terms in the introduction.	yes ______	no ______
I establish an appropriate tone.	yes ______	no ______
I assert my position clearly in the thesis statement.	yes ______	no ______
In body paragraph 1, I predict the counter-arguments.	yes ______	no ______
In body paragraph 1, I provide a rebuttal.	yes ______	no ______
In the other body paragraphs, the topic sentences link with the thesis.	yes ______	no ______
I use different appeals in the development of ideas.	yes ______	no ______
I use an effective variety of evidence types: examples, facts, statistics, anecdotes, experience, outside sources (research).	yes ______	no ______
I have at least three major points in my paper.	yes ______	no ______
Each body paragraph has at least two supporting points.	yes ______	no ______
Each body paragraph provides effective proof for each supporting point.	yes ______	no ______
I use logical transitions throughout the paragraphs.	yes ______	no ______
I use correct in-text citations for my outside sources, according to APA or MLA.	yes ______	no ______
I have a strong summary statement in the conclusion.	yes ______	no ______
I call for action in the conclusion or make a recommendation.	yes ______	no ______
I believe the conclusion is a logical one based on argument I make in the paper.	yes ______	no ______
I have read my final draft at least once out loud to myself.	yes ______	no ______
I have checked the paper for correct use of commas and semicolons.	yes ______	no ______
I have checked the paper for correct use of quotation marks.	yes ______	no ______
I have checked the paper for correct use of colons and dashes.	yes ______	no ______
I have checked the paper for correct spelling.	yes ______	no ______
I have checked for sentence logic.	yes ______	no ______
I have checked for errors in sentences like faulty parallelism, pronoun misuse, dangling modifiers, subject and verb agreement mistakes, and point-of-view shifts.	yes ______	no ______
The look of the final draft meets the requirements set out by my instructor or professor.	yes ______	no ______

WRITTEN ARGUMENT EXAMPLE

Bronstead 1

M. Bronstead
Professor Placque
English 155

23 January 2005

Ban Cigarette Smoking

Have you ever watched Hollywood movies of the 1940s and 50s in which the stars of the film spent most of their time lighting one another's cigarettes? Think of Humphrey Bogart and Lauren Bacall in the 1944 production of To Have and Have Not. More than fifteen scenes centre on cigarettes. Smoking was more than recreation and enjoyment: it was what the stars did, and they were considered cool. However, research begun in the late 1950s began to show the damage that smoking could do to human health, and suddenly, the movies took a different turn. The habit began to be viewed as being socially unacceptable, even harmful. Although smoking rates have declined in the adult Canadian population over the past 20 years, rates for youths have, in fact, increased. Younger people are now smoking, but tobacco companies carry on denying the facts and manipulating their unsuspecting audiences to the real harm smoking can do. Cigarette smoking should be completely banned from all parts of Canada for any citizen, no matter what age.

Supporters of the tobacco industry claim that cigarette smoking is not as harmful as it is made out to be. Groups like Forces Canada declare that the damage done by second-hand smoke is completely unfounded, yet Health Canada reports, based on scientific studies, continue to warn Canadians about the dangers of second-hand smoke, particularly among children living with smokers (8). In addition, supporters state the tobacco industry is a major corporate sponsor. Companies such as Philip Morris, Rothmans, and JTI Macdonald Corp. have been long-term major contributors to sports like figure skating and skiing. Many claim that without this corporate support several world-class events would not be financially possible. Anti-smoking activists, on the other hand, maintain that smoking is a harmful activity that ought not to be promoted by athletes, professional or amateur. They say athletes are models for Canadian youth, and having tobacco companies promote their athletic heroes is akin to suggesting that the athletes are also in favour of smoking. Finally, opponents of anti-smoking bans maintain that removing their right to smokein public places removes a personal right and freedom. The Fraser Institute decries authoritative intervention and suggests "for two decades, a significant amount of political influence has been exercised throughout both Canada and the United States in support of increased regulation" (3). However, these groups do not take the same stance when it comes to other issues of social importance in which governments do "interfere"—international trade, military involvement, and drug regulations. Since interest groups always act for their own benefit, they will not be in favour of anti-smoking campaigns: it becomes more a matter of diminishing profits rather than individuals' rights. For these reasons, it is clear that most opposition to the banning of cigarette smoking stems from self-interest rather than from a commitment to societal good.

Smoking cigarettes damages human health. Individual smokers can expect to suffer terrible diseases like lung cancer brought on by inhaling cigarettes or to die early. Each year approximately 45 000 Canadians will die as a result of cigarette smoking (International Development Research Centre). According to the experts, "Cigarette smoke contains more than 4000 chemicals. At least 43 of these have been identified as carcinogenic in humans or animals, and others have been identified as toxic, so it is no surprise that smoking is so harmful" (International Development Research Centre 8). Furthermore, second-hand smoke is harmful. One study suggests that breathing in second-hand cigarette smoke is actually more destructive than taking in mainstream smoke because second-hand smoke contains higher levels of carcinogens produced at lower temperatures ("Tobacco Smoke"). Pregnant women run the risk of damage to their unborn.

> Nonsmokers are harmed by second-hand smoke, technically known as environmental tobacco smoke (ETS) but sometimes referred to as passive smoking or involuntary smoking. ETS includes both the smoke emitted from the lit end of the cigarette and the mainstream smoke exhaled by a smoker. ETS can cause fatal lung cancer in otherwise healthy nonsmokers and has a particularly harmful impact on children's respiratory systems (International Development Research Centre 10)

Cigarette smoking should be outlawed because it is so costly. First, cigarette smoking is expensive on a social level. The national health care system shoulders the main burden when it comes to paying for the damaged health of cigarette smokers. According to the Aboriginal Youth Network Canada website, "Smokers cost society about $15 billion while contributing roughly $7.8 billion in taxes" (2). The high price of fire insurance and the loss of life in fires started by careless smokers are two other significant issues that

Bronstead 3

affect people and communities. For example, a study conducted by Aligne and Stoddard of the University of Wisconsin declared that "more young children are killed by parental smoking than by all unintentional injuries combined" (652). Besides that expense, there is the cost to the individual smoker. The cost of smoking in 2005 is estimated to be $3000 per year for the average smoker, $6000 for two parents who smoke. Over five years, smoking amounts to $30 000—money that could have been spent on something tangible to improve the quality of family life. Of course, damage done to an individual's health because of cigarette smoking is beyond counting dollars. Besides life-threatening illnesses like cancer, heart disease, and emphysema—all well-documented outcomes of long-term cigarette smoking on human health by countless studies over the past two decades—individuals should consider what sustained smoking does to personal appearance. First, it causes premature aging of the skin ("Gender and Tobacco" 4). Next, the smoke itself yellows teeth and fingers, ruins clothes, and permeates the hair. Also on a personal level, smokers have to deal with the interiors of homes and apartments that require repainting, with furniture that stinks and with damage due to cigarette burns.

Other individuals become the victims of cigarettes. Workers who do not wish to work in a smoke-filled environment have little or no control over their own health. They are fighting back to regain some of that control and with some support from some powerful friends. In January 1, 2000, for instance, the Workers' Compensation Board brought in legislation in British Columbia to ban smoking in the workplace in an attempt to protect workers from the effects of second-hand smoke.

Smoking is an anti-social activity, so it should be legislated as an immoral act. It is irresponsible and immoral to continue to expose innocents like children to the terrible hazards of second-hand smoke. Smoking and drinking are often a paired activity, endangering others in apartment buildings or condominium developments if an intoxicated person passes out with a lit cigarette. Furthermore, some women were encouraged to use cigarettes to suppress their appetites. At the same time, smoking was seen as a way women could assert their independence ("Gender and Tobacco" 15). Encouraging smoking amongst women is tantamount to attacking the social system. Smoking during pregnancy increases the risk of complications, low birth weight, miscarriages, stillbirths, premature births, bleeding during pregnancy, and sudden infant death syndrome. Smoking has been linked to lowered immunity, early menopause, reduced fertility, and peptic ulcers (International Development Research Centre 8). Tobacco is harmful to the environment.

Bronstead 4

In addition to the damage from forest fires, the outdoors has to deal with about 2 billion empty cigarette packages annually, several billion plastic and metallic foil overwraps (used to keep the product fresh), and about 50 billion discarded cigarette butts. The butts are often made with cellulose acetate tow, a substance with poor biodegradability. A vast number of trees are cut down each year to produce cigarette paper, packages, cartons, shipping boxes, matches, and matchbooks (International Development Research Centre 11).

Banning cigarette smoking is the only sensible and moral thing to do. The cost to individuals, communities, and social systems continues to rise due to tobacco abuse. Without more control, medical costs will continue to rise and more people will become sick or die. According to one writer, "Nothing can place a value on the pain and suffering caused by disease, the grief of losing a friend or loved one, or the financial crisis created by the death of a family's wage earner" (International Development Research Centre 13). Moreover, the Government of Canada has the moral obligation to protect the rights of its citizens by assuring fresh water, food, and air. Allowing the continuance of smoking abrogates those responsibilities and instead, places commerce before the health and happiness of a nation's citizenry. Surprisingly, many people continue to deny the facts about smoking. However, rather than engage in a discussion over whose rights should take precedence in the matter, both the federal and provincial governments need to step up and take responsibility for protecting citizens' health. Of all smokers who die prematurely, half will die before age 70 and lose an average of 23 years of life. The half who die after age 70 lose an average of 8 years of life (International Development Research Centre 17).

Smoking must be banned if Canadian citizens are to enjoy a system of health care that can be supported, an atmosphere that is healthful, not toxic, a cost of living that is tenable, and a society that respects an individual's right to be healthy. The Government of Canada, the provincial governments, municipalities, and citizen and community groups must be held accountable before the financial and medical support systems become overburdened and transformed to such a degree that no one except a few corporations benefit.

[word count: 1580]

Bronstead 5

Works Cited

The Aboriginal Youth Network. "The Tobacco Industry in Canada." Tobacco 2000. 25 May 2005 <http://www.ayn.ca/quit>.

Aligne, C. A., and J. J. Stoddard. "Tobacco and Children: An Economic Evaluation of the Medical Effects of Parental Smoking." Archives of Pediatrics and Adolescent Medicine 151 (1997): 648–653.

Forces Canada. July 2003. Canadian chapter, Forces, International Smokers' Rights Movement. 12 June 2005 <www.forces.org/Canada>.

The Fraser Institute. The History of Tobacco Regulation: Forward to the Past. Public Policy Sources, Number 40 (2000): 1–24.

"Gender and Tobacco: Women and Girls." Media Awareness Network. 18 Oct. 2005 <http://www.media-awareness.ca/english/resources/educational/handouts/tobacco_advertising/women_and_girls.cfm>.

The International Development Research Centre. Tobacco or Health: The Consequences of Tobacco Use. 18 Oct. 2005 <http://web.idrc.ca/en/ev-28813-201-1-Do_TOPIC.html>.

"Tobacco Smoke and Involuntary Smoking." IARC (International Agency for Research on Cancer) 83 (2002): 22–27.

REVIEW TEST

Try the following review test. It will help you assess what you have learned from the chapter. Be prepared to share your responses with others in the class.

1. In the following, write "yes" after every effective thesis statement; write "no" after every ineffective one, and provide reasons for your answers.
   - Canadians should be more aggressive on the world's political stage.
   - Vending machines stocking junk food should be removed from all public schools.
   - All rodents should be eliminated.

2. Name the three-step process to construct an argument.

3. What point of view should you use in a written argument?

4. What kind of evidence can you use in your argument?

5. What sources can you use to provide evidence in your argument?

6. Name four logical fallacies to avoid when constructing an argument.

7. What should your introduction look like?

____

____

____

8. Where should you place your counter-arguments?

____

____

____

9. Your instructor will bring in a copy of a persuasive letter to the editor. You will write a short paragraph analyzing the writer's argument. You will write in class.

Assignment

Now that you have read Bronstead's essay, analyze her argument by answering the following questions. Bring your answers to class.

1. According to Bronstead, why should smoking be banned?
2. What evidence does Bronstead provide?
3. Are her sources reliable?
4. Is her source list varied enough?
5. What counter-arguments does she provide?

Bonus Exercise Deductive and Inductive Reasoning

This exercise in deductive and inductive reasoning came from the University of Texas. Try it!

Two women, Anissa and Crystin, and two men, Brett and Donald, are athletes. One is a runner, a second is a skater, a third is a gymnast, and a fourth is a tennis player. One day they were seated around a square table.

1. The runner sat on Anissa's left.
2. The gymnast sat across from Brett.
3. Crystin and Donald sat next to each other.
4. A woman sat on the skater's left.

   Who is the tennis player?

   a) Anissa

   b) Brett

   c) Crystin

   d) Donald

READINGS

Carefully read the two following articles. Think about how each writer constructs an argument. Answer the questions that follow each article.

"Why Johnny Can Never, Ever Read: The Perpetual Literacy Crisis and Student Identity"

by Bronwyn T. Williams

Dr. Williams is a professor of English at the University of Louisville in Kentucky. He writes about popular culture, literacy issues, and the teaching of composition. He is particularly interested in online technology and literacy practices.

Fashion trends and politicians come and go, but one thing that never seems to go out of style is a good old-fashioned literacy crisis. Don't believe me? Then tell me the year of each of the following quotations:

1. Those of us who have been doomed to read manuscripts written in an examination room—whether at a grammar school, a high school, or a college—have found the work of even good scholars disfigured by bad spelling, confusing punctuation, ungrammatical, obscure, ambiguous, or inelegant expressions.
2. If your children are attending college, chances are when they graduate they will be unable to write ordinary, expository English with any degree of structure and lucidity. If they are in high school and planning to attend college, the chances are less than even that they will be able to write English at the minimal college level when they get there.
3. The young people enrolled in middle and high school who lack the broad literacy skills to comprehend and learn advanced academic subjects will suffer serious social, emotional, and economic consequences. As a country, the repercussions of a national literacy crisis will seriously hinder this nation's ability to sustain its social, political, and economic well-being in this century.

The answers are 1.—1879 (Hill, 1995, p. 45), 2.—1975 (Sheils, 1975, p. 58), and 3.—2006 (National Association of State Boards of Education, 2005, p. 4). In fact, it's not difficult to look back over the past 150 years and find a constant and consistent level of concern about the abilities of young people to read and write. This "wailing" does not just happen in the United States—it has made headlines from Australia to Britain. Every generation, upon reaching middle age, finds itself compelled to look at the literacy practices of young people and lament at how poor the work produced today is compared to that of idyllic days gone by. (It does make you wonder, however, that if the ability to read and write has been in such sustained decline for generations, shouldn't we by this point be staring at print in baffled incomprehension?)

THE CAUSES

The causes of the literacy crisis for any generation may vary. On the one hand, there are recurring criticisms of teachers and whatever pedagogies they are using. On the other, there is a common concern about the popular culture of the day from sensationalist newspapers in the 1880s to movies in the 1930s, television in the 1970s, and video games and text messaging today. Each invocation of a literacy crisis, however, makes no mention of previous crises or asks about what happened to students in the crisis-ridden classes of yore as they became adults. In 1983, for example, the U.S. government report *A Nation at Risk* (National Commission on Excellence in Education, 1983) warned that schools, including literacy education, were in a crisis that would undermine the national economy and society in years to come. Yet, as Newkirk (2000) pointed out, nearly 20 years later those students had become adults praised for technological and economic innovation. Of course, now that the students of the "Nation at Risk" generation are adults, they can complain about the literacy crisis among the young.

It is difficult to get a sense of how genuine any of these concerns may be. Complaints about student reading and writing abilities often can be traced to anecdotal evidence and the selective memories of adults. Popular media commentators, who know that there are always ratings to be had in attacking public education, often fan the flames made by such complaints. Others may point to standardized test scores as evidence of decline while ignoring the fact that the tests are poorly constructed instruments for literacy assessment and that they only assess a limited range of reading and writing activities. Meanwhile, more comprehensive and complex ways of assessing literacy, which cover a range of students' literacy practices including those outside the classroom, are usually too expensive to implement and are criticized for their very complexity and nuance by self-appointed defenders of "standards."

To say that literacy is a social practice that is vastly more difficult to define and measure in the same kinds of consistent terms that we would measure something like average rainfall is not an argument against rigorous literacy education or a denial of the utility of designing sophisticated and nuanced assessment processes. But the arguments about how to define and assess literacy are as old and persistent as laments about literacy crises and, while worthy of continued discussion, are not where my thoughts are today.

I'm not arguing that there are no challenges in literacy education or that we don't face important challenges in helping struggling students develop their reading and writing abilities. I am wondering why the "drums beat" about such crises so ceaselessly from one generation to the next when clearly most people by adulthood have acquired adequate levels of literacy. What do such constant concerns tell us about our perceptions of young people as readers and writers? And how do these perceptions of students' identities influence our literacy policies and pedagogies?

THE REASONS

Like so many persistent anxieties, the concerns about literacy are often only surface symptoms of deeper anxieties we are less willing to discuss. Although the conversations are about reading and writing and the arguments about whether young people are acquiring the literacy skills to be "competitive in the world market"—whatever that means—the underlying anxieties are not about instrumental literacies necessary to perform in a job. In fact, the level of instrumental literacy necessary to engage in most jobs has changed little over the past half-century (Newkirk, 2000). Despite a century of a perpetual literacy crisis, the economy has grown, adapted, and flourished.

If the problem is not instrumental levels of reading and writing, what is it that drives society's anxiety about reading and writing? I would argue that many of the complaints about a literacy crisis in fact reflect middle class anxieties about status and privilege. After all, the "wailing" about deficient reading and writing abilities comes not from the affluent. They rest easy in the knowledge that the elite, private schools they send their children to will provide them with the appropriate literacy experiences. Neither are the poor the ones we hear complaining about literacy education, if only because the poor have no voice or political clout. Instead, the alarm about declining literacy skills most often comes from the middle class.

Yet walk into most middle class public schools and talk to the students, and it is hard to believe that they do not know how to read and write. In fact, even brief conversations often reveal that they are reading and writing a great deal outside of the classroom. And, still, the rhetoric of the perpetual literacy crisis would ask us to look at these students and see inept, struggling readers and writers and ignore other forms of literacy they have mastered. If we identify these young people as "in crisis," rather than confident and adventurous readers and writers, how does that influence how we approach our teaching and our means of assessment?

LITERACY AS CULTURAL CAPITAL

The issue, then, is not what Scribner (1984) described as "literacy as adaptation" or the functional literacy "conceived broadly as the level of proficiency necessary for effective performance in a range of settings and customary activities" (p. 8). The anxiety comes from whether young people are acquiring what Scribner described as "literacy as power" and "literacy as a state of grace" (p. 7). Scribner argued that such conceptions of literacy connect the ability to engage in certain literacy practices with certain professional class virtues and social power. It is the potential loss of these literacy practices that serve as markers of cultural capital and professional status that worries the middle class.

This helps explain why concerns about declines in reading and writing are often only about particular kinds of literacy practices—those that are invested with the kinds of cultural capital that are recognized as belonging to middle and upper classes. Students might read and write a great deal online and communicate well with people around the world through instant messaging, but these activities are not considered legitimate literacy practices. Such students, Scribner (2004) argued, are not mastering the literacy practices that make a person literate in a way that reveals refined virtues. For example, the National Endowment for the Arts (2004) report, *Reading at Risk*, which charted the decline of literary reading, received a great deal of media attention as another indication of a literacy crisis. The definitions of *literacy* and *literary reading* in the report were laughably narrow, and many of the people calling attention to the report probably rarely read such literature themselves. And yet the report gained public attention because it seemed to be another indicator that young people were not acquiring the necessary cultural capital to maintain their middle class status. Literacy was implicitly defined as the reading of great books that make one a great person rather than as rhetorically effective communication.

In an economy that is increasingly focused on communication and information, cultural capital is a growing factor in determining status for the middle class. While the affluent worry little about losing their class standing because they have abundant economic capital, the middle class understands that the key to a professional or white-collar job and the attendant economic security it entails rests largely on how one displays cultural capital. Middle class life for many rests not on accumulated wealth but on the ability to convincingly adopt and perform a set of bourgeois conventions of behavior. For example, understanding that an office worker should wear a suit rather than shorts and a T-shirt is one such convention. Language use is another obvious class marker. Unconventional speech or language is regarded in the larger culture as an indication of lower class status, and any person who uses it is penalized in terms of economic opportunities. A person could fall from the middle class if he or she loses the ability to use language in a conventional way. Middle class identity is not primarily about economic status. Middle class identity, first and foremost, is the ability to display certain kinds of cultural capital in certain contexts.

It's no surprise that anxieties over unconventional language use are often at the forefront of literacy crisis rhetoric. Complaints about supposed declines in standardized grammar use are often coupled with calls for a return to the "basics," which usually means "drill-and-kill" grammar instruction and worksheets. New forms of writing, such as e-mail or text messaging, along with overly lenient teachers, are often blamed for the crises in correct grammar. These complaints are rarely based on research but are more often anecdotal in nature. In fact, research into instant messaging, for example, indicates that students are able to switch back and forth between conventional and less conventional grammar and spelling depending on the context of the discussion (Takayoshi, 2006).

You may have noticed that I've been using the word *conventional* rather than *correct* to describe language use. I do this because language use is a matter of convention and context. Although some people like to pretend that there are constant, "a-contextual" rules for grammar, in fact we know that the effect of using language in unconventional ways depends on who is using it and in what context (Harris, 1997; Hartwell, 1985; Williams, 1981). I am a tenured professor so I can get away with splitting an infinitive or other "errors" because my position causes people to think that my unconventional writing is intentional. Even sentence fragments.

Yet there are some conventions, such as subject-verb agreement, that I cannot break. The editors of this journal would "correct" these mistakes because they might seem jarring to readers. (The fact that there are editors to review my work is another example of how my position of power benefits me when it comes to language use.) When we teach students that there are sets of unbreakable rules of grammar we deny to them what we know—that some conventions are more important in terms of marking cultural capital and social class than others. Problems with subject-verb agreement or shifting tenses within a sentence can have consequences in the performance of cultural power. And yet it is clear—given what I read and hear every day—that few care anymore that, according to my dictionary, *loan* is a noun and *lend* is a verb.

As teachers, then, we should help students understand that grammar is not a rigid set of rules but a set of conventions that connect identities and status to language use. Of course, we should teach them that unconventional sentences could obscure meaning. Yet when we talk about grammar and language use we should teach them as matters of style and convention. We should make students aware that different cultural settings call for different conventions of language use. We should also make them aware that using language in unconventional ways in the wrong context results in more than a red mark from a teacher's pen—it marks the identity of the author in a particular way for the audience. As a consequence, we should also teach students which conventions are the most important in terms of cultural capital when displaying a professional or academic identity. And we should teach students these conventions as elements of effective writing and rhetoric rather than on grammar worksheets (the latter might teach students how to fill out worksheets but will have little effect on student writing).

THE SOLUTION

If we allow ourselves to get caught up in the hysterical rhetoric of the most recent literacy crisis it distracts us from teaching what we know to be important in reading and writing. If we want to serve students best in their literacy education we should not scare them with tales of the literacy crisis of their generation but instead teach them how to understand how language, culture, and identity work together. Then students can read and write in any context, making their language choices with knowledge and power.

References

Harris, J. (1997). *A teaching subject: Composition since 1966.* Upper Saddle River, NJ: Prentice-Hall.

Hartwell, P. (1985). Grammar, grammars, and the teaching of grammar. *College English, 47,* 105–127.

Hill, A.S. (1995). An answer to the cry for more English. In J.C. Brereton (Ed.), *The origins of composition studies in the American college 1875–1925: A documentary history* (pp. 45–57). Pittsburgh, PA: University of Pittsburgh Press.

National Association of State Boards of Education. (2005). *Reading at risk: The state response to the crisis in adolescent literacy.* Alexandria, VA: Author.

National Commission on Excellence in Education. (1983). *A nation at risk: The imperative for educational reform.* Washington, DC: U.S. Government Printing Office.

National Endowment for the Arts. (2004). *Reading at risk: A survey of literary reading in America.* Washington, DC: Author.

Newkirk, T. (2000). *Presidential candidates engage in education myth-making.* Retrieved May 5, 2007, from www.unh.edu/news/news_releases/2000/october/tm_20001005edu.html

Scribner, S. (1984). Literacy in three metaphors. *American Journal of Education, 93*, 6–21.

Sheils, M. (1975, December 8). *Why Johnny can't write. Newsweek, 92*, 58–63.

Takayoshi, P. (2006, October). *Youth culture, slang, and instant messaging.* Paper presented at the Thomas R. Watson Conference on Rhetoric and Composition, Louisville, KY.

Williams, J. (1981). The phenomenology of error. *College Composition and Communication, 32*, 152–168.

Comprehension Questions

1. What is a "literacy crisis" (underlined)?
2. According to Williams, what are the causes of a literacy crisis?
3. What evidence is there of a literacy crisis?
4. How does Williams define the underlined term "cultural capital?"
5. What does Williams say about language conventions?

Critical Comprehension

1. Who is best served by claiming a "literacy crisis," and why?
2. How are ideas about language use shaped?
3. Analyzing the argument:
   - In 150 words, summarize Williams's argument.
   - Think of three counter-arguments that opponents might make to Williams's argument.
   - How do you think Williams would rebut the counter-arguments? Provide examples.

The Dark Side of Shopping

by Pamela Klaffke

Pamela Klaffke is a writer and editor. She is currently the literary editor of the *Calgary Herald* and writes a column about popular culture trends. Her writing style is breezy and fun, yet informative. Of *Spree: A Cultural History of Shopping, Maclean's* said it "combines a whimsical history of milestones in shopping . . . with a witty and insightful look at its place in modern life." In the following selection, Klaffke examines shoplifting as a disturbing new trend in Canada and the United States.

Politically correct types take note: kleptomaniacs are definitely shoplifters, but most shoplifters are not kleptomaniacs. In other words, it is both politically and medically incorrect to label someone who steals a "klepto." Whether they be the teen truant who lives down the block and steals chocolate bars at the corner store or the movie star who suffers a very public arrest for swiping loads of designer clothes from a fancy department store, chances are if they steal, they're a shoplifter, not a member of the tiny percentage of the world's population that fits the clinical definition of kleptomaniac.

A rare psychiatric disorder causes true kleptomaniacs to steal, but not because they need or even desire the items they pinch. Their acts are not premeditated; it's an impulse reaction, a compulsion similar to other addictions like alcoholism and drug dependency. They often steal to relieve an overpowering sense of tension and anxiety, and experience a rush from the act of theft, but are quickly left deflated, with feelings of guilt. Sometimes, a kleptomaniac's guilt is so encompassing that they will even return to the scene of the crime and attempt to return the merchandise to the shelves.

Evidence of kleptomania dates back to the mid-1800s, not coincidentally at around the same time as the rise of commercial shopping and the Industrial Revolution. In fact, a rash of what was labeled kleptomania late in that century was witnessed among middle-class and well-to-do Victorian women. It was known as a "women's disease" and the term was tossed around casually, with no distinction made between kleptomania and shoplifting.

It was believed that the women who stole were biologically predisposed to do so simply because of their gender, and as a result, the female "klepto" became the butt of many jokes and the target of comedy sketches of the time. The women who stole didn't do so out of need or want but because they were so entranced by the orgy of consumer delight that was the department store. Shopping was a spectacle and although many female shoppers of the day did indeed make legitimate purchases, they also frequently pocketed extra items that were not paid for.

It's unlikely that all—or even a majority—of the light-fingered women were textbook kleptomaniacs, but rather shoplifters who stole because modern consumer society was still in its infancy and the rules were unclear. As Elaine S. Abelson points out in her definitive 1989 book on the subject, *When Ladies Go A-Thieving: Middle Class Shoplifters in the Victorian Department Store*, many women when caught would offer the excuse that "everyone is doing it."

Everyone may have been doing it then, and kleptomania was written off as a female condition that couldn't be helped, but today it is estimated that only one percent of shoplifters are kleptomaniacs. And even when the term is evoked in medical or legal situations, there is always an expert skeptical of its validity.

In the case of Beverly McGill, an Ogden, Utah woman who was arrested in 1998, experts were split regarding her diagnosis (and subsequent defense) of kleptomania.

McGill, the common-law wife of a police officer, stole daily, even using her children as decoys. She knew the blind spots of various stores (the areas that a security camera can't see), she was known to put electrical tape over alarm sensors, and eventually was caught with over $250,000 worth of stolen merchandise in her home.

The stolen goods filled a warehouse of the Ogden Police Department, and three large trucks were necessary to cart all the goods away. The prosecution in her case alleged that she was a personal shoplifter who stole on demand, taking orders from clients and selling the merchandise for profit. When her home was searched, police found a vast array of items—from 102 scented candles to five bridesmaid's dresses.

Her common-law husband confessed he knew of her habit (how could he not?), but couldn't stop her. As a result, he was found guilty of theft by concealment, served six months in jail, and lost his job as a police officer. McGill, too, was found guilty and is serving a 15-year sentence.

Whether McGill fit the definition of kleptomaniac is up for debate. Certainly, she displayed certain traits, but when a typical kleptomaniac steals the act is unplanned, and McGill undoubtedly knew she was going to steal when she hit the shops armed with electrical tape, her two daughters in tow to throw security watchdogs off her scent.

But like any mental illness, there is no test that can offer indisputable proof of kleptomania, which is perhaps one of the reasons kleptomania and compulsive or addictive shoplifting is misunderstood.

Shoplifters, unlike their kleptomaniac cousins, have an agenda when they hit the shops. A small number of shoplifters steal out of need, and it's usually staples such as food and clothing that they're after. But only an estimated one in 10 shoplifters fall into this category, according to the *Allure* magazine article "Crimes of Fashion" by Simon Dumenco, published in April 2002. The other 90 percent is comprised of a hodge-podge of thrill-seeking teenagers, drug addicts, and professionals who covet pricey designer goods to enhance their lifestyle, and shoplifters with obsessive-compulsive personalities.

Statistics are sketchy. Stores don't often care to speak publicly about shoplifting issues, but the Retail Theft Trends Report in 1999 stated that teenagers account for 25 percent of all shoplifters and only one in 35-to-50 is caught.

One of the reasons stores are so reluctant to divulge shoplifting data is that it is believed much of the retail theft in the United States is an inside job, with store employees doing the stealing. The 2001 National Retail Security Survey conducted by the University of Florida estimated that the average non-employee shoplifting incident resulted in a loss of $195.75; for store employees that number jumped to $1,445.86 per incident.

Retailers will acknowledge, however, that shoplifting is a bigger—and more costly—problem than ever before. The National Retail Federation pegs shoplifting loss at about $10 billion each year in the U.S. alone, and numbers are on the rise, jumping more than 21 percent from 2000 to 2001.

To combat shoplifters, merchants invest in sophisticated security systems, although it's usually only the big chains with big money that can afford a team of floorwalkers, consultants to redesign their space to best deter thieves, electronic sensor tags, and a bevy of security cameras and monitors. Although there are no hard numbers, it is widely believed that department stores, discount chains, drug stores, and supermarkets nab the highest number of shoplifters.

Regardless of a store's security system, there will always be shoplifters. Unlike the rash of female shoplifters in the 1800s, today's shoplifter is just as likely to be a man as a woman. More than half are under 25 and don't be surprised if they're wearing oversize clothing, carrying empty (or nearly empty) shopping bags, and—yes, the cliché does prove to be true—wearing sunglasses. The highest number of shoplifting incidents take place on Fridays and Saturdays, in the early afternoon; the most commonly stolen item in the U.S. is lipstick, though CDs and jewelry are also popular.

Incidents of shoplifting rise during the holiday season and during times of economic recession, but not necessarily for the reasons you'd think. Shoppers may be pressed for cash, maxed out on their credit cards, or unemployed, but it's often stress that triggers stealing.

Like kleptomaniacs and compulsive shoppers, the majority of shoplifters (the 90 percent who are not motivated to steal out of poverty) experience feelings of tension, anxiety, and stress before stealing, then a release—a high—during and immediately following the act. The next phase is guilt or depression, which leads back to the tension, anxiety, and stress that prompted them to shoplift in the first place.

Shoplifters differ from kleptomaniacs in that they are completely conscious of their behavior, perhaps even planning a day of thievery before heading to the mall. They may study security systems, learn the ideal time to steal from a certain store, or bring along helpful tools to aid the removal of sensor tags.

However creative, naïve, or clever a shoplifter may be in eluding capture, they probably had some sort of plan when they walked into the store.

Shoplifting is not in itself a psychological disorder, but habitual shoplifters often suffer from depression, come from abusive homes, and have self-esteem issues or anxiety related troubles. According to the organization Cleptomaniacs & Shoplifters Anonymous, the common motives for shoplifting include "feelings of anger, revenge, or entitlement, to fill a sense of emptiness due to grief or loss, to try to make life seem fair, or as a thrill or high to escape problems, numb feelings, or ease depression." As Michael Nuccitelli, executive director of New York's SLS Wellness Center, told *Allure*'s Simon Dumenco, "Shoplifting means something negative is going on inside."

And whatever is going on inside the minds of shoplifters is certainly more powerful than any existing deterrent. Most shoplifters aren't even caught, let alone punished, and those who are rarely see the inside of a cell. Most offenders are fined and put on probation. Many will steal again.

Until recently, there was little support available for shoplifters, but support groups like Cleptomaniacs & Shoplifters Anonymous (which was founded in Detroit by recovering shoplifter Terrance Schulman) and advocacy groups such as Shoplifters Alternative strive to educate retailers, the public, and the shoplifters themselves about the problem and the reasons behind it.

Source: Pamela Klaffke, "The Dark Side of Shopping," *Spree: A Cultural History of Shopping* (Vancouver: Arsenal Pulp Press, 2003) 178–182. Reprinted with permission.

Comprehension Questions

1. What was the occupation of Beverly McGill's common-law husband?
2. Without using a dictionary and using context clues, what does the underlined term "security watchdogs" mean in the selection?

3. What percentage of shoplifters are motivated out of poverty?
4. How can you tell a kleptomaniac from a shoplifter?
5. Will there come a time when shoplifting is eliminated?
6. Evaluate evidence that shoplifting should be considered a crime.

Critical Comprehension

1. What assumptions does Klaffke make about shoppers?
2. How does surveillance enter into the issue of shoplifting, and does it infringe on personal rights and freedoms?
3. Analyze the argument:

   Prepare two paragraphs of about 150 words each:

   - The first paragraph should outline Klaffke's claims and her supporting evidence.
   - The second paragraph should provide counter-arguments to Klaffke's claims that you have outlined. You should also provide reasons that an opponent might make for the counter-arguments.

Assignment

- Prepare an argument using one of the following topics.
- Use a conventional five-paragraph essay format.
- Use a third-person point of view.
- Use the suggested scheme outlined in this chapter: thesis that clearly states your position; body paragraph 1 that provides your opponent's counter-arguments, reasons, and your rebuttal; body paragraphs 3 and 4 that develop clear claims or points with supporting reasons/evidence; a conclusion that logically follows.
- Do some research to support your views.
- Use either APA or MLA documentation to reference your research. (See Chapters 14 and 15 for more information about APA and MLA.)
- Your paper should be 1000–1100 words long.

Suggested Topics

1. In Ontario, pit bull laws should/should not be repealed.
2. Canada should/should not be sending more foreign aid to other countries.
3. Internet security for personal privacy issues should be/should not be government regulated.
4. The local school board should/should not adopt a four-day school week for its students.
5. Seniors should/should not receive free medications.
6. Foreign doctors should/should not be allowed to practise in Canada.

7. Salaries of professional hockey players should/should not be capped.
8. Provincial exams should/should not be eliminated.
9. Outdoor education should/should not be compulsory for all Canadians.
10. All post-secondary education should/should not be free of tuition.
11. The health care system should/should not include pets.
12. Workers should/should not be allowed to drive their cars to work in urban areas.
13. Space should/should not be weaponized.
14. Satellite television signals should/should not be free.
15. Every Canadian should be able/should not be able to afford her own home.
16. Canada should/should not export water.
17. The North American Free Trade Agreement among the Government of Canada, the Government of the United Mexican States, and the Government of the United States of America should/should not be abandoned.
18. Canada should/should not privatize the health care system.

CHECKOUT

Here are some of the ideas you will take away with you after you have completed the chapter:

1. Write and organize accurate notes while searching the internet.
2. Structure argument papers clearly, and support major claims with reasons.
3. Be aware that readers can be put off by writers' venting, sarcasm, or sermonizing.
4. Carefully select transitions to show the reader a logical flow of ideas.
5. Include correct APA or MLA in-text citations for any outside sources you include.
6. Make sure that your conclusion follows logically from your argument.

Mastering the concepts in this chapter will also help you develop and apply the following employability skills highlighted by the Conference Board of Canada in *Employability Skills 2000+*:

Communicate

- read and understand information presented in a variety of forms (e.g., words, graphs, charts, diagrams)
- use relevant scientific, technological and mathematical knowledge and skills to explain or clarify ideas

Think & Solve Problems

- seek different points of view and evaluate them based on facts

Source: Adapted from *Employability Skills 2000+* Brochure E/F (Ottawa: The Conference Board of Canada, 2000).

chapter 12

Researching

Chapter Objectives

After completing this chapter you will be able to

1. recognize what research writing is;
2. detect different documentation styles in research writing;
3. recognize a research paper according to an accepted style of documentation;
4. discover different styles of documentation required in different academic courses;
5. check the latest handbooks, reference books, or online sources to learn about updated requirements.

INTRODUCTION

Researching and research writing has become part of daily life at home and in the workplace. An important critical skill for today's professional is the ability to carry out, manage, and report research in various forms. The Conference Board of Canada cites the following employability skills as needed in today's work world, in particular the ability to

- locate, gather, and organize information using appropriate technology and information systems;
- decide what needs to be measured or calculated;
- assess situations and identify problems;
- evaluate solutions to make recommendations or decisions;
- set goals and priorities balancing work and personal life;
- plan and manage time, money and other resources to achieve goals;
- work independently or as a part of a team;
- carry out multiple tasks or projects;
- plan, design, or carry out a project from start to finish with well-defined objectives and outcomes.

All of your research projects in post-secondary courses incorporate these employability skills. When you write a research paper, you know how to locate and gather information. You must sometimes work as a team to complete your project. You have to make choices about how to use the information you have gathered. You must be able to acknowledge potential problem areas, if data fits, for example, or if data is reliable and serves your purpose. You must solve problems along the way and check periodically to see if your solutions are working. You have to set goals on a daily, weekly, and overall basis in order to meet specified deadlines, and you have to set priorities and limits so that you use time and energy effectively. Above all, you must meet the standards; meet the assignment deadline; meet the assignment's purpose; use the style of documentation your professor names, whether it is APA, MLA, Chicago, or some other style; and present the paper according to the specifications. Indeed, these steps are very much like the ones you will take in your professional life to accomplish a project in your workplace. In other words, the skills you learn in researching will be transferable skills to the work world and to the life world.

Research writing has its own sets of rules and practices. You will learn that when you use other people's words or ideas in your research papers and essays, you must acknowledge or cite your sources, and you must follow a particular style of showing those sources in your work. Two of the most common documentation styles used in post-secondary research writing are APA (American Psychological Association) style and MLA (Modern Language Association) style. Each documentation style has its own guidelines to use in specific writing situations. It is not practical to try to remember every detail connected to APA and MLA style documentation. You can look up a detail you need when you need it by checking a reputable English handbook or writer's reference, or by looking up a reliable internet site, particularly those from university or college libraries or writing centres.

However, you should know about the important features of these two documentation styles and be able to set them up for your papers. Your instructor or professor will expect you to be able to do so. Chapter 14 discusses using the APA style of documentation. Chapter 15 discusses MLA.

Learning to research requires practice. The more practice you get in doing research, the more confident you will become in your ability to format a paper effectively according to the documentation style. This chapter will introduce you to researching. You will not be an expert after completing the chapter, but you will know the basics of a research paper. You will look at how papers are documented in the two styles, what in-text citations are and what they look like, and how to set up a References or Works Cited sheet at the end of your paper.

WHAT IS RESEARCH?

In everyday life, you often need to find the answer to something. You might have to look something up on the internet or in books. You might also need to ask an expert. Many activities in your daily life include this type of informal "research." Researching a garage sale find—an antique vase—to find out if it might be an original William Morris worth $1500, for example, is informal research. Researching an employer in order to decide if you want to apply for a job with the company is also informal but practical research. Academic researching, however, is very different, particularly at the graduate level, where you will be adding to original research on a specialized topic.

At the undergraduate level in post-secondary education, you will be exploring the rudiments of academic researching. Here, doing "research" does not mean you are going to add original new data or information to a field of study. In fact, what you will be doing is learning to use sources and resources to discover facts and pieces of information on a specific topic to answer a research question you have set up. What *will* be original will be your interpretation of what you have gathered as it relates to your research question.

Leedy, Newby, and Ertmer (1996), in their *Practical Research: Planning and Design* from Prentice Hall publications, define research in this way: "Research is a process through which we attempt to achieve systematically and with the support of data the answer to a question, the resolution of a problem, or a greater understanding of a phenomenon" (p. 7). For two-year programs or for undergraduate degree programs, students are not expected to create an original research project, collect the original data, interpret the original data, and then draw conclusions (and write a thesis). Instead, students learn to work with the academic data and material currently available to them in sources in order to answer a question. Sources for academic research information include online databases, professional journals, textbooks, periodicals, films, interviews, the internet, television, and radio.

Working with academic databases and studies does not mean simply transferring facts from journals into a research essay, using a required documentation style. It does not mean cutting ideas from one source and pasting them into your paper. What it does mean is collecting information that helps to promote and solve your research question and then interpreting the information in some way. When you research as an undergraduate student, you are also learning about the established theories in your discipline and how scholars write about those theories. Your research papers will reflect how well you are able to use relevant material in order to demonstrate your understanding and analysis of important basic concepts in a field.

In your first few years of researching, you will be learning some extremely important skills:

- how to work at becoming an expert in using sources and resources available at your institute or online;
- how to use academic databases online;
- how to read scholarly articles in a variety of disciplines;
- how to take effective notes;
- how to interpret what you have read or watched;
- how to communicate your findings;
- how to follow a required format, such as APA, MLA, Turabian, or others.

WHAT TYPES OF RESEARCH ARE THERE?

As mentioned, individuals can engage in formal academic research or informal research. Academic research is reported in professional journals that are only available in an academic library or online through an academic website. As you begin to read academic research articles, you will notice how extensive online databases are. They contain tens of thousands of articles from all academic disciplines. In fact, a single online database can contain literally thousands of academic journals, each containing several years' worth of academic articles. Some online databases are repositories for newspaper articles. Others may specialize in law research only, while others may contain articles for medical and nursing students only.

To understand how academic research is organized, you should know some general information about it. Researchers must use particular conventional methods, called **methodologies**, in conducting their research. They must also report their findings in what are called **academic studies** published in periodicals called academic journals. The form of reporting is also discipline-specific, and each discipline adopts a specific style. Other academic studies or other sources used in the preparation of the study must be reported in a specialized format.

Academic research is generally divided into two types of methodologies: **qualitative** and **quantitative research**. Qualitative research is most often used to explore the "why" and "how" of human experience, most often in the social sciences, nursing, and education. Qualitative research investigates a phenomenon in order to gain understanding. Researchers observe people where they are doing some activity or activities in relation to their work, family roles, community role, and so forth. In other words, people are observed in context. Qualitative researchers are interested in what people have to say about their experience, so their methodology often includes interviews and surveys. They might also work with small groups of people called **focus groups**. These groups might report back on their experiences or might comment on what something in their lives is like for them. Qualitative researchers believe that the world is not full of certainties that can be measured in strict terms. Instead, they believe in interpretations of the world. These researchers tend to be more subjective in the interpretation of their data.

Quantitative research, on the other hand, uses statistical data and designed experiments as part of its methodology. Quantitative researchers believe that their studies and experiments should be testable and reproducible. They are interested in the "what," "where," and "when" research questions. Sciences, psychology, mathematics, and often business will use hard data and experimental design in their research studies. Quantitative researchers will interpret data based on statistical principles; they are more objective in their interpretations.

As a student preparing a research paper, you will come across studies in your discipline that use either a qualitative or quantitative approach or a combined approach. Recognize when you are reading a scholarly article from a professional journal that an article may be based on qualitative or quantitative methodology (or a combined approach), and pay attention to how researchers set up their work and the conclusions they draw from it. Although you do not have to set up anything like this until you are in graduate school, you should be somewhat familiar with how academic research is designed and reported in order to be able to read it with any sort of facility. You will notice that the reading that comes at the end of this chapter is based on a particular research design.

WHAT DOCUMENTATION STYLE SHOULD I USE?

Academic research reporting has rules. Researchers cannot simply report their research in any format they want; they must adhere to the guidelines set up in their discipline. Documenting your sources is an important part of academic research. The documentation style refers to the style you use in showing your sources and in setting up or formatting your paper. Each discipline has its own documentation style. If you are taking courses from more than one discipline, then you will have to use a specific documentation style for each discipline. This means your research paper in psychology, for example, will have a different documentation style from the one in business or history or linguistics.

You must check with your instructor to find out which documentation style you are expected to use in your papers.

The three most commonly used documentation styles are as follows:

- APA (American Psychological Association) for use in psychology, social sciences, nursing, education, and sometimes business;
- MLA (Modern Language Association) for use in English, language studies, linguistics, and art;
- Turabian or Chicago style, used primarily in history but also used in other disciplines.

Chapter 14 discusses APA format in detail, while chapter 15 provides information on MLA style.

WHAT FORMAT SHOULD I USE?

Research papers use essay format for courses in history, education, nursing, business, psychology, sociology, political science, criminology, anthropology, English, language studies, and philosophy. All research papers must contain a list of sources used in the preparation of the paper. In APA style, that list is entitled **References**; in MLA format, it is called **Works Cited**. You will notice as you read research articles in professional journals that these References sheets or Works Cited sheets are found at the ends of articles. They are an excellent source of information because you can use these as sources to look up yourself.

Your research paper will have the following parts in an essay framework:

- an introductory paragraph with a clear thesis statement that indicates your research question in a statement form;
- body paragraphs organized around the research categories you have developed, containing direct quotations or summaries from source material (these are called **in-text citations** or *parenthetical citations* because they appear in parentheses in the body of your paper);
- a conclusion that follows logically from your paper's development and helps to close discussion on your research question;
- a References (APA) or Works Cited (MLA) sheet.

HOW DO I USE RESOURCES EFFICIENTLY?

In order to do beginning research, you must know what sources you can use. It will take considerable time and energy to do all the reading, note-taking, and writing to complete a single research paper. It is conceivable that in one semester you may have one or two major research papers to do in each course. If you are taking five courses per semester, you could be facing five or more research papers. At first glance, that may not seem like too many. However, each paper will take many hours to prepare. You should know how to access sources, use databases, take efficient notes, and read research articles. The more you practise, the more efficient you will become.

To start off, you should make a point of touring your campus. Some schools offer tours for all new students; take part in one because you will learn what resources are available, where they are housed, and who the key resource people are. Visit the library, learning and writing centres, general computer lab areas, help centres, counselling areas, student society area, and bookstore. Your library or writing, learning, or help centre may offer short courses on researching, including "how to" workshops on a number of research topics. By checking out what is available on your campus, you will know where you need to go when you need help or access to material.

WHAT RESOURCES DO I USE?

You will find the most common resource materials housed in the library or placed online.

Library Resources

Post-secondary libraries are different from public library systems because they contain materials to support students and faculty in their studies. An academic library refers to a smaller library in a college or small university where materials are kept to support students in their course work. A research library is found in larger institutions and provides support to students in their studies and to faculty in their research.

Your school library offers tours of its facilities to explain how material in the library has been organized, what materials are available, and what key resource people are there to assist students.

Following is a list of resource areas in the library:

1. *Periodicals*: an area containing all current issues of professional journals, trade magazines, general circulation magazines, and newspapers from Canada and other countries. The periodicals room also shelves back issues of journals and magazines for the current year. Back issues older than one year may be stored in the Archives section of the library.

2. *Books/textbooks*: shelved throughout the library. These shelves are often referred to as "the stacks."

3. *Digital collections*: an area with computers. These collections provide access to electronic journals, web versions of newspapers, scanned images of photographs, maps, and other documents.

4. *Reference area*: houses books that cannot be removed from the library and must be used on site. Here you will find dictionaries, encyclopedias, atlases, and other material that readers use only as a reference to gather facts or specific bits of information.

5. *Special collections*: an area found in large-school libraries; houses rare documents or materials of special interest.
6. *Government publications:* stores documents and materials related to municipal, provincial, and federal government affairs.

Exercise 1 Locating Resources

Use the previous section to answer each of the following questions. Be prepared to share your answers.

In what section of the library would you find the following materials related to a particular assignment? Write the section's name after each question. Some questions may have more than one possible answer. Check your answers with the Answer Key.

1. Where would you find a star map to help you with your astronomy assignment?
2. Where would you find information on gum disease for your dental hygiene course?
3. Where would you find Einstein's theory of relativity for your physics course?
4. Where would you find a discussion on changing weather patterns in the flood plain regions of Canada?
5. Where would you find literary criticism articles on George Metcalfe for your Lit Crit 200 course?
6. Where would you find examples of the earliest political cartoons for your Journalism 170 class?
7. Where would you go if you wanted to find out the atomic weight of gold for your Chem 070 course?

The library also has highly qualified and highly skilled personnel. Reference librarians have graduate degrees in library science and information retrieval. They can help you locate information or can suggest pathways for searching. If you are stuck in your library search, remember to ask one of the available resource people for help.

Online Resources

Of course, you are familiar with using the internet to find out information, but you may not be familiar with the resources available in your library's digital collection. Your library offers you online databases for your studies. You may need some help learning how to access and use these databases, and someone in the library will assist you if you ask for help. Your library also offers online tutorials for researching, using databases, and accessing electronic information. In addition, your library produces handouts for you to take with you.

Here is a sample of some of the databases you will be able to access at your library or from home (once you receive your password from the library):

- Academic Search Premier (EBSCO*host*), with access to about 4500 journals
- JSTOR, with access to about 700 journals in 45 disciplines
- ProQuest, with access to behavioural sciences journals, newspapers, and other journals

- LexisNexis Academic, with access to legal articles, internal newspapers, and U.S. and major newspapers
- ERIC, with access to education articles for education professionals
- Philosophers database for access to articles on philosophy
- WorldCat, with access to bibliographic information on a database with over 56 million records

Not all material, however, can be used as research sources. Some newspapers, magazines, websites, blogs, television programming, and so forth are not considered trustworthy in terms of accurate information. Check with your instructor or professor to find out if the department has a list of sources that are not recommended. For example, many schools will not accept *Wikipedia* as a reliable source, even though most students try to include it as a source in their References or Works Cited list.

A Caution about Plagiarism

If a material is copyrighted, then you must respect the copyright. In others words, you must never use someone else's words and claim them as your own. If you do so, you are guilty of plagiarism. The issue of plagiarism is mentioned several times in this text because it is so important.

Here are some tips to avoid plagiarism:

- Always copy the author's name, the title of the article, the title of the text or name of the journal or source, the volume number, the date of publication, the publisher, and the page numbers of the source from which you are taking notes.
- Cite the author's name automatically when you use quoted or summarized material—note the citation details (page numbers, date of publication). Even if you use your own words, you may be using someone else's idea, so be sure that you cite your source.
- Use a brightly coloured highlighter and place bullets beside all material you have copied or summarized from other sources. These bright spots will alert you to double-check that your sources have been documented. When you are preparing the final draft of the paper, you can remove the bright bullets.
- List each author's name as you are reviewing your paper. Then double-check your list against your citation materials. Have you included all the source information required? Have you spelled authors' names correctly? Have you included all pertinent page numbers?
- Check your References or Works Cited page against the sources mentioned in your paper.

HOW DO I READ FOR RESEARCH?

Reading for research means you are reading for some specific purposes. First, you are reading to determine whether or not the source material is what you are looking for to complete your research paper. Second, you are reading to gather information for your paper. Third, you are reading for specific quotations or information that you can use and cite directly in your paper. Therefore, when you read like a researcher, you are reading carefully with these purposes in mind.

Primary and Secondary Sources

A **primary source** is the original source material. For example, if you were studying the work of John Stuart Mill in a philosophy course, you would most likely be asked to read some of his essays. When writing your philosophy paper, you would refer to Mill's original essays, perhaps quoting from them or summarizing parts of them. Therefore, you would be working with a primary source.

However, if you wanted to read what someone else had written about John Stuart Mill's essays, then you would be consulting a **secondary source**. Secondary sources are generally an interpretation of a primary source. For example, if you were researching what Mill had to say about human nature and were investigating what others had to say about Mill's ideas on the topic, you would be using secondary sources, such as this one: Janice Carlisle, *John Stuart Mill and the Writing of Character*. Athens, GA: University of Georgia Press, 1991.

Scholarly Articles

You will find scholarly articles in professional journals in your library or online through an academic database. Each discipline has its own method of documentation—that is, using APA, MLA, Turabian (Chicago style), or other. As well, professional journals have panels of experts who decide which study they will publish in their journals. When researchers submit their studies to professional journals, they must adhere to the rules set out by their discipline and the demands of the journal. For the most part, studies in all professional journals have similarities. Generally speaking, they have the same parts.

THE ABSTRACT

An abstract is a summary of the study. It includes the purpose of the study, how the research was conducted (methodology), a brief description of the results, and a recommendation. If you do not know if an article in a professional journal will suit your purposes, read the abstract first.

THE INTRODUCTION

This portion of the study provides the research question and the researcher's context. The section often includes a **literature review**. A literature review means the researchers have to survey the research in the field as it connects to their own research proposal. They must then explain how their research fits into the research picture.

METHODS OF METHODOLOGY

In this section, researchers describe how their research was conducted. They also tell what protocols, materials, and processes were chosen and used in their experiment or study. Researchers will also cite theory from qualitative or quantitative research that supports their methods.

RESULTS

Researchers provide the studies' data in chart or table form. They also include an explanation of what statistical principles were used to calculate their data. In this section, researchers describe what happened in their studies. They tell what outcomes they observed or what data they collected and tabulated.

DISCUSSION

In this section, researchers bring together the results and their research questions. They explain the connection between the two.

CONCLUSION OR RECOMMENDATION

Researchers draw conclusions about their studies in this section. They also recommend what other research needs to be done.

REFERENCES OR WORKS CITED

All sources used as background research and in preparation of studies are listed as the last pages in research articles. Researchers will use the ascribed documentation style, usually APA, MLA, or Turabian (Chicago style) throughout the professional article and in the preparation of the source list.

The parts of a research article or study are given as headers in the article, so you can choose which section you might want to read. For example, you might read only the results section or only the methodology, depending on your research. However, it is almost always important to read the abstract first because it lets you know if the article is suitable to your research project.

Exercise 2 Practising Reading

This is an exercise in reading, so it will not have a set of "right" answers attached to it. Choose a research article from chapters 3, 6, or 8 of this text. Find the parts of the article. Read the abstract. Does knowing the function of each part help you understand the overall article?

Exercise 3 Reviewing Articles

Review the articles from chapters 6 and 7. What comments can you make about how the research was conducted? Which one seems to be more scholarly? Why? Be prepared to share you answers.

Critical Reading and Thinking

Reading like a researcher means keeping your purposes for reading constantly in mind. You must also practise your skills as a critical thinker and reader. Review some of the critical reading strategies provided in chapter 1. Try to apply those to your reading as you read for research purposes.

Here are some tips for reading for research:

- Read the abstract first. Does it suit your research needs?
- Read with a pencil. Think as you read and take clear notes.
- Ask, "What does the author tell me?"
- Ask, "What are the author's arguments?"
- Ask, "What is the author's research question?"
- Ask, "How do the author's findings fit with other studies I've read?" "Are they different? How? Why?"
- What do secondary sources say about this writer's work? What criticisms are given?
- Ask, "Does the author's work support or not support my own research question?"
- Read the first and last paragraphs of sections to get the gist of the discussion. If the paragraphs seem relevant to your research needs, then read in great detail.

Do not try to read scholarly works as if they are light novels. You must develop a different strategy for this type of reading. Good readers have different reading techniques for different purposes. You must be able to use specific techniques like skimming (finding particular facts), scanning (getting the general gist of something), being selective (reading abstracts, headings, introductory and concluding paragraphs only) while keeping in mind your purpose for reading.

Note Taking

Being an excellent note-taker is part of being a good researcher. Take clear and accurate notes. Here are some tips:

- Write down all the citation details, that is, the title of the article or book, the author's name, the date of publication, the publisher's name, the city of publication, the pages (if the material is an article from a journal or text).
- Write direct quotations word for word. Be sure you include the page number or numbers.
- Write careful summaries. Be sure you include the page number or numbers.
- Look up words you do not know to be sure you understand the notes you are taking. Write new words and their definitions in a margin.
- There are many good educational sites on the internet that provide really valuable information on note taking. Here are some sites to visit:
    1. **http://sas.calpoly.edu/asc/ssl/notetaking.systems.html**
       This site from Student Academic Services at California Polytechnic State University is excellent because it shows you five different methods of note taking.

2. **www.accd.edu/sac/history/keller/ACCDitg/SSnote.htm**
   This site is from an American community college and lists some basic note-taking strategies. They explain the SQR3—survey, question, read, recite, and review—method of note taking.
3. **www.uleth.ca/ross/counselling/study_skills_handouts.html**
   This page from the University of Lethbridge gives a variety of tips on taking notes from textbooks and from lectures.
4. **www.coun.uvic.ca/learning/note-taking/index.html**
   The University of Victoria, Counselling Services, offers information on the Cornell method of note taking with handouts that you can download.
5. **http://extend.unb.ca/wss/**
   The University of New Brunswick, College of Extended Learning, has a number of useful links related to note taking and study skills.

You can find many more valuable sites in the .edu domain. These websites are from colleges and university study skills, writing, learning, and counselling centres. All have information and links that can help you become a better note-taker and reader.

REVIEW TEST

Try the following review test. It will help you assess what you have learned from the chapter. Be prepared to share your responses with others in the class.

1. What is academic research?

   ___

   ___

   ___

2. Name three important skills you will develop by researching.

   ___

   ___

   ___

3. Name two methodologies used in academic research.

   ___

   ___

   ___

4. What is a documentation style? Name two styles that are commonly used.

   ___

   ___

   ___

5. How is a research paper set up? Name the parts of a research paper.

____

____

____

6. Name four resource areas you can find in your school's library.

____

____

____

7. What is an online academic database?

____

____

____

8. Describe the setup of academic articles found in academic journals.

____

____

____

READING

The following article describes a community-based research project for medical interns undertaken by Aboriginal communities in northern Ontario, the Government of Ontario, and McMaster University. Dr. Kelly's article clearly shows the parts of a research article: an introduction, the methodology (or program description), discussion, conclusion, and references. Research articles in scholarly journals in medicine, nursing, business, social sciences, and education generally follow this pattern, although researchers often include a section called "recommendations." A research article is a kind of report on a particular research project.

Read Dr. Kelly's article carefully, and answer the questions that follow. Pay particular attention to how the research was carried out and to the details of the research. This piece of research contains data in the form of two tables. When researching, you will find many scholarly articles contain statistical or numerical data in their studies.

Researching Rural: Research Interns in Northern Ontario

by Len Kelly & Natalie St. Pierre-Hansen

Dr. Len Kelly is an associate professor of clinical sciences in the Northern Ontario School of Medicine in Sioux Lookout, Ontario. He is also associated with the department of family medicine at McMaster University. Dr. Kelly was recently given the D.M. Robb Research grant by the College of Family Physicians of Canada in recognition of his outstanding work in Aboriginal palliative care. Natalie St. Pierre-Hansen is a research intern, Northern Ontario School of Medicine, Sioux Lookout, Ontario.

INTRODUCTION

Canada's newest medical school has developed an interesting way to promote community-based research and rural professional development. The Northern Ontario School of Medicine (NOSM) welcomed its charter class of 56 students in 2005. In 2006, the school initiated a community-based research internship program by partnering with government agencies.

PROGRAM DESCRIPTION

Twelve recent university graduates have been placed in rural communities across northern Ontario through a partnership with FedNor (Industry Canada's economic development initiative for Northern Ontario)[1] and the Northern Ontario Heritage Fund Corporation (a provincial agency mandated to foster job creation in northern Ontario).[2]

The year-long internship is designed to provide the interns with valuable work experience and to help them develop relevant research skills applicable to their region. Many NOSM research interns had previously left the north to pursue a university education. This internship facilitated a return to the rural northern Ontario communities for these researchers, opening the door to a rich and diverse research experience valuable to future career development.

NOSM espouses interdisciplinary cooperation, community partnerships and an emphasis on the cultures and characteristics of northern Ontario.[3] A variety of projects from qualitative to clinical research involve a cross-section of health care workers and use community-driven approaches. Application of the CIHR Guidelines for Health Research Involving Aboriginal People[4] and collaboration with community leaders and First Nation organizations lead to research processes that are truly community owned. The spinoff for local research initiatives can—and does—affect program development at local hospitals. Issues as focused as throat swabs and as in-depth as palliative care and obstetrical services can inform local and regional centres that face similar issues.

Cross-cultural and rural issues are often underrepresented in research funding. Rural physicians often lack the time, funding and expertise to examine questions that raise curiosity in clinical challenges. Previous summer-long research internships have had documented success in stimulating rural clinicians to increase scholarly activity.[5]

The presence of continuous, yearlong research support in rural communities is both novel and exciting. In one community, more than 10 local physicians with limited prior research experience are working on a variety of meaningful projects. Their research intern has been able to participate in relevant workshops and report back to physicians unable to attend. Both the clinician and the local hospital have benefitted by looking at challenges in a more systematic manner: elaborate the question, perform a literature search, systematically gather the data, collaborate with the stakeholders and proceed toward solutions, including funding applications for further research.

DISCUSSION

Other successful initiatives enabling community-based research are occurring at the University of British Columbia, where the Department of Family Medicine recognized it was "an unrealistic expectation that family practitioners could devote themselves to research without pay while maintaining a clinical practice."[6] They subsequently developed several 1- to 3-year clinical investigator programs with funding, in addition to program support for research coordination and statistical expertise. The 3-year Community-Based Clinician Investigator program has had over 20 graduates since 2000 and the R3 research clinical investigator positions support re-entry for experienced clinicians to develop research projects. Additionally, British Columbia's newly minted Centre for Rural Health Research has focused on rural maternity care, combining research with networking with policy-makers and with patients and caregivers from 20 rural communities. With these multifaceted endeavours, a culture of primary care research is developing in rural areas.

There are research institutes in various provinces that are involved in primary care studies.[7–10] Their challenge is to reach out in a distributed fashion to the communities they study and to encourage healthy, supported nodes of excellence in community-based research. Some programs support family doctors by protecting 50% of their time and salary support to engage in research.

Performing literature searches is one of a rural researcher's earliest tasks. As disparate as the definitions of "rural" that currently exist, so too are the medical subject headings (MeSH) terms and databases available for searching rural topics. Table 12.1 and Table 12.2 may be of use to others interested in rural research.

Table 12.1 Medical subject headings term searches for rural references

	No. of references						
MeSH terms* for rural	HealthStar	MEDLINE	PubMed Central	EBMR	CINAHL	EMBASE	PsycINFO
Hospitals, rural	2928	3023	3016	13	745		
Rural area					5748	12 955	
Rural health	16 009	17 420	17 393	268	1793		
Rural health care						2898	
Rural health centres					40		
Rural health nursing					1150	5	
Rural health personnel					219		
Rural health services	4809	4900	4889	101	1893		
Rural population	23 429	25 239	25 103	364		4168	
Rural hygiene						110	
Urban rural difference						1588	
Rural environments							7062
Total distinct references (all MeSH terms combined with Boolean "OR")	45 547	48 937	48 790	729	10 205	20 540	7062

CINAHL = Cumulative Index to Nursing and Allied Health Literature; EBMR = Evidence-Based Medicine Reviews; MeSH = medical subject headings.

**The various databases have their own unique MeSH terms. Multiple MeSH within a database exist for a single term, yet each MeSH is distinct from others, therefore all relevant terms should be selected. For example, on MEDLINE there were 17 420 references found under the term "rural health" and 25 239 found under "rural population"; only 220 references were indexed under both MeSH terms.*

Table 12.2 Keyword search for rural references

	No. of references						
Text word*	HealthStar	MEDLINE	PubMed Central	EBMR	CINAHL	EMBASE	PsycINFO
Rural	61 407	68 086	75 834	1783	13 440	34 729	16 327

CINAHL = Cumulative Index to Nursing and Allied Health Literature; EBMR = Evidence-Based Medicine Reviews.

**A text word search retrieves articles that contain the word anywhere in the available text of the reference (title, abstract or main body).*

CONCLUSION

Resourcefulness and creativity are key components of successful research and scholarly activity. These essential ingredients can lead to quality community-driven research through sustainable networks and partnerships. Resources for rural researchers are much like the database tools: an understanding of how to access and use them to their full capacity can lead to rewarding outcomes. The much-needed infrastructure is just developing, and rural doors are being opened for meaningful research opportunities. Several key funding components for the clinician investigator and infrastructure support are needed to sustainably "research rural."

References

FedNor. Youth internships—not-for-profit fund. Available: http://fednor.ic.gc.ca/epic/site/fednor-fednor.nsf/en/fn02300e.html (accessed 2008 Mar 13).

Northern Ontario Heritage Fund Corporation. Youth internship and co-op program. Available: www.mndm.gov.on.ca/nohfc/program yiacp_e.asp (accessed 2008 Mar 13).

Northern Ontario School of Medicine. At a glance. Available: www.normed.ca/about_us/glance.htm (accessed 2008 Mar 13).

Canadian Institutes of Health Research. *CIHR guidelines for health research involving Aboriginal people.* Ottawa (ON): Her Majesty the Queen in Right of Canada; 2007. Available: www.cihr-irsc.gc.ca/e/documents/ethics_aboriginal_guidelines_e.pdf (accessed 2008 Mar 13).

Kelly L., Rourke J. Research electives in rural health care. *Can Fam Physician* 2002; 48:1476–80.

The University of British Columbia. The Vancouver Foundation (BCMSF) community-based clinician investigator salary award request for applications. Available: www.familypractice.ubc.ca/research/documents/cbci_rfa_2007.pdf (accessed 2008 Mar 13).

The University of British Columbia. Centre for Rural Health Research: Rural Maternity Care New Emerging Team (RMNET). Available: www.familypractice.ubc.ca/documents/External_Review 2007/Unit_Self_Study_Reports_Spring 2007/SelfStudyReport2007-Research-Rural_Maternity.pdf (accessed 2008 Mar 13).

Centre for Rural and Northern Health Research. About CRaNHR. Available: www.cranhr.ca/profile.html (accessed 2008 Mar 13).

Queen's University Centre for Studies in Primary Care. Available: www.queensu.ca/cspc/index.html;jsessionid=6E8E05B50FD367E6F786DB589899E9E (accessed Mar 13).

Memorial University. Primary Healthcare Research Unit. Available: www.med.mun.ca/phru/pages/welcome.html (accessed 2008 Mar 13).

Source: Len Kelly & Natalie St. Pierre-Hansen, "Researching Rural: Research Interns in Northern Ontario," Canadian Journal of Rural Medicine *2008; 13 (2): 86–88. © 2008 Society of Rural Physicians of Canada.* Reprinted by permission of Dr. Kelly, Len and Natalie St. Pierre-Hansen.

Comprehension Questions

1. What is "community-based research"?
2. What is an internship?
3. What is the mandate of NOSM?
4. What positive spinoffs do the local initiatives have?
5. Why are not more rural physicians doing research?
6. What were the steps used to conduct the local research?
7. What is a "literature survey"?
8. Review Table 1. What does it describe?
9. Review Table 2. What does it describe?

Critical Comprehension

1. Why is community-based research so important, particularly in Canada's North?
2. How can research and practice connect?

Assignment

Research a community-based project in your own community. In a 500-word essay, describe the project and its impact.

CHECKOUT

Here are some of the ideas you will take away with you after you have completed the chapter:

1. Researching and research writing are needed in today's workplace.
2. Being able to locate reliable sources for your paper is vital.

3. Learning to research does require practice and perseverance.
4. From time to time, documentation style guidelines are updated.
5. Good time-management skills are necessary in order to plan and organize a project so that you complete it effectively and in a timely fashion.
6. Guidelines for formatting papers are complex and can be confusing, so consult with your instructor before you start your paper.

Mastering the concepts in this chapter will also help you develop and apply the following employability skills highlighted by the Conference Board of Canada in *Employability Skills 2000+*:

Communicate

- read and understand information presented in a variety of forms (e.g., words, graphs, charts, diagrams)
- share information using a range of information and communications technologies (e.g., voice, e-mail, computers)
- use relevant scientific, technological and mathematical knowledge and skills to explain or clarify ideas

Manage Information

- locate, gather and organize information using appropriate technology and information systems

Think & Solve Problems

- assess situations and identify problems
- seek different points of view and evaluate them based on facts

Be Responsible

- plan and manage time, money and other resources and other resources to achieve goals

Be Adaptable

- work independently or as a part of a team

Participate in Projects & Tasks

- plan, design or carry out a project or task from start to finish with well-defined objectives and outcomes
- work to agreed quality standards and specifications
- select and use appropriate tools and technology for a task or project

Source: Adapted from *Employability Skills 2000+* Brochure E/F (Ottawa: The Conference Board of Canada, 2000).

chapter 13

Writing the Research Paper

Chapter Objectives

After completing this chapter you will be able to

1. plan and write a research paper using several simple, discrete steps;
2. take the time to write clear and concise notes when you are doing your research;
3. stick to a practical classifying idea for note taking as an important strategy;
4. recognize the need to plan steps and manage time effectively when you write a research paper.

INTRODUCTION

Different disciplines have different styles of documenting sources in academic papers. Once you learn about one style, you will not find it difficult to learn another. As an academic student, you must pay attention to which style of documentation is accepted in programs and courses. Following is a list of various styles in current use:

- Biology—*Scientific Style and Format: The CSE Manual for Authors, Editors, and Publishers* (Council for Science Editors)
- Business—*APA Publication Manual* or *AMA Style Guide for Business Writing* (American Management Association) and sometimes MLA
- English and the humanities—MLA
- Geology—*Geowriting: A Guide to Writing in Earth Science*
- Government—*The Canadian Style: A Guide to Writing and Editing*
- History—*The Chicago Manual of Style* (CMS) or *A Manual for Writers of Research Papers, Theses, and Dissertations*, Seventh Edition, by Kate L. Turabian, Wayne C. Booth, Gregory G. Colomb, and Joseph M. Williams
- Journalism—*The Canadian Press Stylebook*
- Law—*Canadian Guide to Uniform Legal Citation*
- Mathematics—*The AMS Author Handbook* (American Mathematical Association)
- Medicine—Canadian Medical Association (International Committee of Medical Journal Editors)
- Political science—*Style Manual for Political Science*
- Psychology and the social sciences—*APA Publication Manual*

Writing a research paper will take time and effort. It is best to plan and write the research paper using simple, discrete steps. Since a research paper is a complex writing task, it makes sense to break it down. This chapter discusses steps and planning for writing a research paper.

GENERAL TIPS

1. Learn to be a careful researcher. Take two sets of notes: one from a source showing accurate quotations, authors, and page numbers, and another for the References (APA format) or Works Cited (MLA format) with more detailed information about publisher and so forth. Chapter 14 discusses APA style, and chapter 15, MLA.
2. If you find a good source in a periodical, immediately write down the author, the title of the article or book, the title of the journal or magazine the article appears in, the volume and issue numbers, the date of the publication, and the page numbers of the article. Use the same notebook for all your notes.
3. If you find a good source on the internet, immediately write down the author, the title of the article, the title of the website, the sponsor of the website, the date of the website launch and the last update, and the URL. Date your entry. Use the same notebook for all your notes.
4. Keep source cards. If you find a source you like, use a file card or make a note in a separate section of your notebook. Write down all the citation information needed on one side of the card. On the other side of the card, write a short abstract for your own purposes. An abstract is a brief summary. These abstract cards are also called bibliography cards. They are a useful personal reference tool because they provide summaries of sources you have researched. You will add to your source cards, and over the months, you will consult the cards for a variety of research writing purposes.

A Source or Bibliography Card

Side One:

Jemma, Lawrence. The Life of Snails. Toronto: Prentice Hall, 2008.

Side Two:

Your abstract: This book contains an excellent description in chapters 1–3 on the life cycle of snails. Chapter 17 also lists known parasites and diseases.

5. Use effective, relevant citations.
6. Practise good time management. Get help from a learning skills resource person on campus if you need it. The internet is also an excellent source of information in terms of .edu websites, especially from learning centres, writing centres, or libraries.

7. Follow APA or MLA formatting guidelines to the letter. Your instructor will deduct marks if you do not follow the documentation format required for your research paper.

8. Keep your research question clearly in focus. This question guides you and reminds you what you are looking for in your searches.

9. Use the academic databases available through your school library. See a resource person in the library to gain access to the databases if you do not know how to find or use them.

NINE STEPS TO WRITING YOUR PAPER

Use these nine steps as a guideline to help you write your research paper. Information about the steps is mentioned in chapters 12, 14, and 15 of this book. Read some of those chapters if you need additional help in working through one of the steps covered here.

Step 1: Select an Effective Topic

You may decide to pick a topic that has something to do with a career you plan to enter. This is a useful approach since it will familiarize you with the discourse community in that discipline. On the other hand, you may have a strong interest you want to explore that stems from work or from personal experience. Maybe you have not had the time to investigate the area before but now decide it is worth your time. Some students discover research topics through everyday life. For example, if you have an interest in fishing, that pastime may lead you to a line of investigation: licensing practices, conservation practices and policies, fish farms, overfishing, international laws, restocking projects, equipment, new techniques, and so forth.

If you do not have a topic in mind, you need to find an interest and develop a topic. One idea is to spend some time just browsing through the library or a bookstore, looking through various sections, including the periodical or magazine sections. In this way, you may uncover an engaging subject. You may prefer to do some online browsing to generate ideas.

Start by visiting some newspapers online. Skim the first pages. Note any area that captures your interest. After about an hour, check your list. Are there any topics you've listed more than once? If so, you may want to narrow your initial search to two or three of those areas. Another tactic is to browse with keywords. For example, type in *fishing*. Sift through some of the websites and take one- or two-word notes as you glance through sites. You might also want to copy webpage addresses to a file. Above each web address, you can add a few notes like "This site is an official site for provincial fishing stats."

You may also want to discuss ideas with personnel from the writing centre or library on campus. These resource people are trained professionals and can help you. Don't forget: the library itself is a great place to start.

It is important in the end to select a topic that really interests you. Do not select a topic because you think it will please the instructor. If you are interested in the topic, then you will plan well, spend time researching, write, revise, edit, and use the correct application of the documentation style. By doing so, you will produce a paper worth reading.

Step 2: Clarify the Assignment

Reread the instructions for your assignment. Be certain you can answer the following questions:

1. What style of documentation am I supposed to use?
2. How long is the paper supposed to be?
3. Does my professor or instructor specify which sources to use?
4. Does my professor or instructor specify which sources not to use?
5. Does my professor or instructor specify how current the sources have to be?
6. Does my professor or instructor specify which topics may be unacceptable?
7. What is my deadline date?
8. Is a peer review expected? When will the peer review be?
9. Am I expected to hand in an outline? When?
10. Does my professor or instructor specify criteria for the final presentation?

If you are in doubt at all about any aspect of the assignment, consult with your professor well in advance of the deadline date. You may visit him or her during office hours, or you may make an appointment to talk outside of office hours.

Before you visit your professor, be clear what it is you want to know. What aspect of the assignment is not clear to you? Write down questions you want to ask. It is important to be organized because your professor's time is limited.

Step 3: Form the Research Question

A research question helps you to focus your attention on your research in a specific way. For example, if you are a student about to enter the nursing program in your institute, you have probably selected a topic from health care—pediatric nursing, for instance. However, that topic is too broad.

Narrow down your topic. Suppose you think prenatal nursing is the area you want to investigate. Think about what it is you want to know about it. Write down the questions. Review them. Then settle on the one that is of greatest interest to you, and start there. For example: How has the care of premature babies changed in pediatric nursing over the past 10 years in Canada? This question now helps you centre your attention on what is most pertinent to you in your research.

The process in this example, then, has worked something like this:

Broadest topic: Pediatric nursing

↓

Prenatal care

↓

Changes in pediatric nursing in Canada

↓

Narrowest topic: Changes in past decade in caring for premature babies in Canada

↓

Research question: How has the care of premature babies changed in pediatric nursing over the past 10 years in Canada?

Now you have an excellent starting point with a clear research question. After having narrowed the topic and after forming a question connected with it to serve as a guide, you might want to check its workability with your instructor.

Step 4: Prepare a Preliminary Outline and a Project Plan

You will need two guides for your research project: a preliminary outline and a project plan. The preliminary outline will guide your research, note taking, and writing; the project plan will organize your whole research project by setting out the steps and deadline dates for each step.

Consider your preliminary outline to be like a sketch. In other words, it is a tool to help you get started. You will do your sketch in broad strokes because you are forming a general direction for your plan, not the fine-line details.

Your preliminary or sketch outline should contain these components:

- Your research question at the top of the page
- The general ideas your research question brings to mind
- The broad sections of your paper
- What sources you plan to use

Example Preliminary Outline:

Research question: How has the care of premature babies changed in pediatric nursing over the past 10 years in Canada?

I. What are some of the features of the history of preemie care in Canada?
- Who?
- What?
- Where?

II. What has the philosophy of preemie care been in the past in Canada?
- What?
- Who?
- Why?

III. What impact has technology had?
- What?
- How?

IV. What specific changes have come about in the past decade?
- What?
- How?
- Why?
- Who?

V. Sources to check:
- Nursing journals
- Parenting magazines
- Parenting websites
- Health care databases (through library, StatsCan, medical databases)
- Internet searches

The second tool is the project plan. Use the nine steps as suggested in this chapter. Write down the steps. Estimate the time it will take you to complete, making note of the deadline for the completed assignment. In your daily appointment book, write down what you expect to accomplish each day. Write down when the step is to be completed.

Example Project Plan:

Assignment due date: March 1

Step 1: Select a topic—one week—January 4–8

Step 2: Clarify the assignment—one day—January 11

Step 3: Form the research question—three days—January 12–14

Step 4: Prepare the preliminary outline and project plan—one day—January 18

Step 5: Research the topic—two weeks—January 19–February 1

Step 6: Refine the outline based on research—two days—February 2–3

Step 7: Write the first draft—two weeks—February 4–18

Step 8: Get feedback and do revisions—one week—February 19–25

Step 9: Prepare the final draft—two days—February 26–27

Hand in completed paper for March 1

Step 5: Research the Topic

Use your research question and your preliminary outline to guide you in the process of gathering information. You will use the library and the internet for your research.

USING THE POST-SECONDARY LIBRARY

The first activity is to visit the library and discover what is available on your topic. You can then make a list of sources. Familiarize yourself with the layout of holdings in a library: take some time to wander through to get a sense of how things are arranged. The computer catalogue is set up simply so that anyone can use it. Directions are clearly displayed around the various terminals. As previously mentioned, many libraries offer excellent handouts to students for free. These information sheets can be really helpful when you are first learning to do research.

Your library will likely use these abbreviations and categories in its electronic catalogue:

1. TIL—Title or Heading
2. AUT—Author
3. SUB—Subject
4. NUM—Call number, ISBN
5. KEY—One word taken from Title, Author, or Subject

You may begin your search by typing in the number of the category you wish to investigate. If you do not have the title of a specific book in mind, or the name of an author, then choose to browse under the category, *Subject*. Key in the name of the subject you are looking for. For example, if you are interested in looking into what Ottawa was like in 1915, then key in *Ottawa*. You will then receive a list of all books under this category.

You can call up each listing separately if you want to know what the book contains because there is a short entry for each of the listings. Copy down the call numbers of selections that seem relevant to your research. Then go to the section of the library where that information is housed, and hunt for your materials.

After you have found the sources you are looking for, sit down and browse through each one. Look at the Table of Contents or the Index; decide which materials are useful to you. Visit the library over several days. Ask a resource person in the library for help if you need it. Use various sources of information, not just textbooks.

Browse through the wide selection in the periodical section of the library. Look through professional journals, newspapers, and other magazines shelved there. Most university libraries offer many different newspapers from all over the country and the world; in addition, the library archives back issues of major newspapers. Available to readers, too, is an article file and a pamphlet file.

Continue to investigate. Remember to choose a variety of sources, such as magazines, clippings, periodicals, films, and videos. Locate the material in the library, and then spend some time just looking through the material more closely. Have your preliminary outline with you as you read. Take down all the citation information along with the material's call number.

If you have time, take notes from the sources you have selected. Remember that not all books can be taken from the library; some are labelled "reference," and must be used on location. It is also important to write down the author's name or names, the title, the city of publication, the publisher, the date of publication, and the call number while you have the material in your possession. This habit of note taking will save you work and confusion later on.

USING THE INTERNET

You will also work with online sources. Begin by doing a general search, but use the advanced search function to eliminate unwanted sites. Quickly work through the results of each search by using the summary lines and the domain names. Try to train yourself to keep on task; it is really easy to get distracted by other interesting items when you are searching on the internet.

Also use the databases available online. Academic Search Elite, CBCA, Canadian Newsstand, Eric, Web of Science, and JSTOR are some of the databases currently accessible through most post-secondary libraries. Students are also able to access these databases from home, using the remote access function. Talk to a resource person from the library to get a password in order to get remote access to the library's database.

TAKING NOTES

It is important to take the time to make clear and concise notes. Your research paper is like most projects: the more time you take at the front end of the project, the easier the project becomes toward the end. Take notes based on your research question and preliminary outline. As you read and take notes, you will revise your preliminary outline and perhaps even your research question, particularly if you cannot find enough information on your topic. Revising your preliminary outline is part of research because as you research, you discover ideas and information. These discoveries often force you to rethink what you are doing or how you are approaching your research. This activity is a natural part of research.

However, one caution to remember is that too many changes can throw off your project plan completely. As you make changes to your preliminary outline and research question, make adjustments in your project plan. You may have to change deadline dates more than once, but be aware that the final deadline date drives how much time you can budget.

Of course, it is really important to take a good set of notes right from the very start of your research. You will not have time to go back and retrace your steps.

MAKING A SOURCE LIST FOR YOUR REFERENCES OR WORKS CITED SHEET

The first set of notes is really a list of all of the materials you have used in the preparation of your paper. Record all pertinent information about each material along with a comment from you. You can use index cards or a notebook to record your citations. Some students find index cards work well because they are portable, cheap, and easy to flip through. Other students prefer notebooks or computer files.

On the same card, notebook, or computer file, you can write a brief abstract. This abstract tells what the source is generally about and gives your personal comment on its use. These abstracts are very useful because you can skim through them whenever you have a research project assigned. Some sources will be applicable in a number of ways. For example, a source for psychology might also be an excellent source for a history paper.

A Source Card

BF1022F 77	The call number
Francis, Earle. (2005). *The Lives of Swans.* Toronto: House of Anansi.	The citation
Abstract: The life cycle of swans, the species found in Canada, those on the endangered list, disturbance of habitat.	General summary
Excellent information for breeding habits.	Your comment on why the book is useful to you.

USING NOTE CARDS FOR IN-TEXT CITATIONS

These notes are actual quotations, summaries, or paraphrases you plan to use in the body of your text. **In-text citations** are quotations from sources you have imbedded in your text.

Cross-reference the material to the information on your source cards by writing the last name of the author on the top upper-left-hand part of the card. Write the general category for the note directly under the author's name. The general category refers to your preliminary outline: it is the section of your paper in which you plan to use the quotation.

Below is a sample of a reference note card taken from the same imaginary book as the one given in the previous example.

A Reference Note Card

Francis (2005)	Refers to the author's last name and the date of publication—cross-reference to the source card
Mating Habits	Refers to a category and section of your paper
Francis tells us that "mating is generally for life" (p. 88) and that "mating rituals are varied and sustained over long spring periods of one to three weeks" (p. 165).	The quotation in APA style

It is certainly possible to categorize ideas while you are taking notes. As you investigate and reflect back to your research question, you may begin to think of new categories. As you gather information, you write in notes according to those categories. You will then sort your in-text citation note cards into main piles according to the categories.

Example:

Research question: Is the swan endangered in southern Ontario?

Emerging categories according to the preliminary outline and the research:

- Mating habits
- Natural habitat

- Impact of development
- Impact of loss of wetlands
- Impact of pesticides

The researcher will then have five categories and five different piles of note cards for in-text citations.

This classifying idea is an important strategy. If you gather notes willy-nilly, you will be overwhelmed by trying to organize all of the entries into some sensible order. On the other hand, if you make notes according to a series of rough categories, you can quickly determine whether you will have ample evidence for your paper. If you do not, you can substitute another category for the one with insufficient information.

AVOIDING PLAGIARISM

Always cite your sources for any material you use in your research. If you do not, you are committing plagiarism. Copy exactly what you see in an article, text, magazine, or newspaper if your intention is to quote the material. Quotations must be precise. If you are paraphrasing an idea or putting it into your own words, then you must also credit the author.

For example, if you were to take the quotations above and use them in the text of your paper, you might use them in one of four ways:

- **Direct Quote—Parenthetical: APA Style**

  Previously mating habits of swans were largely unknown, but today, scientists have observed "mating rituals are varied and sustained over long spring periods of one to three weeks" (Francis, 2005, p. 165).

- **Direct Quote—Introduced by signal phrase: APA Style**

  Francis (2005) reports that "mating rituals are varied and sustained over long spring periods of one to three weeks" (p. 165).

- **Indirect Quote—Summary: APA Style**

  The mating habits vary but continue over several weeks in the spring (Francis, 2005, p. 165).

  Use the page number if possible.

- **Indirect Quote—Paraphrase: APA Style**

  Use approximately the same number of words as the original writer. Cite your source in the parentheses.

Step 6: Refine Your Outline Based on Your Research

After you have completed a few days' research, compare what you have found—your source cards and your reference note cards—against your preliminary outline. What kind of fit do you find? Does it look as if the sketch outline is still workable, or does it need adjusting?

Look for gaps and inconsistencies between what you have discovered in your research and what you have estimated in your sketch outline. Did you discover new categories to add to your outline? Did you find some categories had little or no information available? Is your research question still workable?

Review your purpose. Make adjustments to your research question or your sketch outline. You may find you need to do more research on a specific point or category.

Consult your project plan to see how you are managing your time. Make adjustments to your project plan, too, if needed.

Step 7: Write the First Draft

Now you can gather all of your notes under your categories to determine how much information you have. Cluster each group of notes under each category into points—that is, each category may have subcategories. For example, the major category Mating Habits may have subcategories, such as "known or documented" and "presumed or speculated." Thus, you may be able to make other categories under the general ones and then fit your notes into these subcategories.

Some notes may not seem immediately useful. Do not discard them; you might decide to use them someplace else. Here's a good rule of thumb: don't throw anything away when you are working on a large project until the project has been completed.

Follow the steps suggested below in writing your first draft:

1. Form a clear thesis statement from your research question.
2. Revise your preliminary outline so that it now contains the supporting information from your reference note cards. Sort your cards according to category. Develop paragraph outlines for body paragraphs, and use your notes to guide you as to what will be in each paragraph.
3. On your outline, write the main points for each paragraph. After each main point, reference which note card supports the point.
4. Review the organization of your paper. Are the body paragraphs arranged in a logical order?
5. Do you have enough supporting evidence for each body paragraph?
6. Bundle up the source cards you will use for your References or Works Cited sheet.

BEGIN TO WRITE

Gather your revised outline and your sets of note cards. Set aside at least one hour for the first session. Write, using your outline and notes to guide the process. Make revisions as you wish, but keep in mind that you want to complete the first draft before you start making too many improvements. Do not worry about editing at this stage.

Try to pay attention to the evidence as you incorporate it into the body of your text. Is it relevant? Is it convincing? Also, apply the documentation style guidelines you have learned. If you are preparing your paper in APA style, then use the correct format for parenthetical citations.

Avoid dropped quotations: you must integrate or introduce in-text citations. You should not simply drop a quotation into a passage, even if the quotation is a complete sentence. You must introduce each quotation with a signal phrase, such as "Professor Expert suggests," "Professor Expert claims," "Professor Expert argues," and so forth, or, instead, you may integrate the quotation into your own sentence in a smooth and grammatical way.

Step 8: Get Feedback and Do Revisions

After you complete the first draft, set it aside for a short time. Take a break. When you return to the first draft, reread it. You may make some minor changes (micro-level), but try to think more globally about your draft (macro-level).

- Is the thesis sentence clear and directing?
- Is the organization effective?
- Is the evidence convincing?
- Have you provided enough evidence?
- Have you answered your original research question?

Get feedback from a friend or colleague. Your instructor may ask you to bring your first draft to class for a peer editing session and may provide you with a checklist for the session. If you do not have such a session, set up your own feedback session with another student from the class or with a friend. Develop a checklist to take along—the checklist will help focus discussion.

After the feedback session, make revisions and incorporate suggestions into your paper. You may not agree with all of the suggestions, but you will want to make some adjustments to your paper according to the feedback you have received.

Some instructors advise having several feedback sessions. Each time you take part in getting or giving feedback, you will learn something valuable about your writing and your approaches. You will also learn to master certain aspects of writing that give you trouble. One of the common complaints students have is that they believe they cannot organize information effectively.

Feedback sessions will offer you opportunities to strengthen your organizational skills. Readers will tell you why they are having difficulty following a section of your paper. They will express their ideas for improvement. Instead of being defensive in the sessions, take a positive stance: ask creative questions and learn what works and what does not. Remain cheerful and optimistic. Soon, you'll discover your writing is really improving.

Step 9: Prepare the Final Draft

After having gone through the drafting process several times and having at least one peer editing session, you are ready to begin to prepare your final draft.

Use a checklist approach for your final draft because there are many details requiring your attention.

Checklist for Organization and Style

1. Is my thesis clear and directing? yes ______ no ______
2. Do I have clear topic sentences in my paragraphs? yes ______ no ______
3. Do I provide good points in my paragraphs? yes ______ no ______
4. Do I provide effective support for each point in my paragraphs? yes ______ no ______

5. Do I make good use of transitions and transitional phrases or sentences? yes ______ no ______
6. Do I have an effective introduction? yes ______ no ______
7. Do I have an effective conclusion? yes ______ no ______
8. Do I use an appropriate point of view? yes ______ no ______
9. Do I use the appropriate tone? yes ______ no ______
10. Do I use concise vocabulary? yes ______ no ______
11. Do I use a variety of sentence patterns? yes ______ no ______
12. Do I use a variety of sentence lengths? yes ______ no ______

Checklist for APA-Style Final Draft

Use the techniques you have learned for editing and proofreading your final draft. The following checklist may be useful:

1. I have a title page with a running head. yes ______ no ______
2. The paper is paginated. yes ______ no ______
3. I have referenced all my sources according to APA style. yes ______ no ______
4. I have included a References sheet at the end of the paper. yes ______ no ______
5. I have followed the APA guidelines for citing internet sources. yes ______ no ______

Checklist for MLA-Style Final Draft

1. I have a first page with a running head and title. yes ______ no ______
2. The paper is paginated. yes ______ no ______
3. I have referenced all my sources according to MLA style. yes ______ no ______
4. I have included a Works Cited sheet at the end of the paper. yes ______ no ______
5. I have followed the MLA guidelines for citing internet sources. yes ______ no ______

Checklist for Grammar and Mechanics

1. I have checked for run-on sentences. yes ______ no ______
2. I have checked for fragments. yes ______ no ______

3. I have checked for comma splices. yes ______ no ______
4. I have checked for faulty parallelism. yes ______ no ______
5. I have checked for pronoun reference problems. yes ______ no ______
6. I have checked for point-of-view shifts. yes ______ no ______
7. I have checked for correct comma use. yes ______ no ______
8. I have checked for correct semicolon use. yes ______ no ______
9. I have checked for correct apostrophe use. yes ______ no ______
10. I have checked for the correct use of quotation marks. yes ______ no ______
11. I have checked for the correct use of colons. yes ______ no ______
12. I have checked for pronoun agreement errors. yes ______ no ______

SUMMARY OF STEPS: HOW TO WRITE A RESEARCH PAPER

Step 1: Select an effective topic.

Step 2: Clarify the assignment.

Step 3: Form the research question.

Step 4: Prepare a preliminary outline and a project plan.

Step 5: Research the topic.

Step 6: Refine your outline.

Step 7: Write the first draft.

Step 8: Get feedback and do revisions.

Step 9: Prepare the final draft.

General Tips for Researching

1. Decide on a topic.
2. Develop a research question.
3. Using the research question, investigate online sources, including the library's databases, periodicals, and texts in the library, newspapers, films, television and radio presentations, or interviews.
4. Make sure your paper has a minimum of FIVE sources. Be sure to use a variety of sources, not only e-sources. Check with your instructor.
5. As you collect information, record all important information on the citation. Remember: you need to cite all your sources.
6. Take careful notes.
7. Summarize or use direct quotations with correct page numbers.
8. Set a limit to the amount of time you will research. One week should be ample time.

General Tips for Writing

1. Create an outline. It is important to have an outline that will guide the organization of your writing.
2. Fit notes or quotations into the appropriate places in your outline.
3. Be sure to use APA- or MLA-style documentation or whichever your instructor specifies.
4. Write your first rough draft.
5. Prepare your References or Works Cited sheet.

General Tips for Revising

1. Have a peer or friend read your draft and make comments.
2. Reread your draft, making revisions as needed.
3. Give yourself a break from your paper for a short time.
4. Then come back to it and reread it.
5. Use a checklist to be sure your paper contains all the elements it should.
6. Review correct MLA- or APA-style formatting.
7. Review your References or Works Cited sheet for accuracy.
8. Be sure to avoid any form of plagiarism: double-check that you have carefully documented all your sources.
9. Set a time limit for revising.

General Tips for Polishing

1. After revisions, reread your paper out loud.
2. Edit for errors. Look for errors in a systematic way:
   - Look for point-of-view shifts.
   - Look for correct use of commas.
   - Look for correct use of semicolons.
   - Look for subject–verb agreement errors.
   - Look for pronoun agreement errors.
   - Look for parallelism faults.
   - Look for misplaced modifiers.
   - Look for sentence logic errors.

- Look for spelling errors.
- Look for other errors you usually make.

3. Prepare a clean and effective title page for APA.
4. Prepare an effective Works Cited or References page.

General Tips for Presentation

1. Follow the APA and MLA guidelines set out for format.
2. Use clean, white paper for your final presentation.
3. Use a running head for page numbers.
4. Staple the paper in the upper left-hand corner.
5. Be sure your title reflects the focus of your paper. It takes some thought to come up with a good title.

REVIEW TEST

Try the following review test. It will help you assess what you have learned from the chapter. Be prepared to share your responses with others in the class.

1. Name three documentation styles.

____

____

____

2. What is a citation? What is an in-text or parenthetical citation?

____

____

____

3. Name the nine steps to writing a research paper.

____

____

____

4. What is a research question? Why should you form one?

____

____

____

5. What is a project plan?

____

____

____

6. What tips can you suggest for taking notes for a research paper?

____

____

____

7. What is the difference between a reference note card and a source card?

____

____

____

8. What steps are the most important when you are writing a research paper? Why?

____

____

____

In-class writing assignment: Your instructor will ask you to write a short in-class essay of about 500 words. The essay will discuss how to write a research paper using APA or MLA style.

Assignment

Write a research paper of 1500 words or whatever length your instructor specifies. Choose a topic of interest. Depending on the type of font you use and your margins, you may have between 250 and 300 words per page. Thus, your paper may be five to six pages long, excluding the title page and References or Works Cited page. Use the documentation style your instructor or professor specifies. If your instructor does not want a title page, use the correct format for the first page of your paper as suggested in the APA- and MLA-style chapters. Use the steps outlined in this chapter and the information provided in chapters 14 and 15 to help you prepare your paper. You may be asked to include the word count at the end of your paper.

Bonus Exercise Dropped Quotations

You will recall that to avoid dropped quotations, you must *integrate* or *introduce* in-text citations. You should not simply drop a quotation into a passage, even if the quotation is a complete sentence.

Decide if the quotations in the following passages are dropped quotations or not. If you find a dropped quotation, repair the error, using one of the two methods of in-text citations. Check your answers with the Answer Key.

1. Often children under three will feel threatened by the presence of a change in their routine. "Biting, sudden shouting, and loud crying are not always symptoms of a tantrum" (Judi, 2004, p. 165).
2. According to some experts, gambling is on the increase. "From 2004–2006, gambling activities on the internet expanded by 400%" (Clarkson, 2006, p. 66).
3. Detective fiction has been popular for over 100 years, but some still insist the genre is the work of hobbyists. "Mystery writing is not a pastime—it is a calling" (Summerside 75).
4. The familiar natural world is disappearing. "Backyard birds are disappearing at the rate of 14% per year since 2003." The Department of Natural Resources, 2005, Government of Canada in "Preserving Nature," page 9.

READING

The following research article is from biology. Read it carefully to determine what the research is describing. Pay attention to the documentation format and to the structure of the article. Be prepared to discuss and share your answers to the questions that follow.

The Art of Concealment

Camouflage is used as a standard example of adaptation in biology textbooks. Until recently, though, many of the assertions made about camouflage were based on very limited scientific work. New studies are starting to change this.

by David M. Wilkinson and Thomas N. Sherratt

David M. Wilkinson is reader in Environmental Science, in the School of Biological and Earth Sciences, Liverpool John Moores University, UK. Thomas N. Sherratt is professor of Evolutionary Ecology in the Biology Department at Carleton University, Ottawa, Canada.

According to the American artist Abbott H. Thayer, "All naturalists perceive the wonderful perfection of the twig mimicry by an inchworm, or of bark by a moth" (Thayer, 1909). The observation that some animals are hard to see because they look like part of their environment, such as a twig, or alternatively blend into the general background colour of their environment, must be of great antiquity. Indeed the idea is so familiar from school science and TV nature programmes that it is easy to assume animal camouflage is fully understood. However in recent years various biologists have pointed out that many of the textbook assertions about how camouflage works have been subject to few, if any, formal tests.

A SHORT HISTORY OF CAMOUFLAGE

The evolutionary ideas of Charles Darwin provided a mechanism for understanding the remarkable camouflage of many animals. Indeed Darwin saw such animals as a striking example of the power of natural selection, writing in *On the Origin of Species:* "When we see leaf-eating insects green, and bark-feeders mottled-grey; the alpine ptarmigan white in winter . . . we must believe that these tints are of service to these birds and insects in preserving them from danger." Darwins' theories focused the attention of some biologists onto studying the fit of organisms to their environment through processes such as camouflage. For example, during the mid 20th century the well known rise (and fall) in the frequency of dark forms of the peppered moth *Biston betularia,* due to populations evolving to match a soot blackened industrial landscape, became a classic textbook example of evolution by natural selection. While some details of this example have been questioned in recent years, the general textbook story still stands up to critical analysis (Ruxton *et al,* 2004).

Several of the influential figures in the history of the study of camouflage in nature combined interests in both natural history and art. For example, Abbott H. Thayer was a fashionable painter in the USA during the later part of the nineteenth century. He also made significant contributions to the study of animal camouflage including the idea of 'ruptive' (later known as 'disruptive') patterns. Like many people with good original ideas, he tended to over-apply them to cases where, with the benefit of hindsight, they were clearly inappropriate. For example, Thayer's ideas were reviewed and popularised in a book published by his son, who was also a gifted natural history illustrator (Thayer, 1909). The frontispiece of this book is a painting of a Peacock *Pavo cristatus* by Abbott Thayer shown in a highly contrived pose, which attempts to convince the viewer that these brightly coloured birds are really cryptic—its blue neck is portrayed against the blue sky while its striking tail is blended into similarly patterned foliage!

The leading figure in the mid-twentieth century was the Cambridge zoologist, wildlife artist and photographer Hugh B. Cott. His book *Adaptive colouration in animals* (Cott, 1940) was the definitive work in this area for many years and is still widely cited for its scientific content as well as its historical importance. Cott was one of several biologists who used their knowledge of animals to advise the military on camouflage during the Second World War.

Another such was the naturalist and artist Peter Scott, who was involved with naval camouflage and noted that some of it was so successful that it was sometimes blamed for causing ships to collide! The military have been greatly interested in camouflage since the early twentieth century; indeed the word 'camouflage' in our modern usage comes from the First World War where the specialist French military artists charged with disguising troops and equipment were referred to as 'camoufleurs' (Newark, 2007). At the same time, the Natural History Museum in London was holding master classes in camouflage for the British military. Clearly there are fascinating overlaps between the studies of biologists and naturalists and the use of camouflage by the military, artists and even the use of camouflage patterns by the fashion industry.

CLASSIFYING CAMOUFLAGE IN BIOLOGY

There are a variety of different ways by which organisms render themselves inconspicuous to potential predators (or to their own prey). Here we briefly review the major strategies suggested in the literature (mainly following the reviews of Ruxton *et al,* 2004, and Stevens, 2007). Clearly an organism can potentially use several of these approaches in combination: indeed there may well be a continuum with the different "types" of camouflage grading into one another.

Probably the most obvious approach is for an animal to match the colour of its background—technically referred to as "crypsis" or "background matching." It is well known that some organisms can actually change their colour to match the environment as they move around: examples include octopi, crab spiders and chameleons. While this seems an ideal way to remain hidden, very few organisms actually manage to follow this approach—presumably because of physiological challenges and/or costs in changing body colour. This means that most cryptic animals have a potential problem in that they may be exposed to predators when in parts of their environment which do not match their body colour.

The other widely known approach to camouflage is disruptive colouration—the familiar mottled "battle dress" pattern, which aims to break up an organism's (or soldier's) outline. Closely related to this is the idea of "dazzle," bold patterns on an animal's body. Thayer was one of the first to describe this idea; however dazzle was brought to particular prominence during the First World War by the work of the artist Norman Wilkinson in designing painting schemes intended to protect shipping from submarine attack (Behrens, 1999). Martin Stevens (2007) considers that this idea is logically distinct from disruptive colouration which tends to work alongside crypsis in hiding an animal; while dazzle patterns may prevent recognition of the whole (as either an animal or war ship) they potentially also make judging an object's speed and direction difficult—important if you want to avoid being torpedoed by a U-boat!

The third main approach to concealment is countershading (also known as "self-shadow concealment" or "obliterative shading"), a concept that can be traced back to 19th century work by both Edward Poulton and Abbott Thayer. The idea is that if an animal has an underside lighter in colour than its dorsal surface then, when illuminated from above, it will cease to look three dimensional and so increase its chances of avoiding detection.

Crypsis, disruptive patterns and countershading all try and hide an organism from its predators. Another approach, referred to as "masquerade," is to look like something else entirely—such as a stone or bird dropping. The military have also used this idea; for example in the First World War the British used fake tree stumps as lookout posts in the trenches. In modern civilian life, some mobile phone transmitter masts in rural areas are now disguised to look like trees. Other possibilities for camouflage include being transparent, which is an option mainly available to some aquatic species—although the many insects with transparent wings may also be using this approach to make themselves harder to detect. Some fish may also rely on "silvering," that is, having a reflective body surface which may make them difficult to see when viewed from the side. These approaches have been the subject of little recent work and so are not discussed further in this article.

WHAT'S NEW IN CRYPSIS?

Although the phenomenon of crypsis seems intuitive, several new questions are currently being asked, and tested, in rather novel ways. For example, one problem with background matching is that many organisms are likely to be viewed against a variety of different background types. Since crypsis is background-specific, then there will inevitably be a trade-off between crypsis in one habitat and crypsis in another. To take an applied example, in 2002 the Canadian military began to use the Canadian Disruptive Pattern for clothing all of its personnel, adopting two very different cryptic forms—"temperate woodland" and "arid region." It seems highly likely that arid region uniform would not provide as much protection as temperate woodland uniform in a temperate woodland, and vice versa! In 1999 Sami Merilaita and colleagues used a simple mathematical model to formally show that the optimal solution, if you have to live in both habitats, is either an appearance which closely matches just one of the two backgrounds (a specialist), or some form of compromise solution with intermediate matching of both backgrounds (a "jack-of-all-trades" generalist). The best solution depends crucially on the nature of the "trade-off" involved between surviving in one habitat and another.

To test this idea further we (Sherratt *et al,* 2007) created a system in which populations of artificial self-replicating web-based prey were allowed to evolve over time, subject to "attacks" by visitors to our internet site. When prey were presented against a simple uniform environment then they rapidly evolved to match their background because good background matchers tended to leave more offspring than poor background matchers. However, when the environment comprised an alternating mixture of two background types then, as predicted, the prey that evolved were either specialists or generalists, depending on the precise nature of the trade-offs we had contrived.

Computer-based studies have also recently been used in a rather different way, this time to help understand why certain species of cryptic prey (such as many species of moth) come in so many different forms. When predators are hunting for cryptic prey, it is believed that they often develop a "search image" for the most common prey types—that is, they learn to recognise the prey's features and how they can be distinguished from the background. If predators overlook rare prey types and consume an excess of abundant ones, then one might expect that this would generate selection to look different. Alan Bond and Alan Kamil (2006) have been testing these sorts of ideas with a system where blue jays *Corvus cristatus* effectively play computer games; pecking at virtual prey on touch-sensitive screens. Sure enough, polymorphisms evolve above and beyond what one would expect were there no predation, and the authors have been successful in pinning down many of the behavioural reasons for this evolution.

Many questions remain to be addressed, such as what the optimally cryptic solutions look like when there are not two but many contrasting habitats. There is also general acknowledgement that more work should be done to understand the costs associated with a cryptic life-style, such as having to stay in one place. So, there may be more to crypsis than meets the eye!

WHAT'S NEW IN DISRUPTIVE CAMOUFLAGE?

Although the concept of disruptive coloration is regularly presented in classrooms around the world, until recently there has been remarkably little evidence that it actually works to reduce detection rates in natural prey. Interestingly the British and USA military were also uncertain about this idea in the mid-twentieth century and largely abandoned disruptive battle dress for some years (Newark, 2007). To test the effectiveness of disruptive marks, Silherglied *et al* (1980) experimentally obliterated the white (and potentially disruptive) wing stripe on the palatable Banded Peacock butterfly *(Anartia fatima)* and found that these modified individuals survived as well as controls. As the authors noted at the time, "Few concepts in the theory of adaptive coloration are as well accepted, but as poorly documented, as that of disruptive coloration."

Things began to change with a paper quantifying the distribution of white markings in the marine isopod *Idotea baltica* (Merilaita, 1998). According to Cott, patterns on the body's edge should be more effective in reducing detection than equivalent patterns placed randomly, since the characteristic edges are thereby better obscured. After carefully quantifying the distribution of marks on a large sample of isopods, Merilaita argued that white spots on the isopod touched its body outline more often than would be expected by chance. From this, he proposed that the isopods were indeed employing disruptive coloration to help enhance their camouflage.

Merilaita's work re-awakened interest in disruptive coloration, but one drawback was that the study did not look directly at predation rates. This was to change in 2005 when Innes Cuthill and colleagues carried out an elegant series of well-replicated experiments in which they pinned out artificial moths (mealworms placed on patterned cards), and compared the survival rate of moths that were patterned in different ways.

One of the challenges in this field of research is to separate the benefits of background matching with those of disruptive coloration, since the two forms of camouflage often occur simultaneously. By comparing the survival rate of moths with patterns that equally matched the proportion of light and dark in tree bark, but with different distributions of marks, the authors showed that edge-overlapping patterns helped to reduce moth detection rates by birds. As such, this experiment was (and still is), the most compelling evidence that disruptive coloration is an effective means of camouflage, above and beyond the benefits of background pattern matching.

Like all good ideas, the success of Cuthill *et al*'s experiment has since spawned a whole series of follow-on studies, testing whether pattern symmetry plays a role (it does—asymmetrical patterns are less easily detected although they remain rare in biology, presumably for reasons unconnected to camouflage), whether disruptive coloration can work in the absence of good background matching (it can, but there are limits), whether the mealworms themselves created any contrasting marks (similar results arise in experiments not involving mealworms), and whether we can understand the phenomenon of disruptive coloration using computer models of birds' visual abilities (it appears we can).

So, disruptive coloration is now on a much surer footing, but what does the future hold? Comparative studies are already beginning to shed light on the habitat that particular forms of patterning tend to be associated with—for example, speckled coats with forest. Likewise, it has often been argued that disruptive coloration may allow individuals to survive on the more variable visual backgrounds, thereby allowing them to generalise, but so far there have been no formal tests. Finally, almost nothing has been done to understand the optimal scale of the blotches used to break up an outline.

WHAT'S NEW IN COUNTERSHADING?

If you thought people had taken the benefits of disruptive coloration somewhat for granted, this is doubly the case for countershading. In fact, the evidence that it actually works has been rather limited. Tentative support comes from the observation that some species that rest in what we might think of as an upside down position—such as hawk moth caterpillars—show darker coloration on ventral (bottom) rather than dorsal (top) surfaces. However, there are a number of plausible alternative hypotheses to explain the general phenomenon, each being based on differential selection pressures on the dorsal and ventral surfaces. For example, for countershading to work in the way proposed, an organism must be regularly viewed side on; however, many apparently countershaded animals may often be viewed from above or below (in the case of birds and fish) and may have this colour pattern for improving crypsis when viewed against two different backgrounds.

One of the best modern tests of the advantage of countershading in reducing detection rates was carried out by Edmunds and Dewhirst (1994), who presented four types of cylindrical pastry baits on lawns to birds—some of which were countershaded. It is still hard to imagine birds seeing the baits side on, but there may have been some advantage to concealing one's shadow because the countershaded baits "survived" best of all.

Nevertheless, Mike Speed *et al* (2005) recently carried out a similar experiment, concluding that countershaded baits did not experience a lower attack rate than other types of bait. Recently Speed and his collaborators (Rowland *et al,* 2007) have attempted to resolve these discrepancies by conducting modified versions of both sets of experiments, and the authors have come down firmly in favour of the view that countershaded prey do indeed survive better than other prey types.

So, there may be something in countershading after all! However, it is clear that we should be extremely cautious—not all species which appear countershaded have evolved this way because of self-shadow concealment. A lot more experimental work is needed in this area to evaluate just how common self-shadow concealment truly is. Perhaps then we can begin to ask more specific questions, such as what levels of contrast in counter-shading provide optimal concealment in given light environments?

NEW DIRECTIONS

The study of camouflage is advancing in a variety of directions. First, thanks to the pioneering work of John Endler, there is a greater awareness of the importance of considering the visual and cognitive abilities of predators, and how they shape camouflage. For example, unlike humans birds can see ultraviolet light, so what looks like camouflage to a human may not be so to a bird and vice-versa. Mathematical models of visual processing are now helping us to gain insights into how natural predators see the world, but there is still a need for experiments to evaluate how predators interpret this information.

Second, there is a growing appreciation that the different forms of camouflage may be inter-related (Stevens, 2007). For instance, disruptive coloration appears to work best when the contrasting colours also match that of the background, and perhaps counter-shading also facilitates concealment by breaking up characteristic body edges. It may be that some objects seen from a distance are camouflaged yet close up they are conspicuous, allowing a distasteful organism to signal its defence only when it is forced to reveal its cards. Perhaps classical mimics, such as harmless hoverflies that mimic wasps, are harder to detect on flowers than non-mimetic flies, and therefore gain an advantage through avoiding detection, as well as through mimicry? Exploring the inter-relationship between these different forms of signal will be an important area of future enquiry.

Finally, we need to think about the possibility of camouflage targeting senses other than sight, and researchers also need to widen their nets to consider camouflage in non-animal systems. For example, many animals rely on smell as well as sight in finding prey and it is possible that some prey have responded by evolving (or reducing) odours, making them harder to detect. Some plants appear to be cryptic and there is the unstudied possibility of camouflage in microorganisms—since the larger protozoa have some predators who use sight we could ask, "are many protozoa largely transparent as a defence against such animals?"

So, the principles of camouflage are not as straightforward as one might first think and a full understanding of how they work requires elements of physics, psychology, biology and old-fashioned natural history. The subject area has been advancing rapidly in recent years, but many more questions are awaiting answers.

References

Behrens R R (1999) The role of artists in ship camouflage during World War I. *Leonardo*. 32, 53–59.

Bond A B and Kamil A C (2006) Spatial heterogeneity, predator cognition, and the evolution of color polymorphism in virtual prey. *Proceedings of the National Academy of Sciences USA*. 103, 3214–3219.

Cott H B (1940) *Adaptive colouration in Animals.* London. Methuen.

Cuthill I C *et al* (2005) Disruptive colouration and background pattern matching. *Nature*. 434, 72–74.

Edmunds M and Dewhirst R A (1994) The survival value of countershading with wild birds as predators. *Biological Journal of the Linnean Society*. 51, 447–452.

Merilaita S (1998) Crypsis through disruptive colouration in an isopod. *Proceedings of the Royal Society of London B*. 268, 1925–1929.

Merilaita S, Tuomi J and Jormalainen V (1999) Optimization of cryptic colouration in heterogeneous habitats. *Biological Journal of the Linnean Society*. 67, 151–161.

Newark T (2007) *Camouflage*. London. Thames and Hudson.

Rowland H M, Speed M P, Ruxton G D, Edmunds M, Stevens M, Harvey I F (2007) Countershading enhances cryptic protection: an experiment with wild birds and artificial prey. *Animal Behaviour*. 74, 1249–1258.

Ruxton G D, Sherratt T N and Speed M P (2004) *Avoiding Attack: The Evolutionary Ecology of Crypsis, Warning Signals and Mimicry*. Oxford. Oxford University Press.

Sherratt T N, PolUtt D and Wilkinson D M (2007) The evolution of crypsis in replicating populations of web-based prey. *Oikos*. 116, 449–460.

Silberglied R E, Aiello A and Windsor D M (1980) Disruptive coloration in butterflies; lack of support in *Anartia fatima*. *Science*. 209, 617–619.

Speed M P, Kelly D J, Davidson A M and Ruxton G D (2005) Countershading enhances crypsis with some bird species but not others. *Behavioral Ecology*. 16, 327–334.

Stevens M (2007) Predator perception and the interrelationship between different forms of protective coloration. *Proceedings of the Royal Society B*. 274, 1457–1464.

Thayer G H (1909) *Concealing-coloration in the animal kingdom*. New York. MacMillan.

Source: David M. Wilkinson and Thomas N. Sherratt, "The Art of Concealment," Biologist, 55 *(1), February 2008: 10–15. Copyright of the Institute of Biology, UK.*

Comprehension Questions

1. What does the underlined term "crypsis" mean?
2. Summarize in 25 words the work of Merilaita (1998) mentioned in the article.
3. What did Cuthill (2005) discover in his experiment on disruptive colouration?
4. What are three main approaches to concealment Wilkinson and Sherratt mention in their article?
5. How do Wilkinson and Sherratt structure their article? What form of documentation do they use? How do the headers frame the structure?
6. Name three examples of your own of animal crypsis.
7. Provide three examples of how the military have made use of nature and the research on camouflage.

Critical Comprehension

1. In the same terms used in the article, describe in 100 words the crypsis used by a walking stick, and discuss whether the insect is a generalist or specialist in regard to crypsis.
2. What are some of the puzzles in crypsis that scientists have yet to solve?

Assignment

Research an animal, looking for how it uses crypsis as a defence and how it adapts to prey attacks. Write a paragraph of about 200 words, organizing the paragraph around your findings. Use APA format and provide a References sheet.

CHECKOUT

Here are some of the ideas you will take away with you after you have completed the chapter:

1. It is a good idea to choose a research topic within your chosen field of academic study.
2. Before you start a paper, discuss the workability of the thesis with your instructor.
3. Set a limit to the amount of time you will research.
4. Keep all your data and notes for at least one semester.
5. Use two tools to guide the process: a sketch outline and a project plan.
6. Use a nine-step process.
7. Read other students' research papers to see how the students constructed their papers.
8. Planning, writing, and revising over several weeks will produce good results.
9. Learn to be a good note-maker and note-taker.

Mastering the concepts in this chapter will also help you develop and apply the following employability skills highlighted by the Conference Board of Canada in *Employability Skills 2000+*:

Communicate

- read and understand information presented in a variety of forms (e.g., words, graphs, charts, diagrams)
- share information using a range of information and communications technologies (e.g., voice, e-mail, computers)
- use relevant scientific, technological and mathematical knowledge and skills to explain or clarify ideas

Manage Information

- locate, gather and organize information using appropriate technology and information systems

Think & Solve Problems

- assess situations and identify problems
- seek different points of view and evaluate them based on facts

Be Responsible

- plan and manage time, money and other resources in order to reach goals

Be Adaptable

- work independently or as a part of a team

Participate in Projects & Tasks

- plan, design or carry out a project or task from start to finish with well-defined objectives and outcomes
- work to agreed quality standards and specifications
- select and use appropriate tools and technology for a task or project

Source: Adapted from *Employability Skills 2000+* Brochure E/F (Ottawa: The Conference Board of Canada, 2000).

chapter 14

Research Papers: APA Style

Chapter Objectives

After completing this chapter you will be able to

1. recognize and apply APA style documentation guidelines;
2. recognize different documentation styles in research writing;
3. format a research paper according to APA style of documentation;
4. consider different styles of documentation required in different academic courses;
5. consult the latest handbooks or reference books to learn about updated requirements.

INTRODUCTION

As you will recall from the previous chapter, two of the most common documentation styles used in college and university research writing are APA (American Psychological Association) style and MLA (Modern Language Association) style. Each documentation style has its own guidelines to use in specific writing situations. It is not practical for you to try to remember every detail connected to APA- and MLA-style documentation. You can look up a detail you need when you need it by checking a reputable English handbook or writer's reference, or by looking up a reliable internet site, particularly those from university or college libraries or writing centres. When researching, remember that when you use other people's words or ideas in your research papers and essays, you must acknowledge or cite your source; otherwise, you will be plagiarizing. Plagiarism is not tolerated in your institution.

You should know about the important features of these two styles in order to be able to document your papers correctly. Your instructor or professor will expect you to be able to do so. Learning to research requires practice. The more practice you get in doing research, the more confident you will become in your ability to format a paper effectively according to the documentation style.

This chapter will give you practice with APA style and structure. You will not become an expert after completing the chapter, but you will know how APA papers are documented, what in-text citations are and what they look like, and how to set up a References sheet at the end of your paper. In addition, the chapter will develop critical reading and researching—finding information, analyzing it, and synthesizing the appropriate parts—all vital Employability Skills in the life of a modern professional.

WHAT IS APA STYLE?

APA style is a form of documentation used in the social sciences. Typically, education, anthropology, psychology, criminology, sociology, nursing, and social work use this style, but many colleges and universities are adopting it more widely. Since English departments are working with other departments within their colleges or universities to help their students become better writers, they have developed writing-across-the-curriculum strategies and new curriculum guidelines. Therefore, many post-secondary institutes have now accepted APA style as the standard for research papers in every department.

The American Psychological Association has developed the guidelines for APA-style documentation in research writing: *The Publication Manual of the American Psychological Association* (fifth edition). The book is available for purchase online and at college and university bookstores. Information from the manual is also available at APA online at **www.apastyle.org**. If you expect to attend college or university for a number of semesters and plan to study for a career in the social sciences, education, or nursing, you should consider buying your own copy. After all, sometimes you may not have access to a computer and may need to look up an item about APA in your manual.

Another recommendation is to purchase a good English handbook. An English handbook contains information about grammar, mechanics, spelling, writing conventions, composing and revising, research writing, and documentation styles. *The Ready Reference Handbook* by Jack Dodds is excellent, but many others are also available. Try to select a Canadian one.

Since so much information is available electronically, it is important to know how to document online sources in your research writing. The internet is relatively new, so the guidelines relating to documentation are emerging. The APA-style online website is updated regularly, so it is important to check the site from time to time to see if a guideline has been added or changed.

The following section does not contain every detail about APA-style documentation, but it will provide you with general guidelines and format. Please consult the APA manual, the website, or *The Ready Reference Handbook* if you need more detailed information.

You will use two types of references or citations in your APA-style paper: The first type includes the direct quotations, summaries, or paraphrases you use in the body of your paper. This type is called an **in-text citation** or in-text reference. The second type of reference is a complete list of all the sources you quoted, summarized, or paraphrased in your paper. This is called the **References** sheet, which appears at the end of your paper. The next section discusses each type in more detail.

WHAT IS APA STYLE FOR DOCUMENTATION IN THE TEXT (IN-TEXT CITATIONS)?

A direct quotation, summary, or paraphrase of another writer or speaker's words in the body of your text is an in-text citation or in-text reference. You must cite the author, the year the work was published, and the page number. Use parentheses to enclose citation information.

Hint:

You must remember *to introduce* or *integrate* your quotation. Use an appropriate **signal phrase** to introduce your quotation or to incorporate the quotation smoothly and grammatically into your sentence. Dropped quotations are not acceptable in academic writing.

Example of a dropped quotation:

Error: Several experiments proved unsuccessful. "After 119 attempts, the chemical combination could not be identified," explained Turner (2006) (p. 400).

Correction: Several experiments proved unsuccessful because "after 119 attempts, the chemical combination could not be identified" (Turner, 2006, p. 400). (integration)

Correction: Several experiments proved unsuccessful because, according to Turner (2006), "after 119 attempts, the chemical combination could not be identified" (p. 400). (introduction of the quotation by the signal phrase "according to")

Common Signal Phrases

To make your paper read more smoothly and to prevent dropping in quotations without properly introducing them, use signal phrases.

Examples:

Azu (2008) claimed that "not all children under five begin to join play groups spontaneously" (p. 312).

Many believed that baboons formed rather loose kinship relationships based on gender, but Monksy (2007) noted "many of the youngsters were drawn to the extroverted members of the troupe" (p. 160).

According to Henstein and Mox (2009), "Eighty-two percent of the recipients of the cash award spent it within 24 hours" (p. 99).

Jasonovitch and Lee (2008) have argued "such micoorganisms as Type T cannot exist in oxygen-rich atmosphere" (p. 852).

Following is a list of handy phrases and verbs that you can use as signal phrases. Note that APA style generally uses past tense for verbs that introduce or signal the quotation. You may add *has* or *have* if you wish to use present perfect tense.

affirmed	argued	asked	agreed
has/have affirmed	has/have argued	has/have asked	has/have agreed
determined	asserted	warned	suggested
contended	reported	noted	declared
disputed	disagreed	concluded	revealed
explained	maintained	ascertained	said
defined	advised	advocated	calculated
clarified	discovered	documented	emphasized
established	explained	observed	reasoned

Common In-Text Citations

To create an in-text citation, place the last name of the author first, followed by the publication date in parentheses. Cite the author's name only once in a quotation; you do not need to include the author's name in the parentheses if you have already used the author-date combination earlier in the quotation. The following gives examples of the most common citations you will use. For more detailed information, look in the APA manual, your English handbook, or online.

WITH QUOTATIONS

A Single Author:

Block (2005) suggested that "Eighty percent of seed samples sold in bulk in stores contain weed seeds" (p. 87).

Some scientists believe weed control should start at the local level since "Eighty percent of seed samples sold in bulk in stores contain weed seeds" (Block, 2005, p. 87).

Two Authors:

Block and Tweed (2005) suggested that "Eighty percent of seed samples sold from bulk bins contain weed seeds" (p. 87).

If you place the authors' names in the parentheses, then use an ampersand (&) between the two names.

Consumers need to be aware of the potential spread of noxious weeds through their purchases since "Eighty percent of seed samples sold from bulk bins contain weed seeds" (Block & Tweed, 2005, p. 87).

Three or More Authors:

According to Plath, English, Connors, and Beveridge (1999), "The process of critical thinking for social work is more than analysis; it is informed action" (p. 208).

If you cite the same source later on, you may use the first author, followed by *et al.*, which means "and others." Remember to include the date in parentheses after the author's name.

Plath et al. (1999) found "creativity, awareness of personal values, confidence in preparing and defending a position, being open-minded and flexible and being able to engage in active listening were all identified as aspects of effective critical reasoning" (p. 216).

Corporate Author:

The Canadian Dental Hygienists Association (CDHA) (2007) called upon the federal government "to commit 36% of total oral health spending ($2,972 million) for categorical national oral health promotion and disease prevention programs for low-income Canadians, including those receiving social assistance and those working, children, persons with disabilities, and seniors" (p. 13).

According to the CBC (2006), "Canadians spend more time than any other nation at the hardware store" (*The National,* April 12).

Cite the publication or broadcast produced by the corporation. Use the name of the company, corporation, organization, corporation, or group in situations where a collective appears to be the author.

No Author:

A few species once thought to be extinct have been rediscovered in unlikely places like "the ivory-billed woodpecker sighted in Arkansas in 2004 and then in 2005" ("Ghost Bird," 2006).

If you cannot find an author for the written material, use a shortened form of the title for the in-text citation.

An Unknown Author:

In "Marketing for Babies" (2004), the author suggests that only 5 percent of supermarket sales stem from baby products (p. 13).

Only 5 percent of supermarket sales stem from baby products ("Marketing for Babies," 2004, p. 13).

More than One Source in a Reference:

Theorists have contended that critical thinking cannot be detached and drilled but must become a part of every day classroom reality (Brookfield, 1988; Freire, 1973; Paul, 1990).

In some cases you may find that more than one source has contributed to an idea or to emerging research. Place the sources in alphabetical order inside the parentheses, and insert a semicolon between them.

Personal Communication:

Referring to sleep disruption during peri-menopause, one woman reported, "I haven't slept more than four hours straight per night in over three years because I keep waking up over and over again" (S. McLoft, personal communication, December 9, 2007).

Any information that is not accessible to your readers falls under the category of "personal communication"—telephone calls or interviews, emails, personal letters, or conversations. You may refer to them in parenthetical in-text citations, but do not include them in your references list.

Summarized or Paraphrased Material:

Holmes (2002) observed that tools to encourage reflective practice in nursing include journalling, storytelling, and writing of critical incidents (p. 78).

Even though you may summarize or paraphrase in your own words another person's words, you must cite your source. If you do not, you are plagiarizing their ideas. APA instructs you to include the page numbers from which you have developed paraphrases or referenced material if possible.

A Source within a Source:

Many Canadians feel the financial worry caused by a failing American economy, the rising Canadian dollar, and the cost of crude oil, so politicians are paying attention: " 'Given the uncertainty in the global economy, now is the time to provide additional tax relief for Canadians' " (Flaherty cited in Yalnizyan, 2008, p. 42).

If someone else's words are quoted in the original source, use the name, date, and quotation but include "cited in" and your original source within parentheses.

WITH ELECTRONIC SOURCES

Generally, you will cite an electronic source using the same author-date style used in APA. However, there are a few exceptions. The following section will provide you with some basic guidelines for using APA and online sources. Because instructors have different preferences, consult with your instructor for clarification if you need it.

No Page Numbers:

Although compact fluorescent lighting has become popular in homes today, users may find bulbs are hazardous during disposal (Greenway, 2008, para 22).

According to Babock (2004), "Workplace literacy came into its own during the 1990s when employers worked specifically with the Government of Canada" (¶ 3).

Often, online sources do not include page numbers, particularly if the documents are in html. If you cannot locate a page number, use the paragraph number instead. Use the abbreviation *para* or the paragraph symbol (¶) before the number. Give the name of the blogger and date of the blog if you use a blog site.

No Author or Date Given:

One source suggested that "a brain injury occurs in Canada every two minutes" ("Brain Injuries," n.d.).

The Canadian Mental Health Association (2005) suggested that the disease is on the rise, saying, "Striking most often in the 16- to 30-year age group, affecting an estimated one person in a hundred, schizophrenia is youth's greatest disabler" (¶ 7).

If there is no author's name on the electronic source, use a shortened version of the title in the parenthetical citation or use the corporation, group, or organization as the author. If no date is given, write n.d. (no date) after the title.

However, be sure the online source you are using is a reliable one. Write out the name of the institution or organization, the date, and the page number if available on the website. If no page number is available, refer to the chapter, section, or paragraph.

Note that when you list the source on your references list, you must show the URL or web address and the date you retrieved the material. Do not include the URL in your in-text citations.

WHAT IS APA STYLE FOR QUOTATION LENGTH?

In APA style, a quotation longer than 40 words must be set as a **block quotation**. The APA manual recommends the following guidelines for incorporating block quotations:

- Use a block of typed lines, double-spaced.
- Do not use quotation marks around the block quotation.

- Indent the block quotation five spaces from the left margin.
- In the case of block quotations, place the period before the parentheses containing the page number or other reference information.

Example:

Freedman (2003) summarized the issue like this:

> Interestingly in the latter part of the 1980s, following a long period of good performance by the Japanese and German economies, a number of authors argued in various books and articles that the German and Japanese model of bank-led financing was superior to the "Anglo-Saxon" reliance on markets because of its ability to take a longer-term outlook and to support corporations through temporary difficulties. (p. 5)

WHAT IS APA STYLE FOR UNDERLINING?

APA recommends using italics for the titles of books, the names of journals, or other longer works. Some APA experts suggest using italics rather than underlining because italics help to distinguish titles. They argue underlining of titles might be confused with the underlining that represents an active hypertext link in online publications or websites.

Consult with your instructor or writing centre resource person if you are in doubt whether underlining is acceptable in your APA-style paper.

WHAT IS APA STYLE FOR HEADINGS?

You can include headings in your APA-style research paper. The APA guidelines suggest from one to five levels of headings, depending on how complicated and detailed your writing is. Most undergraduate research papers using APA style contain only one or two levels of headings.

Level-one headings are the broadest, while level-five headings are the most detailed. According to the *Publication Manual of the American Psychological Association*, fifth edition (2001), there are different rules for different types of publications. It suggests that in your undergraduate papers, you will probably require only two levels of headings:

- The first level should be centred and in title case.
- The second level is set to the left margin, italicized, and in title case.

Example:

Level one heading: Title case and centred

Canadian Indigenous People's Art

Level two heading: Set to the left margin, italicized, and in title case

Metis Beadwork

However, the guidelines for heading use in APA-style papers are complex and can be confusing, so consult with your instructor. Some instructors discourage headings in

APA-style writing while others require heading use. You may also wish to review the official APA manual or website or your English handbook to see what they have to say about the use of headings.

WHAT IS APA STYLE FOR THE REFERENCES SHEET?

The last page of your research paper is a list of the sources you used in your paper. APA style calls this page the References sheet. Readers can use the References sheet to locate any source you have used.

Use the following guidelines to prepare your references:

1. Use a separate sheet for references. At the top centre of your page, type *References.* Do not underline the word or put quotation marks around it.
2. Double-space your list.
3. Use the left margin for the first line of each entry. If the entry has more than one line, the following lines should be indented five spaces.
4. Using alphabetical order, type the last name of each author first, followed by a comma and the initials of the first name.
5. Use (Ed.) after the name to show a person or persons (Eds.) are the editor or editors of a volume.
6. Use the first letter of a corporation's or organization's name to determine alphabetical order. Do not alphabetize by *a*, *an*, or *the* if one of these words begins the name.
7. Include the date of publication in parentheses after the author's or corporation's name.
8. Give the title of the book or article, but do not use quotation marks around the titles of articles.
9. Some handbooks suggest underlining the title of the book, journal, or longer work. However, other APA experts recommend using italics for the titles. Check with your instructor on this point.
10. Do not use title case in the article or chapter titles. Instead, capitalize only the first word of the article and the first word appearing in the subtitle (after a colon).
11. Pay attention to the use of commas and periods between parts of the citation information. For specific information, see your APA manual or your English handbook.
12. Include the volume and issue of a periodical where available.
13. When you reference a book, include the city followed by a colon and then the publisher's name.
14. Include the page numbers of an article.
15. When citing an article or chapter from a journal or anthology, first put the author's name and the date, followed by the title of the article or chapter. Then put the editor's or editors' name or names, followed by the title of the book, the city of publication, the publisher, and the page numbers of the article or chapter.
16. When citing information from the internet, include the date you retrieved the information and the URL of the website. Check APA online for more specific details. For blogs, include the name of the blogger, the blog's date, the date you retrieved the material, and the URL.

Review the following sample section taken from a References sheet.

Drugs and Debt 12

References

Canadian Mental Health Association. (2004). Dealing with addiction. Retrieved May 21, 2005, from http://www.cmha.ca/english/info_centre/mh_pamphlets/mh_pamphlet_15.html.

Cohen, D. (2008). Wednesday, January 23, 2008. CanadaVisa: Canadian Immigration blog. Retrieved January 24, 2008, from http://www.canadvisa.com/canada_immigration_blog.

Cohen, L. (2002). Another day older and deeper in debt. *Alberta Newsmagazine, 29*, 41–42.

Finlayson, A., & Martin, S. (1993). *Card tricks*. Toronto: Viking Press.

Quinn, M. R., Stinski, P. Y., Flannigan, R. R., & Marsh, L. W. (2005). The wonderland express: Worries over paying the bills. *Canadian Money Journal, 15* (3), 88–97.

Renn, J. M. (Ed.). (2005). *Money monkeys*. Toronto: Hickson Press.

Vilopovich, D. S. (2005). Who stole the keys? In Renn, J. M. (Ed.), *Money monkeys* (pp. 239–269). Toronto: Hickson Press.

WHAT IS APA STYLE FOR THE FINAL PRESENTATION OF A PAPER?

Your instructor or professor may have slightly different guidelines for format than the ones given below. Check to be sure before you write your paper.

Your final draft must

1. be typed and double-spaced;
2. be on standard, white paper, 22 cm × 28 cm ($8\frac{1}{2} \times 11$ inches);
3. have one-inch margins on the sides;
4. have a title page, followed by your text, and end with a References sheet;
5. include page numbers in the upper-right corner of each page, beginning with the title page;
6. include a page header in the upper right-hand corner of each page: insert a two- or three-word title that represents the focus of your paper, then insert five spaces, and follow with the page numbers;
7. include a References sheet beginning on a new page with the word *References* centred at the top;
8. include a date on your title page if requested by your instructor.

Consult a checklist to be sure you have included all the required components for your paper. Chapter 13 provides checklists for APA- and MLA-style final drafts.

Sample Title Page for an APA-Style Paper

The page header is Learning Moves.

Learning Moves 1

Running head: LEARNING MOVES IMPACT OF DANCE

Centre your title, with your name, and college or university. Most instructors like you to include the date as well.

Learning Moves:
Impact of Dance on Youth Offenders

Stanley P. Goodley
Canadawide College

[date]

REVIEW TEST

Try the following review test. It will help you assess what you have learned from the chapter. Be prepared to share your responses with others in the class.

1. What does APA stand for?

____

____

____

2. What is an in-text citation?

____

____

____

3. Which disciplines use APA documentation?

____

____

____

4. What is a dropped quotation?

____

____

____

5. What is a signal phrase?

____

____

____

6. What is a block quotation?

____

____

____

7. Does APA style include a title page? Draw a sample title page.

____

____

____

8. Set up the following citation information as it should appear in your References list:

   You have selected a quotation from an article in a book. The book is *Understanding Obsessive-Compulsive Disorder.* The book is edited by Jacqueline Perdis and Frieda Helfmann. It was published in 2008 by Grenier Publishing of Montreal. The article is by Estella Mendez. It is called "Bedtime Habits of OCD Children under 12." It is found on page 123 and ends on page 149.

   ____

   ____

   ____

Assignment

Answer the following questions after you have read the example paper.

1. What are the main strengths of Fendworthy's paper?
2. Has he used effective APA style of documentation?
3. Evaluate his sources. Is there a good variety? Are they current?
4. Evaluate the evidence he cites in his paper. Does he use specific proof? What examples did you find effective?
5. Evaluate Fendworthy's conclusion. Does the conclusion summarize his main points? Does it leave you with a satisfactory closing?
6. How can Fendworthy improve his paper? Provide some specific suggestions.

READING

The following reading is a student essay written in APA style. The student was in a first-year English composition course at a Canadian post-secondary institute when he wrote the paper. Read the paper carefully, looking for APA-style structures, the writer's argument and evidence, language expression, and organization. Be prepared to answer the questions that follow.

A SAMPLE APA-STYLE PAPER

The following is an APA style paper with level one headings. Review the paper.

Running head: CHANGING FACE OF FAST FOOD

Changing Face of Fast Food

Thane Fendworthy
Campus College
Professor Eva Rose Tenez

December 9, 2008

Page Header → Changing Face 2

Introduction → In 2008, the fast food industry has most of the countries of the world covered. According to the McDonald's Canada official website, McDonald's has more than 1400 restaurants in Canada with more than 77 000 employees and 31 000 restaurants all over the globe, employing over 1.5 million workers (McDonald's Canada, para. 2). Canadians spent $14.4 billion in 2005 at quick-service restaurants (Intini, 2006, p. 36) and $15.7 billion in 2006 (Pooley, 2007, p. 26), while "Americans now spend more money on fast food than on higher education, personal computers, computer software, or new cars" (Schlosser, 2005, p. 3). Canadians continue to patronize fast-food restaurants in surprising numbers: Bradbury (2006) points out that "25% of Canadians reported eating at a fast food restaurant within the last 24 hours while 33% of teenagers between 14 and 18 say the same thing" (p. 27). However, despite the love of "gulp and go" products, the fast-food industry is adapting to new demands. Thesis Statement → The fast-food world is changing due to environmental, health, and ethical issues.

Level 1 Heading →

A New Emerging Consumer Base

The fast-food industry is doing some fast learning, but the bottom line has to remain profitable. Although millions of North Americans still tend to eat fast food every day, the fast-food customer base is changing. The industry is moving to bigger markets with larger profit margins, fewer consumer complaints, and almost no regulations. Yum! Brands, which owns KFC, Pizza Hut, and Taco Bell, now gets 50 percent of its business from overseas markets; that amounts to about $824 million net, or 12 000 restaurants in 110 countries outside of North America and China (Cullen, Powell, & Mascarenas, 2008, p. 25). China represents an enormous marketplace with billions of potential fast-food consumers. The fast-food giants have noted that "emerging economies throughout the world are a prime expansion target for fast-food chains. China, with one-fifth the world's population, has a significant segment of it experiencing rising personal wealth because of the country's strong economy" (Fat Margins, 2007, p. 14).

Page Header → Changing Face 3

Level 1 Heading → Fast Food and Environmental Issues

Poor land-use practices and food production sustainability are critically linked to the fast-food industry. With fast-food production comes dramatic shifts in the way food is grown, harvested, and shipped for efficient production. In the United States, the number of independent ranchers has dwindled significantly. Today the world's largest purchaser of beef is McDonald's, which has led to the consolidation of the meat-packing industry and the disappearance of the independent rancher (Schlosser, 2007, pp. 136–138). In fact, the fast-food industry has gained control of American agriculture (Schlosser, 2007, p. 8). Smith and MacKinnon (2007) have pointed out that "industrialization, most intensive from 1950 onward, accounted for one-half of America's lost farms" (p. 56). Canadian farms are faring no better. It is cheaper and faster to import tomatoes, picked by migrant workers in Florida for less than minimum wage, ship the produce to Canada for production of tomato sauce, and use in burgers than it is to use tomatoes grown in southern Ontario (MacLachlan, 2006, p. 32).

Many environmentalists and food scientists urge consumers to think about just how sustainable such production is. Smith and MacKinnon (2007) have estimated that the "food we eat now typically travels between 1,500 and 3,000 miles from farm to plate" (p. 4). Experts advise shoppers to pay attention to where their food is coming from, how it is grown, and whether growing practices are ethical. Canadians have little understanding of the traceability in the foods they consume. "Traceability" is a "measure of how close or how distant one is from one's food. The majority of the world's farmers, saving their own seeds and cultivating, raising, and harvesting the plants and animals they themselves eat, have total traceability" (Smith & MacKinnon, 2007, p. 54).

Although the cattle industry in Canada differs greatly from the Americans', fast-food patrons must understand that giant fast-food chains can import most of their beef from American sources. They are unaware of or unconcerned by the contamination of ground water by gigantic feedlots, some containing over 100 000 head of cattle, and by consequent take-over of food crops like corn and grain to feed these

Page Header → Changing Face 4

animals (Schlosser, 2005, p. 151). Farm and ranch lands are disappearing and being replaced by the needs of mega-monster meatpacking plants. Such practices are enormously damaging to soil and water, and quick production of feed crops also means tonnes of herbicide and pesticides being pumped into the soil, into the food sources, and into underground water reserves.

Level 1 Heading → Fast Food and Health

It is no secret that obesity rates are rapidly rising in Canada and the United States. Bradbury (2006) has suggested that "eight percent of children today between two and 17 are obese, versus three percent 20 years ago. Fourteen percent of adults were obese in 1979, a figure that doesn't compare well with today's 23 percent" (p. 28). In fact, 1 in 20 Canadians is now considered clinically obese (Finn, 2007, p. 4).

As a result of the high saturation of fat, salt, and sugar in fast foods, frequent eaters of these products become obese and often develop other health problems. Diseases often associated with obesity include heart disease, high blood pressure, diabetes, and some forms of cancer. Diabetes, for example, is increasing with "60 000 new cases diagnosed each year" (Potpourri, p. 93). Eating quickly under stress takes its toll on digestion and wellness. However, many Canadian workers seem to need to "speed-eat" because of the pace and demands of the modern workplace. Many workers get barely 30 minutes for lunch breaks, so they cannot afford to wait in long line-ups or to be seated in restaurants, vying for the attention of servers. Consequently, they must grab their food and dash if they haven't prepared their own lunches. Drive-through outlets must now more than ever compete for customers in a big way. According to Pachner (2007), industry research now suggests that if there are more than three cars in the drive-through lane, drivers will pull away. The average transaction time at the fast food drive-through is 3.5 minutes (Pachner, 2007, paras. 3 and 18), so outlets have to provide efficient service and hot food to its customers. If quick eating was not the norm, then fast food chains would not offer the service.

Page Header

Fast Food Fitness and Wellness

Level 2 Heading

The biggest challenge to the fast-food industry in the past 10 years has been the controversy over trans fat. Intini (2006) has noted that

> trans fats—made from partially hydrogenated vegetable oil, and found in taco shells, fried chicken, doughnuts, pizza dough, and French fries—have been declared public health enemy No. 1. Although they're cheap and increase the shelf life of food, trans fats raise bad cholesterol and lower good cholesterol, and are now blamed for tens of thousands of heart attacks. (p. 36)

However, the harmful health effects of trans fat in foods have been known since the 1970s, but without federal legislation and public awareness of the effects, the fast-food industry has been unwilling to change its practices. Once legislation was passed regarding the banning of trans fats in food products, fast-food companies were fearful of litigation. In the United States, eight recent successful "fat lawsuits" have made the industry wary (Intini, 2006, pp. 37–38). Restaurants scrambled for a replacement fat that would not compromise texture and taste. A&W Food Services was one of the first fast-food chains to eliminate trans fats (Lazurus, 2007, p. 4). KFC Canada replaced their trans fat with canola oil, a crop that Canadian farmers can readily grow (Intini, 2006, p. 37).

Level 2 Heading

Changes towards Healthy Eating Trends

Many Canadian consumers have become far more picky about the types of foods they eat. Many people want foods not grown with pesticides or herbicides; they wish to order meals in restaurants that do not contain additives. Gulli (2007) has indicated that the "organic food industry was valued at $1.7 billion in 2005 in Canada and is predicted to rise 20.6 per cent a year until 2015, according to Agriculture Canada" (para. 3). She has claimed "organics have gone mainstream . . . especially in urban centres such as Toronto where organic food sales are 'growing like crazy'" (para. 12).

Page Header → Changing Face 6

Many warn that the industry needs "a more proactive approach to health concerns" (Pooley, 2007, p. 25). In a bid to stay competitive, today most fast-food chains offer salads or lower calorie choices on their menus. Chains like *Lettuce Eatery* are now catering to eaters who want custom salads—that is, low-fat, healthful eating. *Choice* is the buzzword in the industry, with many fast-food restaurants offering side orders of salads, baked potatoes, or veggie chili rather than French fries.

Level 1 Heading → The Ethics of Fast-Food Eating

Plaguing the industry are some major ethical concerns. Animal-rights activists demand that if consumers want meat, then they should be concerned about how these food animals are raised and treated. Famous celebrities, such as k.d. lang, Oprah Winfrey, and Pamela Anderson, have spoken out against cruel practices in the raising and slaughtering of food-production animals, such as cattle and chickens. Because the celebrity comments and activities became so quickly advertised by the electronic media, the fast-food industry had to take notice. In addition, changes in how animals are raised are coming about because of pressures from organizations like PETA (People for the Ethical Treatment of Animals). The fast-food industry is now itself lobbying for "factory-farming reform in a bid to stay ahead of consumer sentiment" because "fast-food companies buy a lot of meat, and thus have tremendous influence over the industry as meat suppliers must quickly fall in line to maintain lucrative contracts" (Campbell, 2007, p. 35).

Level 2 Heading → *Ethical Business Practices and the Fast-Food Industry*

Globalized food chains can easily edge out smaller competitors. The mom-and-pop fast-food operations with only a single restaurant can no longer remain profitable because they do not have the drawing power of the giants. McDonald's for example, purchases its food items in unimaginably vast quantities. In addition, its marketing and advertising capability far outdoes anything in the world. To survive, other industries have taken on the same practices. Because of these pan-global marketing

Page Header →

and purchasing systems, healthy competition no longer exists, leaving the consumer with few choices. In fact, Schlosser (2005) has pointed out "the basic thinking behind fast food has become the operating system of today's retail economy, wiping out small businesses, obliterating regional differences, and spreading identical stores throughout the country like a self-replicating code" (p. 5).

The fast-food industry has helped to escalate the exploitation of workers. Schlosser (2005) called the workers in the meatpacking and fruit industries: the "new industrial migrants" (p. 160). Two-thirds cannot speak English and one-third cannot read or write in any language. Most come from Mexico (Schlosser, 2007, p. 161). Workers' injuries in the meatpacking factories and on meatpacking plant cleaning crews are horrific, including beheadings, torn limbs, fatal stabbings, and gassings (Schlosser, 2007, pp. 172–189). Farm workers who pick tomatoes in Florida for chains such as Taco Bell and McDonald's make about $7500 per year while the companies exploit their labour, making billions of dollars in profit every year (MacLachlan, 2007, p. 11). These brutal working conditions are slowly changing. Fast-food corporations have come under negative public scrutiny, so they have made efforts to improve working conditions, morale, and opportunities for promotion. However, fast-food workers remain the lowest paid in North America.

Level 2 Heading → *Fast Foods and Traditions*

The fast food "grab and go" replaces the traditional sit-down family meal, the traditional foods people once ate, and the sense of self-respect, independence, and community. A great deal has been lost, and while Canadians pride themselves on their multicultural heritage, few recognize what has been left behind.

That traditional knowledge is carried in Canadian literature. In the writing of Austin Clarke and his depiction of Barbadian cuisine, Canadians understand how food is central to family and community life. In the work of Eden Robinson, readers learn about her ancestral Aboriginal roots and the connection of time, place, and food gathering; and in the work of

Page Header

M.J. Vassanji, Canadians can read about his memories of Indian cuisine growing up in Kenya. Roch Carrier and other French-Canadian writers help readers understand how central traditional foods are to the Canadian way of life. Providing a sense of home, food and place are deeply connected. Aboriginal traditional ways of life involved all in the community in food gathering and preparation. The health and well-being of the community are connected to their food practices because "Food, community, identity, and place are intricately woven" (Padlosky, 2005, p. 26). Sadly, fast food has displaced much of that knowledge. Padlosky (2005) described it this way:

> Issues of globalization intersect with ethnicity and food in a number of ways. Conglomerate food companies whether on the production (Monsanto) or consumption (McDonald's, Coke) side obviously have an impact on societies and cultures around the world, with the danger of effacing ethnic and even national differences into a homogenized sameness, the so-called McDonaldization or Coca-Colonialism (Bell and Valentine 1997, 190) of the global village. (p. 28)

In an attempt to recapture part of that heritage, some fast food chains are offering regional items on the menu that might appeal to new demographics. Consumers might find sushi in their local 7-Elevens in Richmond, B.C., or poutine on the menu in their local McDonald's in Quebec City. Tim Hortons might provide the clubhouse atmosphere of the curling rink or hockey arena with special sandwiches, hot "homemade" soup, and strong coffee.

Many fast-food restaurants are attempting to appeal to the idea of a family meal by reorganizing and redecorating their interiors, making them seem like more inviting places to eat. Gone are the plastic red seats and bright colours of most McDonald's restaurants, replaced by earthy tones and wooden furniture. Canadians seem to be wanting to reconnect with the past because "the dinner table has been identified as an important site for the socialization or 'civilization of children'" (Bell & Valentine cited in Padlosky, 2005, p. 23).

Page Header →

The slow food movement is opposing the philosophy of fast food thinking. The slow food movement seeks to reconnect people with what they eat. Advocates say that marketers "depreciate food by standardizing its taste and distancing consumers from producers" (Bradbury, 2006, p. 27). Youth, it seems, need a counterbalance and an education about what meals are all about. Stratford Northwestern High School in Ontario, for example, advocates a slow food movement by rejecting fast foods and fast-food contracts for its cafeteria. Instead, students grow their own vegetables in a school garden, cook, and serve them in their own school café, The Screaming Avocado (Bradbury, 2006, p. 28). Students learn the harmony between production of food in the natural sense and the benefit of community well-being and responsibility.

Traditional practices, flavours, and food that have been lost to industrialized food are of central interest to many cultural groups. Cultural identities are being transformed. For example, food sharing among Inuit, once utterly critical to survival, is slowly disappearing. Searles (2007) has observed that "in the Inuit world of goods, foods as well as other objects associated with hunting, fishing, and gathering are more or less communal property, belonging not to individuals, but to a larger group, which can include multiple households (Dahl 2000; Nuttal 1992; Searles 1998b)" (p. 61). To re-establish past practices, some groups of Inuit have moved away from larger settlements to live in traditional hunting camps, where they can fish and can hunt for marine mammals, such as walrus and seal. These groups strongly believe that these traditional foods are linked to their physical and spiritual well-being. Furthermore, in traditional farming communities, some groups are beginning to reintroduce a number of heritage varieties to the marketplace, so that consumers have more choice and genetic pools are widened. For instance, The Ark of Taste is an international branch of the slow food movement that is interested in re-establishing important foods and flavours lost as food production became more and more industrialized. Red Fife, for example, a once forgotten strain of heritage wheat, has now been successfully re-introduced into Saskatchewan (Bradbury, 2006).

Page Header → Changing Face 10

Level 1 Heading → Conclusion

The fast-food industry, worth billions of dollars, is here to stay. Despite the bottom line, public outcry for more ethical business practices, for better working conditions, for ingredients that are more nutritious and not damaging has led to some marked changes. Consumer demand for the right to know what goes into our food production has made the fast-food world pay attention. Rising health care costs associated with disease stemming from increased obesity, the disastrous harm to the environment through poor land use, the corporate practices of raising livestock, added legislation, and the loss of community and traditional foods have all applied pressure where none had been felt before. Cultural integrity continues to suffer, and many, including Canada's indigenous peoples, are conflicted. As Searles (2007) has described,

> The amount of soda and candy consumed by residents of Nunavut continues to grow every year, a trend that some Inuit parents are trying to change. But it is difficult to impose limits on children, as parents find themselves in their own cultural logic of not interfering with the choices of others. (p. 71)

References

At Play. (2007, November 11.), *Time Canada 170*(22), 15–19.

Bradbury, D. (2006). Pace yourself: Cooking up slow food in a fast food nation, *Alternatives Journal, 32*(3), 27–28.

Campbell, C. (2007). This burger lived a happy life . . . really. *Maclean's, 120*(15), 35.

Cullen, L. T., Powell, B., & Mascarena, D. (2008, January 28). When eat meets west. *Time, 171*(4), 23–28.

Fat margins in fast food. (2007, March /April). *Shareowner*, 4.

Finn, E. (2007, April). A weighty matter: When 'fast' food displaces good food, the fat piles on. CCPA *Monitor*, 4–5.

Gulli, C. (2007, Sept.10). The truth about organic food. *Maclean's, 120*(35/36). Retrieved December 20, 2007, from http://www.macleans.ca/article.jsp?content=20070910_109141

Intini, J. (2006, December 25). Healthier, whether you like it or not. *Maclean's, 119*(51), 36–38.

Lazurus, E. (2007). A&W cuts trans fat. *Marketing, 112*(2), 4.

MacLachlan, A. (2006, December). Tomato Workers not loving McDonald's. *Presbyterian Record, 130*(11), 32.

McDonald's Canada. (2008). FAQs. Retrieved Feb 2, 2008, from http://www.mcdonalds.ca/en/aboutus/faq.aspx

Pachner, J. (2007, March). Faster hotter sooner. *Financial Business Post*, 34–8. Retrieved January 6, 2008, from http://proquest.umi.comezp. camosun.bc.ca:2048/pqdweb?index+52&

Padolski, E. (2005). You are what you eat: Ethnicity, food, and cross-cultural spaces. *Canadian Ethnic Studies, 37*(2), 19–31.

Pooley, E. (2007). A recipe for change. *Canadian Business, 80*(21), 25–26.

Potpourri. (2007), *The Canadian Grocer. 121*(7), 93.

Schlosser, E. (2005). *Fast food nation: The dark side of the all American meal.* New York: Houghton Mifflin, Harper Perennial Edition.

Searles, E. (2002). Food and the making of modern Inuit identities. *Food & Foodways, 10*, 55–78.

Smith, A. & Mackinnon, J. (2007) *The 100-mile Diet.* Toronto: Vintage Canada.

Comprehension Questions

1. Approximately how much money did Canadians spend on fast food in 2006?
2. Why are so many North American fast-food companies moving offshore?
3. What are some of the environmental issues that relate to fast-food production?
4. What are some of the health issues related to eating fast food on a regular basis?
5. What are some of the ethical issues surrounding the production and consumption of fast food?

Critical Comprehension

1. What assumptions does Fendworthy make about fast food?
2. In what ways is the fast-food industry intricately linked to the economy?
3. What impact would the removal of all fast food from Canada have?
4. Should businesses become more ethical in their practices? How can they do so?
5. Do ethical practices have a price? Discuss what the costs might be.

CHECKOUT

Here are some of the ideas you will take away with you after you have completed the chapter:

1. APA-style format is used commonly in post-secondary research papers.
2. APA uses headers.
3. You can find many useful current references about APA on authoritative online websites.
4. Your References list must show all the sources you used in your paper and must be up-to-date.
5. Writing an APA-style paper requires planning and organization, so it's important to allow adequate time for a writing project.

Mastering the concepts in this chapter will also help you develop and apply the following employability skills highlighted by the Conference Board of Canada in *Employability Skills 2000+*:

Communicate

- read and understand information presented in a variety of forms (e.g., words, graphs, charts, diagrams)

- share information using a range of information and communications technologies (e.g., voice, e-mail, computers)
- use relevant scientific, technological and mathematical knowledge and skills to explain or clarify ideas

Manage Information

- locate, gather and organize information using appropriate technology and information systems

Think & Solve Problems

- assess situations and identify problems
- seek different points of view and evaluate them based on facts

Be Responsible

- plan and manage time, money and other resources in order to reach goals

Be Adaptable

- work independently or as a part of a team

Participate in Projects & Tasks

- plan, design or carry out a project or task from start to finish with well-defined objectives and outcomes
- work to agreed quality standards and specifications
- select and use appropriate tools and technology for a task or project

Source: Adapted from *Employability Skills 2000+* Brochure E/F (Ottawa: The Conference Board of Canada, 2000).

chapter 15

Research Papers: MLA Style

Chapter Objectives

After completing this chapter you will be able to

1. recognize and apply MLA-style documentation guidelines;
2. recognize different documentation styles in research writing;
3. format a research paper according to the MLA style of documentation;
4. consider different styles of documentation required in different academic courses;
5. consult the latest handbooks or reference books to learn about updated requirements.

INTRODUCTION

MLA-style guidelines come from the Modern Language Association. Its website, at **www.mla.org**, has some useful information, although it is limited since the association wants writers to purchase the official handbook. However, if you cannot locate the information you are looking for on the official site, you will find that most large university library and writing-centre websites provide extensive information on MLA style.

You may wish to purchase the official handbook because you are a humanities student who will be at college or university for several semesters: the *MLA Handbook for Writers of Research Papers* (7th edition) was published in 2009. When researching, remember that when you use other people's words or ideas in your research papers and essays, you must acknowledge or cite your source; otherwise, you will be plagiarizing. Plagiarism is not tolerated in your institution.

This chapter will give you practice with MLA style and structure. Although you will not be an expert in MLA-style documentation after completing the chapter, you will know how MLA papers are documented, what in-text citations are and what they look like, and how to set up a Works Cited sheet at the end of your paper. In addition, the chapter will develop critical reading and researching—finding information, analyzing it, and synthesizing the appropriate parts—all vital Employability Skills in the life of a modern professional.

WHAT IS MLA STYLE?

MLA format is taken from the guidelines set out by the Modern Language Association. MLA is primarily used in English and languages. The study of literature, comparative literature, linguistics, and modern languages all use MLA. Other disciplines, such as art history, philosophy, and sometimes history also require MLA. However, most history professors require a style using footnotes and endnotes based on *The Chicago Manual of Style*. It is important to check with your instructors in each course to find out which documentation style you will be expected to use.

Like APA, MLA has its own rules, which you must follow carefully and accurately for your English papers. You do not need to memorize the rules, but you should know how to apply them. If you do not plan to buy the official *MLA Handbook for Writers of Research Papers*, Seventh Edition, then use the internet. A reliable source on the web is one having an *.edu* or *.org* extension because these extensions indicate educational institutes or trustworthy organizations. You may also choose to visit the official MLA site at the address given above or at **www.mla.org/style**. Although, as mentioned, the information on the official MLA site is limited, the site does have a useful "Frequently Asked Questions" page and an update on citing electronic sources. You will find excellent sources at university and college writing centre, library, or learning centre sites.

The following section does not contain every detail about MLA-style documentation, but it will provide you with general guidelines and format. Please consult the official handbook or its website.

You will use two types of citation in your MLA-style paper:

- in-text, sometimes called parenthetical citations because they are placed within parentheses in the body of your paper; and
- a Works Cited sheet, which is your list of sources found at the end of your document.

A citation is the information you provide that fully identifies a source you have used. Citations are required for two main purposes—so that the sources can be located and so that credit is given to the person who originated the ideas and research.

WHAT IS MLA STYLE FOR DOCUMENTATION IN THE TEXT (IN-TEXT CITATIONS)?

A direct quotation, summary, or paraphrase of another writer's or speaker's words in the body of your text is called an in-text citation, in-text reference, or parenthetical citation. You must know how to set up in-text citations by using an English handbook, the official MLA handbook, or trusted reference sites on the internet, such as those from universities or colleges, according to the specifications of the documentation style requested by your instructor or professor.

When you set up an in-text citation, you must cite (name) the author and the page number. Unlike APA, you do not need to include the date in-text in MLA. Also, you do not use a comma between the author's name and the page number.

Hint:

You must remember *to introduce* or *integrate* your quotation. Use an appropriate signal phrase to introduce your quotation, or incorporate the quotation smoothly and grammatically into your sentence.

Examples of In-Text MLA-Style Quotations:

- Introduction of quotation with appropriate signal phrase:

Thinking about the confusing possibilities of punctuation, Lynne Truss writes, "Now, so many highly respected writers adopt the splice comma that a rather unfair rule emerges on this one: only do it if you're famous" (88).

According to Maywicki, "More than 19 000 students registered for foreign language classes in southern Ontario from 2002–2007" (505).

Unlike the "buffoonery of trumped up diplomats of earlier times" (Hedgley 17), the new graduates learn through the careful mentorship of their elders.

Notice that the first two examples introduce the quotation and provide a page number in parentheses. The third example integrates the quotation into a newly constructed sentence and shows the author and page number in parentheses directly after the quotation.

- Inside a body paragraph of your essay, you may see an in-text citation that works like this:

Some experts believe that the Canada–U.S. relationship has been one-sided during the past 25 years. John Gorry believes that "Canadians must lose their co-dependence on the United States" (A6).

Common In-Text Citations

Place the name of the author first. In MLA style, the publication date is not needed in parentheses as in APA in-text citations. Cite the author's name only once in a quotation; you do not need to include the author's name in the parentheses if you have already named the author earlier in the quotation. The following gives examples of the most common citations you will use. For more detailed information, consult the MLA handbook, your English handbook, or reliable online sources.

WITH QUOTATIONS

One Author:

Marian Makke suggests that "composition scores have steadily increased in college-level entry tests in the province of Alberta from 2000 to 2005" (67). (integrated quotation)

Some experts believe that "composition scores have steadily increased in college-level entry tests in the province of Alberta from 2000 to 2005" (Makke 67). (parenthetical citation)

Remember: you do not insert a comma between the author and page number in parenthetical citations using MLA.

Two Authors:

Makke and Knight claim that "93% of composition errors are as a result of poor editing" (89).

Four or More Authors:

Makke et al. point out that most entering college students could benefit from critical reading studies since the average reading comprehension score is now below grade 11 (353).

Use *et al.* to stand for the other authors' names; it is Latin for "and others." In your Works Cited sheet, you will show the names of all authors.

A Writer in an Anthology:

In "Hidden Lessons," David Suzuki observes, "In spite of the vast expanse of wilderness in this country, most Canadian children grow up in urban settings" (128).

Notice that for MLA when you cite shorter articles from anthologies or journals, you place quotation marks around them. When you cite the title of longer works, such as books, novels, plays, films, journals, television series, magazines, newspapers, or long musical compositions, you italicize or underline them.

Refer to the writer and his work within the anthology, not to the editor of the anthology.

No Author:

A good long-term investment is one that spans more than ten years, has few risks attached to it and earns the highest rate of interest at initial set-up ("Your Money" 13).

If no author is given for the material, use a shortened version of the work's title.

Indirect Sources:

Jazciewski points out that since 2003, 73 percent of Hollywood blockbuster films have been panned by the critics (qtd. in McMannon 412).

If you wish to use a source that has been quoted inside another source, use "qtd. in" and the name of the author in whose work you found the source.

Corporate Author:

According to the Ministry of Agriculture, Food and Rural Affairs in Ontario, poison hemlock, nightshade, and common yew are "extremely toxic to horses and all grazing animals" (3).

If there is no author named, but the material appears to represent a group, organization, institution, government agency or corporation, use the title of the corporation in your signal phrase or in parentheses.

No Page Number Is Given:

Idlywide indicates that "Eighty-two percent of respondents were unaware of how their local water was treated" (par. 7).

If the source material on the website is not given PDF files or if no page numbers are given, according to the official MLA site "you cannot cite numbers when you borrow from it." In such cases, MLA suggests incorporating the relevant information (e.g., the name of the author or editor needed to locate the entry in Works Cited) into the text instead of placing it in parentheses. If your source page has numbering or shows numbered paragraphs, you may use the abbreviation "par." to refer to the paragraphs or paragraph number.

WHAT IS MLA STYLE FOR THE WORKS CITED SHEET?

At the end of a paper on a separate sheet, you must list all of the sources cited in the paper. This list is called a Works Cited sheet. The Works Cited sheet also has a particular format that you must follow:

- Sources appear in alphabetical order, sorted by the writers' last names, corporations' or organizations' names, or in the case of unknown authors, the titles of the works.
- Start each entry at the left margin.
- If the entry has more than one line, indent the next lines five spaces, a half inch, or one tab setting. Use a consistent length of indent each time.
- Use a separate sheet.
- At the top of the sheet, centred, type *Works Cited.* Do not underline the word, and use the same-sized font as the rest of your paper.
- Double-space.
- Only cite sources used in your paper.
- Give the medium (print, Web, CD-ROM, DVD, personal interview, etc.)

Guidelines for Setting Up a Works Cited Sheet

Book by One Author:

Findley, Timothy. *Stones*. Markham: Penguin Books, 1989. Print.

Book by Two Authors:

Lee, Allen P., and Fransica Meadows. *Squirrels.* Vancouver: Nature House Books, 1990. Print.

Book with Four or More Authors:

Avery, H., et al. *Thinking It Through: A Practical Guide to Academic Essay Writing.* 2nd ed. Peterborough: Trent University, Academic Skills Center, 1989. Print.

Encyclopedia Article, Signed:

Fox, A. L. "Black Holes." *The World Book Encyclopedia.* 1987 ed. Chicago: Field Enterprises. Print.

Encyclopedia Article, Unsigned:

"Abalone." *Encyclopedia Britannica.* Encyclopedia Britannica Premium Service. 2005. Web. 19 October 2005.

Magazine Article, Signed:

Kohl, Helen. "Saving Graces." *Images* Sept. 1990: 35. Print.

Show the date of the issue of the magazine as day (if applicable), month (abbreviated, except for May, June, and July), and year. Then show the page number or numbers after the date preceded by a colon.

Article in Periodical, Unsigned:

"Victoria: Canada's Tropical City." *Beautiful British Columbia* Summer 2000: 68-70. Print.

Newspaper Article:

Gorry, John. "Helping Ourselves." *Globe and Mail* 19 Mar. 2005: A6. Print.

Short Work within an Anthology:

Redhill, Michael. "Human Elements." *Canadian Short Stories.* Eds. Russell Brown and Donna Bennett. Toronto: Pearson Longman, 2005. 436-54. Print.

Government Publication:

Canada. Department of Finance. *GST and You.* Sept. 1990. Print.

Pamphlet:

Proper Septic Systems. Vancouver: GRVD Waste Management Committee, 2003. Print.

Television Program:

Elliott, Don. "Safe Car Seats for Toddlers." *MarketPlace.* CBC. 5 Sept. 2001. Television.

Film:

Batman Begins. Dir. Christopher Nolan. Prod. Larry J. Franco. Warner Bros. Pictures, 2005. Film.

Personal or Telephone Interview:

Ashton, Dr. Liz. Personal interview. 23 Nov. 2004

You can find more detailed information in your *MLA Handbook* or reliable online sources, such as university or college library and writing-centre websites.

With Electronic Sources

Using reliable online sources of information is now common, but guidelines for documentation are still emerging as new situations arise. For the best available and most current information about using online sources in your research paper, check the official MLA website or the most current *MLA Handbook*.

The following section will provide you with a few basic guidelines for using MLA and internet sources on your Works Cited sheet. Because instructors have different preferences, consult with your instructor for clarification.

A Corporate or Group Author on a Website:

Government of Canada. "Domestic sales of refined petroleum products." *The Daily.* Statistics Canada. 5 July 2005. Web. 10 July 2005.

Start with the name of the corporation, group, government and agency, or organization, followed by the title of the document, the name of the site (italicized), the publisher or sponsor of the site (or *N.p.* if unavailable), the date of the last site update, the medium of publication (Web), and the date you retrieved the information. Note that MLA style now omits the url unless the source can't be located without it or your instructor requires it.

A Web Page with a Single Author:

Kwok, Stephanie. "Surgery for Obesity: What Is It?" *Dietitians of Canada.* N.p. 23 Aug. 2005. Web. 24 Aug. 2005.

An Online Magazine:

Intini, John. "Livin' large sellin' suds." *Macleans.ca.* Macleans, 15 Aug. 2005. Web. 20 Aug. 2005.

Online Professional Journal:

MENC: The National Association for Music Education. *Journal of Music Teacher Education.* MENC, fall 2005. Web. 19 Oct. 2005.

Sample Works Cited Sheet

Following is a sample of a Works Cited sheet. The Works Cited sheet must be on a clean, separate sheet of paper.

Huang 9

Works Cited

Furberg, Jon, and Richard Hopkins. *College Style Sheet.* Vancouver: Vancouver Community College Press, 1998. Print.

Galica, Gregory S. *The Blue Book: A Student's Guide to Essay Exams.* Orlando: Harcourt Brace Jovanovich, 1991. Print.

Hammond, Kyle P., Keith Stainsbury, and Lola Fenski. *Teaching Composition to First-year College Students.* Regina: Burning Bridge Publishing, 2005. Print.

Solomon, Gregory. "The Illusion of a Future." *Film Comment* Mar.–Apr. 1992: 35-40. Print.

MLA Style and Italics

Previous editions of the *MLA Handbook* recommended using underlining in the Works Cited page for longer works: book titles, titles of journals, anthologies, magazines, newspapers, plays, and television and radio series. However, the current *MLA Handbook* suggests using italics, although underlining remains acceptable in research papers. Whichever you choose, be consistent in your use.

Consult with your instructor about italics and underlining in MLA style if you are in doubt, or check the most current *MLA Handbook*.

WHAT IS MLA STYLE FOR THE FINAL PRESENTATION OF A PAPER?

Check your *MLA Handbook* or a trusted website for detailed information on MLA format. Also, your instructor or professor may have special requirements for the preparation of your paper, so be sure to check for this information in the handouts and outlines your instructor provides.

You should follow these guidelines for final presentation:

1. Double-space your paper.
2. Use standard-sized white paper: 22 cm × 28 cm ($8\frac{1}{2} \times 11$ inches).
3. Set margins around the edges of your text at approximately one inch.
4. Do not include a title page for MLA-style papers, unless your instructor or professor asks you to include one.
5. Create a header in the upper right-hand corner of your page, and include page numbers.
6. Before the page number, include your last name as part of the running head.
7. At the top of the first page only, type your name, your professor's name, the course name and section number, and the date at the left margin. Double-space.
8. Type your title two lines down from the date. Centre the title. Use title case.
9. Your instructor may specify other requirements. Follow whatever guidelines your instructor or professor provides.

REVIEW TEST

Try the following review test. It will help you assess what you have learned from the chapter. Be prepared to share your responses with others in the class.

1. What does MLA stand for?

____

____

____

2. Which disciplines use MLA style of documentation?

____

____

____

3. What is a Works Cited sheet?

____

____

____

4. Do you include the date of publication in an MLA in-text quotation?

____

____

____

5. Do you insert a comma between the author and page number in an MLA parenthetical citation?

____

____

____

6. Do you include a title page in MLA style papers?

____

____

____

7. Set up the following information as it should appear in your Works Cited list:

____

____

____

You have selected an article online from a website. The website is called thestar.com. The article you selected is called "Canada Goose Provides Cold Comfort." It was posted on August 24, 2007. The author of the article is Bernadette Morra. You accessed the site on May 8, 2009. The site publisher is *Toronto Star*.

Assignment

Use the following citation information to create the appropriate documentation format as you would expect to see it in MLA style.

1. You have taken notes from an article. The name of the article is "Bullying: A national problem" and it appears on pages 11–17. The author's name is Francis J. Lee. The article was published in 2009 issue 5. The name of the periodical is *Education Today.*

2. You wish to use a textbook as part of your references list. You select a nursing textbook, published in 2008. The textbook is called *Modern Nursing.* It is written by Selma Kirk, Madelaine Feldstein, Marnie Singh, and Wendy Yee. It was published in Toronto by Longman and Pearson. The quotation you want to use is on page 433.

3. You are writing a literature paper. You want to include information from an interview with Carol Shields. The interview took place on October 14, 1997, on the CBC television network. The show was a television series called *Writers' Lives.* The interviewer was Peter Gzowski.

4. You find an article on the internet about credit card abuse. The site is sponsored by the University of Toronto. The site is called "Credit: The Big, Bad Picture of Personal Debt." The writer is Professor Edward G. Davies. The article is five pages long. You want to use a quotation from paragraph 5. There are no page numbers. The website was launched on February 2, 2004. It was last updated on March 11, 2005. You retrieve the page on April 9, 2005.

5. You are writing a poetry paper for your English 180 class. You want to use a quotation from a chapter found in a book about P. K. Page. The chapter was written by T. R. Ako. The title of the book is *Modern Canadian Poetry.* The book was published in Toronto by Academic Press in 2001. The title of the chapter is "Thinking Poems and P. K. Page." The book is edited by George Transon and Margot Dubois. The quotation is on page 303.

READING

The following reading is a sample paper written by a first-year student at a Canadian university. The student is in a general arts program.

A SAMPLE MLA STYLE PAPER

Page Header → Sandez 1

Moxie Sandez
Dr. E. Lipinski
English 155

17 March 2009

Godzilla Revealed : Anti-Hero, Action Hero, and Bully

Godzilla, the colossal saurian creature resurrected by an atomic blast, was popularized throughout Japan, the United States, Canada, Germany, Britain, and Scandinavia in 28 different films. For over 50 years, the King of Monsters has fascinated audiences. During this time, Godzilla has become more than the leading character in a B-movie. The original *Gojira* of 1954 evolved according to changing cultural contexts and the big-money economics of movie making. More than the tragic figure of *Gojira* and the lead in "monsters-on-the-loose" films, Godzilla morphed into a metaphor of war, a symbol of the destructive potential of unbridled technology, and the "secure horror" (Tsutsui 201) franchise that lasted five decades. Through various transformations and changing social milieus, Godzilla grew to be an anti-hero, an action hero, and a bully.

The original *Gojira* had a frightening impact on Japanese viewing audiences. Produced and distributed only nine years after the atomic bomb was dropped on Hiroshima in World War II, the film brought Japanese audiences to tears. Japan had suffered the fate of being the first nation on earth to experience the consequences of a nuclear blast: such devastation had never been known before. Ryfle provides a picture of that experience when he observes:

> By the war's end, entire cities were leveled and the magnitude of the casualties was astonishing: an estimated 1.8 million dead, another 680,000 wounded or missing. Factories were destroyed, crippling the economy. Japan's massive Pacific empire was now just a memory, and six million soldiers and civilians returned home to a country whose spirit was crushed. (50)

Page Header → Sandez 2

Like the atomic bomb, Godzilla produced a track of destruction. His radioactive breath reduced Tokyo to rubble and left its citizens poisoned and terrified. As Snider suggests, "Gojira was the physical embodiment of the atomic bomb. He had atomic breath. He created fire. He devastated buildings. He left radiation sickness in his wake. And, as was true in Hiroshima, hospitals were filled with his victims" (67). Corliss suggests that "Gojira is a political metaphor that roars majestically to life" (5). To the Japanese of 1954, Godzilla represented the atomic bomb. For director Ishiro Hondo, who had been through the ruins of Hiroshima on his way home from a prisoner of war camp in WWII, "Godzilla was not a metaphor for the bomb but a physical manifestation of it" (Ryfle 52).

Gradually, Japanese viewers began to see the 1954 Godzilla in a different light. The monster itself became a kind of anti-hero. Typically, the anti-hero is seen as an individual who stands alone and takes a stand but lacks the poise, grace, and nobility of purpose of the traditional hero. Instead, the anti-hero is flawed. He may be weak, confused, and deceitful in his actions. Yet oddly, he is still capable of drawing audience sympathy. According to Furst, an anti-hero poses "extreme self-consciousness, in his disillusioned questioning, in his confrontation of nothingness, in his destructiveness, and self-destructiveness" (67).

In *Gojira*, Godzilla as anti-hero appears dazed and bewildered as he crashes through Tokyo and the power lines that are set up to destroy him. He appears bent on destruction but shows little or no emotional reaction to his own violence. His latex face is unreadable: the audience cannot gain any clues to his mental state or to his intention. He drags his floppy feet through the streets, over citizens' houses and through the towers of corporate structures with equanimity, while emitting a screeching warble unlike anything filmgoers had heard before—a machine-like staccato, the trumpeting of some crazed electronic elephant. The more Godzilla destroys, the more likely he will come to be destroyed. The audience cannot fathom his motivation, yet strangely, as Godzilla is killed by the scientist's Oxygen Destroyer in the final scenes of the film, the audience feels sadness for his predicament and for the world's loss. The audience is

Page Header

Sandez 3

drawn to his power, his unstopability, his bravado, while fearing him at a safe distance.

Audiences may have responded to *Gojira* because the creature gave voice to their feelings and fears. Tsutsui proposes that Godzilla was a "means of 'making radiation visible', of giving tangible form to unspoken fears of the Bomb, nuclear testing, and environmental degradation" (33). In a sense, audiences appreciated Godzilla's exploits because they released their own apprehensions about the future. Viewers were drawn to the acts of the anti-hero and were grateful for the vicarious experiences he provided. Moreover, since the Americans occupied Japan from 1945–1952, perhaps Godzilla became the anti-hero who provided an opportunity for the Japanese to mourn their losses publicly. Finally, Godzilla's senseless destruction fit with the haphazard and long-term devastation of nuclear bombs. The Americans were continuing to test weapons of mass destruction after World War II. In 1954, they exploded a 15-megaton hydrogen bomb on Bikini Atoll in the South Pacific, and the intensity and proximity made the Japanese fearful.

The business of movie making began to transform Godzilla into an action hero. Joseph E. Levine bought the North American rights to *Gojira*. However, the Americans did not want its Godzilla film to be dark and heavy; instead, they wanted an action movie. Since action heroes have a "tendency toward destruction" (Hunter 1), Godzilla's behaviour toward annihilation fit. However, the Americans wanted the new Godzilla films to be less "talky," with more screen time for the monsters and more action-packed sequences. Therefore, the American marketing campaign promoted the movie as "a pure action pulse-pounder that would wow audiences with its realistic, spine-tingling effects" (Tsutsui 40); the advertising posters publicized Godzilla as a mammoth circus freak. In 1956, *Godzilla, King of the Monsters* was released. It was a combination of new American dialogue, a few North American actors like Raymond Burr, quick cutting from the original *Gojira*, and a message that humans would prevail over the forces of nature.

Page Header

Sandez 4

The Japanese responded to the Americanization of Godzilla. With the advent of television in the mid-1950s, the number of moviegoers in Japan decreased dramatically. As memories of WWII faded with new generations, youthful Japanese movie audiences wanted what was up on the screen to be fun. And as the years passed, "the target audience of the Godzilla films grew younger and younger, while production budgets (and by extension, overall quality—special effects, scripts, acting talent) grew leaner and leaner" (Tsutsui 51). According to Tsutsui, "Catering to the short attention spans and schoolyard sensibilities of Japan's young moviegoers, the Godzilla films became increasingly action oriented" (52).

Mast and Kawin suggest that "the heroes of action adventure films affirmed the power of the myths and mythic values" (556). Those values are constituted to protect and serve dominant cultural structures. Traditionally, "'heroes' primarily have been defined in one of two ways: because of some outstanding act they perform or because of their relevance to individuals" (Sullivan and Venter 101). Heroes are admired and "heroes influence individuals when heroes are defined in terms of their relevance to individuals' self-views" (Sullivan and Venter 103). David Mamet calls a hero "a genius of morality—to remain pure while involved in the conflicting rewards and temptations of power, to avoid arrogance and despair in the face of human corruptibility" (46). Thus, Godzilla as action hero was a protector, powerful and amoral. He did not abide by the same codes as his viewers, but ironically, drew their admiration because he fought to keep them safe from harm while at the same time destroying whatever was in his path. As an action hero, Godzilla was unknowable. Hunter suggests "that the price of heroism, of domination, of certitude, of command, was loneliness—or possibly, since they were so disconnected from their emotions they'd never acknowledge such a thing—aloneness" (1). Godzilla stood alone against the terrors of the universe, and audiences admired him for it. What is more, perhaps the success of Godzilla may be partly explained by the fact that it is difficult to replace action heroes, so franchises can help ensure their continuance for as long as they live and beyond. Queenan notes, "Bankable actors who so completely dominate a

Page Header → Sandez 5

genre that when they fade away or die" make it "hard to replace them" (par. 2). The new films had the "hope and wonder of childhood; they set out to recapture or invent a kind of innocence" (Mast and Kawin 557).

In the 1960s and 1970s, Godzilla was an unabashed hero and protector of Japan. Audiences cheered his exploits to protect the country from other terrors and monsters. In fact, "children saw Godzilla as a wholesome and goofy father figure, a radioactive Fred McMurray without the two-piece suits" (Tsutsui, 84). Even Godzilla's appearance transformed into a friendlier version that children could love and admire. He lost his fangs, had larger, rounder eyes like a pet, developed a slight smile, and had a body shape more like a baggy clown suit than a terrifying, giant reptile. His actions became entertaining and rather silly, and so "the violence of Godzilla thus became safe, humorous, and ritualized" (Tsutsui 53). Hence, Godzilla reinvented as a likeable, funny hero, could never be defeated, no matter the threat. According to Tsutsui, he became the "guardian of postwar Japan's prosperity" (86).

Gradually through the films of the 1980s and 1990s, Godzilla took the shape of a bully. Bullies often act out aggressively because someone has provoked them; they usually pick on victims much smaller and weaker than themselves who look different (Frisen, Jonsson, and Persson 751–59). In the latest films, Godzilla turns away from protecting others' interests to protecting his own. Once human provocation and interference cross Godzilla's path, the creature becomes a monster unassailable in its terror and fury. In the 1998 American film, *Godzilla,* for example, the monster is deemed to be a female—a bully mother intent on protecting her spawn deep in the underground tunnels of the New York subway. She is viciously unrelenting in her attacks, not only on skyscrapers and subway trains but also on the little humans who "stand" in her way. Audiences understand that humans and ancient dinosaurs can never be alike, so appearances between them cannot "normalize." Thus, Godzilla's bullying can never end.

Page Header → Sandez 6

The bully Godzilla rips apart the prosperity of Japan in the 1980s and 1990s. Japan made an historic and unprecedented economic turnaround, taking it from the devastation of WWII to economic success within two decades. By the 1990s, Japan had become one of the richest countries in the world. Godzilla was always a reflection of his times, and in the Reagan era superpower threat, he "reemerged as the bully in *Gojira* (1984), to become the big, butch, pissed-off badass once again" (Tsutsui 64). The Godzilla of this era was bent on revenge of one sort or another, and he was a monster without conscience who destroyed indiscriminately. Once again, Godzilla emerged as the symbol of a threat.

Tsutsui implies the following:

> In an even larger sense America has been an intimidating and ambivalent presence in Japan's collective consciousness over the past sixty years. On the one hand, the United States has been a protector and a model, a generous benefactor and a dependable market; but it has also been a bully and an object lesson, an arrogant autocrat and a threatening nuclear power. (98)

Godzilla capitalizes on the human need for spectacle. Through the art of the movies, audiences can watch in safety as the destructiveness of a monster is unleashed. As Sontag observes, "Science fiction films are not about science. They are about disaster, which is one of the oldest subjects of art. . . . The science fiction film . . . is concerned with the aesthetics of destruction, with the peculiar beauties to be found in wreaking havoc, making a mess" (211). Perhaps as Corliss suggests, "Monster-movie parables were the Pop Art of the early nuclear age."

Part anti-hero, part action hero, and part bully, Godzilla remains an enigma. The impact of the original film is now lost on today's moviegoers for a number of reasons: the majority have not lived through the horrors of nuclear attack; nuclear threat does not pervade the lifeworld as it once did, and changes in technology, particularly in movie-making through computer graphics and digitalized sequencing have changed the viewing

Page Header → Sandez 7

experience. Because today, "heightened realism is taken for granted" (Ryfle 54), something has been lost in the movie-going experience.

The Gojira of 1954, protector and hero of Japan, became the goofy action clown that charmed young audiences in the 1960s and '70s, and the object of terror and destruction in the 1980s and '90s. Godzilla, mute in his capability to tell the viewers who he is, remains an interesting mystery, capable of changing with societies' desires and movie-maker economics. As Tsutsui offers,

> Godzilla's fundamental character—and charm—may well be his ambiguity, his ambivalence as a symbol, and his frustrating elusiveness as a subject of interpretation. Rooted both in a specific history and in the dispersed imagination of tens of millions of fans, Godzilla seems at once reassuringly real and magically ephemeral. (111)

Page Header → Sandez 8

Works Cited

Corliss, Richard. "6 Best Sea Monster DVDs Ever." *Time*. Time, 165.26 27 June 2005. Web. 19 October 2007.

Frisen, Anna, Anna-karin Jonsson, and Camilla Persson. "Adolescents' Perceptions of Bullying: Who Is the Victim? Who Is the Bully? What Can Be Done to Stop Bullying?" *Adolescence* 42.168 (2007): 749-61. Print.

Furst, Lilian R. "The Romantic Hero, or Is He an Anti-Hero?" *Studies in the Literary Imagination* 9.1 (1976): 53-67. Print.

Godzilla. Dir. Roland Emmerich. Prod. Kelly Van Horn and Peter Winther. Centropolis Film Productions, TriStar Pictures and Toho Film, 1998. Film.

Godzilla, King of the Monsters. Dir. Ishiro Hondo. Prod. Joseph E. Levine. Embassy Pictures, 1956. Film.

Gojira. Dir. Ishiro Hondo. Prod. Tomoyuki Tanaka. Toho Film Co., 1954. Film.

Gojira, 1984. Dir. Koji Hashimoto and R.J. Kizer. Pro. Norio Hayashi and Kiyomi Kanazawa. Toho Company and Toho Eizo, 1984. Film.

Hunter, Stephen. "The Lost Action Hero: Strong, Stoic, Feared: Alas, Hollywood Doesn't Make 'Em Like It Used To." *Washington Post*. Washington Post, 3 Sept. 2006. Web. 9 Dec. 2007.

Mamet, David. *Bambi vs. Godzilla: On the Nature, Purpose, and Practice of the Movie Business*. New York: Pantheon Books, 2007. Print.

Mast, Gerald, and Bruce F. Kawin. *A Short History of the Movies*. 6th ed. Needham Heights: Simon & Schuster, 1996. Print.

Queenan, Joe. "The Last Action Heroes." *Guardian*. Guardian, 19 Feb. 2008. Web. 3 Aug. 2008.

Ryfle, Steve. "Godzilla's Footprint." *Virginia Quarterly Review* 81.1 (2005): 44-63. Print.

Snider, Mike. "Godzilla Arouses Atomic Terror." *USA Today*. USA Today, 29 Aug. 2006. Web. 14 Jan. 2008.

Page Header

Sandez 9

Sontag, Susan. "The Imagination of Disaster." *Against Interpretation and Other Essays*. New York: Picador, 2001. 209-25. Print.

Sullivan, Michael P., and Anre Venter. "The Hero Within: Inclusion of Heroes into the Self." *Self and Identity* 4.2 (2005): 101-11. Print.

Tsutsui, William. *Godzilla on my Mind: Fifty Years of the King of Monsters.* New York: Palgrave MacMillan, 2004. Print.

Comprehension Questions

1. How many films featured Godzilla?
2. What country originated Godzilla?
3. Why was Godzilla so popular?
4. What has Godzilla symbolized over the years?
5. How did Hollywood transform Godzilla?

Critical Comprehension

1. What assumptions does Sandez make about the movie viewer? About watching movies?
2. Does Sandez link representation with reality? How?
3. What impact does violence depicted in movies have on viewers? What evidence can you provide to support your view?
4. How are movies "Pop Art?" How would you define "Pop Art"? Provide some examples of Pop Art.
5. What B-movies have had a noticeable influence on movie makers and on audiences? What influences have they had? How have they influenced the industry?
6. What relationship is there between viewer and film? What does Sandez suggest? Do you agree with her position? Why or why not?

Assignment

Answer the following questions after you have read the example paper.

1. What are the strengths of Sandez's paper?
2. What are the weaknesses?
3. Evaluate the evidence she uses in her paper. Is it effective? Why or why not?
4. Evaluate the sources Sandez has used in her paper. Are they reliable?
5. What suggestions could improve her paper?

CHECKOUT

Here are some of the ideas you will take away with you after you have completed the chapter:

1. It is valuable to visit the official MLA websites.
2. It is helpful to have a good English handbook.

3. Learning to research requires practice, persistence, and careful planning.
4. From time to time documentation style guidelines are updated.
5. Guidelines for formatting papers are complex and can be confusing, so consult with your instructor before you start your paper.
6. Have someone look over your research plan.
7. Have someone read your first draft.
8. Have someone evaluate the sources you have used.
9. Avoid plagiarism at all costs.

Mastering the concepts in this chapter will also help you develop and apply the following employability skills highlighted by the Conference Board of Canada in Employability Skills 2000+:

Communicate

- read and understand information presented in a variety of forms (eg., words, graphs, charts, diagrams)
- share information using a range of information and communications technologies (eg,. voice, e-mail, computers)
- use relevant scientific, technological and mathematical knowledge and skills to explain or clarify ideas

Manage Information

- locate, gather and organize information using appropriate technology and information systems

Think & Solve Problems

- assess situations and identify problems
- seek different points of view and evaluate them based on facts

Be Responsible

- plan and manage time, money and other resources in order to reach goals

Be Adaptable

- work independently or as a part of a team

Participate in Projects & Tasks

- plan, design or carry out a project or task from start to finish with well-defined objectives and outcomes

Source: Adapted from *Employability Skills 2000+* Brochure E/F (Ottawa: The Conference Board of Canada, 2000.

chapter 16

Editing and Style Notes

Chapter Objectives

After completing this chapter you will be able to

1. edit your papers to meet academic standards of mechanics and grammar;
2. keep a record of the types of errors you make in your papers and assignments;
3. schedule your editing activities before an assignment is due;
4. use a checklist to help you edit your computer document file;
5. obtain useful feedback about your writing from peer editing;
6. refer to the 11 categories of common errors students make in their writing.

INTRODUCTION

The final phase of your writing includes editing and proofreading. **Editing** means you review the paper in terms of how paragraphs fit together as a whole, how whole passages might sound, or how sentences within paragraphs work. When you **proofread**, you will be checking your spelling, grammar, punctuation, and capitalization. You will also be reviewing the format to be sure it meets your instructor's or professor's specifications. In other words, in the last phase you are preparing your paper for the final presentation.

As you are editing, you are also paying attention to particular elements of your writing style. You may do some small revisions in phrasing at this stage, but for the most part, you do not usually take on major reworking of your material. You are also interested in meeting the academic writing standards for mechanics and grammar.

This chapter introduces you to some techniques you can adopt when you are editing and proofreading your work and suggests 11 common errors to pay attention to as you edit. It provides some writing style notes to assist you in improving your writing style and ends in editing exercises to develop your skills in editing sentences, paragraphs, and an essay. Chapter 17 will provide in-depth information on English grammar; if you think your grammar needs more review than chapter 16 offers, please read and review chapter 17, too.

TECHNIQUES FOR EDITING

Tips for Editing

1. Keep a record of the type of errors you make as your papers and assignments are returned to you. Keep a special file on computer, or use a notebook. List the kind of error you made, with an example if possible.

2. When you are ready to edit a paper, take out your errors record. Which errors do you make most often? Least often?
3. Be sure you understand why something is considered an error. If you do not, get clarification and explanation by reviewing your text, the internet, and library reference materials, or by asking your instructor or professor, or a resource person in your writing or learning centre on campus. Learn how to repair your mistakes, too.
4. Leave ample time for editing. Too often students do not leave a window of at least a few hours before an assignment is due. They often lose marks due to editing and proofing errors.
5. Print the pages of your document. It is preferable to be able to write on your pages.
6. As you begin to proofread, first look for the most common error you make.
7. Edit and proofread line by line.
8. Most writers find it helpful to edit out loud. Sometimes it is easier when you hear yourself say the words; you notice the error more easily than when you read silently.
9. Using a brightly coloured highlighter, mark any sections you change. The highlighting will be easy to spot.
10. Read the paper several times, looking for different errors each time.
11. Take breaks when you are editing.
12. Use checklists as tools. Use the checklists from *Spotlight on Critical Skills in Essay Writing, Second Edition* or from the internet. As an alternative, develop or customize your checklists, store them on your computer, and print them as you require them. You may also work from a paper checklist as you edit on computer.

Using Peer Editing

As mentioned in the chapter on essays, peer editing is a valuable exercise because it can provide you with useful feedback on your writing. Instructors do not merely say, "Go ahead and evaluate each other's paper now." Instead, instructors will often demonstrate how to go about being a peer editor for another student. Your instructor may provide you with a variety of checklists to use at different stages of evaluation.

Try searching on the internet for samples of peer-editing worksheets and exercises. There are some very good sites available. Type in "peer editing" and restrict your search to *.edu* sites. Your search engine will bring up a number of university and college writing-centre websites; most are excellent.

Outside of class, you may also want to have someone else peer-edit your paper. Perhaps you can exchange papers with another student from your class, agree on a checklist, and then read one another's paper. One caution is to be careful not to expect someone else to find and fix all of your errors. Such an expectation would be inappropriate and dishonest. However, the peer editor can make general comments to the writer, such as, "I saw a lot of subject–verb agreement errors in your paper," or "I think you should review the spelling errors." Such general guidance, along with comments about organization, structure, evidence, format, and style can be really helpful to you.

Typical Peer-Editing Checkpoints

- Is there a clear thesis?
- Is there an interesting introduction?
- Is there specific evidence to support major ideas in paragraphs?
- Has the writer used correct documentation style? MLA? APA?
- Are there at least three body paragraphs?
- Is the conclusion satisfying?
- Is the argument convincing?
- Do the arguments flow logically?
- Is there good use of transitional devices?
- Is the tone appropriate?
- Who is the intended audience?
- Is the editing thorough?
- Does the format fit the instructor's or professor's guidelines?
- Is the presentation professional looking?

COMMON ERRORS TO LOOK FOR WHEN EDITING

The following section discusses 11 categories of common errors students make in their writing. You will recognize which errors trouble you. Read slowly through each category, and add to your error record the ones appropriate to your own writing needs. The errors have not been arranged by most commonly occurring to least commonly occurring; rather, they are simply listed and discussed. Most students will have difficulty with one or more of them.

Pronoun Agreement Errors

Make pronouns agree in number and gender with their **antecedents** (the words to which pronouns refer).

Example:

Error: Sometimes a person feels lonely when they are away from home.

Correction: Sometimes people feel lonely when they are away from home.

The antecedent is *person*. To avoid sexism and awkward construction, use a third-person, plural point of view—*people* and *they*.

Indefinite pronouns do not refer to specific persons or things. Be sure indefinite pronouns agree with their references.

These indefinite pronouns are singular:

anybody	everybody	somebody
anyone	everything	someone
anything	neither	something
each	nobody	
either	no one	

These indefinite pronouns can be singular or plural depending on the words to which they refer:

all	most
any	none
more	some

Examples:

Error: Everybody should be allowed to bring their own supplies.

Correction: Everybody should be allowed to bring his or her own supplies.

Error: All of the children ate his or her banana cream pie.

Correction: All of the children ate their banana cream pie.

Error: All of the jacket had lost their colour.

Correction: All of the jacket had lost its colour.

Correction: All of the jackets had lost their colour.

If *or*, *nor*, *neither/nor*, or *either/or* joins singular nouns, make sure pronouns agree.

Example:

Error: Neither Patrick nor Sandu have organized their schedules for the project.

Correction: Neither Patrick nor Sandu has organized his schedule for the project.

Ambiguous Pronoun Reference Errors

Pronouns must have clear antecedents. If a sentence appears to have more than one antecedent for a pronoun, the sentence may be interpreted incorrectly. This error is called ambiguous pronoun reference.

Example:

Error: Roberto told Jim he had won the lottery.

Correction: After Roberto won the lottery, he told Jim.

He can refer either to Roberto or to Jim, resulting in ambiguous reference on the part of the pronoun.

Point of View Shifts

Point of view is the position from which a writer sees and writes about something. When you write paragraphs, or essays, you must consistently use the same point of view throughout the writing. A **point of view shift** is a change in person in the middle of a sentence or paragraph.

First-person point of view: *I* or *we*
Second-person point of view: *you*
Third-person point of view: *he*, *she*, *it*, *one*, or *they*

Examples:

Error: Workers who work late night shifts know you must adjust sleep patterns.

Correction: Workers who work late night shifts know they must adjust sleep patterns.

Error: One does not know how one will react until they are in an emergency situation.

Correction: One does not know how one will react until one is in an emergency situation. (This is rather awkward with *one* as the point of view. Most instructors will not accept *one* as the main point of view in a paper.)

Correction: You do not know how you will react until you are in an emergency situation. (Many instructors discourage a second person point of view.)

Correction: People do not know how they will react until they are in an emergency situation.

Sentence Fragments

In academic writing, all sentences must be complete. Sentence **fragments** are incomplete.

Example:

Error: Because the chairperson was late.

Correction: The committee felt anxious because the chairperson was late.

You can choose three ways to correct sentence fragments:

1. If appropriate, join the fragment to the sentence before it.
2. If appropriate, join the fragment to the sentence after it.
3. Revise the sentence to make sure it completes a whole thought and contains a complete subject-verb set.

Example:

Error: It was a rather unusual Thursday morning. The committee felt anxious. Because the chairperson was late. No one spoke.

Correction: It was a rather unusual Thursday morning. The committee felt anxious because the chairperson was late. No one spoke.

Dangling and Misplaced Modifiers

A **dangling modifier** has no clear word to modify. The modifier seems to be implied, but the sentence's meaning is unclear.

Example:

Error: Hunting for his glasses, Theo's pockets were fumbled.

Correction: Hunting for his glasses, Theo fumbled through his pockets.

In the error sentence, there is no clear modifier for the phrase hunting for his glasses. In the correction, hunting for his glasses modifies Theo.

A **misplaced modifier** is a word or phrase that is incorrectly positioned in a sentence, making it confusing or illogical. Place modifiers appropriately to relate to the words they modify.

Examples:

Error: The orange juice we bought at the corner store with extra calcium is past its stale date.

Correction: The orange juice with extra calcium we bought at the corner store is past its stale date.

Error: The puppy was playing with the small boy with floppy ears in the striped T-shirt.

Correction: The puppy with floppy ears was playing with the small boy in the striped T-shirt.

Subject–Verb Agreement Errors

A verb must agree with its subject in number. Plural subjects require plural verbs; singular subjects require singular verbs.

Most of the time, you will not have difficulty matching subjects and verbs; however, some sentence constructions can be confusing. Once you have reviewed special subject-verb situations, you will be able to apply the guidelines to your own writing.

SITUATION 1

As mentioned earlier, you will notice that indefinite pronouns can be singular or plural subjects. Match the verb and any other pronouns in the sentence to the correct number of the indefinite pronoun.

Examples:

Error: Everything in the bags were stolen.

Correction: Everything in the bags was stolen.

Some of the cabbage was rotten. (refers to a single cabbage)

Some of the cabbages were rotten. (refers to a number of cabbages)

SITUATION 2

Do not use the object of prepositional phrases as the subject of your sentence. Prepositional phrases may divide the subject and verb.

Example:

Error: A group of hikers were turned back from the dangerous trail.

Correction: A group of hikers was turned back from the dangerous trail.

Of hikers is a prepositional phrase, not part of the subject and verb set.

SITUATION 3

Collective nouns are words referring to a group of things. Collective nouns are singular when referring to the unit as a whole or plural when referring to members of the group.

Examples of Collective Nouns:

committee	clergy	company	enemy	band
group	family	flock	public	number
team	class	herd	audience	crowd

Examples:

The family is planning a holiday at the beach. (acting as a unit)

The family were arguing over money. (acting as different members)

SITUATION 4

If your subjects are singular and joined by *or*, use a singular verb.

Examples:

Loading furniture or digging in the garden is hard labour.

Katrina or Denise is expected to arrive by seven.

If one subject is singular, the other plural and joined by *or*, match the verb to the last subject in the series.

Example:

The landowner or the officials are holding up the sale.

The officials or the landowner is holding up the sale.

SITUATION 5

If your subjects are joined by *and*, use a plural verb.

Example:

The officials and the landowner are holding up the sale.

Comma Errors

COMMA SPLICES AND RUN-ONS

Comma splices are faults since commas are inserted to join two independent clauses. Because commas cannot be used to join two independent clauses, use semicolons or conjunctions instead. A run-on sentence is two independent clauses without correct punctuation or connectors.

Example:

Error: Rufus was my favourite pet snake, he died at the ripe old age of six. (comma splice)

Error: Rufus was my favourite pet snake he died at the ripe old age of six. (run-on)

Correction: Rufus was my favourite pet snake; he died at the ripe old age of six.

Correction: Rufus was my favourite pet snake, but he died at the ripe old age of six.

SUPERFLUOUS COMMAS

Superfluous commas are extra commas that interrupt or confuse meaning.

Within Dates

If the date consists of only the month and the year, omit commas.

Example:

Error: Marcus left the company in March, 2008.

Correction: Marcus left the company in March 2008.

If the day comes before the month, omit commas.

Examples:

Error: 4 May, 2009 is Peggy's retirement date.

Correction: 4 May 2009 is Peggy's retirement date.

COMMAS WITH NONRESTRICTIVE ELEMENTS

Use commas around these elements: a nonrestrictive clause, an appositive, or a parenthetical expression.

- A **nonrestrictive clause** is a clause not essential to the meaning of the sentence. Use commas to set it off from the rest of the sentence.
- An **appositive** is a phrase that modifies and clarifies the meaning of the noun next to it. Use commas around the appositive.
- A **parenthetical expression** is a phrase that interrupts the meaning or flow of a sentence in order to add emphasis.

Examples:

Nonrestrictive clause set off by commas:

Monique, <u>who comes from Quebec</u>, loves to ski.

<u>Who comes from Quebec</u> is a nonrestrictive clause. It is not essential to the meaning of the sentence and merely adds information.

Appositive surrounded by commas:

Mrs. Weinz, the announcer at the conference, proposed a 50-minute lunch.

Differences in meaning—restrictive and nonrestrictive clauses:

Men who are insensitive do not make good husbands.

Men, who are insensitive, do not make good husbands.

In the first sentence, who are insensitive is not set off by commas; therefore, it is a restrictive clause. What does the first example sentence mean? What does the second example sentence mean? The commas make all the difference!

Sometimes it will be up to you as the writer to decide what elements will be restrictive and what will be nonrestrictive.

Parenthetical expressions surrounded by commas:

Dudley, I believe, was the first person in line to receive free corn chips.

Some typical parenthetical expressions are *of course*, *you can imagine*, *I believe*, *as a matter of fact*, *indeed*, and *after all.*

COMMA OMISSIONS

In Compound Sentences

Leaving out a comma in a longer compound sentence is considered an error.

Example:

Error: A new head coach was hired for the Toronto Maple Leafs and he held a news conference to discuss his goals.

Correction: A new head coach was hired for the Toronto Maple Leafs, and he held a news conference to discuss his goals.

Notice *and* is the conjunction joining the two independent clauses, and notice the comma before the conjunction.

In a Series

You will clarify the meaning of the elements in a series if you use a comma before the *and.* This comma is called the "Oxford comma" or "series comma." Using the Oxford comma helps keep items in a series distinct.

Example:

Error: The children's baseball team ordered chocolate, raspberry, vanilla and banana ice cream cones. (The lack of comma before *and* makes the meaning confusing. "Vanilla and banana" could be one flavour.)

Correction: The children's baseball team ordered chocolate, raspberry, vanilla, and banana ice cream cones. (The Oxford comma separates the last two items to make it clear that four, not three, flavours were ordered.)

After an Introductory Element

Omitting a comma after introductory words or phrases is an error.

Examples:

Error: Next apply the gauze to the wound.

Correction: Next, apply the gauze to the wound.

Next introduces a new step. It is a transition.

Error: On the other hand Raita insisted on paying the bill.

Correction: On the other hand, Raita insisted on paying the bill.

On the other hand is a phrase that introduces the sentence.

Error: Having so little to spend Marshall decided to get another job.

Correction: Having so little to spend, Marshall decided to get another job.

Having so little to spend is a participial phrase that introduces the sentence.

Within Dates

Separate the day of the month from the year, and then separate the year from the rest of the sentence by the use of commas.

Example:

Minnie left on May 12, 2006, and was gone for several months.

If only the month and the year appear, it is not necessary to use a comma.

Example:

Minnie left in May 2006 and was gone for several months.

Within Geographical Names

If a city is followed by the name of a province, use a comma after the name of the province. Use a comma to separate the city from the province and the street address from the city.

Example:

Error: A new arena is to be built on River Street, Prince Albert, Saskatchewan in the summer of 2009.

Correction: A new arena is to be built on River Street, Prince Albert, Saskatchewan, in the summer of 2009.

With Postal Codes

Do not use a comma to separate the postal code from the name of the province.

Example:

Error: The package was sent to AckAck Advertising Company, Studio B, 5757 Bumbledom Street, Calgary, Alberta, T5R 3V9 on June 25, 2006.

Correction: The package was sent to AckAck Advertising Company, Studio B, 5757 Bumbledom Street, Calgary, Alberta T5R 3V9, on June 25, 2006.

Apostrophe Errors

Use an **apostrophe** followed by *s* to show possession after a singular noun or plural noun not ending in *s*. Place the apostrophe after the *s* in plural nouns ending in *s*. Notice that in the English language, some plurals are irregular and do not end in *s*.

Examples:

the goose's neck

some children's toys

the girls' fitness club

men's basketball

cheese's flavour

cheeses' flavours

Use possessive cases for pronouns or a possessive noun in front of a gerund.

Example:

Frodo's snoring kept his dog awake.

His snoring kept his dog awake.

Snoring is a **gerund**, a verb that functions as a noun. (*Snoring* is the subject of the sentence.)

Do not use an apostrophe when you pluralize nouns.

Example:

Error: I ordered 10 carton's of mandarin oranges.

Correction: I ordered 10 cartons of mandarin oranges.

There is no possession shown in the sentence, so you do not need an apostrophe.

Do not use apostrophes when you are naming decades.

Example:

Error: 1990's

Correction: 1990s

Use an apostrophe in dates when the century is not stated.

Example:

Error: 90s

Correction: '90s

Semicolon Errors

A **semicolon** joins two related and independent clauses. Do not use a semicolon as a separator (comma).

Example:

Error: The harp is a complicated instrument to play, it is not particularly popular, however.

Correction: The harp is a complicated instrument to play; it is not particularly popular, however.

The two independent clauses are the harp is a complicated instrument to play and it is not particularly popular, however. A comma cannot join the two clauses (comma splice). However, a semicolon is appropriate if no conjunction is used.

SEMICOLONS WITH CONJUNCTIVE ADVERBS

Conjunctive adverbs require the use of a semicolon in compound sentences. Remember, if you can move a word from its position to another position in a sentence, then the word is not functioning as a strong conjunction.

Example:

Error: Hampton was a dedicated pianist, however, he found time for friends and family.

Correction: Hampton was a dedicated pianist; however, he found time for friends and family. (A semicolon is added before *however*.)

Moving the Conjunctive Adverb

Hampton was a dedicated pianist; he found time for friends and family, however.

However, a weaker conjunctive adverb, can be moved to another position in the independent clause. Therefore, the semicolon remains to join the two independent clauses.

Conjunctive Adverbs

consequently	however	then	moreover	therefore
hence	finally	otherwise	thus	still
meanwhile	nevertheless	besides	anyway	furthermore

Colon Errors

The **colon** has two main purposes: it indicates that a list or quotation will follow, or it precedes an independent clause that adds further explanation to a previous clause. In the second use, the colon sets up anticipation or expectation in the reader's mind.

Examples:

Error Purpose 1: The magazine rack contained only four kinds of publications gardening, sports, home, and hunting.

Correction Purpose 1: The magazine rack contained only four kinds of publications: gardening, sports, home, and hunting.

Error Purpose 2: It was time for Talbot to face his demons, his addiction was destroying his life. (comma splice)

Correction Purpose 2: It was time for Talbot to face his demons: his addiction was destroying his life. (An em dash [—] would also be appropriate.)

Correction Purpose 2: It was time for Talbot to face his demons—his addiction was destroying his life.

Do not use a colon that splits a subject and object or subject complement. Whatever comes before the colon should be a complete, independent clause.

Example:

Error: Genda will bring: the DVDs, tapes, and posters.

Correction: Genda will bring the DVDs, tapes, and posters.

Correction: Genda will bring the following: the DVDs, tapes, and posters.

Notice in the second correction, Genda will bring the following is a complete, independent clause.

Faulty Parallelism

Correct **sentence parallelism** means that grammatical structures are in balance in all parts of the sentence. If you wish to write a number of items in a series in a sentence and you use a particular grammatical pattern in the first sequence, you must repeat that same sequence in the rest of your list; otherwise, you will have committed an error called **faulty parallelism**. Often, you will notice that a sentence "sounds wrong" when faulty parallelism occurs.

Examples of Correct Parallel Structure:

1. William has a generous heart, a willing hand, and an open smile.

   You can see three adjective-noun combinations in the series.

2. Many students have learned to read better, write effectively, and manage their time more appropriately.

   Three infinitive phrases are in the series.

Examples of Faulty Parallel Structure:

Error 1: The new instructor is organized, friendly, and has a good sense of humour.

Error 2: Ahmed loves to dance, play the guitar, and swimming.

Error 3: Moshe can cook just as well as, if not better, than Duke.

Can you spot the parallelism errors in the previous sentences? Can you repair the errors? Discuss your answers with other students. Can you decide together what will solve the parallelism problems in these sentences?

TIPS FOR ELIMINATING FAULTY PARALLELISM

1. Match grammatical structures in all parts of a sentence. Examine the structure in the first part of the sentence, then check to see if the structures that follow are the same.

   Example:

   Loving her new grandson, planning for his future, and helping to care for him occupied Charleen's time. (all gerund phrases)

2. Balance comparisons. Make one structure parallel in form to the other structure you are comparing.

   Example:

   Error: The study showed that boys spend more time on playing games than girls.

   Correction: The study showed that boys spend more time than girls on playing games.

3. Balance the modifiers, so that the sentence is logical and the structures parallel. If you write sentences containing quite a few modifiers, try to pay attention to the meaning and pattern of your grammatical sequences.

   Example:

   Error: The firm wanted a secretary and chef.

   Correction: The firm wanted a secretary and a chef.

4. Balance verb forms and tenses.

   Example:

   Error: Norbert placed an ad in the local paper for an antique rug, purchased one, and is paying a reasonable price for it.

   Correction: Norbert placed an ad in the local paper for an antique rug, purchased one, and paid a reasonable price for it.

5. Balance the two *correlatives—neither-nor* and *either-or* constructions. What is on one side of the correlative must match the other side.

   Example:

   Error: Feelie not only finished the researching but also the writing.

   Correction: Feelie finished not only the researching but also the writing.

   Correction: Feelie not only finished the researching but also finished the writing.

EDITING EXERCISES

The following section will give you the opportunity to practise editing the types of errors discussed in the early part of the chapter. Review the notes in the chapter for each type of error; then try the editing exercises.

Exercise 1 Editing Sentences

Complete the following editing exercise. Find the errors, and then repair them. You may find that some errors can be repaired in more than one way. Use a separate sheet of paper for your work. Check your answers with the Answer Key.

1. I noticed a delicious-looking chocolate cake as I drove up the ramp in the bakery window.
2. Granular fertilizer's excellent for many bedding plants cannot be used in all conditions', however some of the granular fertilizers releases enough nutrients to meet the customer's demand.
3. One of the circus performer's caught their toe on the wire as it drooped over the edge of the grandstand.
4. Anybody who want to pay their locker fees: either send in an email request, or bring a cheque to the student's lounge office, students with outstanding fees will have his library privilege's revoked.
5. Writers know you have to develop techniques to handle one's insecurities, or bolstering your confidence, otherwise we can soon feel: lost, afraid and dazed.
6. Wandering around the parking lot a shopping cart crossed my path.
7. If Davids friends or his sister invite Cherie to the party. You'd better warn her her former boyfriend Buffo plans to attend.
8. The rising flood waters the spread of disease and what people do to loot causes the disaster area to become more dangerous, therefore visitors' should stay away.
9. Shoppers, who steal, will be charged to the laws full extent, moreover you will be barred from entering the shopping mall until September, 2009.
10. The Great Western Railway of course is considered by some to be the first Canadian system, 27, January, 1854 a line was built from London Ontario to Windsor Ontario.
11. Having a place in the traditional stories of the Tsimshian people the kermody a rare white subspecies of black bear is sometimes called the spirit or ghost bear by the Aboriginals relying on old-growth forests to survive.
12. Roy Stanbury the coach from Westside Community League said the boy's basketball team from Edmonton Alberta won more games during the 1990's than the men.
13. The concert held at 112 Water Street Halifax Nova Scotia was thrilling, unusual and most enjoyed it.

Exercise 2 Editing Out Faulty Parallelism

Find all parallelism errors in the following sentences. Correct each error by rewriting the sentence to eliminate the fault. Check your answers with the Answer Key.

1. Not only is our computer service faster but also superior to theirs.

___

___

2. Huey was playing in the backyard, stumbled and twists his ankle.

___

___

3. The article explained that teenagers own more cars than senior citizens.

___

___

4. The college hired a librarian and plumber.

___

___

5. The veterinarian not only prepares her own ointments but also herbal remedies.

___

___

6. The villain was evil, hated squirrels, and trapped them for dinner.

___

___

7. The taxi had been waiting for several minutes and pulls out unexpectedly.

___

___

8. Florentine is clever, quick-witted, and has a lot of energy.

___

___

9. The photographer either takes many digital pictures at the aquarium or videos.

___

___

10. Working with horses is challenging, thrilling, and provides surprises.

___

___

Exercise 3 Editing an Essay

The following is an essay written about the play *Letters from Wingfield Farm.* Below you will see the number and types of errors found in the essay. This is an exercise in editing. You are to look for errors in grammar, usage, spelling, and punctuation in the following student essay. Do not consider stylistic changes. Work in pairs. Find the errors and correct them. Be prepared to share your answers.

Error Types and Counts:

punctuation: 6	parallelism: 2	fragments: 3
usage: 3	run-ons: 2	spelling: 6
subject–verb: 2	pronoun reference: 1	comma splices: 2

Walt Wingfield is a man who goes through many changes throughout the course of the play called *Letters from Wingfield Farm.* Walt Wingfield, a man who has lived a large portion of his life as a stock-broker change his outlook on life and goes into the business of running a farm. This change of heart creates conflict in his life and the life of others. Walt Wingfield, the main character in this book, will find that he will go through many transformations throughout the course of his farming career, some of these changes will cause conflict in his life.

Walt's decision to become a farmer instead of a stock-broker causes trouble from the very beginning of his endevour. Walt is a very successful stock-broker, and brings in alot of money for the firm that he works for. The head of his firm discovers that Walt wants to go and persue life on a farm, and this fact bothers him. If Walt were to leave the firm he would loose a lot of money. Naturally, there is a conflict between them. This type of confict is known as "man against man". Two opposing views between people will often bring a situation where conflict can arise. Because of this change in Walt. Walts' boss wants him to stay. Walt not only has the conflict with his boss but as he goes about his new farming career, he finds another conflict.

Walt finds that many of his animals provides conflict for him in his day-to-day life just as easy as any human being can. Walt's change from a businessman to a farmer not only creates conflict between himself and his employer, but it also creates conflict in his two horses, he has specially designated them to plough in the "old-time" way. Walt discovers that his horses do not want to work they are perfectly happy with their life of standing around a pasture all day doing nothing. The conflict between the two arise when Walt tries to hook up the horses to a plough the author, Dan Needles, shows an example of what Walt thinks as he tries to get the horses to do some real hard work around the farm: "The hard part was trying to convince those horses that God created them to actually do some work in life" There are many examples of the conflict between the horses and Walt in this play. For example, while trying to coax the horses into pulling a sled around the field. Walt ends up with a smashed barn door when the horses bolt. Also, when Walt bring's in a person who has some experience with horses.

TECHNIQUES FOR STYLE

Using Active and Passive Voice

Voice or mood is a term used in relation to verbs. **Active voice** in a sentence means the subject performs the action. **Passive voice** means the subject is removed from direct action: the subject is acted upon.

Examples:

Active voice: A police officer controlled traffic at the intersection during the power outage.

Passive voice: During the power outage traffic at the intersection was controlled by a police officer.

In the sentence with active voice, a police officer is the subject of the sentence. The officer performed the action: he or she *controlled* the object, *traffic*.

In the second sentence, using passive voice, the subject of the sentence is traffic. Action is removed and made passive. A police officer is now placed in a prepositional phrase—by a police officer. In this sentence, the real person or thing doing the action has been moved to the end of the sentence and placed in a minor position—as the object of a preposition.

If you use active voice in your writing, you make the action more direct for the reader, more meaningful in a sense. On the other hand, if you use passive voice, you are eliminating direct action, and by so doing, some experts say, you effectively rid the subject of responsibility or agency. Some discourse theorists believe that authoritative bodies like government agencies, social and educational institutes, and corporations use the passive voice in two cases: whenever necessary to de-emphasize their responsibility for action and to remove agency from others.

Consider the Following Examples:

1. Riot police used rubber bullets to quell some of the potentially dangerous protestors. (active voice)
2. Potentially dangerous protestors were quelled by the riot police, using rubber bullets. (passive voice)

What are the differences in meaning between these two sentences? What is achieved by using passive voice over active voice in this case?

In academic discourse, you use active voice whenever you can. Active voice makes your message more immediate: your reader sees the subject as the agent of action or as the focus of a sentence. When you use active voice, you help to clarify meaning, too. Passive voice can camouflage meaning rather than make it more visible. In fact, the real agents of action are often omitted in passive constructions.

Newspaper, television, and radio news reports often use passive constructions like these:

1. A man was hit late last night about 11:00 p.m. while walking down Centre Street.
2. Airline passengers will be asked to fill in an information sheet just outside the entrance of the main terminal building in downtown Main City.

3. Federal tariffs will be imposed on 11 softwood lumber products exported to the United States.
4. Lobster fishing in the area near the Bay of Fundy is temporarily off limits.
5. The park was blockaded for the summer months by local developers while initial surveys were carried out.

Hints

- Use active voice whenever possible in your academic writing.
- Avoid shifting between the active and the passive in sentences.
- Use passive voice only when you do not know who the subject is or when you want to de-emphasize the subject.

Exercise 4 Uses of Active and Passive Voice

Form a group of three to five. For each of the following topics, get together and write one sentence in the active voice and another in the passive voice. Be prepared to share your answers and discuss the differences in meaning. One member from the group should record your group's answers. Another member should share the answers with the rest of the class.

1. An oil spill
2. Cutbacks to post-secondary education
3. A new gadget in technology
4. Daycare for children under four
5. Supermarkets
6. Government subsidies
7. Cellphones
8. A traffic accident
9. Fast foods
10. Bank machines

Exercise 5 Changing Voice

Change each of the following passive constructions to active voice. Rewrite each sentence. Be prepared to share your answers. Think of how meaning shifts as you reconstruct the sentences.

1. A lost, emaciated dog was found roaming on the campus along Kelly Avenue.
2. Bradshaw House has been closed for the season.

3. The Speaker of the House was forced to resign on Thursday, October 5, 2009.
4. The door had been badly smashed in by the thief.
5. The winner will be contacted by mail.
6. Due to unforeseen difficulties, service to persons with physical disabilities will no longer be available at the centre.
7. A bag of lost mail was retrieved along the side of the main highway near Calgary.
8. The government spokesperson could not be reached for comment.
9. Our burgers are comprised of the finest and freshest ingredients.
10. He was pulled from the wreckage of his car.
11. The Winter Garden was buried under an enormous mound of blasted steel, glass, and wreckage from the collapse of the north tower of the World Trade Center.
12. The customer was fooled into buying a computer with low bus and system speed.
13. The children were given only 20 minutes to eat their lunches each day.
14. Several suspects in the robbery were spotted in the downtown region near the bank.
15. They were given a glimpse into the future.

Avoiding Wordiness

Use economy and conciseness: in effective prose, every word counts. No words occupy space without contributing something to the work. Economical and concise expression comes, then, not simply from using fewer words, but from choosing words that work. They earn the space they take in the sentence. **Wordiness** simply means you have used too many words where a few will do.

Student writers often include the following:

1. Awkward and meaningless repetition of an idea (redundancy).

Examples from Student Writing:

six in number	resultant effect
large in size	recur again
each and every	complete absence
absolutely nothing	red in colour
true fact	habitual custom
important essential	biography of his life
at the age of 10 years old	tiny, little girl
irregardless	totally useless

2. Delay in the focus of the sentence by using *there is* and *there are* constructions.

Examples from Student Writing:

There are many students who cannot afford the books.

(Better) Many students cannot afford the books.

There is a person I know who climbs mountains.

(Better) A person I know climbs mountains.

3. Wordiness or fancy phrasing.

Examples from Student Writing:

He spoke to me concerning the matter of my future.

(Better) He spoke to me about my future.

A large percentage of people are gullible.

(Better) Many people are gullible.

4. Jargon or gibberish or puffed-up, pretentious language that is full of long words and expressions, usually intended to impress the reader or audience.

Examples from Student Writing:

She rendered a vocal selection.

(Meaning) She sang.

He could not discharge his financial obligations.

(Meaning) He couldn't pay his debts.

He victimized his paramour with his verbal misrepresentations.

(Meaning) He lied to his lover.

The weather bureau predicts precipitational activity.

(Meaning) It might rain.

It is not without regret that I bid you farewell.

(Meaning) I am sorry to say goodbye.

5. Wordiness in clauses—the case of too many connectors.

Examples from Student Writing:

The wind which whistled through the cracks made a whistling sound.

(Better) The wind whistled through the cracks.

As he walked through the crowd, he bumped with his shoulders people who were in the way.

(Better) He shouldered his way through the crowd. (one neat clause)

John was out of patience and he was also out of breath; he was so angry that he stammered.

(Better) John, out of patience and breath, stammered angrily.

6. Vague and inexact wording.

Examples from Student Writing:

He walked down the street in an unsteady way.

(Better) He tottered down the street.

The water came into Barbara's apartment in large quantities.

(Better) The water gushed into Barbara's apartment.

The teacher leaned on the little stand that held her notes.

(Better) The teacher leaned on her lectern.

The conductor lifted the stick that he uses to direct the orchestra.

(Better) The conductor lifted his baton.

7. Trite or overused expressions.
Avoid clichés or tired expressions. Your writing will be much crisper without them.

Examples from Student Writing:

tired but happy	with bated breath	doting parents
home sweet home	strange but true	can't teach an old dog new tricks
pretty as a picture	tired as a dog	fast and furious

Using Logical Constructions

Your sentence construction must be logical and sensible. Sometimes placing words in the wrong position (misplaced modifiers), omitting words, or changing word order will result in confusion in meaning.

Example:

Error: As we sped along the highway, we almost discovered we were out of gas.

Correction: As we sped along the highway, we discovered we were almost out of gas.

Exercise 6 Making Logical Constructions

Repair the sentences below so that each is logical. Work in pairs. Be prepared to share your answers.

1. I bought fresh flowers at the store which I gave to a dear friend.
2. I saw a destitute lady walking down the streets in raggedy clothes and pushing an old grocery cart.
3. Although smaller than expected, parents who did turn out for the rally were very angry.

4. Jogging along the circular path, a motorcycle hit a young man.
5. The bank almost sent me a letter, telling me I was out of money.
6. I can remember not having fairy tales told to me when I was a child.
7. Covered in a blue checked tablecloth, the baker decorated the cakes from a bowl of icing.

Varying Sentence Structure

You can improve your writing style by examining the sentence patterns you use. Reading your work out loud helps you to hear repetition or monotonous rhythm.

1. Vary the length of the sentences you write. Use some short sentences among long ones or occasional long sentences if most of them are simple, short sentences. This passage from *Circus in Town* by Sinclair Ross illustrates the technique:

    There was a side door, and near it a ladder to the loft. No one saw her. She lay limp in the hay, listening to her heart-beat subside, letting the little core of pain in her breast that had come from running away slip through her senses like the cool grains of wheat that sometimes she sat in in the granary trickling through her fingers. It was a big, solemn loft, with gloom and fragrance and sparrows chattering against its vault of silence like boys flinging pebbles at a wall. And there, in its dim, high stiffness, she had her circus. Not the kind that would stop off at a little town. Not just a tent and an elephant or two. No—for this was her own circus; the splendid, matchless circus of a little girl who had never seen one.

    Source: Sinclair Ross, "Circus in Town," The Lamp at Noon and Other Short Stories *(Toronto: McClelland and Stewart, 1968).*

2. Mix loose and periodic sentences. In loose sentences, the sentence continues after the main thought has been expressed:

    We know that the young prince died, although we know little more.

    In periodic sentences, the meaning is suspended until the end of the sentence:

    Although we know little more, we know that the young prince died.

3. Change the order of words in sentences to a more unusual but acceptable order.
    - He could never forgive this.
      (to) This he could never forgive.
    - At the last minute Sally rushed in.
      (to) At the last minute, in rushed Sally.
    - He met an interesting traveller at the party.
      (to) At the party he met an interesting traveller.
    - Consequently, Alicia is no longer interested in Alfredo.
      (to) Alicia is, consequently, no longer interested in Alfredo.
    - The children, breathless and excited, waited for the clown to appear.
      (to) Breathless and excited, the children waited for the clown to appear.
      (or) The children waited, breathless and excited, for the clown to appear.

Using Transitions

Remember that transitional words, phrases, and sentences help the reader through your ideas. They are like bridges that carry the meaning from one point to another in your writing. Use transitions within paragraphs and between body paragraphs. Using such devices helps your writing to be more coherent and more fluid.

REVIEW TEST

Try the following review test. It will help you assess what you have learned from the chapter. Be prepared to share your responses with others in the class.

The following sentences contain errors of different types. Using a separate sheet of paper, correct the errors by rewriting each sentence.

1. Chewing on a breadstick a problem was on my mind.
2. Often a person feels annoyed when they have to line up for fast food.
3. Everybody should be prepared to accept their own failures.
4. All of the tourists brought his or her own bottle of water.
5. Neither Isha nor Philip have opted to stay out of the insurance plan.
6. Lorne told Bobo he had been promoted.
7. One clings to one's friends when you are in trouble.
8. Proprietors of pubs know you must not serve more alcohol to customers under 19.
9. Although the storm has passed.
10. The apprentice was disappointed. Because Merlin would not reveal his secrets.
11. Arriving late for an appointment, my cellphone rang loudly.
12. The stylist was arranging the food for the photograph shoot harvested from fall vegetables.
13. Everything in her career and family life were planned carefully.
14. A group of red finches were eating niger seed from the tube feeder.
15. Celebrating birthdays or cooking feasts were my mother's favourite occasions.
16. The dog howled at the moon the sound sent shivers down my spine.
17. Elroy joined the band in August, 2007.
18. 4 November, 2009 the company was disbanded.
19. The science student who prefers to study alone is a brilliant medal winner.
20. The play I believe will closed after only two performances.
21. One of the driving instructors taught me a technique for driving on black ice and I have found it useful in a number of rather dangerous situations.

22. After the president's long speech we felt too tired to ask questions.
23. There are a set of plates' with a country cottage motif on sale at my favourite store.
24. Most of the orchestra did not like their new contract; they planned on taking action.
25. Mushrooms grow wild in the early spring, however, not all of them are edible.
26. She gave us: new towels, curtains, and three toss cushions for our new condo.
27. His manner was rather surprising he was rude and overbearing.
28. We decided we would order: clam chowder, fresh biscuits, and a green salad.
29. The country singers new DVD is inventive, original, and has power.
30. The class interviewed an architect and truck driver.
31. The crew almost ate three dozen doughnuts at coffee break.

Assignment

Improve the style of the following piece of writing by correcting passive voice constructions, making sentences logical, eliminating wordiness, and repairing faulty parallelism, subject–verb agreement errors, fragments, point of view shifts, and punctuation faults. Be prepared to share your answers.

I have one main problem in my life. The fridge being of great embarrassment. Because it might be incredibly almost empty with hardly anything in it except for only a few pathetic bottles of condiments and swing open to view. When inviting friends over for dinner the fridge door refuses to close. Making some strange sounds late at night, I feel bothered by it. I find that even if I clean it you never know when it's going to rebel against me. I try and try to make friends with it but it refuses to acknowledge your existence instead it continues to whirr with such a loud whine it makes your teeth rattle. Wiping off its shelves cleaning out the chunks of ice from its freezer compartment and I give it a wash with lemon cleanser does not make it happier. One week it was cleaned by me four times. Somehow my fridge seems to sense that I want to get rid of it and dispose of it as soon as possible. So it protects itself by reminding you of its existence.

Bonus Exercise Commonly Confused Words

The following sets of words are often confused in usage.

all ready and already	fewer and less
number and amount	maybe and may be
whose and who's	it's and its
lay and lie	accept and except
affect and effect	among and between
definitely and defiantly	continuous and continual
loose and lose	than and then

Work in pairs. Look up each pair of words in the dictionary. Then write a sentence for each one. Be prepared to share your sentences with others.

CHECKOUT

Here are some of the ideas you will take away with you after you have completed the chapter:

1. A peer editor should make general comments, not find errors or fix them.
2. Concise expression comes from choosing words that earn the space they take.
3. When you use active voice, you help to clarify meaning.
4. Reading your work out loud helps you to hear monotonous repetition and clarify meaning.
5. Transitions carry meaning from one point to another.
6. Good editing and proofreading will improve your marks.

Mastering the concepts in this chapter will also help you develop and apply the following employability skills highlighted by the Conference Board of Canada in *Employability Skills 2000+*:

Communicate

- write and speak so others pay attention and understand
- use relevant scientific, technological and mathematical knowledge and skills to explain or clarify ideas

Be Adaptable

- learn from your mistakes and accept feedback

Learn Continuously

- set your own learning goals

Work with Others

- understand and work within the dynamics of a group

Participate in Projects & Tasks

- work to agreed quality standards and specifications

Source: Adapted from *Employability Skills 2000+* Brochure E/F (Ottawa: The Conference Board of Canada, 2000).

chapter 17

Grammar Fundamentals

Chapter Objectives

After completing this chapter you will be able to

1. recognize the basic parts of speech in the English language, i.e. nouns, pronouns, verbs, adjectives, adverbs, conjunctions, prepositions, phrases, and clauses;
2. use the correct forms of pronouns, verbs, adjectives, and adverbs;
3. edit sentences based on your knowledge of the basic parts of speech;
4. identify parts of sentences, i.e., subjects, predicates, direct and indirect objects, and subject complements;
5. edit sentences based on your knowledge of the parts of sentences;
6. identify the four types of English sentences;
7. construct the four types of English sentences;
8. utilize the common marks of punctuation, i.e. the comma, semicolon, colon, apostrophe, hyphen, dash, and quotations marks;
9. edit sentences based on your knowledge of common punctuation marks.

INTRODUCTION

Learning the essentials of English grammar is important. Having this knowledge will assist you when you are editing your own work or the work of others. It will also help you to write more accurately and correctly. Your writing will be evaluated, both as a student and as a professional. Academic writing demands precision with language, so you will notice that understanding the basics of English grammar will support your needs as a learner, writer, critical thinker, and reader.

This chapter contains a review test after each major section. The review tests will help you to recognize what you have learned in each section. You will need to do some review before you try each test.

PART 1: PARTS OF SPEECH

Traditionally, English grammar has been divided into eight categories of words based on how they are used in sentences. These are called the **parts of speech**: nouns, pronouns, verbs, adjectives, adverbs, conjunctions, prepositions, and interjections.

Nouns

Nouns name something. They can name things in the world (**concrete nouns**), or they can name ideas, emotions, or concepts (**abstract nouns**). Nouns can be **singular** (one) or **plural** (more than one).

Examples:

unusual weather	the City of Saskatoon	Annette and Sima
modern dance	Canadian maple	sacks of cash
a terrific bargain	the sound of running water	basic grammar

Usually, if you can place *a*, *an*, or *the* in front of a word, it is a noun. Nouns can be **proper**, i.e., they give a specific name, or they can be **common**; that is, they name a general group of things.

Examples:

Common Nouns	Proper Nouns
city	Montreal
dog	Musty
singer	Shania Twain

Nouns function as subjects or objects in sentences. You will learn more about subjects and objects in the next section, Sentence Parts.

Example:

The manager of the new recreation facility gave the children a tour.

manager	facility	children	tour
subject	object of the preposition	direct object	indirect object

Collective nouns are nouns that refer to a group of things. Generally, collective nouns are used in the singular, but in some cases, collective nouns may refer to members of the group and so are considered plural.

Examples:

jury	faculty	committee	board	team	band
group	class	public	audience	flock	staff

A group of students want some information on registration dates and times.

(All students in the group want the same information.)

A group of students wants some information on registration dates and times.

(Different members of the group want different pieces of information)

Exercise 1 Identifying Nouns

Underline all of the nouns in the following sentences. Check your answers with the Answer Key.

1. Iron oxides are used commercially in the glazing of ceramics, but synthetic iron oxides must be used in cosmetics to safeguard consumer health.
2. One of Canada's past prime ministers, Paul Martin, is an avid sailor and golfer.
3. Batteries should be taken to a recycling depot and should not be thrown out in the trash because some are very toxic to the environment.

Exercise 2 Using Nouns

Write sentences according to the instructions given. Label your answers. Be prepared to share your answers. The answers will vary greatly, so your instructor may ask you to check your sentences with other students.

1. Write a sentence that contains two common nouns, two proper nouns, and one concrete noun.
2. Write a sentence about getting to campus; use two proper nouns, one collective noun, and one abstract noun.
3. Write a sentence about the worst job you ever had; use one proper noun, two common nouns, one collective noun, and one abstract noun.

Pronouns

Pronouns take the place of nouns in sentences. The nouns that pronouns replace are called their **antecedents**.

Examples:

Some of the spectators were not pleased by the band's performance.

Some of them were not pleased by it.

Unless athletes drink plenty of water, they can suffer from a loss of volume in the blood. (*athletes* is the antecedent of *they*)

PRONOUN CASES

Pronouns have particular *cases* and forms, depending on how they are used. There are three cases of pronouns: *subjective* or *nominative* if the pronoun is used as the subject in a sentence; *objective* if the pronoun is used as an object; *possessive* if the pronoun is used to show ownership.

	Subjective or Nominative	Objective	Possessive
first person	I	me	my or mine
second person	you	you	your or yours
third person	he	him	his
third person	she	her	her or hers
third person	it	it	its
first person (pl)	we	us	our or ours
second person (pl)	you	you	your or yours
third person	they	them	their or theirs

Example:

She (subjective) thought that the speech would be too difficult for her (objective), but to her (possessive) surprise, she discovered her (possessive) gift.

RELATIVE PRONOUNS

That, *which*, *who*, *whom*, *whomever*, *whoever*, and *whichever* are called **relative pronouns.** They introduce clauses. They are placed next to nouns to which they refer.

Examples:

The receptionist said whomever we wished to interview would be available in 20 minutes.

We noticed whoever yelled loudest got served first.

Behaviours that reflect poorly on people are usually discouraged.

This is the bridge that was first destroyed by fire in 1842 and then bombed in World War II.

Our equipment, which was damaged by water, could no longer indicate depth of field.

The students who arrived from Hong Kong were visitors to our campus.

The dental hygienist tells the dentist whichever X-rays need review.

INDEFINITE PRONOUNS

Some pronouns refer to unspecified persons or things. These are called **indefinite pronouns**: *all*, *any*, *another*, *anybody*, *anything*, *anyone*, *everybody*, *everyone*, *everything*, *nobody*, *someone*, *somebody*, *each*, *few*, *many*, *some*, *none*, and *several.* Sometimes some of these words function like adjectives.

Examples:

Although Mr. Rochester may have been in love with Jane Eyre, he did not do anything to woo her at first.

The surgeon told nobody about his fatal condition.

Dr. William Osler, a famous early Canadian doctor, taught <u>everyone</u> the method of teaching students at patients' bedsides.

<u>Few</u> (adjective) people in Canada earn more than $500 000 per annum.

<u>Some</u> (adjective) purses are individually designed for clients.

Exercise 3 Identifying Pronouns

Change each of the following underlined words to pronouns, paying attention to using the correct case. Check your answers with the Answer Key.

1. Originating in the 1880s in Canada and the United States, <u>vaudeville</u> died in the 1930s as a form of variety entertainment with the advent of film and cinema-going.
2. One of the <u>speakers</u> stepped down from the podium and addressed the audience directly.
3. The provincial government and the federal government can rarely agree on <u>policies</u>.
4. <u>Hilroy</u> was famous for <u>Hilroy's</u> 15-pepper chili.

Exercise 4 Finding Antecedents

Draw an arrow from each pronoun to its antecedent in each of the following sentences. Be prepared to share your answers with the class.

1. A weekend retreat can be refreshing to most people if it takes place at least 30 miles from home.
2. Raccoons may appear daring, but they are not usually aggressive except during mating season or when defending their offspring; however, their intelligence, strength, teeth, and claws equip them to defend themselves efficiently if needed.
3. Although the campers had doused their fire with water, it was still smouldering in the early afternoon when a park warden came to check it.

Exercise 5 Using Pronouns

Write sentences as instructed in the directions given below. Be prepared to share your answers.

1. Write a sentence about a holiday; use one indefinite pronoun and one relative pronoun in your sentence.
2. Write a sentence about a movie you saw recently; use one possessive pronoun and underline an antecedent in the sentence.
3. Write a sentence about a favourite recipe; use one objective pronoun, one relative pronoun, and one indefinite pronoun in your sentence.

Verbs

Verbs express action or describe a state of being. They express time as past, present, or future tenses. They have particular forms within each tense. These forms are simple, progressive, perfect, and perfect progressive.

Present Tense

Simple present: Tells that an action or condition is taking place now.

Present progressive: Tells that an action or condition is continuing.

Present perfect: Tells that an action or condition that started in the past, continues in the present.

Present perfect progressive: Tells that an action or condition continuing in the past continues in the present.

Present

Simple	Progressive	Perfect	Perfect Progressive
I sing	I am singing	I have sung	I have been singing
you sing	you are singing	you have sung	you have been singing
he/she, it sings	he is singing	he has sung	he has been singing

Past Tense

Simple past: Tells that an action or condition is completed.

Past progressive: Tells that an action or condition was continuing in the past.

Past perfect: Tells that an action or condition that started in the past was finished before another action or condition took place.

Past perfect progressive: Tells that an action or condition continuing in the past began before some other action or condition.

Past

Simple	Progressive	Perfect	Perfect Progressive
I sang	I was singing	I had sung	I had been singing
you sang	you were singing	you had sung	you had been singing
he/she/it sang	he/she/it was singing	he/she/it had sung	he had been singing

Future Tense

Simple future: Tells that an action or condition will take place.

Future progressive: Tells that an action or condition will be continuing in the future.

Future perfect: Tells that an action or condition started in the past will complete in the future.

Future perfect progressive: Tells that a continuing action or condition started in the past will complete in the future.

Future

Simple	Progressive	Perfect	Perfect Progressive
I will sing	I will be singing	I will have sung	I will have been singing
you will sing	you will be singing	you will have sung	you will have been singing
he/she/it will sing	he will be singing	he will have sung	he will have been singing

Examples:

We followed (simple past) the trail until we reached (simple past) a small river.

Unfortunately, none of the water fowl that had been nesting (past perfect progressive) on the shores have been seen (present perfect) this year by any of the local birdwatchers' clubs.

Yumi would have been attending (past perfect progressive: *would* is the past of *will*) the Hana Matsuri or Flower Festival in Japan had she not broken her leg (past perfect).

Exercise 6 *Changing Tenses*

Change each of the verbs according to the parentheses in the sentences below. Use a separate sheet of paper for your work, and be prepared to share your answers.

1. Dim sum, widely popular in Canada, is (simple past) of Cantonese origin and is (simple past) a culinary tradition where diners enjoy (simple past) bite-sized portions served in small quantities per plate.
2. Jojo is playing (future progressive) his harmonica in the university's talent night, but he doesn't expect (simple future) to win the contest.
3. My girlfriend's mother has just bought (past perfect) a Havanese terrier, a purebred toy dog that has originated (past perfect) from Cuba.

Exercise 7 *Using Verbs*

Make up sentences according to the directions below. Write your answers on a separate sheet of paper, and be prepared to share your answers.

1. Make up a sentence about flying, using one verb in the future perfect progressive.
2. Make up a sentence about work, using one verb in the present perfect and one verb in the simple present.
3. Make up a sentence about painting, using one verb in the simple past, one verb in the past perfect, and one verb in the past progressive.

TRANSITIVE AND INTRANSITIVE VERBS

A verb can express action. An action verb is called **transitive** if it takes an object and **intransitive** if it does not take an object. An **object** in a sentence receives the action of the verb. (You will learn more about objects in the section called "Sentence Parts.")

However, sentences will not contain objects if the action verb is intransitive, so read the sentence carefully for meaning.

Examples:

Kristina hired three *students* for the summer project in Algonquin Park.

(*Hired* is the action verb; *students* is the object—who or what got hired.)

The supervisor will test the fire alarms to be sure they are working properly.

(*Will test* is the action verb; *fire alarms* is the object—who or what got tested.)

Exercise 8 Identifying Objects of Verbs

Underline the action verbs in each sentence. Then highlight the objects of the action verbs. Not all sentences contain objects of the verb. Check your answers in the Answer Key.

1. Don't burn combustible materials in the open air during the dry season.
2. Monad apologized for his behaviour at the annual general meeting.
3. The grocery store chain distributes frequent-flyer points as customers go through checkout stands.

LINKING VERBS

Not all verbs express action. Some verbs, called **linking verbs**, describe the state or condition of the subjects of sentences. Linking verbs also join the main parts of the sentence together.

Common Linking Verbs

am	was	smell	feel	become	grow
is	were	appear	remain	turn	look
are	sound	seem	taste	get	lie

Examples:

This may sound crazy, but I think I love you.

Does the lake lie beyond the hills?

Homer's homemade rhubarb wine tastes terrible.

Exercise 9 Using Linking Verbs

Use each of the following linking verbs in effective sentences. Use a separate sheet of paper, and be prepared to share your answers.

1. become
2. smell or smells
3. turn or turns

REGULAR AND IRREGULAR VERBS

Verbs have four main parts:

The base form: *study*

Past tense: Jules *studied.*

Past participle: Jules had *studied.*

Present participle: Jules is *studying.*

Regular verbs form their **past participle** by adding *ed.* However, many irregular English verbs do not. Some irregular verbs change forms when expressed in the past. There are over 250 irregular English verbs, but a few common ones are listed below. Check a reliable English handbook or website for a complete list of irregular verb forms.

Examples:

Base	Simple Past	Past Participle
become	become	become
break	broke	broken
catch	caught	caught
choose	chose	chosen
dig	dug	dug
do	did	done
drink	drank	drunk
fly	flew	flown
get	got	gotten
grow	grew	grown
hear	heard	heard
know	knew	known
leave	left	left
lose	lost	lost
mistake	mistook	mistaken
pay	paid	paid
read	read	read
ride	rode	ridden
see	saw	seen
take	took	taken
tear	tore	tore
understand	understood	understood
write	wrote	written

Exercise 10 Using Correct Verb Forms

Write sentences using the correct form of the base verb in parentheses. Use a separate sheet of paper; be prepared to share your answers.

1. Make up a sentence about a game, using *tear* (past participle).
2. Make up a sentence about a sport, using *become* (simple past).
3. Make up a sentence about hot dogs, using *choose* (past participle).
4. Make up a sentence about cash, using *know* (simple past).
5. Make up a sentence about grades, using *mistake* (past participle).

VOICE AND MOOD OF VERBS

The *voice* of verbs refers to whether the subject is completing the action or not. **Active voice** means the agent or doer of the action is the subject. **Passive voice** means that the verb is constructed with some form of *be* and that the subject no longer acts on the verb. You will learn more about subjects in the coming section called Sentence Parts.

Examples:

The fitness instructor demonstrated how to use the equipment safely. (active voice)

The fitness instructor is the subject of the sentence; he or she completed the action *demonstrated*. Here the subject is the agent or doer.

How to use the equipment was demonstrated by the fitness instructor. (passive voice)

Now the verb is constructed with a form of *be*. The *fitness instructor* is no longer the subject of the sentence and has been removed from agency.

You should use the active voice whenever possible in your writing. Using the active voice makes the writing more immediate.

Exercise 11 Changing Passive Voice to Active Voice

Change all of the passive voice constructions in the following sentences to active voice. Check your answers with the Answer Key.

1. The convention was cancelled because an electrical outlet at the hotel had started a small fire.
2. Video painting, a new genre of art employing moving images, is being driven by the emergence of new television technology, such as high-definition TV.
3. In 2006, the falling of many of the trees in Stanley Park in Vancouver was caused by gale force winds that suddenly whipped across the Strait of Georgia.

The **mood** of verbs has to do with how a writer wishes to express the idea in a sentence:

The indicative mood: Provides a fact.

The imperative mood: Gives a command.

The conditional mood: Indicates a condition.

The subjunctive mood: Expresses a desire or suggests a hypothetical situation.

Examples:

Some cats will not eat the same brand of cat food twice in a row. (indicative)

Stop driving fast through school zones. (imperative)

We would have picked up extra tickets for the concert had we known you wanted to go. (conditional)

If I were Queen of Government, I would change the tax laws immediately. (subjunctive)

Notice that in the subjunctive mood, you use *were* rather than *was*.

Exercise 12 Using Mood

Follow the directions below. Use a separate sheet of paper, and be prepared to share your answers.

1. Make up a sentence using the subjunctive mood.
2. Make up a sentence using the imperative mood.
3. Make up a sentence using the indicative mood.

Verbals

A **verbal** is a word that takes the form of a verb but has a different function. Verbals do not express action or link. Instead, they can function as nouns, adjectives, or adverbs. You will learn more about subjects, objects, and subject complements in the Sentence Parts section.

GERUND

Gerunds act as nouns and end in *ing*. Gerunds can also be in phrases.

Examples:

Skiing took up most of Antonio's spare time. (*Skiing* is a gerund and is subject.)

The rules forbade swearing in the locker room. (*Swearing* is a gerund and is object).

His doctor's specialty is diagnosing autoimmune-deficiency diseases. (*Diagnosing autoimmune-deficiency diseases* is a gerund phrase and is the subject complement.)

Playing too much tennis caused Mennah to develop carpal tunnel syndrome. (The gerund phrase *playing too much tennis* is subject of the sentence.)

PARTICIPLE

Participles act as adjectives; they also end in *ing* and sometimes *ed* or *en*. Participles can also be in phrases.

Examples:

The waiting customer suddenly left the service counter in disgust.

(*Waiting* is a participle functioning as an adjective in describing or modifying *customer*.)

Whispering, Leelah voiced her concern about the company's falling sales record.

(*Whispering* modifies *Leelah*, and *falling* modifies the sales *record*.)

Flipping through his mother's old photographs, Colm noticed a picture of the Irish village where his grandfather had been born.

(The participial phrase *flipping through his mother's old photographs* modifies *Colm*.)

INFINITIVE

Infinitives are made up of *to* plus the base form of a verb. They act as nouns, adjectives, or adverbs. They can also be placed in phrases.

Examples:

To compete was his ambition.

(The infinitive is subject of the sentence.)

The autistic child developed the language to respond.

(The infinitive modifies *language*.)

The candidate must debate fiercely to defend his position.

(The infinitive phrase is an adverb modifying *must debate*.)

Exercise 13 Using Verbals

Follow the instructions given below. Use a separate sheet of paper, and be prepared to share your answers.

1. Make up a sentence about swimming that contains a gerund acting as a noun.
2. Make up a sentence about wine, using a participial phrase.
3. Make up a sentence about watching television that contains an infinitive acting as an adjective.
4. Make up a sentence about nutrition; the sentence should contain one participle and one gerund.
5. Make up a sentence about singing; the sentence should contain one infinitive and one participle.

Adjectives and Adverbs

Adjectives modify or describe nouns while **adverbs** modify verbs, adjectives, or other adverbs. Adjectives and adverbs add colour and detail to sentences. These modifiers can also appear in phrases. Adverbs often end in *ly*.

Examples:

A prevalent attitude among many teens is the desire to copy their models.

(*Prevalent* is an adjective, modifying *attitude*.)

Raccoons will work tirelessly to undo latches of doors and clips on garbage can lids.

(*Tirelessly* is an adverb modifying *work*.)

The smell of the incense was so intense that Ethan passed out.

(*So* is an adverb modifying the adjective *intense*.)

Bears can move extremely quickly, a fact that surprises some hikers.

(*Extremely* is an adverb modifying the adverb *quickly*.)

The speeding car crashed through the barricade and landed in the water.

(*Through the barricade* is an adverb phrase modifying *crashed*; *in the water* is an adverb phrase modifying *landed*.)

The sunflower species with the orange corolla is a variety grown for the home decorating market.

(*With the orange corolla* modifies *species*, so it is an adjective phrase. *For the home decorating market* is an adverb phrases because it modifies *grown*.)

Exercise 14 *Using Adjectives and Adverbs*

Write sentences as requested in the instructions below. Be prepared to share your sentences.

1. Make up a sentence about snoring. Use three adjectives and one adverb in your sentence.
2. Make up a sentence about shopping. Use one adverb and one adjective phrase in your sentence.
3. Make up a sentence about school. Use two adjectives and one adverb phrase.

CORRECT USAGE OF ADJECTIVES AND ADVERBS

Use correct usage with adjectives and adverbs in sentences. It is grammatically incorrect to use an adverb form for adjectives or to use an adjective form for adverbs.

Examples:

Incorrect: My Uncle Santi can golf real well for a man of 80.

Correct: My Uncle Santi can golf really well for a man of 80.

Incorrect: The soldier dropped quick to the ground.

Correct: The soldier dropped quickly to the ground.

Exercise 15 Identifying Adverbs and Adjectives

Underline the correct form of the adverb or adjective in each of the following sentences. Check your answers with the Answer Key.

1. Sometimes comma rules confuse Mike, and he guesses (bad, badly).
2. The bus was (nearly, near) full at the end of the shift.
3. Montigue sings so (poor, poorly) that the judges have eliminated him from the contest.
4. I felt (real, really) (bad, badly) when I found out I did not get the promotion.
5. The Canadian Kennel Club lists the top 20 registered breeds of dogs each year, and in 2007, the Labrador retriever (sure, surely) did the best by placing at number 1.

Conjunctions

Conjunctions are words that join words, phrases, and clauses. Different kinds of conjunctions join different kinds of structures. There are three basic types of conjunctions.

COORDINATING CONJUNCTIONS

Coordinating conjunctions are used to join two similar grammatical structures. For example, they might be used to join a series of verbs, adjectives, or clauses. They are also used as the joiner in compound sentences. You will learn more about conjunctions in the upcoming section, Sentence Types.

The Common Coordinating Conjunctions

and	for	nor	yet
but	so	or	

Examples:

According to research cited in *Arctic*, "Belugas rival narwhals in their ability to navigate thick pack ice and explore depths well in excess of 1000 m." (Reeves & St. Aubin, 2001, p. i).

On January 23, 2006, the Ford Motor Company announced it would be closing a major plant in Batavia, Ontario, and paring down an assembly plant in St. Thomas, Ontario, so 5300 Canadian workers would lose their jobs.

Rudi wanted to introduce himself to the new technologist, but he felt too shy and embarrassed to try.

SUBORDINATING CONJUNCTIONS

Subordinating conjunctions join clauses in complex sentences. They show the relationship between clauses. You will learn more about subordinating conjunctions in the section, Sentence Types.

The Common Subordinating Conjunctions

after	although	as	because
before	if	since	so that
though	unless	until	when
whenever	where	wherever	while

Examples:

Whenever my brother is in Las Vegas, he spends too much money.

Although boiling water can sometimes make it safe for drinking, a person must remember to keep the water boiling hard for at least 20 minutes.

Camelot is said to be the famous castle and home of King Arthur and his court, though the actual geographic site has never been found.

Ethylene is a hydrocarbon gas that is produced by fruits as they ripen.

CORRELATIVE CONJUNCTIONS

Correlative conjunctions are words that occur in pairs; they join word or groups of words that are equal.

Common Correlative Conjunctions

neither/nor	both/and	either/or	not only/but also

Examples:

Neither the bell nor the alarm could be heard outside the heavy doors of the building.

Either people had better stop talking so loudly in public on their cellphones, or the municipality threatens to create a noise bylaw to fine them.

Not only must the peppers be hot for salsa, but also the tomatoes must be juicy and ripe.

Exercise 16 Using Conjunctions

Make up sentences as directed below. Use a separate sheet of paper, and be prepared to share your answers.

1. Make up a sentence about car racing, and use the correlative conjunctions *either/or.*
2. Make up a sentence about banks, and use the coordinating conjunction *but.*
3. Make up a sentence about buying groceries, and use the subordinating conjunction *because.*

4. Make up a sentence about teachers, and use the subordinating conjunction *before*.
5. Make up a sentence about travel, and use the correlatives *not only/but also*.

CONJUNCTIVE ADVERBS

Some words are weak joiners and require semicolons to help them join sentence parts effectively. These are called **conjunctive adverbs**. Remember to use a semicolon in front of them and a comma after them in compound sentences.

Common Conjunction Adverbs

otherwise	however	consequently	thus
moreover	therefore	also	

Examples:

The student society was attempting to negotiate extra space on campus; however, they were unsuccessful.

Keeping sanitary is one way to prevent colds; therefore, wash your hands often during the day.

Prepositions

Prepositions are words that add detail of time and place to sentences. They are usually short words and are placed at the beginning of word groups called prepositional phrases. These phrases can act like adjectives or adverbs.

There are more than 50 prepositions in the English language; the list below provides the most common ones.

Common Prepositions

above	across	after	along	among	around
at	before	behind	below	beneath	beside
between	beyond	by	down	during	for
from	in	inside	into	near	of
on	outside	over	through	throughout	to
toward	under	up	with	within	without

Examples:

without proper sunlight
outside the camp
toward the campus cafeteria
over the rainbow
before the dawn
beneath the ocean

Exercise 17 Using Prepositions

Follow the instructions below. Use a separate sheet of paper, and be prepared to share your answers. You may put the prepositions into prepositional phrases.

1. Make up a sentence about bowling. Use the prepositions *toward* and *inside* in your sentence.
2. Make up a sentence about a dream. Use the prepositions *across* and *around* in your sentence.
3. Make up a sentence about a game. Use the prepositions *between* and *down* in your sentence.

Phrases and Clauses

PHRASES

Phrases are groups of words that can function in different ways, but they do not contain subject-verb sets. As discussed earlier, these phrases act as nouns, adjectives, or adverbs:

- Gerunds can be in phrases that function like nouns.
- Participles can be in phrases that function like adjectives.
- Infinitives can be in phrases that function like nouns, adjectives, or adverbs.
- Prepositions can also be in phrases that function as adjectives or adverbs.

Examples:

The girl with the dark, curly hair has won a scholarship to McGill.

(Modifies *girl*, so adjective prepositional phrase)

Time management helps us during stressful times.

(Modifies *helps*, so adverb prepositional phrase)

Prepositional phrases contain an object of the preposition, usually nouns but sometimes pronouns.

Examples:

of the treaty	during the afternoon	between the lines
about the report	across the bridge	throughout the day

The underlined words are objects of their prepositions; they answer "what?" to the prepositions. For example: Of what? Of the treaty. During what? During the afternoon, and so on.

APPOSITIVES

Appositives are phrases or sometimes just single words that describe the nouns or pronouns immediately in front of them. Appositives can help to identify the noun (restrictive), or they can merely add incidental information about the nouns they describe (nonrestrictive).

Examples:

Harry Hardstone, the coach of the Newfield Wingers, is an ex-wrestler.

(The appositive is nonrestrictive because the name already identifies the coach. Use commas around nonrestrictive or nonessential phrases or clauses).

My brother's son Truman is going to law school in Edmonton, Alberta.

(The appositive is restrictive because it indicates the person has more than one son. Of all the sons, Truman is the one going to law school.)

My brother's son, Truman, is going to law school in Edmonton, Alberta.

(The appositive is nonrestrictive because it indicates the person has only one son who happens to be named Truman. The nonrestrictive element requires commas around it.)

Exercise 18 Using Phrases

Follow the directions below. Be prepared to share your answers.

1. Make up a sentence about conversation. Use an adverb prepositional phrase.
2. Make up a sentence about water. Use an adjective prepositional phrase.
3. Make up a sentence about boots. Use a restrictive appositive phrase.
4. Make up a sentence about a book. Use a nonrestrictive appositive phrase.

CLAUSES

Clauses are groups of words containing subject-verb sets that are used to make up parts of sentences. A **main clause** can stand alone. It is sometimes called the *independent* or *principal clause*. A **dependent clause** cannot stand alone and relies on the main clause in a sentence to complete its meaning. Dependent clauses are also called subordinate clauses.

Clauses relate to one another in meaningful ways: they set up conditions, either spatial or temporal, and they also set up causal relationships. You use subordinating conjunctions (previously discussed in Conjunctions) to introduce a dependent or subordinate clause. If a dependent clause comes first in a sentence, use a comma after it.

Examples:

According to Statistics Canada, while "tourism spending reached $70.6 billion at current prices in 2007," Canadians accounted "for nearly four out of every five dollars."

(The highlighted area shows the main clause; the underlined clause is the dependent clause. The subordinating conjunction *while* expresses a temporal, simultaneous relationship between the clauses.)

The Canadian dollar appreciated during February 2008 against the Euro, the Japanese yen, and the British pound, although it lost some ground against the U.S. dollar.

(The main clause is highlighted; the dependent clause is underlined. The subordinating conjunction *although* sets up a causal relationship between the two clauses.)

Noun Clauses

Noun clauses are clauses that act like nouns. In other words, they can function as subjects, objects, or subject complements in sentences. However, they cannot stand alone. Noun clauses can begin with words like *that*, *if*, *how*, *what*, *when*, *where*, *whenever*, *wherever*, *which*, *who*, *whoever*, *whomever*, *whose*, and *why*.

Examples:

That he wanted to be president of the company was clear.

(Noun clause acting as subject.)

The writer knows that she can complete the work.

(Noun clause acting as object.)

The mystery is how he committed the crime.

(Noun clause acting as subject complement.)

Relative Clauses

Relative clauses begin with the **relative pronouns** *that*, *who*, *which*, *whose*, *whom*, and *where*. These clauses refer to specific nouns; they work like adjectives. Relative clauses can be restrictive (essential to clarifying the noun) or nonrestrictive (nonessential).

Examples:

Half of the households in Canada in 2005 returned expired medications to pharmacies and drop-off centres that provided them with hand-outs and disposal tips.

The police officer encouraged the angry drivers who had left their cars to calm down after they discovered that the freeway exit lanes had to be closed for an emergency.

This is the place that serves delicious homemade pasta.

The company whose logo was stolen declared bankruptcy in 2008.

Exercise 19 Using Clauses

Follow the instructions below and write on a separate sheet of paper. Be prepared to share your answers.

1. Make up a sentence about cycling. The sentence should have one dependent clause.
2. Make up a sentence about coffee. The sentence should contain one relative clause.
3. Make up a sentence about friendship. The sentence should contain one dependent clause that is a noun clause. Label how the noun clause is functioning in your sentence.

REVIEW TEST: PARTS OF SPEECH

Complete the following test to check out what you have learned about parts of speech. You will have to use a separate sheet of paper to write your sentences. Your instructor may ask to see your review test.

1. Underline all the nouns in this sentence. Then label the nouns as follows: concrete, abstract, proper, or common.

   Among all the Canadian provinces, Saskatchewan showed the strongest growth in population from 2007–2008 due to new jobs and an affordable housing market.

2. Draw an arrow from each pronoun to its antecedent in the following sentence:

   In 1845, Sir John Franklin and 128 crew members set out to explore the Northwest Passage; however, their Franklin Expedition failed, and they perished when they developed food poisoning from the lead in their tinned goods.

3. Underline the correct pronoun case in the following sentences:

   (We, Us) parents must become more involved in the education of our children if we want a strong and lasting relationship to develop between (us, we).

   The frivolous Hollywood star would lavish gifts on (whomever, whoever) called her beautiful and talented.

4. Make up a sentence about television, and use the past perfect tense.

   ____

   ____

   ____

5. Make up a sentence about napping, and use the future progressive tense.

   ____

   ____

   ____

6. Make up a sentence about rain, and use the past participle of *get.*

   ____

   ____

   ____

7. Change the passive voice in the following sentence to active voice.

   It was reported by the president of the college, Dr. Exeter Fallworthy, that no new student grants would be awarded in 2011 by the Awards and Scholarship Committee.

   ____

8. Make up a sentence about junk food. Use the indicative mood.

9. Make up a sentence about swimming. Use an infinitive acting as the subject in your sentence.

10. Make up a sentence about a lie. Your sentence should contain two adjectives and two adverbs.

11. Underline the correct form in the following sentence:

    Happiness may (well, good) be in the way we spend our lives and resources; either we spend them (bad, badly), or we spend them (well, good) in the service of others.

12. Make up a sentence about driving. Use the coordinating conjunction *and* in your sentence.

13. Make up a sentence about the beach. Use the word *when* as a subordinating conjunction in your sentence.

14. Make up a sentence about computers. Use one adverb prepositional phrase in your sentence.

15. Make up a sentence about a letter. Use a nonrestrictive appositive in your sentence.

____

____

____

16. Make up a sentence about cooking. Use a dependent clause in your sentence.

____

____

____

17. Make up a sentence about a movie. Use a relative clause in your sentence.

____

____

____

PART 2: SENTENCE PARTS

It is important to be able to identify the parts of sentences when you are editing your work or when you are reading difficult text. Grammar rules are based on sentence parts, so having this knowledge will help you avoid or edit out common grammatical errors, such as subject–verb agreement problems. Applying grammar knowledge to difficult sentences can often help you unlock their meaning when you are reading something complex.

Subjects and Predicates

Each English sentence has two principal parts: the **subject** and the **predicate**. The simple subject is the noun or pronoun that does the action. If the sentence does not express action, then the simple subject is what is being described in the sentence. The complete subject contains the simple subject and all its modifiers.

Example:

<u>Born in Newmarket, Ontario, Canadian comedian Jim Carrey</u> got his start at Yuk Yuk's in Toronto in 1979. (complete subject)

Born in Newmarket, Ontario, Canadian comedian <u>Jim Carrey</u> got his start at Yuk Yuk's in Toronto in 1979. (simple subject)

The simple predicate is the principal verb or verb phrase in the sentence. The complete predicate contains the principal verb and all its modifiers.

Example:

Another Canadian comedian, Martin Short, <u>was born in Hamilton, Ontario, received a social work degree from McMaster University, and kick-started his career with the Second City Improv troupe in 1977</u>. (complete predicate)

Another Canadian comedian, Martin Short, was born in Hamilton, Ontario, received a social work degree from McMaster University, and kick-started his career with the Second City Improv troupe in 1977. (simple predicate)

Sentences can have **compound** (more than one) subjects or predicates.

Examples:

John Candy, Eugene Levy, and Dave Thomas are all Canadian alumni of the sketch comedy series, *SCTV, Second City Television* from 1976–1984. (compound subjects)

During its run, SCTV received 15 Emmy nominations and won two for writing and for music. (simple compound predicates)

During its run, SCTV received 15 Emmy nominations and won two for writing and for music. (complete compound predicates)

Exercise 20 Identifying Subjects and Predicates

Underline the simple subjects and the simple predicates in the following sentences. Check your answers with the Answer Key.

1. The Circle of Chiefs is coming to inaugurate the new Aboriginal Sports Complex.
2. David Philips, a senior climatologist for Environment Canada, reports a 15 percent increase in rainfall in the Yukon during the past two years.
3. Adding nutmeg to pumpkin soup gives it a fresh, lightly spicy taste.

Exercise 21 Using Subjects and Predicates

Follow the directions below. Use a separate sheet of paper, and be prepared to share your answers.

1. Make up a sentence about cellphones. Include a compound subject in your sentence. Underline the complete subject.
2. Make up a sentence about computer networks. Include a compound predicate in your sentence. Underline the complete predicate.
3. Make up a sentence about parking lots. Underline the simple subject and the simple predicate.

Direct and Indirect Objects

Direct objects are nouns or pronouns that receive the action of the verb. They answer "what?" or "whom?" after **transitive** (action) **verbs**. Some sentences may contain compound direct objects. However, not all sentences contain objects. Remember that some verbs are *intransitive* (do not transfer action to objects) or *linking* (state of being).

Example:

On February 21, 2008, the prime minister of Canada, Stephen Harper, delivered a speech that stated Canada would continue its military mission in Afghanistan until 2011. (*speech* is the direct object of the verb *delivered; mission* is the direct object of the verb *would continue*. Each answers what? *delivered what? would continue what?*)

Indirect objects are nouns or pronouns placed before the direct objects in sentences. They express for whom or to whom the action is being done. Sentences may contain compound indirect objects, but some sentences may not contain indirect objects at all, depending on whether the verb is transitive or intransitive.

Examples:

Lily gave her daughter extra fruit in her lunch box.

(*Daughter* is the indirect object. It is for whom the action of giving is being done. *Fruit* is the direct object; it is what is being given.)

The stable hand fed the horses and the ponies apples and oats.

(*Horses* and *ponies* are the compound indirect objects. It is for whom the feeding took place. *Apples* and *oats* are the compound direct objects. It is what the animals were fed.)

Exercise 22 Using Direct and Indirect Objects

Follow the instructions below. Use a separate sheet of paper, and be prepared to share your answers.

1. Make up a sentence about reading. Include one direct object in your sentence.
2. Make up a sentence about work. Include one direct object and one indirect object in your sentence.
3. Make up a sentence about clothing. Include two direct objects in your sentence.

Subject Complements

Subject complements are words or phrases that complete the meaning of sentences. They come after linking verbs and help to describe or identify subjects.

Examples:

Newfoundland is rich with natural beauty, history, and culture.

Vicki is an experienced mountain-climber.

"Being green" appears to be a profitable marketing trend.

REVIEW TEST: SENTENCE PARTS

Try the review test to see what you have learned about sentence parts. Your instructor may ask to see your work.

1. Underline the complete subject in the following sentence:

   Confidence and effective preparation are necessary ingredients for making a good speech.

2. Underline the simple subject in the following sentence:

   The majority of Canadians do not want to see falling stock markets.

3. Underline the complete predicate in the following sentence:

   Serge drove his truck through the snowy mountain pass and skidded to a stop just outside the tunnel.

4. Underline the simple predicate in the following sentence:

   Despite the student protests, the administration will raise fees for residence to $13 000 annually.

5. Underline the simple compound subject in the following sentence:

   Popular among Jamaicans and other Caribbean islanders, jerk chicken and jerk pork have a sweet, spicy flavour and very tender meat.

6. Underline the simple compound predicate in the following sentence:

   In 2006, heritage sites in Canada such as history and science museums remained popular and generated over $1 billion in revenue.

7. Underline the direct object in the following sentence:

   Michael Ondaatje's novels explore issues of identity and transnational identities.

8. Underline the indirect object in the following sentence:

   Raita told her classmates a secret.

9. Underline the subject complement in the following sentence:

   Canada is a parliamentary democracy and a constitutional monarchy.

10. Make up a sentence about winter. Include two direct objects in your sentence. Underline the simple subject, and circle the simple predicate.

    ____

    ____

11. Make up a sentence about snoring. Include one subject complement. Underline the complete subject and the complete predicate.

    ____

    ____

PART 3: SENTENCE TYPES

In English grammar, you will find four types of sentences. Studying sentence types will increase your sentence style. It will also help you to become a better editor of your own and others' writing.

Simple Sentences

Simple sentences are one-idea sentences. They have one main clause only with no dependent clauses. They may contain compound subjects and compound predicates. Simple sentences are not necessarily short.

Examples:

The police department released a statement. (The complete subject is highlighted; the complete predicate is underlined.)

After six hours, the police department released a statement and answered questions from the press. (The complete subject is highlighted; the complete compound predicate is underlined. The two verbs are *released* and answered.)

Compound Sentences

Compound sentences are made up of two or more main clauses. They can be joined by **coordinating conjunctions** (see Conjunctions section) or by semicolons. Use a comma in front of the coordinating conjunction in a compound sentence.

Examples:

The Alberta Tar Sands have some of the richest oil reserves in the world, but it is difficult and expensive to extract the crude bitumen oil from the sand. (The comma and *but* join the two main clauses together.)

Some foods, such as brown rice and kale, can boost the immune system; however, they must be unprocessed and fresh. (The semicolon and the conjunctive adverb *however* join the parts of the sentence together.)

Complex Sentences

Complex sentences are made up of one main clause and two or more dependent clauses. You might wish to review the previous section, Conjunctions, to assist you with the following ideas about complex sentences.

How the dependent clauses relate to the main clause is what makes this type of sentence complex. They may relate by time or condition, or they may have a causal relationship between them. Subordinating conjunctions are used in complex sentences.

Examples:

Although bats make up 20 percent of mammals, almost 70 percent of bat species are insectivores. (The main clause is underlined; the dependent clause is highlighted. *Although* is the subordinating conjunction. Use a comma after the dependent clause if it comes first in the sentence.)

Making a dry wall stone fence requires no mortar because the builder uses the natural weight and shape of the stones to hold the fence in place.

Compound-Complex Sentences

Compound-complex sentences have two or more main clauses and one (and sometimes more) dependent clauses.

Examples:

Of Armenian-Egyptian heritage, Atom Egoyan is a remarkable Canadian director whose many films include *Ararat* (2002) and *Where the Truth Lies* (2005), and he is currently distinguished director in the Faculty of Arts and Science at the University of Toronto where he will be teaching until 2009. (The two main clauses are underlined; the two dependent clauses are highlighted.)

REVIEW TEST: SENTENCE TYPES

Complete the following review test to see what you have learned about sentence types. Your instructor may ask to see your review test.

1. Identify what type each of the following sentences is. Write your answer after the sentence.
   - NHL referees can receive annual salaries from $115 000 to $220 000 while referees in the NBA can garner between $90 000 to $225 000 per annum.
   - One suggestion for curing motion sickness is to look out the window of the moving vehicle, and to steady the nausea, the traveller can then fix on the horizon line.
   - Polar bears hunt a variety of seals and feed on the carcasses of whales.
   - Gulrez (2001) stated, "The important conclusion drawn from this study was that preservation of the skin pH may be important to control the bacterial count on the skin surface in patients of acne."
   - The Jack Frost Children's Winterfest occurs in Charlottetown, PEI, during February each year; however, the Carnaval de Québec with the illustrious Bonhomme Carnaval held in Québec City is the more famous.

   ____

   ____

   ____

2. Make up a compound-complex sentence about a party. Underline the main clauses. Highlight the dependent clauses.

   ____

   ____

   ____

3. Make up a complex sentence about dentists.

   ____

   ____

   ____

4. Make up a compound sentence about paying bills.

   ____

5. Make up a simple sentence about fireplaces.

PART 4: PUNCTUATION GUIDE

At one time, writing did not include punctuation, but with the advent of the printing press, things changed. Writing became confusing to readers without correct punctuation marks; therefore, experts began to standardize the use of punctuation in English. Periods, commas, semicolons, colons, apostrophes, dashes, and quotation marks then signalled specific, syntactical meaning to readers.

The following section is a guide to punctuation. Although in some writing cases you may find that correct punctuation does not matter to you, you must use conventional and correct punctuation in your academic writing. In this next section, you will learn the guidelines to the common uses of punctuation.

Commas

Commas are the most commonly used and yet misused pieces of punctuation. Follow the guidelines below.

1. Use commas to separate items in a series.

   The United States, New Zealand, Denmark, Australia, and Belgium are the top ice-cream producers in the world.

   Note: Use an Oxford or serial comma: that is, use a comma between the last two items in your list. Most experts agree that doing so helps to eliminate possible confusion in reading.

2. Use a comma before the coordinating conjunction in a compound sentence.

   Several of the teapots were from ancient China, but one came from the Spode porcelain factory in England.

3. Use a comma after the dependent clause in a complex sentence if the dependent clause comes first.

   If you keep your property clean, free of pet food and garbage, you will discourage black bears from making uninvited visits.

4. Use a comma in separating dates and addresses.

   Tilda can expect to receive the parcel from Brampton, Ontario, on September 8, 2009.

   Margaret Laurence was born on July 18, 1926, in Neepawa, Manitoba.

   However, if the date is written so that the day appears first, you do not need to use commas. You do not need a comma before a month and year if no day is mentioned.

You do not need a comma before a postal code.

WWI ended on 11 November 1918.

She broke her leg in August 2008.

The card was sent to Box 27, Plentiful, Alberta T4B 1Z1.

5. Use a comma after an introductory clause, phrase, or expression.

   Although Quebec City is beautiful, I prefer the excitement of Montreal.

   Without a doubt, Sherlock was always logical.

   Having missed his bus to the game, Newton decided to go home.

6. Use a comma to separate people's names from their title or credentials.

   John Ralston Saul, Ph.D., is famous for his essays.

   Maude Barlow, former Chair of the Council of Canadians, debated the topic, "Water as a Human Right" on CBC on March 24, 2008.

7. Use commas to set off nonessential or nonrestrictive phrases or clauses.

   David Miller, graduate of Harvard University and the University of Toronto, became mayor of Toronto in November 2003.

   The two household cleaners will, of course, explode if they are combined.

8. Use commas between a series of adjectives, especially when the adjectives can be written in any order. If you can say "and" between the adjectives, then you need to put commas between.

   The young curlers experienced exciting, wondrous, and tense times as they took part in the World Curling Championship held in Moncton, New Brunswick.

   The technician removed the damaged television cable from the wall connector.

9. Use a comma to separate tag questions.

   That was the best meal ever, wasn't it?

10. Use a comma after the introduction to someone's direct words.

    Pierre Elliott Trudeau said, "The state has no business in the bedrooms of the nation."

Semicolons

Semicolons (;) have only two main purposes.

1. Use a semicolon to link two main clauses when they are closely associated.

   Canada's immigration policies of the early 20th century changed dramatically; many immigrants came to Canada to farm and expanded the cultivated land by 329 percent in those early years.

2. Use a semicolon along with weak conjunctions, such as conjunctive adverbs. Use a comma after the conjunctive adverb.

   The bald eagle spends many months of the year on southern Vancouver Island; however, it can best be seen during the spring and the fall when salmon are abundant.

Television watchers should spend 30 minutes per day walking; otherwise, they may slowly put on weight without realizing it.

Colons

Use a colon in the following three situations.

1. Use a colon after a main clause if you intend to add a list, make a comment, or further explain what you have said in the first main clause.

   If people want to dye natural materials, such as linen, cotton or hemp, they should use reactive dyes: these dyes are brighter and can be used in cool water, thus preventing shrinkage.

   The best bargains at the local farmers' market today are vegetables: potatoes, turnips, carrots, and cabbages.

2. Use a colon after the address in a business letter.

   Dear Mr. Merchansy:

3. Use a colon between hour and minutes.

   The blueberry-pie-eating contest will begin at 10:45 on the dot, so everyone should be seated by 10:30.

Apostrophes

The most common use of apostrophes is to signal possession.

1. Use *'s* for possession with singular nouns.

   The opera singer's voice was powerful and moving.

2. Use *s'* for possession with nouns that form regular plurals.

   The opera singers' voices were powerful and moving.

3. Use *'s* for nouns that do not form regular plurals by adding s.

   <u>children's</u> books   <u>men's</u> clothing department

   <u>women's</u> studies   the <u>people's</u> rights

4. Use *'s* in a compound word that is singular.

   her sister-in-law's business (only one sister-in-law)

   Do not use apostrophes when you are merely pluralizing a word.

   Incorrect: All of the rabbit's were wandering around the campus and hospital grounds.

   Correct: All of the rabbits were wandering around the campus and hospital grounds.

   Incorrect: Some of the first-year zoology students' were studying the rabbits habits.

   Correct: Some of the first-year zoology students were studying the rabbits' habits.

Hyphens and Dashes

A **hyphen** is generally seen as a mark used for spelling purposes.

USING HYPHENS IN SPELLING

1. Use a hyphen when two words are used as an adjective and are placed before a noun.

   air-borne diseases　　well-known recipe
   red-brown hair　　dewy-eyed youth

2. Use a hyphen when you are using two numbers to signify a unit

   thirty-three-foot long boat　　twenty-nine people

3. Use a hyphen at the end of a line to show the syllable break in a word.

   Many of the account executive were concerned about the letter coming out of the president's office.

USING DASHES

Dashes, on the other hand, are viewed as marks of punctuation. An **em dash** consists of two dashes placed together. When you are typing and want an em dash, type two hyphens and then the next word. The software program will read this as an em dash.

Use a dash as you would use parentheses in order to interrupt or add emphasis to a main clause. However, do not overuse dashes. Most experts agree that in academic writing, it is preferable for you to use commas rather than dashes.

The starling had made its way across the lawn—it had seen the cat—yet was determined to claim its prize.

Many of the applicants—middle-aged people, mostly—looked desperate.

Quotation Marks

Use **quotation marks** to indicate direct speech.

In an online interview with Jeffrey Brown on June 28, 2006, for *PBS Online NewsHour*, Leonard Cohen said, "If I knew where the good songs come from, I'd go there more often."

Place the period inside the closing quotation mark unless you are using APA or MLA.

REVIEW TEST: PUNCTUATION

Complete the following review test to see what you have learned in the punctuation section. Your instructor may ask to see your work.

1. Add commas to the following sentence:

   The harvester ant the pavement ant the wood ant and the large carpenter ant are all members of the formicidae family.

2. Add commas and semicolons to the following sentence:

   According to a Yahoo Canada survey respondents voted the star fruit as the most unusual fruit other votes included the kiwi kumquat and ugli as being the strangest.

3. Add colons and commas to the following sentence:

   It is difficult to administer oral medications to cats veterinarians suggest that an owner position the cat on a table with a slick surface wrap the cat in a towel and tip its head back.

4. Add apostrophes to the following sentence:

   My friends brother-in-laws car won a prize at Calgarys Classic Car Festival.

5. Add dashes to the following sentence:

   Learning to play chess well most people don't simply have the patience takes discipline and motivation.

6. Add quotation marks and commas to the following sentence:

   Robertson Davies once remarked Authors like cats because they are such quiet lovable wise creatures and cats like authors for the same reasons (*Toronto Daily Star*, 21 Nov 1959).

7. Make up a sentence about music. Use one comma, one apostrophe, and one dash in your sentence.

   ____

   ____

   ____

8. Make up a sentence about a spy. Use one quotation and one comma in your sentence.

   ____

   ____

   ____

9. Make up a sentence about pies. Use one colon and one apostrophe in your sentence.

   ____

   ____

   ____

10. Make up a sentence about what you enjoy about summer. Use one semicolon and two commas in your sentence.

   ____

   ____

   ____

CHECKOUT

Here are some of the ideas you will take away with you after you have completed the chapter:

1. Having a basic knowledge of English grammar is important when you have to edit your papers for courses.
2. Having a good foundation in English grammar will help make your writing more accurate.
3. Being able to edit your work or the work of others is an asset in the workplace.
4. Good editing and proofreading skills depend on your having a good foundation in English grammar and mechanics.

Mastering the concepts in this chapter will also help you develop and apply the following employability skills highlighted by the Conference Board of Canada in *Employability Skills 2000+*:

Communicate

- write and speak so others pay attention and understand
- use relevant scientific, technological and mathematical knowledge and skills to explain or clarify ideas

Be Adaptable

- learn from your mistakes and accept feedback

Learn Continuously

- set your own learning goals

Work with Others

- understand and work within the dynamics of a group

Participate in Projects & Tasks

- work to agreed quality standards and specifications

Source: Adapted from *Employability Skills 2000+* Brochure E/F (Ottawa: The Conference Board of Canada, 2000).

chapter 18

Developing a Vocabulary for College

Chapter Objectives

After completing this chapter you will be able to

1. develop a strong and varied vocabulary to achieve better results in your writing;
2. use context clues and basic word parts to help develop your vocabulary and predict the meaning of a new word;
3. understand many English words when you know common Greek or Latin roots;
4. use your knowledge of prefix and suffix meanings along with the meaning of a root word to figure out the meaning of an unfamiliar vocabulary word.

INTRODUCTION

Many studies have concluded that students who develop strong and varied vocabularies tend to achieve better results in papers, exams, and overall post-secondary work. Instructors and professors can be heard to say, "If only my students had more powerful vocabularies, they would be better able to express themselves in clear and concise ways."

Having a robust vocabulary will become more and more important in your professional life, too. Most professionals have to write reports, emails, letters, and summaries; they must also give presentations. In each of these facets of their work, vocabulary takes a predominant role. However, most professional people have learned to develop their word power; they know powerful vocabularies are acquired by dint of awareness and effort. You, too, must develop your vocabulary for college or university and for the communication demands of your career.

This chapter will provide you with two strategies to assist you in your vocabulary development: using context clues and learning some basic word parts. These two strategies will be extremely helpful to you in your language learning and writing development for all your coursework. In addition, you will expand these strategies the more you apply them to new situations.

As you experience language, you become more familiar with commonly used terms of vocabulary. You also gain an understanding of the structure of the language and how ideas are or can be organized. Through the knowledge of structure comes meaning. Also, your experience helps in another way: you build up strategies you can use when you don't understand or "get" the meaning.

Building strategies also means building learning independence. The more you can rely on your own learning strategies and language knowledge, the less you will have to depend on anyone or anything else.

Sometimes learning to improve your language involves making guesses, and guesses gleaned from strategies are more likely to be correct. For example, many times you may not know the exact meaning of a word, but if you predict the meaning of a word because you have studied the word's context clues, you will probably be right.

DEVELOPING THE WORD HABIT

1. Get in every available moment of language experience you can. You should always have a book with you to read. You should take advantage of every opportunity you have to express yourself in writing or in spoken language. In other words, learn to read by all of these methods, but reading means reading! Read the newspaper or parts of it every day. Carry a pocket book with you wherever you go. While you wait for the bus, read. While you wait for your groceries to be checked out, read. While you are waiting for an appointment, read. Instead of watching television for an hour every day, read. Go to the library. Visit second-hand bookstores. Make word gathering and reading a good habit. At first, this will seem like a chore, but the more you read, the easier it will be! Talk to someone about something interesting you have read or are reading. Discuss these ideas.
2. Work at developing the word habit. Your good habits rub off on others, just as well as bad ones do. If you have children, you will be modelling the word habit. Because you read every day, your children will watch you. Soon, they will become interested in reading, too. It is very important that your children become readers by habit. Surrounding you and your family with a reading atmosphere is crucial.
3. Learn strategies. This chapter will teach you some, but you must develop some of your own. Constantly using the dictionary to translate or define word meanings is not very efficient. Don't always use your dictionary; if you do, you are not thinking about what you are reading.
4. Learn to be a good "guesser." Informed and careful guessing can teach you a lot. This chapter will encourage you to guess and predict the meanings of words.
5. Try to enjoy the word habit. Try to gather at least some new words every day through your reading and courses. Share your new words with people at home. Use them in conversation. Try using some new words every time you write.

USING CONTEXT TO GET MEANING

Suppose someone said the following to you:

"I don't really think people in government are doing enough for single mothers. They don't provide enough good daycare centres for the children and training opportunities for the parents. They seem to think these single mothers are lazy and spoiled individuals."

Imagine that someone else walks into the room and only hears the last few words this person has said: " . . . these single mothers are lazy and spoiled individuals." The second person may be very surprised by what she has just heard. She would probably feel offended, particularly if she is a single mom herself.

But what has really happened here? How has the meaning changed? Why has the meaning changed?

The problem described has occurred because the last words were heard out of context. In other words, the listener has heard only the last few words but has not heard the speaker's whole statement. What surrounded these last words is missing.

When we say something is "out of context," we mean that something has been pulled from its surroundings. Most of the time we need to look at the whole set of remarks in order to gain a fair interpretation.

Context gives us meaning. You look at the surroundings in order to understand. As a reader and thinker, this is what you do, too—you read what is surrounding a word, a phrase, a paragraph, or a situation in order to pick up meaning clues.

Suppose that you saw *incognito* by itself. Could you tell what the word means? Since there is no context, no clues to meaning are available.

Now suppose you saw the word in a sentence:

> Geraldo is incognito.

Does the sentence help much? Again, there is not much context or surroundings to help you with the meaning of the word. This sentence is not a very good example; it is much too vague. Fortunately, writers will usually provide much more expansive information; therefore, since it is not practical to look up every word you do not know in the dictionary, keep reading—more clues may be on their way!

Better Example Sentence:

> Geraldo wears dark glasses and a rain hat when he wants to be incognito because he is constantly being pestered by the press.

Write down what you think *incognito* means in the sentence above. Use the context, not your dictionary.

Incognito means ____.

Now check your answer against this definition:

Incognito means your identity is kept secret.

Do you think you understand how context works in giving you the meaning? Let's look at the better example sentence again:

> Geraldo wears dark glasses and a rain hat when he wants to be incognito because he is constantly being pestered by the press.

How did you tell what *incognito* means without using a dictionary?

- Clue one: wears dark glasses and a rain hat.
- Clue two: when he wants to be in a different state—incognito.
- Clue three: constantly being pestered by the press.

When people do not want to be pestered, they will try ways to make themselves unrecognizable—wearing dark glasses and a rain hat might accomplish that! Putting the clues together gives you a better impression of what a word like *incognito* might mean. So, even if you did not understand the exact meaning of *incognito*, you can still understand the passage by continuing to read it and figuring out words as you go. Thus when you are reading, you can often get further explanation from inside a passage itself. Keep reading, looking for clues.

Writers use a variety of context clues to help their readers get the meaning.

Explanation as a Context Clue

As you've just seen, sometimes you can gain lots of meaning about words by reading the entire sentence or passage and putting different clues together.

Exercise 1 Explanation as a Context Clue

Here are some more context puzzles for you to try. Do not use a dictionary. Try to get the meaning of the underlined words by picking up clues (further explanation) that each passage gives you. Check your answers with the Answer Key.

1. Most people tend to mull over difficult decisions. They may spend many long hours or days thinking about the various sides to the issue before their minds are finally made up.

   mull means ______________________________

2. The parquet floor of the palace was beautiful. Different colours and pieces of marble and various precious stones were inlaid to form an intricate pattern.

   parquet means ______________________________

3. The Douglas fir is the hallmark of the Canadian West Coast. The magnificent tree is easily distinguished by any visitor to this region.

   hallmark means ______________________________

Look back at the three passages. Do you see how you can get the meaning by the context? Do you see how the context supplies you with explanations? Do you see that you do not have to use a dictionary?

Exercise 2 More Explanation as a Context Clue

Try these. Read each one. Write down what you think the underlined words mean, but do not use your dictionary. Use context! Check your answers with the Answer Key.

1. The old man had a peculiar gait. He would pull one foot forward as he walked and would pull his shoulders down in a kind of shrug.

   gait means ______________________________

2. Cellulose is the chief part of the cell wall of plants. It is a white, spongy substance that protects the plant cell from the outside.

   cellulose means ______________________________

3. My brother brought home a celestial map from the observatory. It showed the phases of the moon, the position of the planets, and what was visible in the skies during July and August.

   celestial means ____________________

4. Sometimes I crave chocolate. Then I must rush to the store and buy my favourite kind to satisfy myself.

   crave means ____________________

5. The Conservatives tried to filibuster when a new bill, proposed by the Liberals, came up for reading in Parliament; however, the Speaker of the House called them to order.

   filibuster means ____________________

6. The jejune speech made by the Leader of the Opposition put me to sleep in the press box.

   jejune means ____________________

7. Rodney is a complete egoist. All he talks about is himself.

   egoist means ____________________

8. Is Canada really a utopia? Do all Canadians enjoy a full, satisfying life without problems or woe?

   utopia means ____________________

9. The commander of the platoon ordered his company to stop at the bridge. The group of men then stood in rows as the leader explained the battle strategy.

   platoon means ____________________

10. Bigfoot rudely hammered on the service counter and shouted at the attendant; the manager knew that Bigfoot's bellicose behaviour was going to lead to trouble.

    bellicose means ____________________

After you have checked your answers, go back and read each passage again. Can you now get the meaning from context?

You can see that often further explanation in a passage (in context) will be given to help you get the meaning or meanings of words. Context can give meaning in other ways besides explanation.

Restatement as a Context Clue

Sometimes writers of textbooks or technical articles will use other words that mean the same thing right after a term is introduced.

Example:

Fissures, or deep grooves, frequently occur between the toes as a result of dryness and cracking of the skin.

You can tell what fissures means by looking at the words that follow it.

Example:

The nanny or nursemaid wheeled the baby in its carriage.

You can tell from the example sentence above a nanny is a nursemaid—one who looks after children.

Writers restate or use other words to explain an idea, a phrase, or a term. The **restatement** usually appears right after the new term is introduced. You will see restatement used in nursing, dental hygiene, biology, chemistry, psychology, and many other types of textbooks and articles. Sometimes writers will provide an example of the term.

Example as a Context Clue

Sometimes writers give an example rather than a restatement or explanation of a term. The example provides you with help in understanding the term.

Example:

Goldenseal, a medicinal herb, is used in naturopathic remedies to help relieve symptoms of influenza and the common cold.

You can tell from the example that some herbs, like goldenseal, have properties that are used in natural medicine.

Example:

Drug toxicity (deleterious effects of a drug on an organism or tissue) results from overdosage, ingestion of a drug intended for external use, and buildup of the drug in the blood because of impaired metabolism or excretion (cumulative effect). Some toxic effects are apparent immediately; some are not apparent for weeks or months. Fortunately, most drug toxicity can be avoided if careful attention is paid to dosage and by monitoring for toxicity. An example of a toxic effect is liver failure due to the cumulative effect of methotrexate (antimetabolite that is used to treat arthritis and certain types of cancer).

Source: Barbara Kozier, Glenora Erb, and Audery Jean Berman, Fundamentals of Nursing: The Nature of Nursing Practice in Canada, *Canadian Edition (Toronto: Prentice-Hall, 2000) 611.*

The passage about drug toxicity is difficult to read because there are a number of health terms introduced that may be unfamiliar to you. Notice that the writer provides two types of context clues: the first is restatement. The writer first explains what drug toxicity is. Can you find what she says?

You will see right after the term *drug toxicity* these words: "deleterious effects of a drug on an organism or tissue." This is a restatement and tells you exactly what drug toxicity means.

Further along in the passage, you will see that the writer has provided an example. She says, "An example of a toxic effect is liver failure due to the cumulative effect of methotrexate (antimetabolite that is used to treat arthritis and certain types of cancer)." The writer explains what the term *drug toxicity* means; this is the first context clue—restatement. Then the writer gives an example of drug toxicity; this is the second type of context clue—example.

Exercise 3 Using Two Types of Context Clues

Read each of the following passages; do not use a dictionary. Guess what each of the underlined words means by using context to help with meaning. Write down your guesses. Check them with the Answer Key.

1. The visitor was told to wait in the vestibule. This room was not the usual pleasant entrance at all, but was dark and dank smelling.

   vestibule means ______________________________

2. Citrus fruits, such as lemons and oranges, contain Vitamins C and A.

   citrus means ______________________________

3. After the argument, the child was sullen. She sat in the corner of the room and looked moodily out the window.

   sullen means ______________________________

4. The cowboy would wear a neckerchief. When the winds howled and the dust blew, he would wrap it round his face to protect his breathing from the sand in the air.

   neckerchief means ______________________________

5. The police will impound your car if it is left parked on the streets for too long. You will then have to find out where it has been locked up and how much the fine is to get it back.

   impound means ______________________________

6. My brother is a very hospitable person. Whenever you visit him, he makes you feel very welcome and right at home.

   hospitable means ______________________________

7. A finger food like a hot dog or taco is the most popular item served in North American restaurants. It seems most people enjoy the convenience of being able to get a fast snack that they can carry away with them.

   finger food means ______________________________

8. The victim of the car crash received some serious lacerations. This was due to the flying glass from the broken windshield.

   lacerations means ______________________________

9. The band played a medley or mixture of songs that the dancers had requested.

   medley means ______________________________

10. The precipitation or rainfall for our region during the past two months has been seven centimetres.

    precipitation means ______________________________

11. Tomi was mortified! He was standing at the head of a long lineup of people, with a huge order of groceries waiting to be checked out, and he had forgotten his money at home!

    mortified means ______________________________

12. Since Mrs. Minda was a proponent of green space in the city, she spoke vehemently against the city's proposed removal of the small play park for toddlers in favour of a fast-food drive-in restaurant.

    vehemently means ______________________________

13. The flowers I bought are perennials. I'm glad because I needn't replant them every season.

    perennials means ______________________________

14. The argument was over a trivial matter. It seemed ridiculous that adults could fight over such an unimportant thing.

    trivial means ______________________________

15. The sight we saw was ghastly! It was so horrible that we could not bear to look at it.

    ghastly means ______________________________

DEVELOPING VOCABULARY THROUGH KNOWING WORD PARTS

Another strategy for developing vocabulary is to learn about word parts. Sometimes you can "crack" the meanings of words by knowing what the meanings of the prefixes, suffixes, and roots are. This next section will teach you how to use the information about word parts in order to gain meaning and word power.

What Is a Root Word?

A **root word** is the base of a word; it carries the meaning. For example, in the word *reusable*, *use* is the root word because it is the base and it carries the meaning of the word. Most of the words in English are based on Latin or Greek roots, prefixes, or suffixes.

You can look for the meaning of a word by looking for its root meaning.

Examples:

information	Root word: inform
uninspiring	Root word: inspire
dislocation	Root word: locate
multi-dimensional	Root word: dimension
unspeakably	Root word: speak

COMMON ROOT WORDS AND THEIR MEANINGS

Remember that many English words have their origins in Latin or Greek. You don't need to take a course in Latin or ancient Greek, but learning common Greek or Latin roots will help you understand many English words. You will also notice you can use your knowledge of prefix and suffix meanings along with the meaning of a root word. The following chart contains common Latin or Greek root words, their meanings, and some example words containing the roots.

Common Root Words and Their Meanings

Root	Meaning	Example
aud	to hear	auditorium (a place where one hears something)
metre, meter	measure	centimetre (measured in units of 100)
chron	time	chronometer (something that measures time)
cede, ceed	go, move	recede (move back), proceed (move toward)
cred	believe	incredible (not able to be believed)
graph	to write	graphology (the study of writing)
dic	to say	dictation (something said)
ped, pod	foot	pedal (for the foot), podiatrist (one who practises on the foot)
card	heart	cardiac (having to do with the heart)
dent	tooth	trident (three-toothed)
neuron	nerve	neurology (the study of nerves)
psyche	mind	psychology (the study of the mind)
path	suffering	pathetic (inciting a feeling of suffering or pity)
mort	death	postmortem (after death)
phon	sound	telephone (a sound from far away)
rupt	to break	interrupt (to break between)
port	to carry	transport (to carry across)
pel	to push	propel (to push forward)
vert	to turn	revert (to turn back)
ego	I, self	egotist (one who thinks of self)
spect	to see or look	inspect (to look in)
pater	father	paternal (having to do with a father)
mater	mother	maternity (having to do with motherhood)
frater	brother	fraternity (brotherhood)
soror	sister	sorority (sisterhood)

Study the words on the root word chart. Read them over until you think you understand what each means. Then try the following exercise.

Exercise 4 Practice with Root Words in Context

Read each sentence group that follows. One word in each group has been underlined. Do not use a dictionary to do this exercise. After reading each group, answer the question that follows. Use your knowledge of word parts to put together a literal meaning for the underlined words. Check your answers with the Answer Key.

Example:

The court found him guilty of fratricide. He was sentenced to life imprisonment for the murder.

Fratricide means

1. the murder of a friend,
2. the murder of an uncle,
3. the murder of a father, or
4. the murder of a brother.

A. It is often easier to think about things in retrospect.

Retrospect means

1. consider in advance,
2. consider looking backward in time,
3. consider looking forward in time, or
4. not consider at all.

B. The letters were arranged in chronological order.

Chronological order means

1. alphabetical,
2. by name only,
3. time, or
4. amount.

C. Opening the windows will help to dispel the fumes from the cleaner.

Dispel means

1. push away,
2. push forward,
3. evaporate, or
4. push inside.

D. Creatures such as centipedes abound in my garden.

Centipedes means

1. insects that live to be 100,
2. insects without "feet,"
3. insects with 100 "feet," or
4. lying insects.

E. In some cultures, especially Russian, children are often given a patronymic in their names.

Patronymic means named after a

1. sister,
2. mother,
3. brother, or
4. father.

F. The researcher wanted to triangulate the results of her study.

Triangulate means to look at it from this number of directions:

1. three,
2. one,
3. four, or
4. two.

G. Some high-pitched sounds are inaudible to the human ear.

Inaudible means

1. loud,
2. not able to be understood,
3. not able to be heard, or
4. not able to be felt.

H. Because of the stress in society, the type of food people eat, obesity, and the lack of exercise, cardiologists are concerned about the increase in myocardial infarctions.

Cardiologists study

1. the nerves,
2. the heart,
3. the lungs, or
4. the mind.

I. The water will recede during the summer months.

Recede means

1. to move forward,
2. to move back,
3. to move with force, or
4. to stay still.

J. Her <u>podiatrist</u> looks after Lou's plantar fascitis.

Podiatrist means

1. a foot specialist,
2. a heart specialist,
3. a brain specialist, or
4. an internist.

K. The <u>propeller</u> on the boat needed to be repaired.

A propeller is used to

1. push forward,
2. push back,
3. pull back, or
4. not push or pull.

L. Baroque music contains many <u>contrapuntal</u> harmonies.

Contrapuntal means going

1. against,
2. parallel,
3. beside, or
4. with.

M. A <u>psychopathic</u> disease is difficult to treat and cure.

A psychopathic disease is one connected with

1. the lungs,
2. the eye,
3. the mind, or
4. children.

N. Most people dislike Randolph because he is too <u>egocentric</u>.

People do not like Randolph because

1. he talks too much,
2. he talks too softly,
3. he talks about himself too much, or
4. he talks to himself.

O. I do not give <u>credence</u> to his story.

Credence means

1. belief,

2. ideas,
3. attention, or
4. help.

P. Do you doubt that <u>introspection</u> is good for your personal development?

Introspection means examining the

1. inside,
2. outside,
3. angles, or
4. psyche.

Q. The verb *apologize* is <u>intransitive</u>.

Intransitive verbs do not take objects

1. inside,
2. outside,
3. through, or
4. across.

R. My Uncle Ratchit <u>preceded</u> my father in the family business.

Preceded means that Uncle Ratchit

1. worked before my father,
2. worked after my father,
3. worked at the same time as my father, or
4. stole from my father.

S. Games such as basketball, hockey, and football are fantastic <u>spectator</u> sports.

Spectator means these games are

1. fun to play,
2. fun to watch,
3. fun to talk about, or
4. fun to listen to.

T. Many universities have <u>sorority</u> clubs.

These clubs would be

1. for men,
2. for children,
3. for women, or
4. for everyone.

U. They will not accept postdated cheques for your payment.

A cheque that is postdated is dated

1. before the day you are writing it,
2. the same day you are writing it,
3. incorrectly, or
4. after the day you are writing it.

V. Dinosaurs and huge birdlike creatures existed during prehistoric times.

Prehistoric means dinosaurs lived

1. after history was written down,
2. during the time history was written down,
3. before the time history was written down, or
4. while history was being written down.

Exercise 5 Recognizing Root Words

Read the words below. Then decide what the root word of each is. Write the root word on the line. Check your answers with the Answer Key.

Word	Root Word
1. unemployment	______
2. fragility	______
3. redefine	______
4. answered	______
5. unpicked	______
6. building	______
7. forgetful	______
8. children	______
9. unchain	______
10. mistreat	______
11. discharged	______
12. protection	______
13. rocky	______
14. uncomfortable	______
15. spoonful	______
16. disadvantage	______
17. reviewing	______
18. rewritten	______
19. manager	______
20. brownish	______

21. unbendable ____________________
22. worthless ____________________
23. disappointment ____________________
24. unpainted ____________________
25. valuable ____________________

What Are Prefixes and Suffixes?

Did you notice that the root parts of the words in the exercise above have additions to them? The elements added to the beginnings or ends of root words can have a drastic effect on the meanings of the roots. They can become positive or negative; they can turn into adjectives or adverbs; they can become more or less—all because of the addition of prefixes and suffixes.

A part added to the front of a root or base word is called a **prefix**. Every prefix has a special meaning.

Examples:

(un)zip—*un* is the prefix added to the root word *zip*.

(mis)place—*mis* is the prefix added to the root word *place*.

The part added to the end of a root or base word is called a **suffix**. Every suffix also has a special meaning that you will learn about.

Examples:

teach(able)—*able* is the suffix added to the root word *teach*.

price(less)—*less* is the suffix added to the root word *price*.

COMMON SUFFIXES AND THEIR MEANINGS

You will enhance your word study by learning the meanings of some common suffixes. Remember that a suffix also has meaning and that when a suffix is added to a root word, the meaning of the whole word changes.

Common Suffixes and Their Meanings

Common Suffix	Meaning	Example Word
able (adj.)	able to (capable of doing the root)	understandable
ible (adj.)	able to (capable of doing the root)	reversible
er, or (noun)	one who (does the root)	teacher, dictator
ful (adj.)	full of (the root)	hopeful
ish (adj.)	like (the root)	childish
ish (adj.)	close to (the root)	sevenish
ist (noun)	one who (does the root)	psychologist
less (adj.)	without (the root)	worthless
logy (noun)	the study of something	biology
ous (adj.)	qualities of the root	nervous

You can figure out the *literal* meaning of the words by knowing what each suffix means. You do not need to look these words up in a dictionary. A **literal meaning** is the explicit or specific meaning.

Look at the suffixes in the following, and think about how they are used according to their meanings. Suppose you saw the example words in sentences and knew the meanings of their roots and suffixes. It would be quite easy to understand the meaning of the words by working out the meaning of their parts.

1. It is understandable why he resigned.

   understandable—able to understand (able as a suffix means capable of doing the root—capable of being understood, in other words)

2. The tablecloth is reversible.

   reversible—able to be reversed (ible as a suffix means capable of doing the root—capable of being reversed, in other words)

3. The teacher wrote a note on the whiteboard.

   teacher—one who teaches (er, and sometimes the suffix or, means one who does the root—one who teaches)

   The dictator ruled the small island country.

   dictator—one who dictates

4. We are hopeful of getting the job.

   hopeful—full of hope (ful as a suffix means full of the root—full of hope)

5. She made a childish gesture.

   childish—like a child (ish means like the root—like a child)

6. I will meet you about sevenish.

   sevenish—close to or around seven (ish means around the root—around seven)

7. The psychologist gave a lecture on learning.

   psychologist—one who practises psychology (ist means one who does or practises the root—one who does or practises psychology)

8. This chair is not a French antique; it's a replica, so it is virtually worthless.

   worthless—without worth (less as a suffix means without the root—without worth)

9. We will study the biology of cells later in our human physics course.

   biology—the study of living things (logy means the study of the root and bios means life in Latin, so the study of life or living things)

10. Loud noises make me nervous.

    nervous—full of nerves (ous means having the quality of the root—qualities to do with nerves—full of nerves)

Exercise 6 Practice with Suffixes

Study the suffix chart above. Think about meanings of the suffixes in the following words. After you have done that, underline each suffix, then tell what each word means. Do not use a dictionary. Check your answers with the Answer Key.

Example:

adaptable: capable of adapting or being able to adapt

1. enjoyable: ______
2. successor: ______
3. eventful: ______
4. babyish: ______
5. machinist: ______
6. breathless: ______
7. mountainous: ______
8. disposable: ______
9. clownish: ______
10. adapter: ______
11. bleachable: ______
12. plentiful: ______
13. snobbish: ______
14. hypnotist: ______
15. flexible: ______
16. cordless: ______
17. cheerless: ______
18. monstrous:______
19. blondish: ______
20. originator: ______

Exercise 7 More Practice with Suffixes

In this next exercise, the literal meaning is given to you. You create the word needed by taking the root word and adding the correct suffix. Check your answers with the Answer Key.

Example:

able to be accepted; capable of being accepted: <u>acceptable</u>

Hint: Remember to use the root by itself before you add any suffixes. In this example, *accept* is the root word for *accepted.*

1. full of hate: ______________________
2. like a bear: ______________________
3. one who calls: ______________________
4. able to be believed: ______________________
5. full of tears: ______________________
6. able to be bleached: ______________________
7. room that is full: ______________________
8. able to break: ______________________
9. full of beauty: ______________________
10. without fear: ______________________
11. the study of technical things: ______________________
12. without limit: ______________________
13. the study of bacteria: ______________________
14. without a branch: ______________________
15. full of disaster: ______________________
16. one who plays the piano: ______________________
17. full of help: ______________________
18. like a sheep: ______________________
19. close to green: ______________________
20. having the qualities of ambition: ______________________
21. able to bend: ______________________
22. one who separates: ______________________
23. close to ten: ______________________
24. able to employ: ______________________
25. without use: ______________________
26. without harm: ______________________
27. full of care: ______________________
28. one who practises style: ______________________
29. having the qualities of caution: ______________________
30. having the qualities of poison: ______________________

COMMON PREFIXES AND THEIR MEANINGS

You will recall that a prefix is a part added to the front of a root word. When a prefix is added to a root word, the meaning of the whole word changes.

Following is a list of common prefixes. You will learn the meaning of each common prefix. An example word for each prefix is also listed.

Common Prefixes and Their Meanings

Common Prefix	Meaning	Example Word
un	not	unlockable (not able to be locked)
in	not	incorrect (not correct)
im	not	impossible (not possible)
non	not	nontoxic (not toxic or poisonous)
mis	done wrong or badly	misfire (fires badly)
pro	for, forward	propel (pushes forward)
anti	against	antifreeze (works against freezing)
counter	against	counteract (act against)
contra	against	contradict (say against)
pre	before	preview (view before)
post	after	postmortem (after death)
		postwar (after war)
retro	backward	retrospect (looking backward)
inter	between	international (between nations)
trans	across	transport (port or carry across)
re	back or again	redo (do again)
		return (turn back)
dis	away, away from	discomfort (away from comfort)
co	together or with	co-operate (operate together)
tele	far	telephone (far sound)

Number Prefixes

Prefix	Meaning	Example Word
uni	one	unicycle (one cycle)
mono	one	monologue (speech for one person)
tri	three	tricycle (three cycle)
cent	100	century (one hundred years)

Exercise 8 Practice with Prefixes

In each of the following words:

1. Underline the root word.
2. Put parentheses around the prefix.
3. Tell what the literal meaning is.

Check your answers with the Answer Key.

Example:

(anti)poverty = against poverty

1. unimportant = ______
2. pronoun = ______
3. counterattack = ______
4. misinform = ______
5. antisocial = ______
6. nonprofit = ______
7. preschool = ______
8. intercollege = ______
9. prefix = ______
10. counterclockwise = ______
11. transplant = ______
12. unkind = ______
13. co-editor = ______
14. unskilled = ______

Exercise 9 More Practice with Prefixes

Follow the same directions as you did in the previous practice. Remember to put parentheses ( ) around prefixes (and suffixes, if applicable) and to underline the root word. Check your answers with the Answer Key.

Example:

(un)law(ful) = not full of the law

1. unicycle = ______
2. co-chairperson = ______
3. monosyllable = ______
4. pre-employment = ______
5. interdepend = ______
6. counterbalance = ______
7. telephoto = ______
8. prejudge = ______
9. postdate = ______

10. unnecessary = ______________________________

11. co-exist = ______________________________

12. uniform = ______________________________

13. unilingual = ______________________________

14. trilingual = ______________________________

15. unthinkable = ______________________________

REVIEW TEST

Part 1: Context

Try the following review test. It will help you assess what you have learned from the chapter. Be prepared to share your responses with others in the class.

Read each passage. Use context to help you get the meanings of the underlined words. You are not allowed to use a dictionary.

1. After a long illness, the woman was taken to a private hospital in the country. There she could convalesce in the quiet atmosphere and clean air.

   convalesce means ______________________________

2. Using the metric system of measurement is often a hindrance to those who are used to the imperial system. It seems to be awkward and time consuming to switch from one to the other.

   hindrance means ______________________________

3. The lawn tractor cut a swath through the long overgrown grasses.

   swath means ______________________________

4. The shock of the situation made his explanations inarticulate; we could not understand what he was trying to tell us.

   inarticulate means ______________________________

5. The hot sun beat down on the delicate tropical plant. Because it was unused to the bright light and intense heat, its leaves began to wither.

   wither means ______________________________

Part 2: Prefixes, suffixes, roots

Underline the root words in the following words.

1. untitled
2. rearrangement

3. dislike
4. forceful
5. homeless

Part 3: Word part meanings

Give meanings for the following prefixes, suffixes, and roots. Do not use a dictionary.

Example:
non: _not_

1. tri: __________
2. ful: __________
3. uni: __________
4. metre, meter: __________
5. psyche: __________
6. graph: __________
7. soror: __________
8. co: __________
9. mono: __________
10. cred: __________

Part 4: Putting parts together for new meaning

Put together what you know about prefixes, suffixes, and roots to answer these questions. Underline the correct answers. Do not use a dictionary.

1. Mannie gave Donna his excuse for being late, but Donna seemed <u>incredulous</u>. This means
   a. Donna believed him,
   b. Donna ignored him,
   c. Donna did not believe him, or
   d. Donna did not ignore him.
2. An <u>audiometer</u> measures
   a. the heart,
   b. the lungs,
   c. the hearing, or
   d. vision.

3. If you study the <u>mortality</u> rate among infants of a culture, you study
   a. their growth rate,
   b. what they eat,
   c. how they live, or
   d. their death rate.
4. If a smell <u>repels</u> you, you are
   a. attracted to it,
   b. pushed away by it,
   c. interested in it, or
   d. made unhappy by it.
5. <u>Psychosomatic</u> diseases begin in
   a. the heart,
   b. the lungs,
   c. the nerves, or
   d. the mind.
6. The <u>phonetic</u> system of a language is its system of
   a. sounds,
   b. grammar,
   c. meaning, or
   d. spelling.
7. The Greeks and Romans believed their gods were <u>immortal</u>. This means they believed their gods
   a. never lied,
   b. never died,
   c. never lived, or
   d. never suspected.
8. The young mother is experiencing <u>postpartum</u> depression. This means she is experiencing depression
   a. before her child's birth,
   b. after her child's birth,
   c. during her child's birth, or
   d. until her child's birth.

Bonus Exercise *Literal Meanings*

Use the charts on prefixes, suffixes, and root words to help you with this exercise. Answer the following questions. Do not use a dictionary.

Example:

Give a literal meaning for unthinkable.

not able to be thought of

1. Give a literal meaning for preoccupied.

2. Give a literal meaning for interdepartmental.

3. Give a literal meaning for monosyllable.

4. Give a literal meaning for pathology.

5. Give a literal meaning for audiology.

6. Give a literal meaning for preplan.

7. Give a literal meaning for postgraduate.

8. Give a literal meaning for co-chair.

9. Give a literal meaning for monotone.

10. Give a literal meaning for uniform.

11. Give a literal meaning for counterweight.

12. Give a literal meaning for discouragement.

13. Give a literal meaning for co-editor.

____

14. Give a literal meaning for interaction.

____

15. Give a literal meaning for postpaid.

____

CHECKOUT

Here are some of the ideas you will take away with you after you have completed the chapter:

1. Professional writers know powerful vocabularies are acquired.
2. Word gathering and reading are good habits that help build language skills.
3. Constantly using the dictionary to translate word meanings is not very efficient.
4. Try using some new words every time you write.
5. Always have a book with you to read.

Mastering the concepts in this chapter will also help you develop and apply the following employability skills highlighted by the Conference Board of Canada in *Employability Skills 2000+*:

Communicate

- read and understand information presented in a variety of forms

Think & Solve Problems

- be creative and innovative in exploring possible solutions

Learn Continuously

- be willing to continuously learn and grow

Participate in Projects & Tasks

- select and use appropriate tools and technology for a task or project

Source: Adapted from *Employability Skills 2000+* Brochure E/F (Ottawa: The Conference Board of Canada, 2000).

answer key

Answers to the review tests, some bonus exercises, comprehension questions, and critical comprehension questions are in the Instructor's Manual only.

Chapter 2: Writing as Process: Prewriting

EXERCISE 3: ***Purposes in Writing***

1. To explain, evaluate, or investigate; it could also be to convince
2. To explain, evaluate, or investigate
3. To describe; it could also be to narrate
4. To explain, evaluate, or investigate
5. To describe; it could also be to explain, evaluate, or investigate

EXERCISE 5: ***Identifying Tone***

1. Passage 1. Informal; humorous and optimistic—words like *strolling past*, *marvel*, *screaming shade of fuchsia* are positive and fun; it also has amusing examples; point of view is first person.
2. Formal tone; professional, businesslike, and precise—words like *retain*, *effective*, *skills*, *clearly*, *priorities*, *standard* all have to do with efficiency and delivering a professional service; point of view is third person, plural.
3. Informal, although a serious topic; caring and concerned—words like *teach*, *learning*, *reframe*, *empowered*, *feel*, *grieve*, *enhance and enrich*, *perceived* all have to do with thinking about behaviour in a compassionate way; the point of view is mixed—first paragraph is first person, plural; the second and third paragraphs are third person, plural.

Chapter 3: Writing Phases: Planning to Presentation

BONUS EXERCISE: **That *or* Which?**

1. that
2. which
3. that
4. that
5. which
6. that
7. which

Chapter 4: The Paragraph

BONUS EXERCISE: ***A Case of* Who *or* Whom**

1. whom
2. whom
3. who
4. who, who
5. who
6. whom
7. whom
8. whom
9. whom
10. who

Chapter 5: The Essay

BONUS EXERCISE: ***Avoiding Sexist Language***

Your answers might vary with the suggested answers below. Check with your instructor if you are unsure.

1. All people want the freedom to find happiness for themselves.
2. Most of the time, corporations try to find the best people for the job.
3. Everyone decided to vote with his or her own conscience.

4. Everybody should do what he or she can to help.
5. The reporters were trying to find out who was responsible and if the person was available for comment.

Chapter 7: Critical Skills: Evaluating

BONUS EXERCISE: ***The Subjective Tense***

Answers may vary.

1. I wish that Doris were kinder to me.
2. J.K. Ruck, supervisor of parking, requests that Bettina move her car to another parking spot.
3. The health authority wishes that all parents would have their infants immunized.
4. I wish the moon were made of green cheese!
5. The municipality requires that all farms under one hectare be licensed.

Chapter 9: Expository Writing

BONUS EXERCISE: ***Avoiding Double Negatives***

Answers may vary.

1. doesn't want anything
2. because I hardly have any
3. could scarcely walk
4. has been here barely a year
5. could not find anywhere

Chapter 12: Critical Skills: Researching

EXERCISE 1: ***Locating Resources***

Answers may vary.

1. reference or digital collections
2. periodicals or digital collections
3. books/textbooks or digital collections
4. digital collections, reference, or government publications
5. periodicals, books/textbooks, digital collections (e-journals)
6. special collections or digital collections
7. reference

Chapter 13: Writing the Research Paper

BONUS EXERCISE: ***Dropped Quotations***

Answers may vary.

1. dropped quotation
   Repair 1: As one expert suggested, "Biting, sudden shouting, and loud crying are not always symptoms of a tantrum" (Judi, 2004, p. 165). *(APA style)*
   Repair 2: Judi (2004) suggested, "Biting, sudden shouting, and loud crying are not always symptoms of a tantrum" (p. 165). *(APA style)*
2. dropped quotation
   Repair 1: According to some experts, gambling is on the increase since "from 2004–2006, gambling activities on the internet expanded by 400%" (Clarkson, 2006, p. 66). *(APA style)*
   Repair 2: Clarkson (2006) contended that "from 2004–2006, gambling activities on the internet expanded by 400%" (p. 66). *(APA style)*
3. dropped quotation
   Repair 1: Detective fiction has been popular for over 100 years, but some still insist the genre is the work of hobbyists. Summerside insists that "mystery writing is not a pastime—it is a calling" (75). *(MLA style)*
   Repair 2: Detective fiction has been popular for over 100 years, but some still insist the genre is the work of hobbyists. However, some experts insist that it is much more than that because "mystery writing is not a pastime—it is a calling" (Summerside 75). *(MLA style)*
4. dropped quotation
   Repair 1: The familiar natural world is disappearing. In its Department of Natural Resources' publication, "Preserving Nature" (2005), the Government of Canada has noted that "backyard birds are disappearing at the rate of 14% per year since 2003" (p. 9). *(APA style)*
   Repair 2: The familiar natural world is vanishing. As an example, some experts have noted that "backyard birds are disappearing at the rate of 14% per year since 2003" (Government of Canada, 2005, p. 9). *(APA style)*

Chapter 16: Editing and Style Notes

EXERCISE 1: Editing Sentences

1. As I drove up the ramp, I noticed a delicious-looking chocolate cake in the bakery window.
2. Granular fertilizers, excellent for many bedding plants, cannot be used in all conditions; however, some of the granular fertilizers release enough nutrients to meet the customers' demand.
3. One of the circus performers caught her toe on the wire that drooped over the edge of the grandstand.
4. Anybody who wants to pay his or her locker fees can either send in an email request or bring a cheque to the students' lounge office, but any student with outstanding fees will have his or her library privileges revoked.
5. Writers know they have to develop techniques to handle their insecurities or bolster their confidence; otherwise, they can soon feel lost, afraid, and dazed.
6. As I was wandering around the parking lot, I was shocked when a shopping cart crossed my path.
7. If David's friends or his sister invites Cherie to the party, you'd better warn Cherie that her former boyfriend, Buffo, plans to attend.
8. The rising flood waters, the spread of disease, and people's looting cause the disaster area to become more dangerous; therefore, visitors should stay away.
9. Shoppers who steal will be charged to the law's full extent; moreover, they will be barred from entering the shopping mall until September 2009.
10. The Great Western Railway, of course, is considered by some to be the first Canadian system, and on 27 January 1854, a line was built from London, Ontario, to Windsor, Ontario.
11. Having a place in the traditional stories of the Tsimshian people, the kermody, a rare white subspecies of black bear, relying on old-growth forests to survive, is sometimes called the spirit or ghost bear by the Aboriginals.
12. Roy Stanbury, the coach from Westside Community League, said the boy's basketball team from Edmonton, Alberta, won more games during the 1990s than the men's team.
13. The concert held at 112 Water Street, Halifax, Nova Scotia, was thrilling, unusual, and enjoyable.

EXERCISE 2: Editing Out Faulty Parallelism

1. Our computer service is not only faster but also superior to theirs.
2. Huey was playing in the backyard, stumbled, and twisted his ankle.
3. The article explained that teenagers own more cars than senior citizens do.
4. The college hired a librarian and a plumber.
5. The veterinarian prepares not only her own ointments but also herbal remedies.
6. The evil villain hated squirrels and trapped them for dinner.
7. The taxi had been waiting for several minutes and pulled out unexpectedly.
8. Florentine is clever, quick-witted, and energetic.
9. At the aquarium the photographer takes either many digital pictures or videos.
10. Working with horses is challenging, thrilling, and surprising.

Chapter 17: Grammar Fundamentals

EXERCISE 1: Identifying Nouns

1. oxides, glazing, ceramics, oxides, cosmetics, health
2. one, prime ministers, Paul Martin, sailor, golfer
3. batteries, depot, trash, environment

EXERCISE 3: Identifying Pronouns

1. it
2. them
3. them
4. he, his

EXERCISE 8: Identifying Objects of Verbs

1. <u>burn</u> (materials)
2. <u>apologized</u> (no object)
3. <u>distributes</u>; <u>go</u> (points)

EXERCISE 11: Changing Passive Voice to Active Voice

1. The organizers cancelled the convention because an electrical outlet at the hotel had started a small fire.

2. The emergence of new television technology like high-definition TV is driving video painting, a new genre of art employing moving images.
3. In 2006, gale force winds suddenly whipped across the Strait of Georgia and felled many of the trees in Stanley Park in Vancouver.

EXERCISE 15: *Identifying Adverbs and Adjectives*

1. badly
2. nearly
3. poorly
4. really, bad
5. surely

EXERCISE 20: *Identifying Subjects and Predicates*

1. Circle of Chefs; is coming
2. David Phillips; reports
3. adding; gives

Chapter 18: Developing a Vocabulary for College

EXERCISE 1: *Explanation as a Context Clue*

Accept any answer you have given that is similar in meaning.

1. Mull means to consider something very thoughtfully and to turn it over and over in your mind.
2. Here, parquet means pieces that have been inlaid to form a pattern of some sort.
3. Hallmark means a symbol or something that stands for something else. It is like the mark of distinction that sets something apart from something else.

EXERCISE 2: *More Explanation as a Context Clue*

1. gait: Here *gait* means the walk a person has. You get the meaning by reading the whole passage.
2. cellulose: Here the meaning of *cellulose* is actually explained; the sentence tells you directly what *cellulose* means—"a white, spongy substance that protects the plant cell from the outside." Remember that often a term is explained directly in the passage.
3. celestial: *Celestial* is explained by reading the whole passage and getting a sense in general for its meaning. It is having to do with the stars, planets, and skies.
4. crave: You can tell meaning by reading the two sentences together. *Crave* in this passage means to desire something in a very strong and urgent way. You "get" the meaning of *crave* by reading the whole passage.
5. filibuster: *Filibuster* means delaying or preventing a vote by taking up time by talking too much.
6. jejune: *Jejune* means dull or not very interesting. We can tell this because it put even members of the press to sleep.
7. egoist: We can tell that *egoist* means someone who thinks about himself or herself only. We can get the meaning by reading the whole passage and picking up the clues.
8. utopia: We read the whole passage to gain general meaning for this word. A utopia is a kind of paradise, and the passage explains that because it says a life without "problems or woe."
9. platoon: There are several clues to the meaning of *platoon*. First, we see "company"; next we see "group of men." Therefore, a platoon is a group of men led by another.
10. bellicose: *Bellicose* means "belligerent," "aggressive," or "wanting to fight." The clues are "rudely hammered," "shouted," and "trouble."

EXERCISE 3: *Using Two Types of Context Clues*

1. vestibule: The key word for meaning here is *entrance*. Another word helps you with meaning, too; that word is *room*. If you put these two clues together, you have "entrance room." This is what a vestibule is, a kind of small entrance or entry room.
2. citrus: The sentence explains what this means by giving you two examples: lemons and oranges. So you know that citrus fruits are fruits like lemons and oranges that contain Vitamin C and A.
3. sullen: The passage explains *sullen* by giving you an example of how someone would behave if he or she were acting in a "sullen" way. Other words in the sentence like *moodily* also help you with the meaning. You can conclude then that *sullen* means to act in a moody, spoiled way.
4. neckerchief: You can tell from the passage that a neckerchief is something worn. Because it tells you that a neckerchief can be wrapped around

the face, you can tell that it must be a piece of cloth that is long enough to wrap. Therefore, you can put your clues together to know that a neckerchief is a garment worn around the neck (Note: neck-erchief).

5. impound: The passage tells you that if you impound something, you "lock it up." Reread the passage and find where this clue comes.
6. hospitable: You can gather the meaning of *hospitable* from the rest of the passage. Clues are "makes you feel welcome and right at home." Therefore, if someone is hospitable, they welcome you and treat you with kindness.
7. finger food: Two examples of finger foods are given: a hot dog and taco. Therefore, you can tell that a finger food is one that can be eaten from the hand; it does not require a plate or bowl.
8. lacerations: The main clue to meaning here is "flying glass"; another clue is "car crash." If you put these clues together, you can tell that *lacerations* means deep cuts.
9. medley: The sentence tells you by way of a restatement clue that a *medley* is "a mixture."
10. precipitation: The sentence tells you that precipitation is rainfall.
11. mortified: To get the meaning of *mortified*, you must put the whole series of clues together to form a general meaning. The second sentence really gives you a reason and, therefore, the meaning for the word. You can tell that *mortified* means "embarrassed."
12. vehemently: *Vehemently* means "done forcefully and emotionally." Because of Mrs. Minda's beliefs, she would be forceful in her opposition to a fast-food restaurant's replacing a park for toddlers.
13. perennials: The sentence explains that perennials do not need to be planted each season; therefore, you can tell that the word means "plants that grow from season to season."
14. trivial: There is one important clue—"unimportant thing." Therefore, you can tell that *trivial* means "unimportant."
15. ghastly: The sentence tells you that something ghastly is horrible.

EXERCISE 4: Practice with Root Words in Context

A. 2
B. 3
C. 1
D. 3
E. 4
F. 1
G. 3
H. 2
I. 2
J. 1
K. 1
L. 1
M. 3
N. 3
O. 1
P. 1
Q. 3
R. 1
S. 2
T. 3
U. 4
V. 3

EXERCISE 5: Recognizing Root Words

1. employ
2. fragile
3. define
4. answer
5. pick
6. build
7. forget
8. child
9. chain
10. treat
11. charge
12. protect
13. rock
14. comfort
15. spoon
16. advantage
17. view
18. write
19. manage
20. brown
21. bend
22. worth

23. appoint
24. paint
25. value

EXERCISE 6: Practice with Suffixes

1. enjoyable: able to be enjoyed or capable of being enjoyed
2. successor: one who succeeds
3. eventful: full of event (incident)
4. babyish: like a baby
5. machinist: one who works a machine
6. breathless: without breath
7. mountainous: full of mountains
8. disposable: able to be disposed
9. clownish: like a clown
10. adapter: one who adapts
11. bleachable: able to be bleached
12. plentiful: full of plenty
13. snobbish: like a snob
14. hypnotist: one who hypnotizes
15. flexible: able to be flexed; capable of being flexed
16. cordless: without a cord
17. cheerless: without cheer
18. monstrous: having the qualities of a monster
19. blondish: like a blond; close to blond
20. originator: one who originates

EXERCISE 7: More Practice with Suffixes

1. hateful
2. bearish
3. caller
4. believable
5. tearful
6. bleachable
7. roomful
8. breakable
9. beautiful (Note the spelling change. The *y* in *beauty* changes to *i* and the suffix is added.)
10. fearless
11. technology
12. limitless
13. bacteriology (Note the spelling change from *bacteria* to *bacterio*; this is because the word becomes easier to pronounce.)
14. branchless
15. disastrous (Note the spelling change from *disaster* to *disastr*; this change has to do with pronunciation.)
16. pianist (Note the spelling change.)
17. helpful
18. sheepish
19. greenish
20. ambitious (Note the spelling change.)
21. bendable
22. separator
23. tenish
24. employable
25. useless
26. harmless
27. careful
28. stylist
29. cautious (Note the spelling change.)
30. poisonous

EXERCISE 8: Practice with Prefixes

1. (un)<u>important</u> = not important
2. (pro)<u>noun</u> = for a noun
3. (counter)<u>attack</u> = attack against
4. (mis)<u>inform</u> = inform badly
5. (anti)<u>social</u> = against social things or society
6. (non)<u>profit</u> = not a profit; no profit
7. (pre)<u>school</u> = before school
8. (inter)<u>college</u> = between colleges
9. (pre)<u>fix</u> = fix before
10. (counter)<u>clockwise</u> = against the clock; to move in a direction that is against the clock
11. (trans)<u>plant</u> = plant across
12. (un)<u>kind</u> = not kind
13. (co-)<u>editor</u> = a person who edits with another; editors together
14. (un)<u>skilled</u> = not skilled

EXERCISE 9: More Practice with Prefixes

1. (uni)cycle = one cycle
2. (co-)chairperson = a person who chairs together; to chair with another person
3. (mono)syllable = one syllable
4. (pre-)employment = before employment
5. (inter)depend = depend between or among
6. (counter)balance = balance against
7. (tele)photo = photograph from far; a far photo
8. (pre)judge = judge before
9. (post)date = date after
10. (un)necessary = not necessary
11. (co-)exist = exist together
12. (uni)form = one form
13. (uni)lingual = one language
14. (tri)lingual = three languages
15. (un)think(able) = not capable of being thought of; not thinkable

index

B

C

Q

T

U

V

W